Mr. Dooley and the Chicago Irish

Finley Peter Dunne

Mr. Dooley
and the
Chicago Irish

The Autobiography
of a Nineteenth-Century
Ethnic Group

Edited, with a New Introduction,
by Charles Fanning

The Catholic University of America Press
Washington, D.C.

Printed in the United States of America

LIBRARY OF CONGRESS CATALOGING-IN-PUBLICATION DATA

Dunne, Finley Peter, 1867–1936.
  Mr. Dooley and the Chicago Irish.

  Originally published: New York : Arno Press, 1976.
  1. Irish Americans—Illinois—Chicago—Anecdotes, facetiae, satire, etc.   I. Fanning, Charles.   II. Title.
PN6161.D8174   1987   818'.5202   87-13228
ISBN 0-8132-0650-2
ISBN 0-8132-0655-3 (pbk.)

"I know histhry isn't thrue, Hinnissy, because it ain't like what I see ivry day in Halsted Sthreet. If any wan comes along with a histhry iv Greece or Rome that'll show me th' people fightin', gettin' dhrunk, makin' love, gettin' married, owin' th' grocery man an' bein' without hard-coal, I'll believe they was a Greece or Rome, but not befure. Historyans is like doctors. They are always lookin' f'r symptoms. Those iv them that writes about their own times examines th' tongue an' feels th' pulse an' makes a wrong dygnosis. Th' other kind iv histhry is a post-mortem examination. It tells ye what a counthry died iv. But I'd like to know what it lived iv."

—*Observations by Mr. Dooley* (1902)

Contents

Acknowledgments

Thanks are due above all to Thomas N. Brown of the University of Massachusetts at Boston who introduced me to Mr. Dooley and gave so generously of his time and knowledge through the various stages of this project. I am grateful to Daniel Hoffman of the University of Pennsylvania for his considerate direction of my dissertation on Finley Peter Dunne and Mr. Dooley. Special thanks are also due to the extremely helpful librarians at the Chicago Historical Society and the Illinois State Historical Library at Springfield, where most of the research was done. I am deeply obliged to my typist Barbara Doten, who performed the maddening task of transcribing these dialect pieces with miraculous accuracy and good humor. Through Mr. Dooley I have been introduced to a number of latter-day Irish Chicagoans whose friendship and encouragement have been very important to me. My special thanks to Andrew M. Greeley, Lawrence J. McCaffrey, and Ellen Skerrett. Also, I am grateful to Richard J. Shea, whose kind hospitality allowed me to live in Chicago long enough to discover these Dooley pieces. And to my wife, Frances Purcell Fanning, I owe thanks for countless hours of typing, proofreading, map-making, and energetic textual criticism far beyond the call of duty. Without her talents and support, this collection would never have appeared.

Introduction

The earliest Irish voice of genius in American literature is that of Finley Peter Dunne. Although his chosen form was the often ephemeral weekly newspaper column, Dunne created the first truly memorable Irish character in American literature, the aging immigrant bartender Martin J. Dooley, and the first fully realized ethnic neighborhood, Bridgeport on the South Side of Chicago. The Dooley pieces collected here establish Dunne as a pioneering literary realist and social historian.

For years, "Mr. Dooley" has had a secure place in the hearts of historians and journalists as the source of some of the most trenchant short speeches ever delivered on the state of the American nation. Ever since his clearheaded critique of the Spanish-American War brought Dunne's creation to the attention of a national audience, analysts of the American scene have been quoting glittering bits of his wisdom. Stretching from 1898 to the First World War, Mr. Dooley's tenure as resident American comic sage was remarkable both in its length and in the consistent high quality of the mostly occasional commentary. Anything newsworthy in an offbeat way attracted Dunne's gadfly mind: from Teddy Roosevelt's health fads to Andrew Carnegie's passion for libraries; from the silliness of Washington politics to high society frolics at Newport; from the Boer and Boxer Rebellions to the Negro, Indian, and immigration "problems."

For all this, a grateful nation thanked Peter Dunne by making him the most popular journalist of his time. But there was much more to him than the years of center-stage national commentary and celebrity status. Before fame overtook him, Mr. Dooley had had a very productive talking life in his native Chicago. By the time the battleship *Maine* was sunk at Havana, 215 Dooley pieces had already appeared in the Chicago *Evening Post,* and most of them were concerned with Irish American daily life in Bridgeport. When the popularity of his humorous perspective on the "splendid little war" in Cuba made it possible for Dunne to collect his early pieces as *Mr. Dooley in Peace and in War* (1898) and *Mr. Dooley in the Hearts of His Countrymen* (1899), he passed over much of the Bridgeport material because he believed that it would not appeal to his new national audience. However, it is precisely their specific locality that keeps these neglected pieces alive. They illustrate the validity of the creed of Patrick Kavanagh, whose own poetry is rooted in the small farms and fields of his native County Monaghan: "Parochialism is universal; it deals with the fundamentals."[1]

The world of American big-city journalism in the last quarter of the nineteenth century was one of the most exciting places in the history of communications. Because of exploding immigrant populations and rapidly expanding industrialization, cities were where the action was, and of course Chicago had a lion's share. Between its two defining spectacles, the Great Fire of 1871 and the World's Fair of 1893, the city grew from 300,000 to 1,300,000 people, many of them immigrants, and became a world leader in meat-packing, grain and lumber distribution, banking, manufacturing, and merchandising. During these hectic years, Chicago had as many as thirty-two competing daily papers at one time, and one of these, *The Telegram,* hired a sixteen-year-old boy in June 1884 to cover the police beat. He was Peter Dunne, the son of Irish immigrants, born in the shadow of St. Patrick's Church at West Adams and Desplaines streets, and fresh out of the West Division High School where he had managed to graduate last in his class of fifty. Over the next eight years Dunne worked for six different newspapers and moved up fast. At nineteen he was covering the White Sox for the *Daily News,* at twenty-one he was city editor of the *Times,* and at twenty-five, in 1892, he arrived as editorial page chairman at the *Evening Post,* which soon became Mr. Dooley's first home.

---

1. Quoted in Seamus Heaney, "The Sense of Place," in *Preoccupations: Selected Prose 1968–1978* (New York: Farrar, Straus, Giroux, 1980), p. 139.

Dunne had previously experimented with Irish dialect in his political reporting. He often enlivened city council news with comical transcriptions of the brogues of Chicago aldermen. Now, at the suggestion of the *Post*'s managing editor, he began to write a weekly column featuring Colonel Malachi McNeery, a saloon-keeper in the tenderloin district of the city. McNeery was modeled on a friend of Dunne's, Jim McGarry, whose Dearborn Street saloon was a gathering place of newspapermen and visiting celebrities, including boxer John L. Sullivan and actor James O'Neill. The real catalyst for the column, though, was the grandiose 1893 World's Fair, and the colonel's adventures on the exotic midway became so popular that his prototype McGarry ordered Dunne to stop making fun of him. Dunne acquiesced by shipping Colonel McNeery back to Ireland at the end of the fair.[2]

Two weeks later, the *Evening Post* for Saturday, October 7, 1893, carried the first appearance of Mr. Martin Dooley, a saloon-keeper from Archer Avenue in Irish working-class Bridgeport. The shift in location is significant. McGarry's barroom in the Loop was a worldly, exciting place, and Dunne had portrayed Colonel McNeery as a sophisticated friend of the great. On the other hand, a bar out in Bridgeport was likely to be a community institution, dispensing solace and companionship to a stable clientele of Irish mill workers, draymen, and streetcar drivers. Dunne understood the special character of a neighborhood saloon in the very first Dooley piece:

> Business was dull in the liquor-shop of Mr. Martin Dooley in Archey road last Wednesday night and Mr. Dooley was sitting back in the rear of the shop holding a newspaper at arm's length before him and reading the sporting news. In came Mr. John McKenna. Mr. McKenna has been exceedingly restless since Colonel McNeery went home to Ireland, and on his way out to Brighton Park for consolation he bethought himself of Martin Dooley. The lights were shining in the little tavern and the window decorations—green festoons, a single-sheet poster of a Parnell meeting in McCormick's Hall and a pyramid of bottles filled with Medford

---

2. See Charles Fanning, *Finley Peter Dunne and Mr. Dooley: The Chicago Years* (Lexington: University Press of Kentucky, 1978), and Elmer Ellis, *Mr. Dooley's America: A Life of Finley Peter Dunne* (New York: Knopf, 1941).

rum and flies—evoked such cheery recollections of earlier years that Mr. McKenna hopped off the car and entered briskly.

"Good evening, Martin," he said.

"Hello, Jawnny," replied Mr. Dooley, as if they had parted only the evening before. "How's thricks? I don't mind Jawnny, if I do. 'Tis duller here than a ray-publican primary in the fourth ward, th' night. Sure, ye're like a ray iv sunlight, ye are that. There's been no company in these pa-arts since Dominick Riley's big gossoon was took up be th' polis—no, not the Riley that lived down be th' gas-house; he's moved over in th' fifth wa-ard—may th' divil go with him: 'twas him bruk that there mirror with a brick for an' because I said Carey, th' informer, was a Limerick man. This here's Pat Riley, th' big, strappin' kid iv Dominick Riley, that lived beyant the rollin' mills. He was th' 'ell's own hand f'r sport. . . .

"But where 've ye been all these days, man alive? I ain't seen ye, Jawn dear, since ye led th' gr-rand ma-arch in Finucane's Hall, this tin years past."

Immediately, we are in a different world. Mr. Dooley's brogue is thicker than Colonel McNeery's, which signals the social transition from the Loop to "Archey road." There is an assumption by the speaker of knowledge common to the Irish-American community in the references to Parnell and "Carey, th' informer" (who betrayed the Dublin Phoenix Park murderers in 1883). But most important, we are at once in that community, exposed to the flavor of a parochial neighborhood culture, where people are placed by family, geography, and reputation. These are the seeds of Dunne's accomplishment in the Chicago Dooley pieces—the imaginative creation of Bridgeport.

The Irish had first come to Chicago in numbers to work on the construction of a canal joining the Mississippi River and Lake Michigan. The digging had begun on July 4, 1836, a year before the incorporation of the city, and the canal was completed in 1848. By that time, the tiny settlement of Hardscrabble, where the first Irish laborers had raised their shanties, had been transformed into the lively community of Bridgeport, so named for its position at the eastern end of the canal. The construction of a railroad line over the same route provided more work for immigrants; when it began operating in 1851, the railroad opened Bridgeport to industry. Lumber and stock yards appeared in the 1850s, and in 1865 the first steel rolling mill was built at Archer and Ashland avenues. Over the years more yards and factories were opened, until, by the 1890s, the character of Bridgeport was established as a mixture of industrial sites and working-class housing—a place to be left behind on the road to the respectability of St. Patrick's parish. In the nineties, the "new immigrants" from southern and eastern Europe were arriving in Bridgeport, but there was still a sizable Irish community, concentrated at the crossing of Halsted Street and Archer Avenue, just below the South Branch of the Chicago River. It was there that Martin Dooley set up his liquor shop in October 1893.

Mr. Dooley lived on Archer Avenue until 1900, when Peter Dunne moved to New York and the second phase of his career, as a nationally syndicated humorist. In his earlier Chicago setting—his only real home—Mr. Dooley provides many riches unavailable elsewhere. Of first importance here is the issue of the brogue, the background of American and Irish-American dialect writing that Dunne emerged from and repudiated. Dialect was, of course, a major component in the portrayal of the stereotypical "stage Irishman" in nineteenth-century drama. In addition, fiction and journalism also contained numbers of similar broad-brush, condescending caricatures, displaying the familiar, if contradictory, traits of ignorance, wiliness, and garrulity, always in the service of provoking laughter at supposed Irishness.

Writers from the WASP mainstream throughout the nineteenth century made full use of the brogue to help create derogatory pictures of the alien immigrant hordes. Teague O'Regan, the bumbling Sancho Panza figure in H. H. Brackenridge's 1792 picaresque novel *Modern Chivalry,* stands at the head of this line. And there were, as a matter of fact, some particularly unpleasant examples published in Mr. Dooley's day; for example, the 1897 *Shantytown Sketches* of Philadelphian Anthony Joseph Drexel Biddle.³ These were part of the new wave of nativism that swept America in the nineties in reaction against the "new immigration."

3. *Shantytown Sketches* (Philadelphia: Drexel Biddle, 1897) is divided into three sections—Irish, Jewish, and Black—all offensive. A classic of this genre is

In addition, identifiably Irish-American writers also contributed to this vein. Indeed, the first Irish-American novel, *The Irish Emigrant* by "An Hibernian" of 1817, makes use of a familiar linguistic convention of nineteenth-century fiction on both sides of the Atlantic. Aristocratic Irish protagonists speak the King's English while their clownish servants talk with brogues.[4] Again, this convention of linguistic reinforcement of elitist barriers between working-class and lace-curtain Irish characters continued unabated into the 1880s and 1890s, in Irish-American fiction such as George Jessop's San Francisco stories of *Gerald Ffrench's Friends* (1889) and the many popular novels of Maurice Francis Egan, the best-known, turn-of-the-century American Catholic literary figure.[5]

In American journalism, the brogue goes back at least as far as it does in fiction. And again, perhaps because of the general interest in urban local color at the time, there were quite a number of Irish dialect voices in American newspapers in the 1880s and 1890s when Dunne was starting out. John Joseph Jennings's sketches about the Widow Magoogin and her cousin Officer Mike ran in the St. Louis *Post-Dispatch* and *Critic*. For the *Brooklyn Eagle*, Maurice E. McLoughlin created "the Gowanusians," Irish

---

the virulently anti-Irish-Catholic novel, *Thorns in Your Sides* (New York: Putnam, 1884), by Harriete A. Keyser, in which are contrasted the "ignorant Irish Romanists" with thick brogues, "general uncleanness and turbulence," and the Ulster Protestants of an earlier migration. Published in the Chicago anti-immigration periodical *America* in 1888 was a series of ten "Intercepted Letters" to Ireland presenting the urban Irishman as a drunken, dishonest political hack (*America*, May 26–August 11, 1888).

4. *The Irish Emigrant: An Historical Tale Founded on Fact*, By An Hibernian (Winchester, Va.: John T. Sharrocks, 1817).

5. George H. Jessop, *Gerald Ffrench's Friends* (New York: Longmans Green, 1889). Maurice Francis Egan, *The Disappearance of John Longworthy* (Notre Dame: Office of the Ave Maria, 1890); *The Wiles of Sexton Maginnis* (New York: The Century Co., 1909). Other examples of abuses of the brogue by Irish-American writers include *Biddy Finnigan's Botheration; or, That Romp of a Girl*, by Mary Nolan (St. Louis: E. Carreras, 1884). Fresh off the boat, Biddy Finnigan is hired by a WASP family in Philadelphia, who find her kindly, faithful, and a little dense. The author's attempt at brogue does nothing to dispel this impression. A similar brogue-laden servant girl in the midst of upper-class swells appears in *The Bewildering Widow: A Tale of Manhattan Beach* (New York: W. B. Smith, 1881) by Julia E. Dunn.

settlers beside the Gowanus Canal who included the social-climbing McSniffigans and saloonkeeper's wife Mrs. Mulgrew. Ernest Jarrold's "idylls" of ten-year-old Mickey Finn, the son of immigrants to Coney Island, appeared in the New York *Sun* and *Leslie's Weekly*. Mr. Dooley even had dialect rivals in his own city, where "Officer Casey on the City Hall Corner" conversed with "the Connemara cop" in the Chicago *Times-Herald*. Without exception, these dialect columns use an awkwardly insistent brogue and slapstick-comic situations to ridicule the Irish in all the old familiar ways.[6]

In the context of the overwhelmingly negative tradition of Irish dialect writing, the opposition to Mr. Dooley voiced by a number of Irish-American editors in the 1890s becomes understandable. When they saw the brogue, they saw red. Chicagoan John Finerty, who had other reasons for disliking Dunne as we shall see, editorialized in his weekly paper, *The Citizen,* against "the devil of dialectism" in general and Finley Peter Dunne in particular, as the perpetrator of "an atrocious brogue, such as only the very lowest of the Irish peasantry indulge in," the aim of which was "to make fools and bigots laugh."[7] However, had he been able to read Mr. Dooley more objectively, Finerty would have seen the brogue used in new and salutary ways.

First of all, the voice itself is a kind of miracle. Far from being a language expert, Dunne was only trying, as he explained in an 1899 interview, "to make Dooley talk as an Irishman would talk who has lived thirty or forty years in America, and whose natural pronunciation had been more or less affected by the slang of the

6. Several of these dialect series were collected into books, as follows: *Widow Magoogin* (New York: Dillingham, 1900), *The Gowanusians: Humorous Sketches of Every-Day Life among Plain People* (New York: Edmunds Pub. Co., 1894), *Mickey Finn Idylls* (New York: Doubleday & McClure, 1899), and *Mickey Finn's New Irish Yarns* (New York: Doubleday & McClure, 1902). Officer Casey appeared in the *Times-Herald* from April 14 through August 4, 1895, and was revived in the *Chicago Evening Post* in January 1906. Many of these columns echo themes of Mr. Dooley's, thus illustrating that the Irish communities in other cities shared concerns. For example, there are many references to the shift from old-country customs to new American ways. But the brogue and the use of the Irish as comic figures are consistently heavy-handed.

7. Fanning, *Finley Peter Dunne and Mr. Dooley,* pp. 157–59.

streets."[8] Dunne was also aware of the dangers of dialect writing for a general newspaper audience, and here he successfully walked a tightrope, managing to suggest the brogue without sacrificing clarity. Working simply, with a few sure strokes, he made of the Dooley voice a serviceable, flexible medium. The dialect is conveyed by occasional contraction (th' and gettin') and expansion (gr-rand and ta-arget), with a sprinkling of Irish pronunciations (quite [quiet], jood [dude], a cup of tay) and holdovers from the Gaelic (soggarth [priest], omadhon [lout], gossoon [little boy]). Dunne's ear for the rhythms and timing of this Irish American urban speech is everywhere remarkable. In even the slightest Dooley piece, we hear a living voice.

Even more important is the range of tasks to which Dunne set the inimitable Dooley voice. Certainly, although he is the first immigrant city-dweller in the group, Mr. Dooley belongs in the nineteenth-century American tradition of the crackerbox philosopher or wise fool, along with such unlettered dispensers of wisdom in dialect as Major Jack Downing, Petroleum V. Nasby, and Artemus Ward. In addition, Dunne had a few positive precursors in Irish-American dialect writing. For example, he was probably aware of Charles G. Halpine's Civil War dispatches of Private Miles O'Reilly, satirical journalism featuring rollicking songs in broad brogue that had been popular enough to be read at President Lincoln's cabinet meetings.[9] Moreover, although it is much less likely, Dunne may have heard tell of the extraordinary phenomenon of prefamine Irish-American satire. In the 1830s and early forties, a number of sophisticated satiric novels appeared, some anonymously, in which potentially sensitive Irish ethnic issues are treated with refreshing candor and humor. These include *The Life of Paddy O'Flarrity* (1834), which satirizes the immigrant's dream of success and the venality of political aspiration, *Six Months in a House of Correction* (1835), a parody of the nativist

8. W. Irving Way, "Mr. Martin Dooley of Chicago," *The Bookman*, 9 (May 1899):217.

9. Charles G. Halpine, *The Life and Adventures, Songs, Services and Speeches of Private Miles O'Reilly* (New York: Carleton, 1864); *Baked Meats of the Funeral* (New York: Carleton, 1866).

fiction of convent "revelations," and John M. Moore's *Adventures of Tom Stapleton* (1842), which laughs at high, low, and political life among the New York Irish.[10] Dunne shares with these predecessors a common bag of verbal tricks: cacography; juxtaposition of incongruous predicates, nouns, and proper names; misquotation of classics and the Bible. However, Dunne-as-Dooley also significantly broadened the range of subjects and deepened the range of tones able to be sustained in the vernacular dialect voice.

Even when making serious points, as in the Civil War pieces of Nasby, Ward, and Miles O'Reilly, the earlier dialect writers kept themselves wrapped in the protective cloak of humor. To be sure, Mr. Dooley provides a number of classic humorous narratives also, including sketches of family feuding and fear of marriage, rough-and-tumble politicking, and mock-heroic ceremonial occasions such as the St. Patrick's Day parade. And yet, even when he is being funny, Mr. Dooley provokes laughter not because he knows so little, but because he knows so much. He is witty, satirical, cutting. He exposes delusions rather than being victimized by them. In addition, and in contrast to his later manifestation as the purveyor of comic perspective on national issues, Mr. Dooley is funny in only half of the Chicago pieces. He is often utterly serious in theme and tone, dealing with such subjects as starvation in Ireland and Chicago, wanton murder and grim retribution, and heroism both quiet and spectacular, in an appropriate voice that achieves at times a tragic resonance. That Dunne accomplished so much without strain constitutes an expansion of the possibilities for fiction of the vernacular voice. On a smaller scale, Dunne's achievement is comparable to Mark Twain's decision to let Huck Finn tell his own story.

Finley Peter Dunne had Irish as well as Irish-American literary

10. *The Life of Paddy O'Flarrity, Who, from a Shoeblack, Has by Perseverance and Good Conduct Arrived to a Member of Congress* (Washington, D.C.: n.p. 1834). *Six Months in a House of Correction; or, The Narrative of Dorah Mahony* (Boston: Benj. B. Mussey, 1835). John M. Moore, *The Adventures of Tom Stapleton* (New York: Wilson & Co., 1843). This novel was serialized in *Brother Jonathan* (New York) in 1842. For excerpts from all three of these forgotten books, see Charles Fanning, ed., *The Exiles of Erin: Nineteenth-Century Irish American Fiction* (Notre Dame, Ind.: University of Notre Dame Press, 1987).

forebears. A satiric tradition is, of course, central in Irish literature. In Gaelic, satire is pervasive from the curses and character assassinations of the medieval bards to Brian Merryman's hilarious treatment of relations between the sexes in "The Midnight Court" of 1781. In English, it runs from the savage indignation of Jonathan Swift (for example, "A Modest Proposal" of 1729) to the satiric plays of Synge and Lady Gregory and the essentially comic genius of James Joyce. I would say that in his fierce expositions of the suffering of Bridgeport's poor Dunne is akin to Swift, and in his insistent, imaginative verbal playfulness he bears at least a passing comparison with Joyce, the master wordsmith.[11]

In sum, through Mr. Dooley, Finley Peter Dunne made a number of pioneering contributions to American literary realism and social history. As an urban local colorist, he described the life and customs of Bridgeport in the later nineteenth century. As the creator of substantial character sketches of Irish immigrants, he affirmed that the lives of ordinary people were worthy of serious literary consideration. And finally, he brought forth the community and its people through the vernacular voice of a sixty-year-old, smiling, public-house man. Major figures in literary realism's first two generations acknowledged Dunne's part in their movement. Declaring that "no one but an Irish-American could have invented such an Irish-American, or have invested his sayings with such racial and personal richness," William Dean Howells called Mr. Dooley "wise and shrewd and just for the most part," and capable of "the last effect of subtle irony." He confessed to having read the Dooley pieces "with a constant surprise that their very simple formula suffices for the treatment of so many of our social

11. The centrality of the Irish satiric tradition is argued forcibly in Vivian Mercier, *The Irish Comic Tradition* (New York: Oxford University Press, 1962). We know, by the way, that James Joyce admired Mr. Dooley. He even worked Dunne's inseparable Chicago pair into the "Willingdone Museyroom" (Wellington Museum) section near the beginning of *Finnegans Wake:* "This is hiena hinnessy laughing alout at the Willingdone. This is lipsyg dooley krieging the funk from the hinnessy. This is the hinndoo Shimar Shin between the dooley boy and the hinnessy. Tip."

as well as political ills." And Theodore Dreiser wrote to George Ade that "as early as 1900, or before, [Ade's *Artie*] passed into my collection of genuine American realism. . . . In fact, I entered it with your *Fables in Slang,* Finley Dunne's *Philosopher Dooley,* Frank Norris' *McTeague* and Hamlin Garland's *Main Traveled Roads.* . . . These were the beginning of my private library of American realism."[12]

As for the historical contribution, Mr. Dooley takes us as close as we are likely to come to the circumstances, customs, and attitudes of a nineteenth-century Irish-American neighborhood. He measures up very well to his own standard of what history ought to be, which stands as the epigraph to this collection:

> "I know histhry isn't thrue, Hinnissy, because it ain't like what I see ivry day in Halsted Sthreet. If any wan comes along with a histhry iv Greece or Rome that'll show me th' people fightin', gettin' dhrunk, makin' love, gettin' married, owin' th' grocery man an' bein' without hard-coal, I'll believe they was a Greece or Rome, but not befure. Historyans is like doctors. They are always lookin' f'r symptoms. Those iv them that writes about their own times examines th' tongue an' feels th' pulse an' makes a wrong dygnosis. Th' other kind iv histhry is a postmortem examination. It tells ye what a counthry died iv. But I'd like to know what it lived iv."

Dunne's Dooley columns are cameo etchings, with the precision and vividness of illuminated corners of the Book of Kells, of the archetypal Irish immigrant themes and characters. The themes include memories of the Great Hunger, the turbulent voyage out to America, the shattered dream of gold in the streets, the hard life of manual labor, the sufferings of the destitute, the pains of assimilation, the gulf between immigrants and their American children, and the slow rise to respectability. And the characters include Civil War veterans, heroic firemen, stoic, exploited mill workers, rackrenting, miserly landlords, failed politicians who

---

12. William Dean Howells, "Certain of the Chicago School of Fiction," *North American Review* 176(May 1903):734–46. Theodore Dreiser, *The Letters of Theodore Dreiser,* ed. Robert H. Elias (Philadelphia: University of Pennsylvania Press, 1959), 3:949.

lose their money, successful ones who forget their friends, lace-curtain social climbers with pianos in the parlor, and compassionate, overworked parish priests.

The Dooley pieces are populated with a large cast of recurrent characters, many of them modeled after real people. John McKenna was a genial Republican politician from Chicago's Brighton Park neighborhood. His role as chief listener goes back to the Colonel McNeery days and ceases only after the presidential election of 1896. During the Bryan-McKinley campaign, Dunne invented Malachi Hennessy, a working-class Bridgeport Democrat, to argue against McKenna, thereby allowing Mr. Dooley to stand comfortably in the middle, exploiting the comic potential of both sides. After the election, Hennessy took over the listening post, presumably because, as a slow-thinking mill worker with a large family, he was a more typical Bridgeporter than McKenna, and a better foil for Mr. Dooley's wit. Of the other important characters, Police Sergeant John Shea, political kingmaker William Joyce, Aldermen Billy O'Brien and Johnny Powers, and the local parish priest Father Kelly were real-life Chicagoans who lent their names and some of their idiosyncracies to Dunne's cast. And, of course, presiding over all is the saloonkeeper, Mr. Dooley himself: satirist, social critic, and philosopher, generally cynical but specifically kind; at the least (in his own words) "a post to hitch ye'er silences to," at the most, a provider of companionship and solace to bone-weary working people.

By accretion of the weekly Dooley columns, a whole picture emerges, and Dunne has stitched this world together with locating, landmark references throughout the series. All movement for Mr. Dooley is defined in relation to the "red bridge" that joins Bridgeport to the rest of Chicago. Archey Road is a lively main street, extending from Dooley's saloon to his rival Schwartzmeister's "down th' way" to the political capital of Bridgeport at Finucane's Hall. Social position is measured by the proximity of one's home to the rolling mills and the gas house. And meandering backdrops for many scenes are provided by the Chicago River and its swampy runoff, Healey's Slough. It is no wonder that Mr.

Dooley laments the takeover by newer immigrant groups of Bridgeport's "sacred sites." Thus firmly placed in the imagination, Bridgeport blossoms before us as a believable ethnic subculture, with its own customs and ceremonies, a social hierarchy rooted in ancestry, family, and occupation, and a shared perspective on the world.

That subculture takes shape when Dunne's columns are arranged in thematic groups, as they are in this collection. I would venture to call the result the great nineteenth-century Irish-American novel—in pieces. Actually, Dunne tried several times without success to write conventional fiction. In December 1898 he proposed to *Century* magazine publisher Richard Watson Gilder "a series of articles—perhaps a story—of Irish-American life. . . . It seems to me that the job has not been done with real knowledge of the people." But nothing was ever delivered. Dunne also promised to the *Ladies' Home Journal* a long series of related stories starring Bridgeport teenager Molly Donahue. Only four of these appeared (from December 1899 through March 1900), and three were merely extensions of previous Dooley columns about Molly. With the last, the *Journal* printed an apology from Dunne, who claimed ill health and dissatisfaction "with the story as far as it has gone."[13] Always a reluctant writer, Dunne was particularly unsuited for the novelist's long haul. And yet, even though it was never Dunne's conscious ambition, his work constitutes the coming of age of Irish-American fiction.

Indeed, the first great novelist of Irish-American life, James T. Farrell, acknowledged his kinship with fellow-Chicagoan Dunne at the opening of his own first novel, *Young Lonigan* (1932), in the front-porch revery of Studs Lonigan's father:

Nope, his family had not turned out so well. They hadn't had, none of them, the persistence that he had. . . . Well, Pat Lonigan had gone through the mill, and he had pulled himself up by his own bootstraps, and while he was not exactly sitting in the plush on Easy Street, he was a boss painter, and had his own business, and pretty soon maybe he'd even be worth a cool hundred thousand berries. But life was a funny thing, all

13. Fanning, *Finley Peter Dunne and Mr. Dooley,* pp. 210–11.

right. It was like Mr. Dooley said, and he had never forgotten that re-mark, because Dooley, that is Finley Peter Dunne, was a real philoso-pher. Who'll tell what makes wan man a thief, and another man a saint? [14]

Finley Peter Dunne's chronicle of the works and days of Irish Chicago came to its virtual conclusion in January 1898 with a bitter farewell piece in which Mr. Dooley searches his memory for concrete, positive results attributable to his talking career in Chi-cago, and finds none. In the Dooley pieces written through the course of the preceding year there is observable a downhill slide toward the conviction that human suffering cannot be appreciably alleviated with the pen. While some of Dunne's best writing is here, it seems to have become too painful for this thirty-year-old journalist to go on creating parables of poverty and injustice with-out real hope of doing much good. Thus, Mr. Dooley left home rather than continuing to live among neighbors whose troubles he could only observe with impotent anger. At the end of the Janu-ary piece, he locks the door and turns out the lights, "perhaps for the last time."

One month later, in February 1898, the declaration of war against Spain provided a convenient vehicle for the return to con-versation of the man who had confessed in his January farewell piece that " 'tis har-rd f'r me to lave off talkin'." A safe, general topic, the war lent itself to brisk, light handling, with little risk of emotional involvement for Dunne. Thus, with the sinking of the battleship *Maine* in Havana harbor, Mr. Dooley returned to the Chicago newspaper scene. In reality, though, it was only his ghost—a rootless, disembodied voice, not all that different, except for the brogue, from its predecessors in the genre of crackerbarrel dialect humor. The rest of the story is well known. The American people outside Chicago soon loved Mr. Dooley, as they had loved Hosea Biglow, Artemus Ward, and the folksy platform image of Mark Twain; for Dooley's lilting, skeptical voice remained bless-edly lucid and rational.

Moreover, a number of things happened to Dunne himself after

14. *Studs Lonigan: A Trilogy* (New York: Modern Library, 1938), pp. 16–17.

1898 to solidify the new Dooley role as a national figure. He moved to New York, thus cutting himself off from the Chicago genius loci, he embraced syndication with its confining restrictions of topicality and tactfulness, and he began to live a high life among men of wealth and ease at whom his satiric powers might well have been directed. This is not to deny the importance of Mr. Dooley's national commentary. Certainly, America was a better place for these twenty years of laughter and perspective that he provided.

And yet, we ought also to regret and appreciate what was lost. Hence the following chapters, which are presented thematically to organize Finley Peter Dunne's scattered treatments of the various dimensions of Chicago Irish life: 1) memories of Ireland, emigration, and the early years in America, 2) daily life in Bridgeport in the 1890s, 3) the mixed blessings of Irish assimilation into American life, 4) Bridgeport as a culture of poverty, 5) Irish-American politics as seen from Archer Avenue, and 6) the tragicomedy that was nineteenth-century Irish-American nationalism. In addition, the final chapter (7) collects the later (1897) philosophical pieces in which Dunne's view of the world darkened toward pessimism and despair.

Mr. Dooley and the Chicago Irish

Chapter One
The Past: Ireland, Emigration, Early Bridgeport

When he first appeared in the Chicago Evening Post *in 1893, Martin Dooley was already over sixty. In the course of the Chicago pieces, Finley Peter Dunne provided him with a plausible and fairly detailed past history. Mr. Dooley's earliest reminiscence is of a childhood Christmas in Ireland (piece 1). He also recalls the great hunger of the late 1840s with a chilling vignette (2). He must have emigrated from Ireland around this time, because another piece (6) places him in Chicago during the construction of the Illinois and Michigan Canal, which was completed in 1848. He remembers vividly the trip to America (3), his first job-hunting experiences in the new world (4, 5) and the brawling life of old Bridgeport as a canal town (6, 7). Exposure to both systems allows him to compare education in Ireland and early Chicago (8). He also charts the effects on Bridgeport of the Civil War (9, 10) and the Chicago Fire of 1871 (12), and provides a glimpse of one of the community's first citizens, the near-legendary "little priest" who died in the 1867 cholera epidemic (11). Also included here are Mr. Dooley's account of the last of the old-time social extravaganzas, the Faugh a Ballagh Ball of 1872 (13), and a genuine Bridgeport ghost story set in the late 1870s (14). Mr. Dooley was fond of looking backward, and there are many more reminiscences; the others are arranged thematically in subsequent chapters.*

4 *Mr. Dooley and the Chicago Irish*

1. Christmas in Ireland *

In this early piece Mr. Dooley claims Mayo as his home county. Washington Hesing was the owner of the German-language news-paper, the Illinois Staats-Zeitung, *as well as postmaster of Chicago during the second Cleveland administration.*

There was a turkey raffle on Halsted street last night and Mr. McKenna shook fifty-four. He came into Mr. Dooley's with the turkey under his arm and Mr. Dooley, who was mixing a Tom-and-Jerry dope on the end of the bar, paused to inquire: "Where'd ye get th' reed bur-rd, Jawnny?"

"I won it at Donnelly's raffle," said Mr. McKenna.

"Ye ought to've kep' it in a warm place," said Mr. Dooley. "It's shrinkin' so 'twill be a fishball before ye get home. It must be a canned turkey. I've seen th' likes iv that in th' ol' counthry f'r ivrybody that cud get thim wanted turkey f'r Chris'mas, an' if they cuddent get a big fat gobbler with mate enough on him to feed a rig'ment iv Mayo min they took what they got, an' they got wan iv thim little herrin' turkeys like th' bur-rd ye have under ye'er ar-rm. Faith, it wasn't all iv thim wud get that much, poor things. There was places in th' pa-art iv Ireland ye'er people come fr'm, Jawn, with ye'er di'mons an' ye'er gol'-headed umbrella, where a piece iv bacon an' an exthra allowance iv pitaties was a feast f'r th' kids. 'Twas in ye'er town, Jawn, that th' little girl, whin she wanted to remimber something, says to th' ol' man: 'Why,' she says, 'ye remimber 'twas th' day they had mate,' says she. She remimbered it because 'twas th' day they had mate, Jawn. 'Twas like Christmas an' th' Foorth iv July an' Pathrick's day, whin they had mate in ye'er part iv Ireland, Jawn. On other oc-casions they had pitaties an' butthermilk, or, if their neighbors wuz kind, oatmale stirabout. Poor things! Did I iver tell ye about me Uncle Clarence that died iv overatin' reed bur-rds?"

---

* Most of these pieces appeared untitled, under a "Mr. Dooley" by-line of some sort. I have provided headings for all of them, to facilitate identification and refer-

"You did," said Mr. McKenna, surlily, for it was a point upon which Mr. Dooley often jibed him.

"Annyhow," said Mr. Dooley, grinning, "poor or rich alike, th' people iv Ireland never let th' Christmas pass without cellybratin'. Ye'd know th' day was comin' fr'm th' gr-reat coortin' that'd be goin' on ivrywhere. Advint week was always gr-reat coortin' time f'r th' la-ads. They'd make love before Christmas an' get married aftherward if th' gir-rls'd have thim an' they mostly would. That's a way th' gir-rls have the wide wur-rld over.

"Thin ivery man 'd wish f'r a snowy Chris'mas. A green Chris'-mas makes a fat churchyard, says th' good book, an' like as not there'd be snow on th' ground, at laste in Mayo where I come fr'm. An' about Christmas eve th' lads and lasses 'd go into th' hills an' fetch down ivy to hang above th' hearth an' all th' kids 'd go light on the stirabout so's they could tuck in more on th' morrow. Christmas eve th' lads that 'd been away 'd come thrampin' in fr'm Gawd knows where, big lads far fr'm home in Cork an' Limerick an' th' City iv Dublin—come thrampin' home stick in hand to ate their Christmas dinner with th' ol' folks. Dear, oh dear, how I re-mimber it. 'Twas a long road that led up to our house an' me mother 'd put a lamp in th' windy so's th' la-ads could see th' way. Manny's th' time I've heerd th' beat iv th' stick on th' road an' th' tap on th' pane an' me mother runnin' to th' dure an' screamin', Mike, 'r Tim, 'r Robert Immitt an' cryin' on his shoulder. 'Twas, let me see, four fours is sixteen, an' thirty makes forty-six—'twas in the Christmas iv fifty-sivin I last seen me brother Mike—poor fellow, poor fellow.

"We was up early ye may say that, th' nex' mornin'. Some iv th' pious wans 'd go to th' midnight mass an' thim we called 'vo-teens.' But th' kids had little thought iv mass 'til they opened their Christ-mas boxes. Poor little Christmas boxes they was like enough—a bit iv a dolly f'r th' little girls an' a Jack-in-the-box with whiskers like Postmaster Hesing's an' a stick iv candy. There's on'y wan

ence. The date of original publication in the Chicago *Evening Post* is in paren-theses at the end of each piece.

thing ye have over here that we niver had at home, an' that's Sandy Claus. Why is it, d'ye suppose? I niver knew that St. Patrick druv him out with th' snakes, but I niver heerd iv him till I come to this counthry.

"Thin afther th' Christmas boxes th' kids 'd go out in th' road an' holler 'Christmas box' at ivry man they met an' thin wud be off to mass where the priest's niece sung the "Destah Fidelis,' an' ivry man chipped in a shillin' or two f'r th' good man. By gar, some iv thim soggarths was bor-rn politicians, f'r they cud jolly a man f'r givin' big an' roast him f'r givin' little till ivery citizen in th' parish was thryin' to bate his neighbor like as if 'twas at a game iv give-away. Ye'd hear thim comin' home fr'm th' church. 'Th' iday iv Mike Casey givin' tin shillin's whin Badalia Casey borrid a pinch iv tay fr'm me on'y las' week.' 'What a poor lot thim Dugans is. Before I'd be read fr'm th' altar with six pince after me name I'd sell th' shoes off me feet. I heerd Tim Dugan got three poun' tin f'r that litther iv boneens. Did ye notice he wint to his jooty to-day. Faith, 'tis time. I was thinkin' he was goin' to join th' Prowtestants.'

"An' so 'twud go. Thin they was dinner, a hell iv a dinner, iv turkey or goose with bacon an' thin a bottle iv th' ol' shtuff with limon an' hot wather, an' toasts was drunk to th' la-ads far away an' to thim in prison an' to another reunion, an' late at night me mother 'd tuck us all in bed an' lade me father to his room with his jag upon him, singin' 'Th' Wearin' iv th' Green' at th' top iv his voice. Thim ol' days!"

"Well, Martin, good night," said McKenna. "A merry Christmas before I see you again."

"Merry Christmas," said Mr. Dooley. If Mr. McKenna had returned five minutes later he would have found Mr. Dooley sitting on the edge of the bed in the back room wiping his eyes on the bar towel. (December 23, 1893)

2. The Necessity of Modesty among the Rich: A Tale of the Famine

On February 10, 1897, the Bradley-Martins of Troy, New York, hosted the most expensive private party ever given, a masked ball at the Waldorf-Astoria, New York City, the cost of which was estimated at nearly $370,000. As the country was then mired in a severe economic depression, many people criticized the timing of this ostentatious display of wealth. "Pether th' Packer" was an Irish "hanging judge," and Hennessy's opening question was prompted by the fact that one of Bridgeport's aldermen around this time was named Charles Martin.*

"I wondher," said Mr. Hennessy, "if thim Bradley-Martins that's goin' to give th' ball is anny kin iv th' aldherman?"

"I doubt it," said Mr. Dooley. "I knowed all his folks. They're Monaghan people, an' I niver heerd iv thim marryin' into th' Bradleys, who come fr'm away beyant near th' Joynt's Causeway. What med ye think iv thim?"

"I was readin' about th' Prowtestant minister that give thim such a turnin' over th' other night," said Hennessy. Then the Philistine went on: "It looks to me as though th' man was wr-rong, an' th' Bradley-Martins was right. Faith, th' more th' poor can get out iv th' r-rich, th' better f'r thim. I seen it put just r-right in th' paper th' other day. If these people didn't let go iv their coin here, they'd take it away with thim to Paris or West Baden, Indiana, an' spind it instid iv puttin' it in circulation amongst th' florists an' dhressmakers an' hackmen they'll have to hire. I believe in encouragin' th' rich to walk away fr'm their change. 'Tis gr-reat f'r business."

Mr. Dooley mused over this politico-moral proposition some time before he said:—

"Years ago, whin I was a little bit iv a kid, hardly high enough

---

* See also Chapter Four, piece 16.

to look into th' pot iv stirabout on th' peat fire, they was a rich landlord in our part iv Ireland; an' he ownded near half th' counthryside. His name was Dorsey,—Willum Edmund Fitzgerald Dorsey, justice iv th' peace, mimber iv Parlymint.

"I'll niver tell ye how much land that man had in his own r-right. Ye cud walk f'r a day without lavin' it, bog an' oat-field an' pasthure an' game presarves. He was smothered with money, an' he lived in a house as big as th' Audjitoroom Hotel. Manny's th' time I've seen him ride by our place, an' me father'd raise his head from th' kish iv turf an' touch his hat to th' gr-reat man. An' wanst or twict in th' month th' dogs'd come yelpin' acrost our little place, with lads follerin' afther in r-red coats; f'r this Dorsey was a gr-reat huntsman, bad scran to his evil face.

"He had th' r-reputation iv bein' a good landlord so long as th' crops come regular. He was vilent, it's thrue, an' 'd as lave as not cut a farmer acrost th' face with his whip f'r crossin' th' thrail iv th' fox; but he was liberal with his money, an', Hinnissy, that's a thrait that covers a multitude iv sins. He give freely to th' church, an' was as gin'rous to th' priest as to th' parson. He had th' gintry f'r miles around to his big house f'r balls an' dinners an' huntin' meetin's, an' half th' little shopkeepers in th' neighborin' town lived on th' money he spent f'r th' things he didn't bring fr'm Dublin or London. I mind wanst a great roar wint up whin he stayed th' whole season in England with his fam'ly. It near broke th' townsfolk, an' they were wild with delight whin he come back an' opened up th' big house.

"But wan year there come a flood iv rain, an' th' nex' year another flood, an' th' third year there wasn't a lumper turned up that wasn't blue-black to th' hear-rt. We was betther off than most, an' we suffered our share, Gawd knows; but thim that was scrapin' th' sod f'r a bare livin' fr'm day to day perished like th' cattle in th' field.

"Thin come th' writs an' th' evictions. Th' bailiffs dhrove out in squads, seizin' cattle an' turnin' people into th' r-road. Nawthin' wud soften th' hear-rt iv Dorsey. I seen th' priest an' th' 'Piscopal ministher dhrivin' over to plead with him wan night; an' th' good man stopped at our house, comin' back, an' spent th' night with us. I heerd him tell me father what Dorsey said. 'Haven't I been lib'ral with me people?' he says. 'Haven't I give freely to ye'er churches? Haven't I put up soup-houses an' disthributed blankets whin th' weather was cold? Haven't I kept th' shopkeepers iv th' town beyant fr'm starvin' be thradin' with thim an' stayin' in this cur-rsed counthry, whin, if I'd done what me wife wanted, I'd been r-runnin' around Europe, enj'yin' life? I'm a risidint landlord. I ain't like Kilduff, that laves his estate in th' hands iv an agint. I'm proud iv me station. I was bor-rn here, an' here I'll die; but I'll have me r-rights. These here people owes their rent, an' I'll get th' rent or th' farms if I have to call on ivry rig'mint fr'm Bombay to Cape Clear, an' turn ivry oat-field into a pasture f'r me cattle. I stand on th' law. I'm a just man, an' I ask no more thin what belongs to me.'

"Ivry night they was a party on th' hill, an' th' people come fr'm miles around; an' th' tinants trudgin' over th' muddy roads with th' peelers behind thim cud see th' light poorin' out fr'm th' big house an' hear Devine's band playin' to th' dancers. Th' shopkeepers lived in clover, an' thanked th' lord f'r a good landlord, an' wan that lived at home. But one avnin' a black man be th' name iv Shaughnessy, that had thramped acrost th' hills fr'm Galway just in time to rent f'r th' potato rot, wint and hid himself in a hedge along th' road with a shotgun loaded with hardware under his coat. Dorsey'd heerd talk iv the people bein' aggrieved at him givin' big parties while his bailiffs were hustlin' men and women off their holdin's; but he was a high-handed man, an' foolish in his pride, an' he'd have it no other way but that he'd go about without protection. This night he rode alongside th' carredge iv some iv his frinds goin' to th' other side iv town, an' come back alone in th' moonlight. Th' Irish ar-re poor marksmen, Hinnissy, except whin they fire in platoons; but that big man loomin' up in th' moonlight on a black horse cud no more be missed thin th' r-rock iv Cashel. He niver knowed what hit him; an' Pether th' Packer come down th' followin' month, an' a jury iv shopkeepers hanged Shaughnessy so fast it med even th' judge smile."

"Well," said Mr. Hennessy, "I suppose he desarved it; but, if I'd been on th' jury, I'd've starved to death befure I'd give th' verdict." "Thrue," said Mr. Dooley. "An' Dorsey was a fool. He might've evicted twinty thousan' tinants, an' lived to joke about it over his bottle. 'Twas th' music iv th' band an' th' dancin' on th' hill an' th' lights th' Galway man seen whin he wint up th' muddy road with his babby in his arrums that done th' business f'r Dorsey." (February 6, 1897)

3. The Wanderers

"Poor la-ads, poor la-ads," said Mr. Dooley, putting aside his newspaper and rubbing his glasses. "'Tis a hard lot theirs, thim that go down into th' say in ships, as Shakespeare says. Ye niver see a storm on th' ocean? Iv coorse ye didn't. How cud ye, ye that was born away fr'm home? But I have, Jawn. May th' saints save me fr'm another! I come over in th' bowels iv a big crazy balloon iv a propeller, like wan iv thim ye see hooked up to Dempsey's dock, loaded with lumber an' slabs an' Swedes. We watched th' little ol' island fadin' away behind us, with th' sun sthrikin' th' white house-tops iv Queenstown an' lightin' up th' chimbleys iv Martin Hogan's liquor store. Not wan iv us but had left near all we loved behind, an' sare a chance that we'd iver spoon th' stirabout out iv th' pot above th' ol' peat fire again. Yes, by dad, there was wan,—a lad fr'm th' County Roscommon. Divvle th' tear he shed. But, whin we had parted fr'm land, he turns to me, an' says, 'Well, we're on our way,' he says. 'We are that,' says I. 'No chanst f'r thim to turn around an' go back,' he says. 'Divvle th' fut,' says I. 'Thin,' he says, raisin' his voice, 'to 'ell with th' Prince iv Wales,' he says. 'To 'ell with him' he says.

"An' that was th' last we see of sky or sun f'r six days. That night come up th' divvle's own storm. Th' waves tore an' walloped th' ol' boat, an' th' wind howled, an' ye cud hear th' machinery snortin' beyant. Murther, but I was sick. Wan time th' ship 'd be settin' on its tail, another it'd be standin' on its head,

thin rollin' over cow-like on th' side; an' ivry time it lurched me
stummick lurched with it, an' I was tore an' rint an' racked till, if
death come, it 'd found me willin'. An' th' Roscommon man,—
glory be, but he was disthressed. He set on th' flure, with his
hands on his belt an' his face as white as stone, an' rocked to an'
fro. 'Ahoo,' he says, 'ahoo, but me insides has torn loose,' he says,
'an' are tumblin' around,' he says. 'Say a pather an' avy,' says I, I
was that mad f'r th' big bosthoon f'r his blatherin' on th' flure.
'Say a pather an' avy,' I says; 'f'r ye're near to death's dure, avick.'
'Am I?' says he, raising up. 'Thin,' he says, 'to 'ell with the whole
rile fam'ly,' he says. Oh, he was a rebel!

"'Through th' storm there was a babby cryin'. 'Twas a little
wan, no more thin a year ol'; an' 'twas owned be a Tipp'rary man
who come fr'm near Clonmel, a poor, weak, scarey-lookin' little
divvle that lost his wife, an' see th' bailiff walk off with th' cow, an'
thin see him come back again with th' process servers. An' so he
was comin' over with th' babby, an' bein' mother an' father to it.
He'd rock it be th' hour on his knees, an' talk dam nonsense to it,
an' sing it songs, 'Aha, 'twas there I met a maiden down be th'
tanyard side,' an' 'Th' Wicklow Mountaineer,' an' 'Th' Rambler
fr'm Clare,' an' 'O'Donnel Aboo,' croonin' thim in th' little babby's
ears, an' payin' no attintion to th' poorin' thunder above his head,
day an' night, day an' night, poor soul. An' th' babby cryin' out
his heart, an' him settin' there with his eyes as red as his hair, an'
makin' no kick, poor soul.

"But wan day th' ship settled down steady, an' ragin' stum-
micks with it; an' th' Roscommon man shakes himself, an' says,
'To 'ell with th' Prince iv Wales an' th' Dook iv Edinboroo,' an'
goes out. An' near all th' steerage followed; f'r th' storm had done
its worst, an' gone on to throuble those that come afther, an' may th'
divvle go with it. 'Twill be rest f'r that little Tipp'rary man; f'r th'
waves was r-runnin' low an' peaceful, an' th' babby have sthopped
cryin'.

"He had been settin' on a stool, but he come over to me. 'Th'
storm,' says I, 'is over.' 'Yis,' says he, ''tis over.' ''Twas wild while
it lasted,' says I. 'Ye may say so,' says he. 'Well, please Gawd,' says

I, 'that it left none worse off thin us.' 'It blew ill f'r some an' aise f'r others,' says he. 'Th' babby is gone.'

"An' so it was, Jawn, f'r all his rockin' an' singin'. An' in th' avnin' they burried it over th' side into th' say, an' th' little Tip-p'rary man wint up an' see thim do it. He see thim do it." (February 16, 1895)

4. Gold-Seeking: Illusions about America

The day before this piece appeared, news of fabulous discoveries of gold in the Yukon broke in the Chicago papers. Mr. Dooley's immediate reaction was to cast doubt on all such accounts—by recalling his own youthful illusions about America and describing the pernicious effects that wealth would have on Hennessy.

"Well, sir," said Mr. Hennessy, "that Alaska's th' gr-reat place. I thought 'twas nawthin' but an iceberg with a few seals roostin' on it, an' wan or two hundherd Ohio politicians that can't be killed on account iv th' threaty iv Pawrs. But here they tell me 'tis fairly smothered in goold. A man stubs his toe on th' ground, an lifts th' top off iv a goold mine. Ye go to bed at night, an' wake up with goold fillin' in ye'er teeth."

"Yes," said Mr. Dooley, "Clancy's son was in here this mornin', an' he says a frind iv his wint to sleep out in th' open wan night, an' whin he got up his pants assayed four ounces iv goold to th' pound, an' his whiskers panned out as much as thirty dollars net."

"If I was a young man an' not tied down here," said Mr. Hennessy, "I'd go there; I wud so."

"I wud not," said Mr. Dooley. "Whin I was a young man in th' ol' counthry, we heerd th' same story about all America. We used to set be th' tur-rf fire o' nights, kickin' our bare legs on th' flure an' wishin' we was in New York, where all ye had to do was to hold ye'er hat an' th' goold guineas'd dhrop into it. An' whin I got to be a man, I come over here with a ham and a bag iv oatmeal, as sure that I'd return in a year with money enough to dhrive me own ca-ar as I was that me name was Martin Dooley. An' that was a cinch.

"But, faith, whin I'd been here a week, I seen that there was nawthin' but mud undher th' pavement,—I larned that be means iv a pick-axe at tin shillin's th' day,—an' that, though there was plenty iv goold, thim that had it were froze to it; an' I come west, still lookin' f'r mines. Th' on'y mine I sthruck at Pittsburgh was a hole f'r sewer pipe. I made it. Siven shillin's th' day. Smaller thin New York, but th' livin' was cheaper, with Mon'gahela rye at five a throw, put ye'er hand around th' glass.

"I was still dreamin' goold, an' I wint down to Saint Looey. Th' nearest I come to a fortune there was findin' a quarther on th' sthreet as I leaned over th' dashboord iv a car to whack th' off mule. Whin I got to Chicago, I looked around f'r the goold mine. They was Injuns here thin. But they wasn't anny mines I cud see. They was mud to be shovelled an' dhrays to be dhruv an' beats to be walked. I choose th' dhray; f'r I was niver cut out f'r a copper, an' I'd had me fill iv excavatin'. An' I dhruv th' dhray till I wint into business.

"Me experyence with goold minin' is it's always in th' nex' county. If I was to go to Alaska, they'd tell me iv th' finds in See-berya. So I think I'll stay here. I'm a silver man, annyhow; an' I'm contint if I can see goold wanst a year, whin some prominent citizen smiles over his newspaper. I'm thinkin' that ivry man has a goold mine undher his own dure-step or in his neighbor's pocket at th' farthest."

"Well, annyhow," said Mr. Hennessy, "I'd like to kick up th' sod, an' find a ton iv goold undher me fut."

"What wud ye do if ye found it?" demanded Mr. Dooley.

"I—I dinnaw," said Mr. Hennessy, whose dreaming had not gone this far. Then, recovering himself, he exclaimed with great enthusiasm, "I'd throw up me job at th' gashouse an'—an' live like a prince."

"I tell ye what ye'd do," said Mr. Dooley. "Ye'd come back here an' sthrut up an' down th' sthreet with ye'er thumbs in ye'er armpits; an' ye'd dhrink too much, an' ride in sthreet ca-ars. Thin ye'd buy foldin' beds an' piannies, an' start a reel estate office. Ye'd be fooled a good deal an' lose a lot iv ye'er money, an' thin ye'd tighten up. Ye'd be in a cold fear night an' day that ye'd lose ye'er fortune. Ye'd wake up in th' middle iv th' night, dhreamin' that ye was back at th' gas-house with ye'er money gone. Ye'd be prisidint iv a charitable society. Ye'd have to wear ye'er shoes in th' house, an' ye'er wife'd have ye around to rayciptions an' dances. Ye'd move to Mitchigan Avnoo, an' ye'd hire a coachman that'd laugh at ye. Ye'er boys'd be joods an' ashamed iv ye, an' ye'd support ye'er daughters' husbands. Ye'd rack-rint ye'er tinants an' lie about ye'er taxes. Ye'd go back to Ireland on a visit, an' put on airs with ye'er cousin Mike. Ye'd be a mane, close-fisted, onscrupulous ol' curmudgeon; an', whin ye'd die, it'd take half ye'er fortune f'r rayqueems to put ye r-right. I don't want ye iver to speak to me whin ye get rich, Hinnissy."

"I won't," said Mr. Hennessy. (July 17, 1897)

5. Irish County Rivalries and Employment in Chicago

Here Irish geography is seen to have been important in determining American jobs. Mr. Dooley makes many specific references to Ireland: Maynooth (in County Kildare) is the seat of the Catholic theological college; "Connick" is the historical province of Connacht; the "guns in '98" refers to the 1798 rising against the British; and "Lor-rd Frederick" was Lord Frederick Cavendish, chief secretary for Ireland, who was murdered by fanatic nationalists in Dublin's Phoenix Park in 1882.

"How come I to go into th' liquor business?" Mr. Dooley repeated. "How come I to go into th' liquor business? Jawn, I give ye me wurrud I done it to get even with me own people. There's on'y two ways f'r to bate th' Irish. Wan is gowan th' polis foorce, an' th' other is to give thim tay. I had an uncle that was highly thought of at M'ynooth. I cudden't be a polisman.

"Whin I come over here 'twas me intention f'r to have a goold orchard. All I had to do was to plant a handful iv small change an' thin lay undher th' trees an' blow th' tin dollar notes off iv th' bra-anches. Afther I'd been here a month I become scared thinkin' that if I got to coughin' I might be dhrownded in money, so I dhruv a dhray an' was without fear. I niver had enough to eat. Th' hor-rse died on me an' I wint to wurruk in th' Northwistrun freighthouse. I did that. An' 'twas beginnin' there I seen what the Irish was.

"Jawn, I'll tell ye thrue. I'm a Connickman. I'll not deny it. But I was born near enough to th' County Clare f'r to have to take along an ax whin I'd knocked th' hurlin' ball over th' bounds. I'll say that much. But I'll say beyant that, that though Connickmin is put down f'r stealin' hor-ses an' cuttin' th' ligs off cattle they're no wor-rse thin th' rist iv th' counthry is. Divvle th' bit. They was in this here freighthouse a man be th' na-ame iv Casey, an' he was fr'm th' County Kilkenny. 'White stocking an' no money,' d'ye mind. A proud people th' Kilkenny people—too proud to fight, may th' divvle mind them. 'Twas thim that poored wather on th' locks iv their guns in '98, an' opened th' wa-ay f'r Cromwill, or whoever th' 'ell it was, I dinnaw. Annyway I found all th' lead dumped on me thruck an' all the feathers on th' Kilkenny la-ads. I sthruck, I sthruck a ma-an be th' name iv Finley an' th' foreman sthruck me with a hook an' I was in th' hospital f'r wan whole week.

"Thin I wint to wurruk f'r th' Pittsboorg, Fort Wayne an' Chicago Railroad Comp'ny, an' th' foreman was fr'm th' County Limerick. Butthermilks ivery man jack iv thim down to th' switchmin. I always got along with th' butthermilks till thin, but whin they thried to make a couplin' iv me bechune two freightca-ars I wint an' got me time. 'Twas more thin I cud stand. I moved over to th' Alton, d'ye mind. Here 'twas Dublin. Th' foreman'd been a jackeen an' there was divvle the wan iv thim that hadn't dhruv a cab an' didn't know th' raison Lor-rd Friderick was croaked. I said wan day that th' Shannon was beautifuller thin th' Liffey an' they med me ate coal.

"Th' last job I took was in th' Burlin'ton. Well, iv all th' places.

Ye may ta-alk iv May-o min, but th' Waterford la-ads 'd cut th' buttons fr'm their coats. I was surrounded be Shannyvogles an' Perkladdies, an' befure I'd been there a week I had scars on th' back iv me legs fr'm th' points iv their thrucks. I wint to th' foreman, an' says I: 'Thim min is again me,' I says.

"'F'r why should they be?' says he.

"'Because they does be Perkladdies,' says I, 'an' I'm fr'm Connick.'

"'Come,' says he, 'an' we'll roll around.'

"So we rolled. I was up first, but he took tin dollars fr'm me time, an' I wint into the saloon business.

"I had th' plisure three years aftherward iv disfranchisin' him. Me an' Donohue held him on th' flure while big Dochney fed him with raypooblican posthers." (December 22, 1894)

6. The Illinois and Michigan Canal

Two pieces contain substantial recollections of this long-defunct waterway. In the first, Mr. Dooley recalls a pick-and-shovel strike during the construction of the canal; the context is the American Railway Union's sympathy strike in support of the walk-out by workers at George Pullman's Chicago-area plant in June 1894. In the second, a disputed America's Cup yacht race in 1895 prompts the anecdote of a similar altercation between two canal-barge operators.

"Sthrikes used to be for a matter iv principle whin I was younger. Min sthruck because their wages was cut down or because iv some other thing that stirred th' souls iv thim. I remimber well th' sthrike on Dorgan's section iv th' canal. Dorgan got his rollers upon him one night and says he, 'I've been accused,' he says, 'iv hirin' on'y Mayo min,' he says; 'an' I give it out, could an' flat,' he says, 'that anny min, barrin' thim from th' County Clare,' he says, 'can handle a pick undher me.' Well sir, th' nex' day there was th' 'ell an' all to pay. The May-o min held a meetin' an' they goes to Dorgan, an' says Callaghan, th' leader of th' comity: 'Dor-

gan,' he says, 'we've been given to undherstand,' he says, 'that
ye'er discriminatin' again th' County May-o,' he says. 'Why,' says
Dorgan, 'ain't every man on me section from th' County May-o?'
he says. ''Tis true,' says Callaghan, 'but we undherstand ye dis-
criminate,' he says. 'Didn't ye say,' he says, 'that anny man was as
good with a pick as a May-o man?' 'Whin?' asks Dorgan. 'Last
night,' says Callaghan. 'I had a tub 'r two aboord last night,' says
Dorgan, 'but I didn't say that,' he says, 'that I remimber,' he says.
'What I said,' he says, 'was that I'd heer tell of good pick-min,' he
says, 'out iv May-o,' he says, gettin' his back up. 'An' be hivins I
stand by it,' he says, 'Thin,' says Callaghan, 'we strike,' he says.
'We like ye, Cornelius,' he says, 'as a man,' he says; 'but on principle we'll break ye'er back,' he says. An' they thrun him into th'
canal.

"Do ye suppose there was anny wan sthruck f'r sympathy?
Sare a wan. A gang iv Wexford min in th' nex' siction come over
an' offered half a day's wurruk an' th' Roscommon Lith'ry Society
volunteered to fill th' places iv th' sthrikers with min that could
handle a pick betther thin any man fr'm wan ind iv Mayo to th'
other. Dam'd th' sympathy. 'Tis only recent th' lads begun t'
sthrike f'r sympathy. It rayminds me iv Gavin, th' undhertaker.
He closed up his shop an' got dhrunk whin Cassidy, th' roofer,
died, an' bedad it looked f'r a time as if th' poor corpse would have
to go without Christian burial, f'r th' only other undhertakers in th'
neighborhood was prowtestants. As it was, by dad, they planted
poor Cassidy in a crate in a shroud that Mrs. Hinnissy had made
f'r Terence whin he was down with pneumony iv th' lungs."
(June 30, 1894)

"Th' same case [as that of the America's Cup dispute] come up
on th' canal twinty years ago. Mike O'Brien had th' scow 'Long
John' an' Dorsey ownded th' 'Juniata.' Th' mules was dhruv be
their two sons. Wan day Dorsey started out down th' canal, an'
O'Brien come afther him. 'I'll race ye f'r a dollar to the Sag,' says
O'Brien. 'I'll go ye,' says Dorsey. Well, th' two kids whaled away
at th' mules, an' Dorsey an' O'Brien stood on their boats an' yelled

at each other. O'Brien had the fastest mule. He was out iv th' most famous mule on th' canal—Lady Annabel, ownded be a man be th' name iv Clancy. Th' 'Long Jawn' closed down on th' 'Juniata,' an' O'Brien yells out: 'Give way there,' he says. 'Give way nothin',' says Dorsey, th' wise man that'd figured O'Brien couldn't pass him on account iv th' ropes bein' in th' way. Thin he sang 'A wet sheet and a flowin' wind,' an' took a dhrag out iv the jug. 'Dominick,' sings out O'Brien to his boy, 'I, I, pappa,' says th' la-ad. 'I'm goin' to slack out,' says O'Brien; an' he an' th' other mariners aboord shoved off an' wint around th' 'Juniata,' an' faith th' towline took Dorsey on th' whiskers an' carried him th' whole linth iv th' yat. I'm tellin' ye th' thruth. 'Twas so. I'll say this f'r O'Brien, that he took no advantage iv Dorsey. He waited f'r him at Willow Springs, an' they spint an hour or two rollin' each other into th' canal.

"Dorsey wudden't pay an' th' matther was referred to a comity at my place. Hannigan was th' chairman, a thrue spoort. Whin we'd heerd the ividince he says: 'Fr'm repoorts we've had we are convinced that "Long Jawn" deliberately fouled Dorsey's whiskers in crossing its line outside iv "Juniata." Therefore, we decide that Juniata wins, f'r 'tis th' rule iv yattin',' he says, 'that,' he says, 'th' scow that starts first is th' first at th' Sag. Heave two,' an' they heaved at least tin.

"Did O'Brien go back to Ireland? I sh'd say not. He turned in an' won th' dollar fr'm Dorsey shakin' dice." (September 14, 1895)

7. A Canalside Championship Fight

This tale of an epic Irish-German confrontation appeared while Gentleman Jim Corbett and Bob Fitzsimmons were fencing verbally and legally about the arrangements for a heavyweight title boxing match. When they finally did fight, almost two years later, Fitzsimmons won in fourteen rounds.

"Good avenin', Jawn," said Mr. Dooley.

"Good evening," said Mr. McKenna.

"Ye'er late to-night. Annything new downtown?"

"Never a thing."

"How's th' Vinzwalan situation comin' on?"

"No change that I've heard of."

"Has the Cubans done annything, I dinnaw?"

"How do I know?" Mr. McKenna returned with asperity. "Ask Hesing."

"Well," said Mr. Dooley, casting aside pride and his newspaper, "what I want ye to tell me is: Is there annything new about Jim and Bob? There, now."

"They're still getting themselves arrested," said Mr. McKenna. "I think Corbett's got the best of it so far. He's been arrested twice to Fitzsimmons' once."

"They'll niver fight," said Mr. Dooley thoughtfully. "What Hinnissy calls th' noble art iv whalin' somewan has gone to pot in this counthry. F'r why, Jawn? Because 'tis immoral, says I. Because 'tis degradin' to th' youth iv th' land f'r to see two human brutes in a ring injurin' th' best features Gawd give thim. What a horrid spictacle, Jawn. I can hardly think iv me whin I was a young gossoon—an' I cud put up me hands with th' bist of thim in those days, avick; another Donnelly I was—iv me walkin' all th' way out to th' Sag f'r to see Con Murphy, th' champine hivvy-weight iv th' ya-ards, go again th' German blacksmith.

"Oh, 'twas a gran' fight. They was no play-actin' f'r th' boxers in thim days. Sare a plug hat did wan iv thim wear. Murphy was a sticker—an' a good wan—at Armour's an' the German swung a hammer f'r Clancy that we called th' Kerry Gow. They was no pictures iv thim in th' pa-apers. They was niver heerd of but whin a squad iv polismin was sint to arrist Murphy ivery Saturdah night. Murphy trained be shakin' dice all night in Dorney's an' wrastlin' with th' night watchman in th' scrap-iron yard near th' mills, an' th' German got into condition playin' sixty-six an' leadin' thrumps at Schwartzmeister's.

"We didn't have no special ca-ars. Some walked, an' some like th' liftinant iv polis rode out in their horse an' buggy. They was no clubhouse an' no purse. Th' crowd put in what it cud affoord. Th' ring was pitched on th' turf near th' canal, an' whin Sundah mornin' come, frish and pure, an' th' people in town was gettin' ready f'r to go to church, Callaghan, that run th' thing, he says, 'Gintlemin,' he says, 'this is a fight to th' finish,' he says. 'If ayether wan iv th' two laves th' ring while he can walk,' he says, 'I'll have th' law on him,' he says. 'I'm wan iv th' thrustees iv this town,' he says. An' so he was. 'Now, gintlemin," he says, 'remember th' example iv McGraw, th' Fermanagh flail. He wint into th' ring iv a Mundah mornin' an' he niver come out till Saturdah night. They was no bugs on that man. A-are ye ready?' he says. 'I am,' says Murphy. 'Somy,' says th' smith. 'Thin go at it,' says Callaghan, 'an' may the bist man win.'

"Well, Jawn, 'twas to be three-minyit rounds, but th' time-keeper bet his watch on Murphy. 'Twas the on'y watch in th' crowd an' th' stakeholder, being he was f'r th' smith an' th' smith was havin' th' bist iv it, said nawthin' till they'd fought twinty minyits. In th' sicond round, th' German thrun Murphy an' gettin' up give him a kick be way iv good-by. 'Foul,' says a little man in th' crowd. 'What d'ye mane?' says Callaghan. 'He kicked him,' says th' little man. 'An' ye yelled "foul" f'r that an' frightened us half out iv our wits?' says Callaghan. 'Doheny, take that little gazabo an' thrun him into th' canal. This is no chicken fight,' he says.

"Th' match was reshumed. It begin at 4 o'clock in th' mornin'. At tin I come in f'r to see th' folks to church. Whin I got back at wan th' lads was still at it. 'Twas dark whin Murphy's backer put a horseshoe on th' big man's fist. He give th' smith wan puck in th' jaw an' th' gr-reat match was over."

"That wasn't fair," said Mr. McKenna.

"So some iv th' la-ads said," said Mr. Dooley. "But Callaghan put it this way: 'Sure,' he says, 'if I hadn't done it they'd've fought all night,' he says. 'I've got to attind a meetin' iv th' thrustees iv th'

rayform school in th' mornin',' he says. So we give th' stakes to
Murphy. They was twilve dollars an' fifty cints an' a pass on th'
towpath. Murphy was th' champine iv th' parish till he died. Th'
on'y wan that iver licked him was his wife.

"Thim was prize fightin' days, Jawn. Sure Murphy'd take this
man Corbett be th' hair an' pull him around th' block, he wud so."

"You're an expert," said Mr. McKenna with deference. "Who
do you think'll win if they come together?"

"Well," said Mr. Dooley. "If 'tis a long-range fight Corbett
ought to win. But I think Fitz'll get th' money if there's much
in-fightin'. Corbett'd win over a tiliphone but Fitzsimmons 'll
smother him through a speakin'-chube." (November 2, 1895)

8. Education in Ireland and Chicago

*When a University of Chicago professor advocated corporal pun-
ishment at the 1897 National Education Association convention in
Milwaukee, Dunne responded with this piece. The real hedge schools,
illegal, open-air Catholic schools, had disappeared long before Mr.
Dooley's time, but most of his generation did attend private Catholic
schools because the "free schools" that he mentions were government-
run and Protestant-dominated. The Irish teaching order of Christian
Brothers opened an industrial school, the Bridgeport Institute, on
Archer Avenue in 1859.*

"I see here," said Mr. Dooley, laying down his paper, "that
there's a man out in th' hootchy-cootchy colledge on th' Midway
that believes in corporeal punishment f'r childher."

"I seen that," said Mr. Hennessy, "an' I'd like to have him here.
I'd go to th' flure with him. I'll bet he's near-sighted an' is afraid iv
cows. I niver knowed a man that wanted to club little childher
that wasn't. I had me own share iv hoistin' whin I was a kid an' I
swore that if iver a ma-an laid hands on child iv mine I'd inthrojooce mesilf to him be means iv a pickax."

"I was licked good whin I was a kid," said Mr. Dooley solemnly. "I wint to school to an old hedge schoolmasther be th' name iv Larney. There were free schools nearer, but none iv us was sint. Our people paid Larney to polish us off an' he done it. Glory be, he was a rough man, a long-legged, sour-faced ol' man, as hard as his blackthorn stick an' as knotty. He larned us 'A-ah-b-l-e, to be competent' an' 'A-ah-b-e-l, a boy's name.' I can see him now in his knee breeches takin' off his long coat an' callin' out, 'McGuire, give ye'er back to Misther Dooley: I want to teach him th' etiket iv th' house iv larnin.' He used a hoe-handle, an' whin he got through we were in a way to think betther thin to set down. Lord save us, it's fifty years an' more since I laid eyes on him, an' he's been dead most iv th' time, but to this day I dhream iv him an' wake up in terror, with th' cold chills chasin' each other down me back.

"I don't believe in corporeal punishment ayether for teacher or scholar," Mr. Dooley went on. "In th' ol' days whin we had a little school out here f'r thim that was too pious to go to th' public schools most iv th' throuble come fr'm th' scholars lammin' th' teachers. That was befure th' Christian brothers come. I niver knowed a boy to lick a Christian brother. Most iv th' mimbers iv that order wud've gone into th' prize ring if they hadn't landed where they did. I'd match thim again anny body iv men in th' wurruld at annything like their weight. There was wan iv thim wanst, Brother Aloysius, that cleaned out th' whole Hogan fam'ly in Halsted sthreet with th' 'Lives iv the Saints' tied to a booksthrap. But ye raymimber that. 'Twas befure th' Christian brothers come that we had th' little school. They r-run out teacher afther teacher. I've seen a whole procession iv thim pass this very dure.

"Well, afther a while a quite, gentlemanly young man from colledge come along an' offered to take th' school. He was a big man an' a sthrong wan, but he was warned befurehand that he'd have throuble. 'I guess I can get along all right,' says he, with that quite, fearless look iv a man that knows his own strenth. An' he took th' school. F'r a time there was no throuble an' he was an ideel school masther. He inthrested th' childher in their studies, told thim stories an' learned thim to sing songs. He was a gr-reat favorite with th' girls an' the parents swore be him. School life took on a new color an' th' attindance was niver so high.

"But throuble was brewin'. No teacher had iver got away with that school, an' th' rough la-ads did not propose to let this jood from colledge do it. Wan day they was an open revolt. Some wan pegged a lump iv coal at th' school masther an' th' school masther descinded on Tom Mulhern, who was a quite lad, but had been pointed out as th' toughest in th' class. 'Mulhern,' said th' teacher ca'mly, 'come out here,' he says. 'What f'r?' says Mulhern. 'I undherstand ye're quite a fighter,' says the young man in th' same steady voice. 'I want to teach ye a lesson in boxin',' he says. 'Ye're a good, sthrong la-ad,' he says, 'but ye need insthruction in boxin',' he says, with a smile on his face. 'I want th' school to see Tom larn to box,' he says. 'Ivry man sh'd larn th' manly art iv self-defense,' he says. 'All right,' says Tom Mulhern. 'Me father sint me here to larn sums, but,' he says, 'if ye can teach me anny other accomplishmints,' he says, 'I'm ye'er gooseberry,' he says.

"Th' school was silent as a church as th' big, hulkin' rowdy faced th' quite but determined masther. 'Put up ye'er hands,' says th' masther, 'f'r I'm goin' to hit ye har-rd,' he says. 'Poke away, ol' spoort,' says th' lout, an' suddenly th' masther's fist shot out like lightenin'. But just at that moment Tom ducked his head an' comin' up undher th' masther's high gyard he ripped in a stiff right hand punch in th' wind an' cracked him wan in th' nose with th' left. As th' school masther sunk again a blackboard, with th' quite, confident smile turnin' green, Tom hooked him on th' point iv th' jaw an' put him out. Mike O'Grady pulled out a stop watch an' counted. 'Wan, two, three, four, five, six, siven, eight, nine, tin,' he says. 'Th' fight goes to Mulhern,' he says. Ye see, Tom Mulhern was th' welterweight champeen iv Illinye an' only wint to school whin he was not fightin' f'r $50 a corner.

"Afther that come th' brothers, an' whin wan iv thim wint through th' Christian jooty class with a couplin'-pin th' school become ordherly."

"Well, annyhow, I don't believe in lammin' th' kids," said Mr. Hennessy.

"Nayether do I," said Mr. Dooley. "If a lad don't want to go to school I say lave him stay away. There's too much idyacation annyhow. There's twinty men in this counthry that can write pothry to wan that can dhrive a car or hoop a bar'l." (July 10, 1897)

9. Bridgeport in the Civil War

Colonel James Mulligan led Chicago's Irish Brigade of nine hundred men off to the Civil War in July 1861. "Calv'ry" is Calvary Cemetery, just north of Chicago, where most Irish Catholics buried their dead, and Gavin was a real Bridgeport undertaker. Meagher (a veteran of the 1848 Rising in Ireland) and "Shur'dan" (Philip H. Sheridan) were Union generals.

"Jawn," said Mr. Dooley the other evening, "did ye see th' p'rade yesterday?"

"Yes," said Mr. McKenna.

"Was it good?"

"Fine."

"Who led th' polis?"

"Mike Brennan, on horseback."

"Be hivins," said Mr. Dooley, "I wisht I'd been there, f'r when I knowed Mike Brennan he couldn't ride a thrunk without houldin' on. But I've made it a rule niver to go out on Dec'ration Day. It turns the hear-rt in me gray f'r to see th' women marchin' to Calv'ry with their veils over their heads an' thim little pots iv gyraniums in their hands. Th' sojers has thim that'll fire salutes over their graves an' la-ads to talk about thim, but there's none but th' widdy f'r to break her hear-rt above th' poor soul that died afther his hands had tur-rned to leather fr'm handlin' a pick. But thin what's th' odds? Dam'd th' bit iv difference it makes to a man wanst he's tucked away in Calv'ry whether he died f'r his counthry or was r-run over be a brewery-wagon. Whin Gavin nails th' lid on th' crate an' sinds down to th' corner grocery f'r th' pall-bearers we're all akel an' all heroes.

"Ye was a little bit iv a kid, Jawn, durin' th' war and ye ray-mimber nawthin' about it. But to me th' mim'ry iv it is as fr-resh as paint. I wint through it all. I mind as well as if it happened yesterday whin Thomas Duggan came up th' r-road wan after-noon an' says he: 'Barrygard,' says he, 'is firin' on Sumter.' I'd niver hear-rd iv Barrygard an' says I: 'Is he,' I says; 'whin did he lose his job on th' Alton?' I says. 'Tut, tut,' says he. 'Barrygard is a gin'ral,' says he, 'an' Sumter's a fort,' he says, 'an' th' southern states have left th' Union.' 'Ah, well,' says I. 'Let thim go,' I says. 'There's plenty left,' I says. 'Don't mind it, Tom,' I says. 'How's Maggie an' th' little wans?' But he was half crazy with th' news an' whin others come in ye scarce could hould him. 'I'm a dimo-crat,' says he, 'that's voted th' ticket,' he says, 'iver sence I put fut in this counthry,' he says. 'But whin anny man fires on that there flag,' he says, 'I'm a dimocrat no longer,' he says. 'I'm goin' into th' ar-rmy,' says he. 'Is there anny to go along?' he says. Dorgan, the plumber, said he'd go, an' little Kerrigan an' Doherty that worked in th' box factory, an' young Hinnissy, afther he'd found out what it was, he said he'd go along, too. That shtarted Duggan, an' be-fure two weeks was out he had gone up an' down th' r-road an' enlisted fifty men, an' they wint off with Mulligan. I raymimber Mrs. Duggan comin' in to get a pint iv beer th' night they wint away.

"I heerd no more about th' war f'r a long time, f'r I didn't r-read th' pa-apers in thim days, an' bedad, I wisht I'd niver shtarted to r-read thim. There's nawthin' in thim but hell an' hor-rors. But in th' coorse iv a year we heerd tell iv what th' A-archey road lads was doin'. Poor Duggan died iv th' fever an' Dorgan, th' plumber, was made a sergeant an' ye cuddent walk on th' sa-ame side iv th' shtreet with Mrs. Dorgan. Thin wan day a lad with a leg gone an' a face as white as a ghost's came into me shtore. 'Do ye know me?' he says. 'No,' says I. 'I'm Larry Hinnisy,' said he, an' he tould me all th' news iv th' war—how th' south was lickin' th' divvle out iv the north, an' how th' throuble was they didn't make

Thomas Francis Meagher gin'ral iv th' ar-rmy. Hinnissy said th' whisky in th' south was bad.

"Thin me cousin Mick was dhrafted. Ye didn't know Mick, Jawn. He was th' biggest coward an' liar outside iv his brother that iver lived. He always swore he was tin years younger thin me. He'd prove it be an argymint as long as a rope. He'd say: 'I was bor-rn th' year Father Hogan was sint to Curlow, an' 'twas Father Hogan confirmed you. Ye must've been fifteen year old th' night iv th' big wind, f'r I raymimber ye carryin' me out in ye'er arms f'r to see th' bonfires an' that ye stole a little goold watch me father'd give me f'r a prisent. Thin d'ye mind when me brother Dan licked ye so bad, th' night iv th' eviction iv th' Sullivans,' he says, 'I was too small to hould his coat I raymimber.' Well, wan day he comes up to me with tears in his eyes an' says he, 'Martin,' he says, 'how old am I?' 'Fifty years,' I says. 'Ye'er a liar,' he says, 'but will ye swear to it?' he says; 'I'm dhrafted.' 'Ah-ha,' says I, 'there's ye'er game, is it?' I says. 'No, Mick,' says I, 'I'll swear to nawthin',' I says. 'I admit,' I says, 'ye'er only thirty,' I says. Well, sir, ye shud've seen him. He proved be th' year iv th' big potato rot that I was tin year younger thin him. He showed me be letthers he'd wrote that he must be fifty. Be addin' up th' dates he knew ye'd'v thought he was here befure the flood. I made him go down on his knees befure twinty men an' declare on his oath he was between fifty-five an' sixty. Thin I give him th' laugh an' he had to go to Canada f'r to escape th' dhraft.

"Th' la-ads that had gone out so brave an' gay come back wan be wan an' iv'rybody talked war talk. I raymimber th' battle iv Gettysburg well. 'Twas th' day I put in new bar fixtures. Wan night there was a free fight up an' down Archey road because Dan Dorgan said Shur'dan was a betther gin'ral thin Thomas Francis Meagher. Thim was th' only two afther Mulligan was kilt that th' A-archey road cared f'r. Nearly all th' Mayo men was f'r Shur'dan. Well, sir, thin th' first thing we knowed th' war was over. Father Kelly comes in wan day an' says he: 'Praise be to Gawd,' he says, '' tis inded.' 'Th' war?' says I. 'Yis,' says he. 'Well,' I says, 'I'm glad iv it,' I says, an', Jawn, I was that." (June 2, 1894)

10. The Blue and The Gray

On Memorial Day 1895 a monument to the Confederate dead was dedicated at Oakwoods Cemetery, Chicago. An Evening Post *headline declared that "Blue and Gray Clasp Hands." The riots of seventy-seven mentioned here were skirmishes between state militiamen and striking railroad workers in Bridgeport in the summer of 1877.*

"A-ho," said Mr. Dooley, "th' blue an' th' gray, th' blue an' th' gray. Well, sir, Jawn, d'ye know that I see Mulligan's regiment off. Sure I did. I see thim with me own eyes, Mulligan marchin' ahead with his soord on his side, an' his horse dancin' an' backin' into th' crowd; an' th' la-ads chowlder arms an' march, march away. Ye shud've been there. Th' women come down fr'm th' peeraries with th' childher in their arms, an' 'twas like a sind-off to a picnic. 'Good-by, Mike.' 'Timothy, darlin', don't forget your prayers.' 'Cornalius, if ye do but look out f'r th' little wans, th' big wans 'll not harm ye.' 'Teddy, lad, always wear ye'er Agnus Day.' An', whin th' time come f'r th' thrain to lave, th' girls was up to th' lines; an' 'twas, 'Mike, love, ye'll come back alive, won't ye?' an' 'Pat, there does be a pair iv yarn socks in th' hoomp on ye'er back. Wear thim, lad. They'll be good f'r ye'er poor, dear feet.' An' off they wint.

"Well, some come back, an' some did not come back. An' some come back with no rale feet f'r to put yarn socks on thim. Mulligan quit down somewhere in Kentucky; an' th' las' wurruds he was heard to utter was, 'Lay me down, boys, an' save th' flag.' An' there was manny th' other that had nawthin' to say but to call f'r a docthor; f'r 'tis on'y, d'ye mind, th' heroes that has somethin' writ down on typewriter f'r to sind to th' newspapers whin they move up. Th' other lads that dies because they cudden't r-run away,— not because they wudden't,—they dies on their backs, an' calls f'r th' docthor or th' priest. It depinds where they're shot.

"But, annyhow, no wan iv thim lads come back to holler because he was in th' war or to war again th' men that shot him. They wint to wurruk, carryin' th' hod 'r shovellin' cindhers at th' rollin' mills. Some iv thim took pinsions because they needed thim; but divvle th' wan iv thim ye'll see paradin' up an' down Arrchey Road with a blue coat on, wantin' to fight th' war over with Schwartzmeister's bar-tinder that niver heerd iv but wan war, an' that th' rites iv sivinty-sivin. Sare a wan. No, faith. They'd as lave decorate a confeatherate's grave as a thrue pathrite's. All they want is a chanst to go out to th' cimitry; an', faith, who doesn't enjoy that? No wan that's annything iv a spoort.

"I know hundhreds iv thim. Ye know Pat Doherty, th' little man that lives over be Grove Sthreet. He inlisted three times, by dad, an' had to stand on his toes three times to pass. He was that ager. Well, he looks to weigh about wan hundherd an' twinty pounds; an' he weighs wan fifty be raison iv him havin' enough lead to stock a plumber in his stomach an' his legs. He showed himsilf wanst whin he was feelin' gay. He looks like a sponge. But he ain't. He come in here Thursdah night to take his dhrink in quite; an' says I, 'Did ye march to-day?' 'Faith, no,' he says, 'I can get hot enough runnin' a wheelbarrow without makin' a monkey iv mesilf dancin' around th' sthreets behind a band.' 'But didn't ye go out to decorate th' graves?' says I. 'I hadn't th' price,' says he. 'Th' women wint out with a gyranium to put over Sarsfield, the first born,' he says.

"Just thin Morgan O'Toole come in, an' laned over th' ba-ar. He's been a dillygate to ivry town convention iv th' Raypublicans since I dinnaw whin. 'Well,' says he, 'I see they're pilin' it on,' he says. 'On th' dead?' says I, be way iv a joke. 'No,' he says; 'but did ye see they're puttin' up a monnymint over th' rebels out here be Oakwoods?' he says. 'By gar,' he says, ''tis a disgrace to th' mim'-ries iv thim devoted dead who died f'r their counthry,' he says. 'If,' he says, 'I cud get ninety-nine men to go out an' blow it up, I'd be th' hundherth,' he says. 'Yes,' says I, 'ye wud,' I says. 'Ye'd be th' last,' I says.

"Doherty was movin' up to him. 'What rig'ment?' says he. 'What's that?' says O'Toole. 'Did ye inlist in th' army, brave man?' says Pat. 'I swore him over age,' says I. 'Was ye dhrafted in?' says th' little man. 'No,' says O'Toole. 'Him an' me was in th' same cellar,' says I. 'Did ye iver hear iv Ree-saca, 'r Vicksburg, 'r Lookout Mountain?' th' little man wint on. 'Did anny man iver shoot at ye with annything but a siltzer bottle? Did ye iver have to lay on ye'er stummick with ye'er nose burrid in th' Lord knows what while things was whistlin' over ye that, if they iver stopped whistlin', 'd make ye'er backbone look like a broom? Did ye iver see a man that ye'd slept with th' night befure cough, an' go out with his hooks ahead iv his face? Did ye iver have to wipe ye'er most intimate frinds off ye'er clothes, whin ye wint home at night? Where was he durin' th' war?' he says. 'He was dhrivin' a grocery wagon f'r Philip Reidy,' says I. 'An' what's he makin' th' roar about?' says th' little man. 'He don't want anny wan to get onto him,' says I.

"O'Toole was gone be this time, an' th' little man laned over th' bar. 'Now,' says he, 'what d'ye think iv a gazabo that don't want a monniment put over some wan? Where is this here pole? I think I'll go out an' take a look at it. Where'd ye say th' la-ad come fr'm? Donaldson? I was there. There was a man in our mess—a Wicklow man be th' name iv Dwyer—that had th' best come-all-ye I iver heerd. It wint like this,' an' he give it to me." (June 1, 1895)

11. Coxey's Army and the Little Priest

When Jacob Coxey's "army" of "commonwealers" was marching toward Washington in the spring of 1894, Mr. Dooley was reminded of an important figure from the Bridgeport past, the little priest from "up wist iv th' bridge," whose exemplary character is cited in many accounts of old Chicago. "Big Steve" was a favorite Dooley nickname for President Grover Cleveland.

"If that there Coxey gets to Wash'n'ton," said Mr. Dooley, "there'll be 'ell poppin' fr'm wan ind iv Pennsylvania avnoo to th' other, Jawn. There will that. This here Coxey do be a determined man; an' by dad, whin he asks f'r annything an' don't get it 'tis time to call out the mil-ishaw. 'Tis so."

"And what does the man want?" asked Mr. McKenna.

"Faith, ye have me there," said Mr. Dooley. "On'y whativer it is, he wants it that bad 'tis wreckin' his happiness. He do be like Riordan, the plumber, that was in here last week dhrinkin' Jamaica rum an' chasin' it with bock beer. He was talkin' about Dinnis Doolan, mutterin' to hisself an' sayin' be-this-and-be-that what he was goin' to do with him whin they come together. 'Whin I see him,' he says, 'Ma-ark what I tell ye,' he says. 'I'll flay him alive,' he says. 'An' wha-at would ye kill th' poor man f'r?' says I, 'ye big, shtrong ox.' Sure Doolan will take that little goat-faced Kerry man an' r-remove th' shtreetca-ar thracks with him. But 'twas no use to tell Riordan that. 'Twud spoil the sport. 'What ar-re ye goin' to murder him f'r?' says I. Well, sir, Riordan he scratches his head an' looks at me an' says he, 'I got a gredge again him.' 'An' what f'r?' says I. 'I dinnaw,' says Riordan. 'But annyhow I'll break his back with me fut.'

"So be Coxey. Th' omadhon, he gets a lot of gazaboys together an' he says to thim: 'Let's go down to Washin'ton,' says he, 'an' invade it,' he says, 'an' we'll tache thim what's what,' he says. He calls it the commonwheel, he does; an' why, I dinnaw, f'r all iv thim has to walk. By gar, I sh'd think he'd ca-al it th' common fut. 'Tis more thrue to nathure. So they're off, an' whin those iv thim that ain't thrun into th' booby hatch gets down to Washin'ton 'twill be time f'r Cleveland to put on his hat an' coat. F'r if I ain't much mistaken 'twill go ha-ard with him. As I said, this here Coxey is a determined man, Jawn, an' whin he makes up his mind he's as ris'lute as th' parish priest takin' subscriptions f'r a new church. Gawd, be good to me that shouldn't be sayin' th' like iv that. Did I niver tell ye how th' little soggarth up wist iv th' bridge put th' comether on me wan time. He wanted to have a spire on th' church an' I was th' soft ma-ark iv th' parish. He wint out afther me, an' by gar, I made up me mind to escape. I hired Dorney's lad to watch f'r him, an' whin he see th' good man comin' he passed th' wurrud an' I pulled down th' blinds an' sneaked out th' ba-ack way. Well, sir, we had it to an' fro f'r near a month an' I wint to mass all that time in th' little Frinch church beyant where ye'd expect to see th' pastor doin' a jig step ivry time he r-read th' gospel fr'm Saint Jawn. Hivin help me, me tongue's r-run away. Well, sir, th' little soggarth thried be letters an' be missingers to land me, but I stud him off till wan day I was standin' down at th' dure an' see him comin' up th' r-road. I r-run inside an' bolted th' dure. Thin I waited. I heerd him talkin' with th' la-ad an' thin there come a knock. 'Misther Dooley,' says th' kid, 'he's gone.' 'He's not,' says I. 'He is,' says th' little rogue. 'He's gone an' he lef' a goold watch an' chain f'r ye,' he says, says th' la-ad, 'that they voted ye as th' mos' pop'lar man in th' parish.' Well, Jawn, ye know I was dam shtrong in thim days an' I thought it was on th' square an' I opened th' dure. Th' minyit I did in come a good-sized broadcloth leg an' th' smilin' face iv th' little soggarth. Me strenth left me an' I let him all in. 'Well,' I says, 'ye've bate me,' I says. 'But savin' ye'r prisince,' I says, ''tis a strange example ye give.' 'Be what?' says he. 'Be lyin',' says I. 'Sure,' says he, 'I didn't lie,' he says. ''Twas th' la-ad, an' I'll give him a pinance that'll br-eak his back. An' now,' he says, 'about that spire ye wa-ant so bad.' Well, sir, he got me f'r wan hundhred bucks, an' afther all I didn't begredge it, Jawn. He was a good man, the little soggarth that died along in sixty-sivin iv nursin' th' chollery patients. Pax vobiscum."

"But what about Coxey?" queried Mr. McKenna.

"Well, as I say, I dinnaw what th' 'ell's goin' to be-come of big Steve. That there Coxey 'll talk him to death unless"—and here Mr. Dooley stroked his chin—"he can sind congress again him." (April 21, 1894)

12. The Chicago Fire

Mr. Dooley ridiculed the 1897 commemoration of the great Chicago Fire of 1871 by remembering what the fire actually did to the city's poor people. His argument opens with a list of other uncelebrated misfortunes, including the arrival in Chicago of streetcar monopolist Charles T. Yerkes ("Yerkuss") and the election to the gover-

norship of Illinois of John R. Tanner, who was then being criticized widely for his apparent favoritism toward business interests.

"Ar-re ye goin' to attind th' cillybration iv th' fire?" asked Mr. Hennessy.

"Th' cillybration iv th' fire!" Mr. Dooley replied. "An' why shud I cillybrate th' fire? An' why shud annywan? D'ye hear iv people cillybratin' th' famine iv forty-eight or th' panic iv sivinty-three or th' firin' on Fort Sumpter? We've had manny other misfortunes an' they're not cillybrated. Why don't we have a band out an' illuminated sthreet ca-ars f'r to commimorate th' day that Yerkuss come to Chicago? An' there's cholera. What's th' matther with cholera? Why don't we have an ipidimic day, with floats showin' distinguished citizens in convulsions an' a procission iv hearses? That'd be a pretty sight. Sometime I expect to see Tanner's inaug'ration cillybrated because it happened, an' th' people, or manny iv thim, lived through it. We cud have a riprisintation iv Tanner bein' pursued by a yellow fever mickrobe an' durin' th' intertainment mimbers iv th' legislature'ud pass among th' audjience pickin' pockets.

"F'r mesilf, who was here whin it happened, though I see little iv it, th' Chicago fire doesn't stir up anny wild desire to get out an' mar-rch an' shoot off Roman candles. Not much. I'm good f'r th' Foorth iv July an' Pathrick's day, an' other naytional holidays, but I've got to quit at the fire. I'm not up to rejoicin' over th' misfortunes iv me fellow men. Iv coorse I know th' fire was a good thing—Oh! a fine thing, f'r Chicago. It desthroyed old buildin's so that new wans cud be put up. But did ye iver think that th' ol' buildin's was homes f'r poor people? Ye hear iv th' men who be nerve an' interprise took advantage iv th' fire to build up fortunes. D'ye iver think if thim that had no nerve an' interprise afther th' fire to begin new again? Poor souls."

"Was you here during th' fire?" asked young Mr. Aloysius Hogan, who had come in to drink a small bottle of pop and listen to the conversation of the elders.

"I said I was," retorted Mr. Dooley. "I was here, right here. I niver moved. I stayed right on th' old homestead an' heerd about th' fire fr'm men who came in to tell about it. I've heerd about it manny times since. Out this way we didn't pay much attintion to it. Me nex'-dure neighbor was a man be th' name iv Clancy, an' I cud just see th' smoke iv his chimbly on a clear day. But down be Halsted sthreet, where they was as manny as four houses in a block, th' excitemint was turrible. People moved their furniture out on th' sthreet an' poored wather on th' roof. Bimeby they sint a man over th' creek to see how th' fire was goin' on. He come back at night. 'It's all right,' he says. 'Th' fire has swept across DeKoven sthreet an' is now movin' north, desthroyin' th' intire business district an' th' whole North Side,' he says. 'Saved,' cried Malachi Geohegan, that ownded a house about as big as a chicken coop, with nawthin' in it but wan bed, a stove an' a table. 'Is th' coorthouse gone?' says a German named Schmidt. 'It is,' says th' messenger. 'An' th' jail,' he says. 'Thank hivin,' said Schmidt. They was a warrant out f'r him f'r keeping a saloon without a license, an' he wud've been arristed if anny polisman cud be found to put a fut in Bridgeport in thim days. It's all changed now. They'se nawthin' else here but polismin.

"So ivery wan rayturned to his home an' thought no more iv it till th' papers come out. They was about as big as a porous plasther, an' they looked like wan afther usin'. Thin we see what a divvle iv a misfortune we'd been through. Afther a while people we knowed come over an' lived on us till th' winter. Thin we heerd that money was poorin' in an' they wint over to get relieved. Be th' same token, this relieved us too. They got things to eat an' clothes to wear an' manny other conthributions. Wan iv thim that 'd lived with me sint me a hammick an' a pair iv boot trees that he got fr'm th' comity. Those iv thim that wanted a house to wear around got wan. They were more useful as watch char-rms or pocket pieces thin to live in, but a lot iv th' people iv our race took thim over to Goose Island, an' be patchin' thim up with what lumber they found lyin' around loose made a comfortable mansion. Ye can see thim in th' twenty-third war-rd to this day if ye can find thim. I knowed a man be th' name iv Murphy—a clan man—that kept buildin' around th' relief house till now he has a mansion four stories high. I wint over to see him las' year. 'Where's th' little house ye got fr'm th' relief comity afther th' fire?' I says. 'It's th' back stoop on th' third flure,' he says.

"But that's nayther here nor there. What I started out to say was, I'll have no cillybration iv th' fire. I don't care if we did get a new jail. Th' ol' wan was good enough f'r me." (October 9, 1897)

13. A Ball at Finucane's Hall, 1872

Mr. Dooley is provoked into reminiscence by John McKenna's attendance at the County Democracy Ball of 1894, presided over by Mayor John Patrick Hopkins. William Joyce was a king-making politician, who wielded a good deal of clout in Chicago in the nineties without holding office himself.

Mr. McKenna came in very late Wednesday night—it was, in fact, Thursday morning and Mr. Dooley had sat up to read a copy of the Cork *Intelligencer* which his cousin Sarsfield had sent enclosing a bunch of clover. Throwing back his coat the visitor revealed a sadly-rumpled shirt front of great extent and other sartorial evidences of recent engagement in social frivolities.

"By dad," said Mr. Dooley, surveying him narrowly. "Jawn, ye'er lookin' gr-rand. Did ye have a good house?"

"I come from the County Democracy's ball," said Mr. McKenna, disregarding the gibe. "And it was out of sight."

"Was it thin," said Mr. Dooley. "I suppose all th' la-ads was there with their first pa-arty clothes upon thim an' their dimons an' all?"

"They was," said Mr. McKenna. "I never saw so many diamonds in my life. By heavens, the mayor had a horseshoe of diamonds with a big ruby——"

"The dam jood," said Mr. Dooley, contemptuously. "That there Hopkins is that swilled up, by dad, 'tis a wonder to me he don't have to wear a injy rubber suit. An' I knowed him whin he didn't have a coat to his back. I did that, Jawnny. I'm glad I didn't gaw to th' ball, with its dimons an' its r-rubies an' Gawd knows what all. 'Twud make me hear-rt sick thinkin' iv th' days gone by, th' days gone by.

"I usety be th' 'ell an' all f'r parties an' dances whin I was your age, Jawn. I was r-recordin' secretee iv th' Faugh a Ballagh Social Plisure Club, th' principal social plisure iv which was to get out iv a 'lection mornin' an' see how manny votes we cud poll f'r Malachi Riordan f'r constabble iv th' South Town. That was before he become a British spy—th' thraitor. Mind ye, in thim days they was no such a thing knowed as a u-nited democracy. By gar, th' democracy iv th' sixth wa-ard was niver united with th' democracy iv th' fifth wa-ard save an' excipt be way of gettin' their teeth in each other's neck. Each wa-ard had its own social an' polit-ical clubs an' th' shtar iv thim all was th' Faugh a Ballagh that I was recordin' secretee iv an' main guy gin'rally. An' ivry year comin' on Lint we had a ball in Finucane's hall that ye niver see th' like iv f'r fun an' merriment. By hivins they niver detailed liss than twinty polismen f'r it an' th' whole foorce was on reserve whin it come off. Ho, ho, 'twas gorjous!

"Th' last ball they give was on th' Pathrick's night after th' big fire. 'Twas in Lint, but ye know there's a dispensation ivry Pathrick's day so that anny wan iv us can do as we dam please excipt the Dutch. They don't come in on th' dispensation. I usety think 'twas Willum Joyce got th' dispensation, but Grogan's boy that goes over to th' college tells me 'twas St. Pathrick himsilf. It seems that whin he'd done his jooty around through Ireland convartin' th' whole counthry excipt th' County May-o, he wint to R-rome f'r his health an' calls on th' pope. Says th' pope iv Rome, he says to St. Pathrick, mind ye, 'Ye've done gr-rand work,' he says, 'dhrivin' out th' snakes,' he says, 'an' convartin' th' savages be a shamrock,' he says, 'that nobody could convart with logic,' he says. 'Fa-ather Dorney has spoke iv ye very kindly,' he says, 'an' I'd like to do somethin' f'r ye,' he says. 'What d'ye want?' says th' pope iv Rome, he says to St. Pathrick, 'what d'ye want?' he says. 'How wud a bridge strike ye?' 'Thank ye,' says St. Pathrick, 'but there's on'y wan thing I've got to ask,' he says. 'Ye see,' he says, 'the birthday,' he says, 'comes in Lint,' he says, 'an' th' la-ads,' he says, 'would like to celebrate it properly,' he says; 'but they can't,' he says, 'for an' because 'tis in Lint,' he says. 'Now,' says he, 'I'd like to ask ye,' he says, 'to declare,' he says, 'all bets off on that night,' he says. 'I'll do it,' says th' pope, an' he done it. Ye can't believe that, Jawn? Faith, 'tis little ye believe, ye heretic.

"Be that as it may, Jawn, th' Faugh a Ballaghs give a dance on Pathrick's night and I lid th' gr-rand ma-arch with Mrs. Cornelius Flynn upon me ar-rm. They was wan hundhred and eight couples in th' gr-rand ma-arch an' ivry wan had th' divvle's own time till Mike McCloskey took Clarice Hinnesy out to dance. He didn't know no more about dancin' thin a cow, an' before he'd tur-rned three times, bedad, he an' Miss Hinnesy was on th' flure. She gets up an' yells: 'Ye thripped me, ye brute,' an' thin she calls to her brother Redmond, she calls: 'Reddy,' she says, 'will ye let this here shkate insult a lady?' Well, sir, what followed, ye niver see th' like. Th' Hinnesys and the McCloskeys was related to nearly ivry wan on th' flure an' there was no favors. Th' last I see iv th' prisidint iv th' club he was goin' out iv th' window with his head through th' big fiddle. Oh, thim was th' days iv social injyment.

"Are ye goin', Jawn? Well, good night me lad, an' be sure ye button up ye'er coat. If a polisman was to see ye he'd take ye f'r a sleep-walker and r-run ye in." (February 3, 1894)

14. The Quick and the Dead: A Ghost Story

Dunne may have been influenced here by the interest in Irish folklore in the 1890s generated by Yeats, Lady Gregory, and other writers of the Celtic literary revival. The plot of this piece is similar to that of the traditional Irish tale, "Leeam O'Rooney's Burial," which Douglas Hyde translated into English in the collection, Beside the

Fire *(1890)*. *The "A-ho-aitches" is the Ancient Order of Hibernians, an Irish-American fraternal organization.*

Mr. Dooley and Mr. McKenna sat outside the ample door of the little liquor store, the evening being hot, and wrapped their legs around the chair, and their lips around two especially long and soothing drinks. They talked politics and religion, the people up and down the street, the chances of Murphy, the tinsmith, getting on the force, and a great deal about the weather. A woman in white startled Mr. McKenna's nerves.

"Glory be, I thought it was a ghost!" said Mr. McKenna, whereupon the conversation drifted to those common phenomena. Mr. Dooley asked Mr. McKenna if he had ever seen one. Mr. McKenna replied that he hadn't, and didn't want to. Had Mr. Dooley? "No," said the philosopher, "I niver did; an' it's always been more thin sthrange to me that annywan shud come back afther he'd been stuck in a crate five feet deep, with a ton iv mud upon him. 'Tis onplisint iv thim, annyhow, not to say ongrateful. F'r mesilf, if I was wanst pushed off, an' they'd waked me kindly, an' had a solemn rayqueem high mass f'r me, an' a funeral with Roddey's Hi-bernyan band, an' th' A-ho-aitches, I have too much pride to come back f'r an encore. I wud so, Jawn. Whin a man's dead, he ought to make th' best iv a bad job, an' not be thrapsin' around, lookin' f'r throuble among his own kind.

"No, I niver see wan, but I know there are such things; f'r twenty years ago all th' road was talkin' about how Flaherty, th' tailor, laid out th' ghost iv Tim O'Grady. O'Grady was a big sthrappin' Connock man, as wide across th' shoulders as a freight car. He was a plastherer be thrade whin wages was high, an' O'Grady was rowlin' in wealth. Ivry Sundah ye'd see him, with his horse an' buggy an' his goold watch an' chain, in front iv th' Sullivans' house, waitin' f'r Mary Ann Sullivan to go f'r a buggy ride with him over to McAllister Place; an' he fin'lly married her, again th' wishes iv Flaherty, who took to histin' in big wans, an' missed his jooty, an' was a scandal in th' parish f'r six months.

"O'Grady didn't improve with mathrimony, but got to lanin'

again th' ol' stuff, an' walkin' up an' down th' sidewalk in his shirt-sleeves, with his thumbs stuck in his vest, an' his little pipe turned upside down; an', whin he see Flaherty, 'twas his custom to run him up an alley, so that th' little tailor man niver had a minyit iv peace. Ivry wan supposed he lived in a three most iv th' time, to be out iv th' way iv O'Grady.

"Well, wan day O'Grady he seen Flaherty walkin' down th' sthreet with a pair iv lavender pants f'r Willum Joyce to wear to th' Ogden Grove picnic, an' thried to heave a brick at him. He lost his balance, an' fell fr'm th' scaffoldin' he was wurrukin' on; an' th' last wurruds he said was, 'Did I get him or didn't I?' Mrs. O'Grady said it was th' will iv Gawd; an' he was burrid at Calvary with a funeral iv eighty hacks, an' a great manny people in their own buggies. Dorsey, th' conthractor, was there with his wife. He thought th' wurruld an' all iv O'Grady.

"Wan year aftherward Flaherty begun makin' up to Mrs. O'Grady; an' ivry wan in th' parish seen it, an' was glad iv it, an' said it was scandalous. How it iver got out to O'Grady's pew in th' burryin' ground, I'll niver tell ye, an' th' Lord on'y knows; but wan evenin' th' ghost iv O'Grady come back. Flaherty was settin' in th' parlor, smokin' a seegar, with O'Grady's slippers on his feet, whin th' spook come in in th' mos' natural way in the wurruld, kickin' th' dog. 'What th' 'ell ar-re ye doin' here, ye little farryer iv pants?' he says. Mrs. O'Grady was f'r faintin'; but Flaherty he says, says he: 'Be quite,' he says. 'I'll dale with him.' Thin to th' ghost: 'Have ye paid th' rint here, ye big ape?' he says. 'What d'ye mane be comin' back, whin th' landlord ain't heerd fr'm ye f'r a year?' he says. Well, O'Grady's ghost was that surprised he cud hardly speak. 'Ye ought to have betther manners thin insultin' th' dead,' he says. 'Ye ought to have betther manners thin to be lavin' ye'er coffin at this hour iv th' night, an' breakin' in on dacint people,' says Flaherty. 'What good does it do to have rayqueem masses f'r th' raypose iv th' like iv you,' he says, 'that doesn't know his place?' he says. 'I'm masther iv this house,' says th' ghost. 'Not on ye'er life,' says Flaherty. 'Get out iv here, or I'll make th' ghost iv a ghost out iv ye. I can lick anny dead man that iver lived,' he said.

"With that th' ghost iv O'Grady made a pass at him, an' they clinched an' rowled on th' flure. Now a ghost is no aisy mark f'r anny man, an' O'Grady's ghost was as sthrong as a cow. It had Flaherty down on th' flure an' was feedin' him with a book they call th' 'Christyan Martyrs,' whin Mrs. O'Grady put a bottle in Flaherty's hands. 'What's this?' says Flaherty. 'Howly wather,' says Mrs. O'Grady. 'Sprinkle it on him,' says Mrs. O'Grady. 'Woman,' says th' tailor between th' chapters iv th' book, 'this is no time f'r miracles,' he says. An' he give O'Grady's ghost a treminjous wallop on th' head. Now, whether it was th' wather or th' wallop, I'll not tell ye; but, annyhow, th' ghost give wan yell an' disappeared. An' th' very next Sundah, whin Father Kelly wint into th' pulpit at th' gospel, he read th' names iv Roger Kickham Flaherty an' Mary Ann O'Grady."

"Did the ghost ever come back?" asked Mr. McKenna.

"Niver," said Mr. Dooley. "Wanst was enough. But, mind ye, I'd hate to have been wan iv th' other ghosts th' night O'Grady got home fr'm th' visit to Flaherty's. There might be ghosts that cud stand him off with th' gloves, but in a rough an' tumble fight he cud lick a St. Patrick's Day procession iv thim." (May 9, 1896)

Chapter Two

Daily Life in Bridgeport in the Nineties

The Chicago Dooley pieces provide a detailed picture, available nowhere else, of Irish-American city life at the turn of the century. Dunne has observed the Bridgeport passing scene closely, vividly, and with the economy of a born journalist. From the door of Mr. Dooley's saloon, he throws a wide net and catches the colors of the common life: the daily round of mill workers and streetcar drivers, fairs and raffles, sporting events and holiday celebrations, marriages and christenings and funerals.

The Catholic church provided the social as well as the religious center for Bridgeport, and Mr. Dooley attends most of the church-sponsored activities. These include two fairs (pieces 1 and 3) that feature shooting galleries, gambling games, and booths selling everything from religious articles to oyster stew; a parish theatrical production of "The Doomed Markey" starring Denny Hogan (2); the parochial school graduation of "Hennessy's youngest" with Irish music and a recitation of Robert Emmet's speech from the dock (4); and a nonalcoholic "temperance saloon" that lasts exactly one evening (6). Mr. Dooley also describes two of his own ill-fated attempts to give up drink, swearing, and cards during Lent (5, 7).

A variety of secular events are reported, too: a genealogy lecture in the school hall that erupts into a brawl over whose ancestors were kings and whose only dukes (8); a benefit raffle for an ailing bartender on the road (9); a family reunion of Dooleys scattered by emigration, in the course of which the emotional climate shifts from nostalgia to name-calling (10); and the ringing in of the New Year 1897 (11). In addition, Bridgeport interest in sports can be followed in Mr. Dooley's accounts of a football game between the "young Par-nells" and the "young Sarsfields" (12), a baseball game umpired with disastrous results by Hennessy (13), and the 1894 Corbett-Mitchell fight (14), which local observers interpret as an Irish-English vendetta. In other pieces, Dooley and Hennessy go fishing up in Wisconsin (15), ice-skate on a vacant Bridgeport lot (16), and watch an aging friend undergo a hard initiation to bicycling (17). And the athletic heroes of Bridgeport puzzle over what to make of the fashionable new game of golf, which is beyond their means but not their mockery (18).

Mr. Dooley is a fascinated observer of the crooked course of love on Archey Road. Several pieces (19, 20, 21) corroborate his judgment that "f'r an impetchoos an' darin' people th' Irish is th' mos' cowardly whin it comes to mathrimony that iver I heerd tell iv." For balance, he recalls the unrequited love of "Felix Pindergasht" for Molly Donahue (22) and the economically motivated whirlwind courtship of two landed Bridgeport misers (23).

In some of the best pieces, Mr. Dooley illuminates the lives of Bridgeport working men, "th' quite people nayether you nor me hears tell iv fr'm wan end iv th' year to another." He describes the hard-ships faced by streetcar drivers on a winter night (24) and steel-rolling-mill workers in the sweltering summer (25), and his nar-rative of the family history of Shaughnessy, a Bridgeport carpenter, reads like an O'Neill tragedy in miniature (26). Finally, Mr. Dooley acknowledges the importance of the civil service route out of the slough of unskilled labor with a series of vignettes about the fire and police departments, heroes and goats, respectively, to Chicagoans in the nineties, and both predominantly Irish.

Chicago was a wide-open city, full of opportunities for graft, and newspaper campaigns for reform of the police were yearly events in Dunne's time. Mr. Dooley is most often critical, too, though mildly so, perhaps because so many of his neighbors were "polismen." He confuses policemen and robbers in one piece (27), and cannot distin-guish between police control and provocation of rioting in another (28). Moreover, he dispenses faint praise to "th' foorce" only once— when Lieutenant John Shea finds out who stole Hogan's goat (29).

*On the other hand, as Mr. Dooley admits, the situation was "alto-
gether diffrent with th' fireman." In a largely wooden, increasingly
crowded city, his job was indispensable and dangerous. Because he
placed his life on the line daily for the common good, the big city fireman was an Irish-American cultural hero for Bridgeport and greater
Chicago. So it is that Mr. Dooley admires Fire Chief Denis Swenie
on a visit to Bridgeport (30) and responds to two real Chicago fire-
fighting tragedies by creating lasting fictional images of the fireman-
hero (31, 32).*

1. A Parish Fair at St. Honoria's

"Jawn, d'ye know who's th' most pop'lar man in St. Honoria's
parish?" asked Mr. Dooley.

"The little priest ought to be," said Mr. McKenna.

"Well, iv coorse, we ba-ar him. Th' most pop'lar man in th' parish is Cornelius J. Costigan. He bate th' aldherman and Aloysius
Regan. He did that.

"I like Fa-ather Hogan, though he an' Fa-ather Kelly does be at
outs over th' Nicene council an' th' ma-an Hopkins put to wurruk
on th' r-rid bridge. So whin he come over with tickets f'r th' fair
an' I seen he had a game leg fr'm toddlin' around in th' snow
makin' sick calls I bought two an' wint over th' closin' night—
'twas las' Sathurday.

"'Twas a gr-rand fair. They had Roddy's Hibernyun band
playin' on th' cor-rner an' th' basemint iv th' church was packed.
In th' ba-ack they had a shootin' gall'ry where ye got five shots f'r
tin cints. Hogan, th' milkman, was shootin' whin I wint in an'
iverybody was out iv th' gall'ry. He missed eight shots an' thin he
thrun two lumps iv coal at th' ta-arget an' made two bull's-eyes.
He is a Tipp'rary man an' th' raison he's over here is he hit a polisman with a rock at twinty ya-ards—without sights.

"I'd no more thin inthered th' fair thin who should come up but
Malachi Dorsey's little girl, Dalia. 'Good avnin',' she says. 'Won't
ye take a chanst?' says she. 'On what?' says I. 'On a foldin' bed,'

says she. 'Faith, I will not,' I says. 'I'll take no chances on no foldin' bed,' I says. 'I was locked up in wan wanst,' I says, 'an' it took a habees corpis to get me out,' I says. She lift me alone afther that, but she must've tipped me off to th' others f'r whin I come away I stood to win a doll, a rockin' chair, a picture iv th' pope done by Mary Ann O'Donoghue, a deck iv ca-ards an' a tidy. I'm all right if th' combination comes out ayether way fr'm th' rockin' chair to th' doll 'r th' tidy. But I wuddent know what th' divvle to do if I sh'd catch th' pope iv R-rome an' th' ca-ards.

"Th' booths was something iligant. Mrs. Dorsey had th' first wan where she sold mottoes an' babies' clothes. Next to hers was the ice crame layout, with the Widow Lonergan in cha-arge. Some wan touted big Hinnisy again it. He got wan mouthful iv it an' began to holler: 'F'r th' love iv hivin' won't some wan give me a cup iv tay,' he says. 'Me insides is like a skatin' rink.' He wint over an' shtud be th' fire with his coattails apart till th' sexton put him out.

"Acrost th' hall was th' table f'r church articles, where ye cud get 'Keys iv Hevin' an' 'St. Thomas a Kempises' an' ros'ries. It done a poor business, they tell me, an' Miss Dolan was that sore at th' eyesther shtew thrade done be Mrs. Cassidy next dure that she come near soakin' her with th' 'Life iv St. Rose iv Lima.' 'Twas tur-r-rible.

"But I wanted to tell ye about th' mos' pop'lar ma-an. Iv coorse ye know th' ga-ame. Ye've been agin it. Well, they had th' stand in th' middle iv th' flure an' 'twas bossed be Donnigan, th' lawyer. Donnigan is prisidint iv th' Young Married Min's Sodality an' dhraws all th' thrade iv th' parish; he's gettin' rich. Th' names iv th' candydates was on th' blackboord—th' aldherman, Costigan an' Regan. Ye know Regan. Reel estate man. Costigan has made enough conthractin' to be thinkin' iv movin' away, an' th' aldherman was bound to win. Regan is fr'm Kildare, Costigan's a black-hear-rted villain fr'm th' County Mayo an' th' aldherman come fr'm Wexford, though a dacint man. He married a towny iv mine. She was second cousin iv me wife's second cousin, Judy Flynn.

"Th' votes dhropped in mighty fast till iliven o'clock an' thin they poored in. Poor Doheny come fr'm threatin' th' ba-and an' he wint up to vote. 'How much?' says he. 'Fifty cints,' says Donnigan. ''Tis not enough,' says Doheny. 'Niver liss thin a dollar.' He'd hear-rd, d'ye mind, that th' candydates was spindin' money f'r votes an' he'd made a conthract f'r to bring down a lodgin' house. He was that mad.

"Each wan iv th' three had some wan to place his money. Donnigan kept thim runnin' for more. O'Malley'd come r'rushin' up with a bunch iv bills an' roar 'Wan hundhred votes f'r Costigan!' In a minyit they'd be two more rolls undher Donnigan's nose. 'Wan hundhred an' fifty f'r th' aldherman!' 'Wan hundhred an' thirty-five f'r Regan!' Whin we seen odd numbers comin' we knowed Regan was down. He begun borryin' fr'm his frins an' thin he dhropped out intirely, lavin' th' race to Costigan an' th' aldherman. He made an assignmint th' nex' day. Whin th' polls closed th' Mayo man had him beat be two votes, an' half th' people left in disgust."

"For why?" asked Mr. McKenna.

"F'r why?" said Mr. Dooley, scornfully. "Th' idee that anny rayspict'ble parish sh'd allow a May-o man to go around wearin' a diamond stud an' boastin' himself th' mos' pop'lar man! I tell ye what, Jawn, 'tis goin' too far. I'll not knock anny church, d'ye mind, but I'll say this here an' now, that manny nice people was that angry they wint to th' Frinch church, where they cudden't undherstand th' announcement, th' nex' day." (December 29, 1894)

2. "The Doomed Markey"

"Potther Pammer," mentioned here by Mrs. Hogan, was Potter Palmer (1826–1902), Chicago merchant prince and real estate king whose name was synonymous with wealth and social position. The Palmer House hotel still bears his name.

"Did ye iver see th' play iv th' 'Doomed Markey'?" asked Mr. Dooley.

"No," said Mr. McKenna. "Where is it at?"

"I see it at th' school hall undher little Father Kelly's church las' Widnisdah. 'Twas give be th' St. Pathrick's Stock Comp'ny f'r th' binifit iv th' church, an' 'twas a gr-reat show, Jawn. 'Twas a ree-fined show, too, an' I had a fr-ront seat.

"'Twas this here way. Ye see, Mike Kenny was a Frinchman, a markey, d'ye mind, an' a more dishonest an' outhrajous divvle was ne'er bor-rn iv woman—in th' play. Off th' stage he's as quite as a mouse an' head iv th' Sons iv St. Joseph. Well, sir, Dinny Hogan's father died——"

"What's that?" exclaimed Mr. McKenna. "Is old Terence Hogan dead?"

"Ah, musha, Jawn, ye have a head, an' so has a pin," said Mr. Dooley. "Terence is as live as a goat this minyit. 'Twas Dinny's father in th' play that died. He was a rich man an' in th' play he was Mike Kenny's uncle, Mike an' Dinny bein' first cousins. Well, sir, Mike an' Dinny was both in love with Molly Donahue, d'ye mind. She was an orphan—in th' play, Jawn. She was stuck on Dinny an' she thrun th' boots into Mike—turned him down. So what does Mike up an' do but steal th' will."

"Whose will?" asked Mr. McKenna.

"Dinny Hogan's father's will in th' play," explained Mr. Dooley.

"Glory be," said Mr. McKenna. "What did he do that for?"

"So's Dinny wuddent have no money. Ol' man Hogan in th' play, he had a lot iv dough. Well, sir, Dinny was all broke up. 'What,' he says, 'shall I do?' he says. 'What shall I do?' he says. 'What shall I do?' he says. 'What shall I do?' 'Go to wurruk,' says wan iv th' Dorgan twins in th' back iv th' hall. 'I want ye to un-dherstand he has a good job promised to him on th' ca-ars,' said Mrs. Hogan, tur-rnin' round on th' Dorgan twin. ''Tis ye'er own fam'ly 'll be scratchin' a beggar's back whin I'm ridin' up an' down to Mrs. Potther Pammer's without payin' no more thin how-d'ye-do to me own son,' she says. So they thrun out th' Dor-gan twin an' th' play wint on.

"'What shall I do?' says Hogan again. 'What shall I do?' Thin he put his hand to his forehead. 'Lave me think,' he says. Ye cud hear Father Kelly coachin' fr'm behint th' scenes. 'Din,' he says. 'Din, ye big basthoon,' he says. 'This is not where ye think,' he says. 'Ye don't think till th' second act.' 'Tubby sure,' says Dinny. 'Ah, heavens,' he says. 'F'r to think iv me las' night with th' wealth iv creosote in my pockets, coorted, pampered, child iv fortune,' he says. 'With Molly Don—I mane th' Countess iv Tolurum me bride,' he says. 'An' now disinherited, a waif, an' outcast, so poor that th' dogs ba-ark at me,' he says. ''Tis crool,' he says, ''tis crool.' Thin he walked over to set down an' weep an' th' chair give way undher him an' he wint off with a limp.

"Well, th' nex' scene was a wood, an' 'twas made iv them pretty Chris'mus threes in tubs that Schwartzmeister has out in front on th' Foorth iv July. Molly Donahue was walkin' in th' woods, and in come Kenny. 'Fly with me' he says to Molly Donahue. 'I'm rich an' prosperous an' doin' well,' he says. 'Why wud ye sacrifice ye'er young life to that worthless scapegrace?' he says. 'Worthless scapegrace though he be,' says Molly Donahue, 'I'd not give his little finger f'r all ye'er vaunted wealth,' says she in th' play. 'Thin,' says Kenny, 'ye shall be mine,' he says, 'if not be fair means, thin be foul,' he says; an' he made a r-runnin' jump at her. Out come Malachi Cassidy; he had a job with Hogan in th' play. 'Hold,' says Cassidy. 'Low bor-rn caitiff,' says Kenny, dhrawn his soord. At that out comes Cassidy with a cannon. 'Wretch,' he says, 'touch wan head iv yon fair maiden's hair—I mane wan fair head iv yon fair hair—I mane—well, annyhow, ye lave her alone, Kenny, or I'll throw away th' reevolver an' buckle into ye,' he says. I heerd Father Kelly groanin' behind th' scenes, but ol' Cassidy was tickled to death. 'Goo boy, Malachi,' he says. 'Goo boy,' he says. 'Ye'er all right,' he says. Dan Kenny was mad clear through. 'They're givin' Mike th' worst iv it,' he says. 'It ain't right f'r Father Kelly to do that.' 'Sure, who cares,' says Mrs. Kenny. 'Well, he ought to have th' girl,' says he. 'He's th' best actor, two out iv three.' 'Ah,' says she. 'Small loss. She ain't much,' she says. 'A forward thing.' 'Well, annyhow,' says Kenny, ''twas no business iv Cassidy's f'r to stick in his jaw,' he says. An' he was sore all avenin'."

"Well, how did it come out?" asked Mr. McKenna.

"Well, ye see, whin Kenny copped th' will he lost it an' Jawn O'Shea was walkin' through th' woods on his way to th' coort-house—he's a lawyer, in th' play, d'ye mind—an' he picked up th' will. Well, ye see, Kenny was in with Danny O'Connell in hookin' th' will an' whin it was brought back be O'Shea Danny tipped it off. So just as Kenny come to claim th' estate, d'ye mind, in walks a rigimint iv sojers an' pinches him f'r burglary. He was so mortified that he pulled a knife fr'm his pocket an' poked it into his stomach. 'I die,' he says. 'My curses rest on ye.' But he didn't die. He fell down on a tack, an' whin th' curtain wint down he was runnin' up an' down th' stage holdin' on to his leg an' cursin' th' other wan iv th' Dorgan twins that was a sojer an' put th' tack there f'r him.

"I heerd Mrs. Kenny an' Mrs. O'Connell talkin' about th' play. ''Twas a good play,' says Mrs. O'Connell. ''Twas so,' says Mrs. Kenny. 'But I think ye'd be ashamed to have ye'er son an informer.'" (November 16, 1895)

3. Heresy at a Church Fair

This piece had its origin in the shenanigans of Mayor John Mc-Carthy of the Chicago suburb of Lemont, Illinois, who was under attack for sanctioning prostitution and gambling in his town. On July 11, 1895, he had alienated the Chicago press by tearing up a reporter's story of a Lemont citizens' meeting for better government and substituting his own communiqué. In an interview two days later, he declared himself to be the only Democrat in Cook County who could read. Mike McDonald had been the political and gambling boss of Chicago in the seventies and eighties; by 1895 he was in semiretirement.

"Well, Jawn," said Mr. Dooley, laying down his newspaper and pushing his spectacles up over his forehead, "if they'se anny man in all th' wurruld that desarves to be called a hero that man is John McCart'y iv Lemont."

"What has he been doing?" asked Mr. McKenna.

"He beat a church fair," said Mr. Dooley. "He wint again thim at th' wheel iv fortune an' carrid off wan hundherd an' fifty dollars, an' th' bist part iv it was he kep' it. They'se no wan iver done that befure since fairs was sta-arted, f'r th' greater glory iv Gawd. I've played dice with that ruffyan O'Malley whin th' inside iv th' box was that polished ye cud see ye'er face in it, an' I won tin dollars wanst in a game iv cards with three la-ads fr'm th' tinth ward, an' whin I counted th' deck aftherwards they wasn't a face card in it. But I niver beat a church fair. They say Mike McDonald joined th' Jews whin he heerd iv what McCart'y done.

"Wanst I knew a man," said Mr. Dooley, laying down his newspaper, "be th' name iv Burke, that come fr'm somewhere around Derry, though he was no Presbyteryan. He was iv th' right sort. Well, he was feelin' how-come-ye-so, an' he dhrifted over to where we was holdin' a fair. They was a band outside, an' he thought it was a grand openin'. So he come in with a cigar in th' side iv his mouth an' his hat hangin' onto his ear. It was th' last night iv th' fair, an' ivrything was wide open; f'r th' priest had gone home, an' we wanted f'r to break th' record. This Burke was f'r lavin' whin he sees where he was; but we run him again th' shootin' gallery, where ye got twinty-five cints, a quarther iv a dollar, f'r ivry time ye rang th' bell. Th' ol' gun we had was crooked as a ram's horn, but it must 've fitted into Burke's squint; f'r he made that there bell ring as if he was a conducthor iv a grip-car roundin' a curve. He had th' shootin' gallery on its last legs whin we run him again th' wheel iv fortune. He broke it. Thin we thried him on th' grab-bag. They was four goold watches an' anny quantity iv brickbats an' chunks iv coal in th' bag. He had four dives, an' got a watch each time. He took a chanst on ivrything; an' he won a foldin'-bed, a doll that cud talk like an old gate, a pianny, a lampshade, a Life iv St. Aloysius, a pair iv shoes, a baseball bat, an ice-cream freezer, an' th' pomes iv Mike Scanlan.

"Th' comity was disthracted. Here was a man that'd break th' fair, an' do it with th' best iv humor; f'r he come fr'm another parish. So we held a private session. 'What 'll we do?' says Dorgan, th' chairman. They was a man be th' name iv Flaherty, a good man thin an' a betther now; f'r he's dead, may he rest in peace! An' Flaherty says: 'We've got to take th' bull be th' horns,' he says. 'If ye lave him to me,' he says, 'I'll fix him,' he says.

"So he injooced this man Burke to come down back iv th' shootin' gallery, an' says he to Burke, 'Ye're lucky to-night.' 'Not so very,' says Burke. ''Twud be a shame to lave ye get away with all ye won,' says Flaherty. ''Twill be a great inconvanience,' says Burke. 'I'll have to hire two or three dhrays,' he says, 'an' 'tis late.' 'Well,' says Flaherty, 'I'm appinted be th' parish to cut th' ca-ards with ye,' he says, 'whether ye're to give back what ye won or take what's left.' ''Tis fair,' says Burke; 'an', whoiver wins, 'tis f'r a good cause.' An' he puts th' watches an' th' money on th' table.

"'High man,' says Flaherty. 'High man,' says Burke. Flaherty cut th' king iv spades. Burke, th' robber, cut th' ace iv hearts. He was reachin' out f'r th' money, whin Flaherty put his hands over it. 'Wud ye take it?' says he. 'I wud,' says Burke. 'Wud ye rob th' church?' says Flaherty. 'I wud,' says Burke. 'Thin,' says Flaherty, scoopin' it in, 'ye're a heretic; an' they'se nawthin' comin' to ye.'

"Burke looked at him, an' he looked at th' comity; an' he says, 'Gintlemen, if iver ye come over in th' Seventh Ward, dhrop in an' see me,' he says. 'I'll thry an' make it plisint f'r ye,' he says. An' he wint away.

"Th' story got out, an' th' good man heerd iv it. He was mighty mad about it; an' th' nex' sermon he preached was on th' evils iv gamblin', but he asked Flaherty f'r to take up th' colliction." Mr. Dooley thought awhile and then called, "Jawn."

"What is it?" asked Mr. McKenna.

"'Twas all right f'r McCart'y iv Lemont to beat th' church fair, but what does it profit a man if he gains th' whole wurruld an' loses his own soul? I'd not be in his place f'r twice wan hundherd an' fifty, an' I'd kill a man this minyit f'r wan hundherd." (August 31, 1895)

4. A Parochial School Graduation

A transfer of customs from Ireland is evident at this graduation ceremony—in the musical entertainment, the recitation of the sentencing speech of Irish patriot Robert Emmet, and the award of a copy of Carleton's Willy Reilly *(1855), which is not a religious book but a popular novel of Irish peasant life. Toward the end, Mr. Dooley compares the Hennessy boy's oratorical stance to that of a notorious Chicago after-dinner speaker, "Macchew P." Brady.*

"I wint up las' night to th' school hall to see Hinnissy's youngest gradjooate," said Mr. Dooley. "He's a fine la-ad that, an' they do be thinkin' iv makin' a priest iv him. I shouldn't wondher if he'd be a good wan. He's doin' nothin' all th' livelong day but readin' 'Th' Lives iv th' Saints' an' 'Saint Thomas a Kempis.' A fine lad."

"Was it any good?" asked Mr. McKenna.

"It was a pretty good show," said Mr. Dooley. "Near ivry wan along th' r-road was there an' had their best clothes on thim. Father Kelly was th' busyest man ye iver see. He met all th' ol' folks at th' dure an' give thim th' glad hand. 'Twas: 'Ye have a smart boy there, Mrs. Murphy,' an' 'Niver mind about Tim, Mrs. Cassidy. There's worse nor him, an' he's th' divvle an' all at figgers.' Thin he was lecturin' Brother Aloysius about th' way th' stage was fixed up with thim little Christmas trees that grows on'y in tubs, an' hoistin' th' curtain an' lightin' th' footlights till his collar was th' color iv that sponge—an' as wet.

"Th' first number on th' program was th' speech that Robert Immitt made whin they was goin' to hang him. 'Tis a warm speech an' Grogan's boy had to say it. He come out lookin' red an' nervous, an' old man Grogan had a front seat an' begun to applaud most uproaryous. That rattled Micky all th' more an' his voice sounded like wan ye'll hear over a tiliphone whin he said, 'Oh, dear an' vinrated shades iv me departed fathers.' He thrun his hands in th' air an' begun snappin' his fingers. 'Mike,' whispers Grogan fr'm th' front seat. 'Ye'er mitts,' he says. 'Drop ye'er mitts. Mike,' he says louder, 'ye'er mitts,' he says. 'Drop thim,' he says.

'Stop snappin' ye'er fingers,' he says. Thin raisin' his voice he bawls, 'Mike, what in th' name iv goodness d'ye think ye'er do-in'—defindin' Ireland or shootin' craps?' Th' boy was overcome with emotion an' Mrs. Grogan wint home.

"They was other things done be th' lads. Wan iv th' Kelly boys played 'Kathleen Mavourneen' on a flute his father bought f'r him an' th' Saint Ignatius Quartet sang 'Row, Brothers, Row,' that they'd practiced undher me window Sundah nights till I cud near sing it mesilf. Thin they was a conversation bechune young Dimp-sey, Hannigan's Jawnny an' little Tommy Casey. Tommy Casey was a good young man an' Dimpsey was th' divvle an' Jawnny Hannigan was a good angel, d'ye mind. Dimpsey was tryin' to lure Tommy Casey away. 'Come,' he says, 'enjoy ye'erself while ye'er life lasts,' he says. 'Ye'll be dead a long time,' says Dimpsey, 'an' ye might as well have a good time now.' 'But,' says Jawnny Hannigan, 'what availeth a man if he gain th' whole wurruld an' lose his own sowl,' he says. 'Will ye desert me f'r a few days iv vice knowin' that ye'er immortial sowl will be denied happiness to come an' will be condimmed to atarnal torture.' 'Nit,' says Tommy Casey—an' ye sh'd 've seen Father Kelly's face! He was that mad with rage. I dinnaw what he done to Casey, but th' good angel had a black eye this mornin' f'r puttin' him up to it.

"Thin they was a thrajeedy an' all th' lads took th' parts iv play-acthors. 'Twas a hot play; young Murphy was attimpting to walk through the forest whin up comes Malachi Cassidy. 'What,' says Malachi, 'you here?' 'Yis,' says the Murphy kid, 'an' what woulds't with me?' he says. 'What woulds't with me?' 'Die, caitiff,' says Malachi, givin' him a wallup with a tin soord. 'Twas in th' play f'r Murphy to be croaked, but he refused to die, an' his father stood up an' roared acrost th' hall: 'Look here, Cassidy, ye put that boy up to that,' he says. 'I'll not have it,' he says. Father Kelly ran to th' front iv th' stage, an' says he: 'Murphy,' he says, 'if ye don't be quite an' make that la-ad lay down an' die,' he says, 'I'll excom-municate th' both iv ye,' he says. An' he'd iv done it there an' thin. So th' play wint on.

"Afther th' play Hinnissy's youngest spoke his piece. He come out wearin' a long black coat an' a white nicktie an' read his speech with his hand tucked in th' coat like Macchew P. He said that he was lookin' th' future square in th' eye, an' though th' past was bad he'd thry to do the bist he cud f'r th' wurruld. What was needed to be done, he said, was f'r young min to take up th' battle iv life an' fight it out ccɔrajously. He'd been very busy at school for some years, but now that he'd gradjooated he thought he'd have time to put things in ordher. He tipped off a whole lot to us. Father Kelly hung a medal to him an' give him two prizes—relijous books—'Th' Life iv Pope Boniface' an' 'Willy Reilly.'

"His father come over with me afther th' intertainment an' he looked blue. 'What's th' matther with ye?' says I. 'Does it remind ye iv ye'er own boyhood days,' I says, 'whin ye was gradjooated be th' toe iv th' hidge schoolmasther's boot?' I says. 'No,' says he. ''Tis not that,' he says. 'I was on'y thinkin' afther hearin' Joe's o-ration,' he says, 'that I've lived a misspent life,' he says. 'I niver give care nor thought to th' higher jooties iv citizenship,' he says. 'Mebbe,' he says, 'I had to wurruk too hard,' he says. 'Go home,' says I. 'I'm goin' to close up,' I says." (July 6, 1895)

5. Keeping Lent

Mr. McKenna had observed Mr. Dooley in the act of spinning a long, thin spoon in a compound which reeked pleasantly and smelt of the humming water of commerce; and he laughed and mocked at the philosopher.

"Ah-ha," he said, "that's th' way you keep Lent, is it? Two weeks from Ash Wednesday, and you tanking up."

Mr. Dooley went on deliberately to finish the experiment, leisurely dusting the surface with nutmeg and tasting the product before setting down the glass daintily. Then he folded his apron, and lay back in ample luxury while he began: "Jawn, th' holy season iv Lent was sent to us f'r to teach us th' weakness iv th' human flesh. Man proposes, an' th' Lord disposes, as Hinnissy says.

"I mind as well as though it was yesterday th' struggle iv me father f'r to keep Lent. He began to talk iv it a month befure th' time. 'On Ash Winsdah,' he'd say, 'I'll go in f'r a rale season iv fast an' abstinince,' he'd say. An' sure enough, whin Ash Winsdah come round at midnight, he'd take a long dhraw at his pipe an' knock th' ashes out slowly again his heel, an' thin put th' dhudeen up behind th' clock. 'There,' says he, 'there ye stay till Easter morn,' he says. Ash Winsdah he talked iv nawthin but th' pipe. '"Tis exthrordinney how easy it is f'r to lave off,' he says. 'All ye need is will power,' he says. 'I dinnaw that I'll iver put a pipe in me mouth again. 'Tis a bad habit, smokin' is,' he says, 'an' it costs money. A man's betther off without it. I find I dig twict as well,' he says, 'an', as f'r cuttin' turf, they'se not me like in th' parish since I left off th' pipe,' he says.

"Well, th' nex' day an' th' nex' day he talked th' same way; but Fridah he was sour, an' looked up at th' clock where th' pipe was. Saturdah me mother, thinkin' to be plazin to him, says: 'Terrence,' she says, 'ye're iver so much betther without th' tobacco,' she says. 'I'm glad to find you don't need it. Ye'll save money,' she says. 'Be quite, woman,' says he. 'Dear, oh dear,' he says, 'I'd like a pull at th' clay,' he says. 'Whin Easter comes, plaze Gawd, I'll smoke mesilf black an' blue in th' face,' he says.

"That was th' beginnin' iv th' downfall. Choosdah he was settin' in front iv th' fire with a pipe in his mouth. 'Why, Terrence,' says me mother, 'ye're smokin' again.' 'I'm not,' says he: ''tis a dhry smoke,' he says; ''tisn't lighted,' he says. Wan week afther th' swear-off he came fr'm th' field with th' pipe in his face, an' him puffin' away like a chimney. 'Terrence,' says me mother, 'it isn't Easter morn.' 'Ah-ho,' says he, 'I know it,' he says; 'but,' he says, 'what th' divvle do I care?' he says. 'I wanted f'r to find out whether it had th' masthery over me; an',' he says, 'I've proved that it hasn't,' he says. 'But what's th' good iv swearin' off, if ye don't break it?' he says. 'An' annyhow,' he says, 'I glory in me shame.'

"Now, Jawn," Mr. Dooley went on, "I've got what Hogan calls

a theery, an' it's this: that what's thrue iv wan man's thrue iv all men. I'm me father's son a'most to th' hour an' day. Put me in th' County Roscommon forty year ago, an' I'd done what he'd done. Put him on th' Ar-rchey Road, an' he'd be deliverin' ye a lecture on th' sin iv thinkin' ye're able to overcome th' pride iv th' flesh, as Father Kelly says. Two weeks ago I looked with contimpt on Hinnissy fr an' because he'd not even promise to fast an' obstain fr'm croquet durin' Lent. To-night you see me mixin' me toddy without th' shadow iv remorse about me. I'm proud iv it. An' why not? I was histin' in me first wan whin th' soggarth come down fr'm a sick call, an' looked in at me. 'In Lent?' he says, half-laughin' out iv thim quare eyes iv his. 'Yes,' said I. 'Well,' he says, 'I'm not authorized to say this be th' propaganda,' he says, 'an' 'tis no part iv th' directions fr Lent,' he says; 'but,' he says, 'I'll tell ye this, Martin,' he says, 'that they'se more ways than wan iv keepin' th' season,' he says. 'I've knowed thim that starved th' stomach to feast th' evil temper,' he says. 'They'se a little priest down be th' Ninth Ward that niver was known to keep a fast day; but Lent or Christmas tide, day in an' day out, he goes to th' hospital where they put th' people that has th' small-pox. Starvation don't always mean salvation. If it did,' he says, 'they'd have to insure th' pavemint in wan place, an' they'd be money to burn in another. Not,' he says, 'that I want ye to undherstand that I look kindly on th' sin iv'——

"''Tis a cold night out,' says I.

"'Well,' he says, th' dear man, 'ye may. On'y,' he says, ''tis Lent.'

"'Yes,' says I.

"'Well, thin,' he says, 'by ye'er lave I'll take but half a lump iv sugar in mine,' he says." (March 7, 1896)

6. The Temperance Saloon

Father Theobald Matthew (d. 1856) was an Irish priest who became known internationally for his leadership in the temperance movement in the British Isles in the 1840s. As a hold-over from this

movement, the "Father Macchoo society" in Bridgeport is under-
standably prominent in the following piece.

"Over in St. Simeon's," said Mr. Dooley, "they're goin' to petty-
shun th' archbishop f'r a new parish priest."

"What's the trouble?" asked Mr. McKenna.

"Throuble enough," said Mr. Dooley. "They had a timp'rance
rayform movement last week an' near iv'ry man in th' parish took
th' plidge. Hogan was over Choosdah an' he told me all th' dhrink
he'd sold f'r two nights was a can iv butthermilk an' two bottles iv
brown pop. But ye cudden't keep th' lads away fr'm th' saloons.
They was around late an' early playin' dhry forty-fives f'r th' ciga-
ars an' lookin' gloomy at th' ba-ar. Little Father Cassidy, a good
man but as nervous as a hin, seen this, an' says he to himsilf:
'What'll I do?' he says. 'They'll not stay away fr'm th' saloons,' he
says. 'Th' first thing I know they'll be dhrinkin' cider,' he says,
'thin weiss beer,' he says, 'thin weiss beer with a dhrop iv kimmel
into it,' he says, 'thin just wan tub iv lager,' he says, 'an' before
Pathrick's Day th' prisidint iv th' Father Macchoos'll be wallopin'
th' sicritee with a chair leg an' there'll be a scandal in th' parish,'
he says. 'I must do something,' he says to himself. So what does he
do but starts a parlor saloon with a bar in it an' a free lunch an' a
cash register f'r to make it homelike.

"There was no sthrong dhrink to be had in it, d'ye mind.
Nawthin' but hot coffee an' milk an' cocoa an' gruel an' thim
things. But it looked like a saloon an' it done a great business
whin it opened. All th' Father Macchoo society come over in a
body to give it a boost an' dhrunk thimsilves into chollery morbus
with coold limonade. Harrigan, the thrisurer, was laid up with a
game leg, but not to be last to help along th' movement he r-rushed
th' can over f'r a pint iv beef tay. They say it'd 'v done ye'er heart
good to see th' little soggarth's eyes whin th' min at the ba-ar lined
up an' knocked glasses. 'Here's to ye,' says they. 'Dhrink hearty,'
says he, an' th' noise they made pushin' down th' dhrink ye cud
hear on the sidewalk. Thin some wan ordhered a second round iv

cocoa an' they got away with that. Thin they asked f'r th' dicebox an' shook hor-rses. Ivry wan took limonade. Whin they'd got through they shook back an' th' dhrinks was on th' house an' they took sarsprilla pop. At th' tinth round they was pale, but still dhrinkin' ice crame sody, but at the elivinth little Dorsey, th' milkman, set down be th' stove with his hand on his stummick. Harrity, th' lad fr'm th' wather office, said he had to meet a man an' wint over to th' dhrug store on th' corner. Father Cassidy was still game. 'Let's have a song,' he says. 'Give us "Cruiskkeen Lawn,"' he says to Doherty. Doherty thried f'r to sing, but whin he lifted his glass an' see what was in it his voice died in his thrawt.

"At that moment in comes Dinny Bradley, a villain he is, an' loaded to th' ga-ards. 'Good avnin,' he says to th' barkeep. 'Good avnin,' says th' barkeep. 'Give me a dhrop iv th' same thing,' says Dinny. 'We serve on'y timp'rance dhrinks,' says th' barkeep. 'Thin give me a beef-tay fizz,' says Bradley. 'We haven't anny,' says th' barkeep. 'What kind iv a laundhry is this?' says he. 'Can ye make me a cocoa cocktail?' says Dinny. 'No,' says th' barkeep. Bradley looked around him an' says he, 'I'll go down to-morrow,' he says, 'an' have ye'er license took away,' he says. An' he wint out.

"Now whither he had annything to do with what happened aftherward, I dinnaw, but annyhow he was seen talkin' with Hogan. Th' favor-ite dhrink in this parlor saloon was what they called 'maltoroorio,' because it was made iv malt an' tasted like beer an' was beer, ony ye cud 've dhrunk a ton iv it without beatin' ye'er wife. Well, Jawn, so much iv it was dhrunk th' first mornin' that toward nightfall they had to sind f'r another kag. An' that kag was a ringer. It was a ringer, Jawn. Twinty minyits afther it was tapped th' line at th' ba-ar was gettin' gay. Clancy, th' horse-shooer, that'd niver dhrunk a dhrop in his life, was tellin' iv'ry wan that he was goin' to r-run fr' alderman in th' spring. Little Mike Casey had his ar-rms around Dorgan's neck an' was thryin' to convince him he was th' best frind he iver had, an' Sullivan th' cobbler, was singin' 'The Pretty Girl Milkin' th' Cow.' Whin th' good man come back, th' prisidint iv th' Sons iv St. Joseph had th' recordin' secretee iv th' Married Min's Sodality on th' flure.

He r-rushed up to th' ba-ar an' put his nose in wan iv th' glasses. 'Th' Lord help us,' he says, 'it's beer.'

"That night the bartinder run away with th' cash drawer an' th' parlor saloon was closed, but th' parish is up in ar-rms again th' poor, good man. I seen Hogan last night an' he told me he had hired an extry bartinder." (February 23, 1895)

7. Not Keeping Lent

"Well, thin," said Mr. Dooley, "thank hivin that Lint is almost over, Gawd f'rgive me f'r sayin' it. 'Tis very thryin' on the soul—not th' fastin', mind ye; but th' thought, bedad, that ye shud be fastin' whin ye aren't. I suppose, Mr. McKinna, that ye'd think nothing iv tuckin' in a slab iv beef on Good Friday, like anny prowtestant, but f'r me an' th' likes iv me 'tis different. If I was to ate meat this blessed day I'd go th' way Hinnissy's goat wint that thried to di-gest th' hoopskirt. I'd choke to death on that there flure.

"Whin Ash Whin'sday come around I says to mesilf, I says: 'Ma-artin,' I says, 'ye've not been on ye'er good behavior this year.' I says, 'an 'twould be a good thing f'r ye to put in this here holy season of Lint,' I says, 'squarin' ye'erself,' I says, 'be fastin' an' abstainin'.' So, thinks I, I'll stop off swearin', drinkin', smokin' and playin' ca-ards till afther Easter. Well, sir, I done all right through th' wan day, though I was dam dhry f'r a smoke afther me dinner. But th' nixt day, whin I was goin' by th' gashouse, I cracked me shin again a skid an' forgettin' me good intintions I swore till half the women along th' road begun to call in their childher. Iv coorse I had to scratch off swearin' an' thry to play th' shtring out with th' other three. I done all right through th' afthernoon, but at night that big Clare man, O'Toole, he come in. I don't like a hair iv his head an' he knows it, so I says, 'Terence,' I says, 'I'm glad to see ye.'

"'How ar-re ye?' says he. 'I was goin' by,' he says, 'an' I thought I'd come in an' play ye a little game iv forty-fives.' ''Tis Lint,' says

I. ' 'Tis a good excuse,' says he. 'What's that?' says I. 'Oh,' he says, with a laugh, 'I don't blame ye,' he says, with that mane smile iv his. 'I don't blame ye,' he says. 'There's very few min fr'm ye'er part iv Connack that can play games,' he says, 'that ray-quires in-tillegence,' he says. 'Ye'er betther a long way at pitchin' quates,' he says. I was hoppin' made in a minyet. Says I: 'There niver was a man born in th' County Clare,' says I, 'that could bate me playin' forty-fives,' I says. 'Come on,' says I. 'What for?' says he. 'Th' dhrinks,' says I. 'An' th' see-gars,' says he. 'It's a go,' says I, an' there I was, all me good intintions down at wanst. 'Twas a judg-ment on him f'r challengin' me that he lost tin straight games an' had to walk clear to Brighton f'r lack iv car fare.

"An' mind ye, whin a man swears off annything, Jawn, an' falls down wanst, 'tis all over. He goes in deeper than iver, an' be hivins I've done ivrything bad this here Lint but th' wan thing. I've et no meat on a fast day, and 'tis a ha-ard shtrain upon a ma-an like me."

At this moment the boy from Clancy's restaurant came in to find what Mr. Dooley wanted brought over for dinner.

"Mickey," said Mr. Dooley, "tell ye'er father to cuk that big fish I seen in th' window, an' some soft biled eggs, an' some sparry-grass an' a dish uv coffee. Hell-an'-all, I wish Lint was over." (March 24, 1894)

8. A Genealogy Lecture

This discussion of Irish royalty opens with a reference to Queen Liliuokalani of Hawaii, who upset American plans for annexation by attempting to restore the island monarchy after succeeding to the throne in 1891. The "Major Sampson" mentioned later was a promi-nent Chicago racketeer in the nineties.

"I see be th' pa-aper," said Mr. Dooley, "that th' Queen iv Hawhoo have got th' run, an' because she thried to go back on again, they have her up befure th' polis coort an' are libel to give her wan hundherd dollars or two hundherd days.

"'Tis a queer thing to hear iv a queen iv th' rile blood, copped out be a polisman an' booked an' hauled up befure th' justices, as if she'd been caught snakin' off with a dure mat. 'What's this woman charged with?' 'Ye'er onner, at twinty minyutes past nine last night, just afther I pulled th' box, I was thravelin' down be th' gas house an' I see this here winch thryin' f'r to be a queen. So I took her in.' 'Have ye annything to say?' says th' judge. 'Well, ye'er onner,' says th' queen, 'I wint out with some frins to a chris-tenin' an' I took a dhrop iv beer too much an'——' 'Twinty-five dollars,' says th' judge; 'an' I'll suspind th' fine durin' good behav-ior. Ye look like a hard-wurrkin' woman an' I'll let ye off this time. But don't let me see ye here again.' Oho, but 'tis gr-reat sport.

"Ye don't often hear nowadays iv wan iv us sayin' he's de-scended fr'm wan iv th' kings iv Ireland. Who the divvle'd care? A man might as well boast iv bein' a cousin iv Major Sampson. Th' kings an' queens are played out, Jawn. Th' business have run down since th' days iv Brian Boru an' Dermot McMurrough an' Owen Roe O'Neill an' Malachi that wore th' collar iv goold that he won fr'm th' proud invader. A collar iv goold, d'ye mind, Jawn? Th' dam jood.

"'Tis on'y th' ol' foolish la-ads that thinks iv thim. Not that I'm again kings, Jawn, mind ye now. A king is as good as anny other man if he does what's right an' pays his bills. But f'r mesilf I'd as lave have a plastherer f'r a grandfather—me own was marrid to th' niece iv th' parish priest—as th' Imp'ror iv Roosha or th' Sul-tan iv Boolgaria. I would that.

"There was a man up here last week that lictured in th' school hall on th' origin iv th' people iv Ireland. He had a big map on th' wall an' he thraced th' coorse iv th' thribes across th' face iv Eu-rope. He says, says this here man, that all th' counties come fr'm some part in Persia save an' excipt Kerry. 'They was foorced,' says he, 'to lave their native land,' he says. 'Evicted?' asks Hinnissey. 'Mebbe,' says the man. 'But annyhow, they come acrost th' Bos-phorus.' ''Twas wan iv me frinds had th' bridge,' says Gallagher. 'He was wan iv th' sthrongest min in all Persia,' he says. 'He car-ried th' prim'ries again th' polis station.' 'Lave off talkin',' says th' man, 'an' let me go on in peace,' he says. 'Here,' he says, pointin' with his stick to th' map, 'wan iv th' columns wint in,' he says. 'To get a dhrink?' says Hogan, the tailor man. 'Probably yis,' says th' man, mad as a hin at th' la-ads; 'probably yis,' says he. 'If they was anny iv ye'er people,' he says. 'An' they come out immejutely,' he says. 'They didn't have th' price,' he says. That sittled Hogan, an' they was no more interruption till he had th' procission moved up into Germany. ' 'Twas th' intintion iv th' Irish,' he says, 'to sittle in Germany,' he says, 'but th' natives iv that place,' he says, 'dhruv thim out,' he says. 'Not in wan thousand years,' says big Morrisey. 'They niver lived th' Dutchman that cud do it.' Th' man had to take that back befure they'd lave him go on. Whin he'd landed th' Irish over beyant, O'Shea stands up in th' back iv th' hall an', says he, 'ye have lift out th' Kerry min,' he says. 'Where did they come fr'm?' he says. 'They come fr'm China,' says th' man. 'I thought so,' says O'Shea. 'Thin,' he says, lookin' at Tim Reardon, that he had a gredge again, 'am I to understhand that whin Mr. Reardon's at home his name is Wan Lung?' Reardon was up in a minyit, an' he says, says he, 'Wan lung or twinty,' says he, 'it makes no difference,' he says. 'Th' Reardons was niver run on wind,' he says, 'an' if it'll convanience Mister O'Shea,' he says, 'I'll have me name changed to Two Fists,' he says, 'an' make him ate it.'

"That inded th' licture an' some iv th' ol' la-ads come over here an' tould me iv it. 'I make no doubt it's thrue,' says Clancy. 'Th' main guy iv our fam'ly was Murtagh, th' first king iv Connock,' he says. 'An' he had a gr-reat deal iv goold in his threeasury.' 'Me folks is fr'm Owen, the first,' says Robert Immitt Grogan. 'I've heerd till iv him,' says Clancy. 'Me father mintioned his name often,' he says. 'He was a grand jook, Grogan,' he says. 'He wur-rked f'r King Murtagh,' he says, 'an' was a sober, industhrious man,' he says. ' 'Tis a lie,' says Grogan. 'Owen, the first,' he says, 'niver'd take any such job as jook,' he says. 'An', furthermore,' he says, 'no Grogan,' he says, 'iver wur-rked f'r a Clancy,' he says, 'ayether in Persia,' he says, 'in Connock,' he says, 'or in th' rowlin' mills,' he says. An' if I hadn't got in bechune thim they'd been rile blood spilt on that there flure." (March 2, 1895)

9. A Benefit Raffle

In the course of reporting this social event, Mr. Dooley reduces the spoils system to absurdity in noting how a local job-seeker is distressed at the elevation to cardinal of apostolic delegate Francisco Satolli in January 1895.

"They tell me the wagon had eight calls to Donovan's last night," said Mr. McKenna to Mr. Dooley, who was wearing a piece of plaster over his eye.

"Yis, an' twict eight, bad cess to thim May-o min. 'Tis a wondher I got out alive. Harrity, that was Donovan's bartinder, does be down sick with noomony iv th' lungs an' they got up a raffle f'r a dimon pin. I niver see him wear no dimon pin whin he was fillin' out pints f'r Donovan; but they've had it in th' ciga-ar case f'r two weeks, as big as an egg an' shinin' like th' light iv Kinsale. They come ar-round to me an' I bought a ticket an' wint over f'r to see that no wan give me the double-cross. A man who buys a ticket to a raffle an' don't attind 'd bether have a guarjeen appinted.

"Near ivry wan along th' r-road was at Donovan's, f'r Harrity was a pop'lar man who give good measure. Th' aldherman was there, an' th' sinitor, an' th' loot fr'm th' station, an' th' captain iv th' fire depa-artmint—a coorajoos man, that. He niver wint to a fire yet that he didn't sthrip to his red flannel shirt. He wears his hat an' coat indoors, but no wan iver see him with ayether, though th' big wind sh'd blow again, whin on his way to a fire.

"There was gr-reat arguin' iv politics befure th' raffle. Th' aldherman an' th' sinitor come together wanst an' th' loot accused Donovan iv thryin' f'r to have him thrun down. Little Hogan, th' most ignorant man in Bridgeport, was standin' at th' ind iv th' room whin Timothy Clancy wint up to him, an' knowin' how he'd been thryin' f'r a job, says he: 'Did ye hear-r about Satolli?' he says. 'Faith, no,' says Hogan. 'What iv him?' he says. 'He's got a good job,' he says. 'What doin',' says Hogan, tur-rnin' pale. 'He's been appinted ca-ardinal,' says Clancy. 'Th' 'ell he has,' says Hogan, sthrikin' th' ba-ar. 'Thin, by dad, I'll niver vote f'r Casey again,' he says. 'He promised that to me.' Th' ignorance iv him!

"Donovan waited till business slacked up an' thin he says: 'Gintlemin,' he says. 'Attintion,' he says. 'If ye'll pro-ceed in an ordherly manner into th' nixt r-room,' he says, 'we'll have th' raffle f'r this here dimon, valyed be me frind Misther Goldstein here at five hundherd dollars.' At that Hogan said a pather-an-avy an' we wint back. Did ye iver attind a raffle, Jawn? Ah, tell th' thruth! Well, ye take three dice, an' ye take a funnel an' ye take a punch bowl. Thin ye dhrop th' three dice three times through th' funnel, an' th' man that has th' most iv th' spots he wins. Hogan was th' first man. He shook twenty-nine. As he wint out he huv a brick through th' window. Malachi Dimpsey made thirty-five an' waited till Dorgan shook forty, an' they sittled it in th' alley. Th' next throw was Cassidy's. He flung forty-five, an' wint around with his thumbs in his vist till a black Mayo man be th' name iv O'Malley, a man fr'm th' fifth, shook fifty-four. Now, fifty-four is all ye can shake. 'Tis th' high number, an' O'Malley says, 'Give me th' dimon.' 'I'll give ye nawthin',' says Donovan; 'there's twinty more to shake.' 'I've shook fifty-four an' no wan can beat it,' says O'Malley. 'Some wan can tie ye,' says Donovan. 'No wan here can tie me,' says O'Malley, fr'm th' fifth ward an' Mayo, an' he ups an' swallows th' dice. Well, sir, they was ructions. Whin I wint out with that there little scut iv a Mahoney, that I've lint manny's th' dollar to, buttin' me in th' stomach, Donovan was on top iv th' ice chist, th' aldherman was rollin' bar'ls on th' sinitor, an' that divvle of an O'Malley was doin' th' joynt swing fr'm the shandyleers, an' flurin' ivery wan that come within tin feet iv him. I met th' hurry-along wagon on me way home, loaded with polismin."

"And what became of the diamond?" asked Mr. McKenna.

"'Twas dam pec-uliar. Some way it got near th' stove they cook th' horse-mate sausages on an' it milted an' r-run all over th' flure.

Ye don't belave me? Ask Donovan. An', Jawn, I go to no more raffles." (January 12, 1895)

10. The Dooley Family Reunion

"Why aren't you out attending the reunion of the Dooley family?" Mr. McKenna asked the philosopher.

"Thim's no rel-ations to me,' Mr. Dooley answered. "Thim's farmer Dooleys. No wan iv our fam'ly iver lived in th' counthry. We live in th' city, where they burn gas an' have a polis foorce to get on to. We're no farmers, divvle th' bit. We belong to th' indus-threel classes. Thim must be th' Fermanagh Dooleys, a poor lot, Jawn, an' always on good terms with th' landlord, bad ciss to thim, says I. We're from Roscommon. They'se a Dooley family in Wixford an' wan near Ballybone that belonged to th' constabulary. I met him but wanst. 'Twas at an iviction; an', though he didn't know me, I inthrajooced mesilf be landin' him back iv th' ear with a bouldher th' size iv ye'er two fists together. He didn't know me aftherwards, ayether.

"We niver had but wan reunion iv th' Dooley fam'ly, an' that was tin years ago. Me cousin Felix's boy Aloysius,—him that aftherwards wint to New York an' got a good job dhrivin' a carredge f'r th' captain iv a polis station,—he was full iv pothry an' things; an' he come around wan night, an' says he, 'D'ye know,' he says, ''twud be th' hite iv a good thing f'r th' Dooleys to have a reunion,' he says. 'We ought to come together,' he says, 'an' show the people iv this ward,' he says, 'how sthrong we are,' he says. 'Ye might do it betther, me buck,' says I, 'shovellin' slag at th' mills,' I says. 'But annyhow, if ye'er mind's set on it, go ahead,' I says, 'an' I'll attind to havin' th' polis there,' I says, 'f'r I have a dhrag at th' station.'

"Well, he sint out letthers to all th' Roscommon Dooleys; an' on a Saturdah night we come together in a rinted hall an' held th' reunion. 'Twas great sport f'r a while. Some iv us hadn't spoke frindly to each other f'r twinty years, an' we set around an' tol' stories iv Roscommon an' its green fields, an' th' stirabout pot that was niver filled, an' th' blue sky overhead an' th' boggy ground undherfoot. 'Which Dooley was it that hamsthrung th' cows?' 'Mike Dooley's Pat.' 'Naw such thing: 'twas Pat Dooley's Mike. I mane Pat Dooley's Mike's Pat.' F'r 'tis with us as with th' rest iv our people. Ye take th' Dutchman: he has as manny names to give to his childher as they'se nails in his boots, but an Irishman has th' pick iv on'y a few. I knowed a man be th' name iv Clancy,—a man fr'm Kildare. He had fifteen childher; an', whin th' las' come, he says, 'Dooley, d'ye happen to know anny saints?' 'None iv thim thrades here,' says I. 'Why?' says I. 'They'se a new kid at th' house,' he says; 'an', be me troth, I've run out iv all th' saints I knew, an', if somewan don't come to me assistance, I'll have to turn th' child out on th' wurruld without th' rag iv a name to his back,' he says.

"But I was tellin' ye about th' reunion. They was lashins iv dhrink an' story-tellin', an' Felix's boy Aloysius histed a banner he had made with 'Dooley aboo' painted on it. But, afther th' night got along, some iv us begun to raymimber that most iv us hadn't been frinds f'r long. Mrs. Morgan Dooley, she that was Molly Dooley befure she married Morgan, she turns to me, an' says she, ''Tis sthrange they let in that Hogan woman,' she says,—that Hogan woman, Jawn, bein' th' wife iv her husband's brother. She heerd her say it, an' she says, 'I'd have ye to undherstand that no wan iver come out iv Roscommon that cud hold up their heads with th' Hogans,' she says. ''Tis not f'r th' likes iv ye to slandher a fam'ly that's iv th' landed gintry iv Ireland, an' f'r two pins I'd hit ye a poke in th' eye,' she says. If it hadn't been f'r me bein' between thim, they'd have been trouble; f'r they was good frinds wanst. What is it th' good book says about a woman scorned? Faith, I've forgotten.

"Thin me uncle Mike come in, as rough a man as iver laid hands on a polisman. Felix Dooley was makin' a speech on th' vartues iv th' fam'ly. 'Th' Dooleys,' says he, 'can stand befure all th' wurruld, an' no man can say ought agin ayether their honor or their integrity,' says he. 'Th' man that's throwin' that at ye,' says me uncle Mike, 'stole a saw fr'm me in th' year sivinty-five.' Felix paid no attintion to me uncle Mike, but wint on, 'We point proudly to th' motto, "Dooley aboo—Dooley f'river."' 'Th' saw aboo,' says me uncle Mike. 'Th' Dooleys,' says Felix, 'stood beside Red Hugh O'Neill; an', whin he cut off his hand,—' 'He didn't cut it off with anny wan else's saw,' says me uncle Mike. 'They'se an old sayin',' wint on Felix. 'An' ol' saw,' says me uncle Mike. 'But 'twas new whin ye stole it.'

"'Now look here,' says Aloysius, 'this thing has gone far enough. 'Tis an outrage that this here man shud come here f'r to insult th' head iv th' fam'ly.' 'Th' head iv what fam'ly?' says Morgan Dooley, jumpin' up as hot as fire. 'I'm th' head iv th' fam'ly,' he says, 'be right iv histhry.' 'Ye're an ol' cow,' says me uncle Mike. 'Th' back iv me hand an' th' sowl iv me fut to all iv ye,' he says. 'I quit ye,' he says. 'Ye're all livin' here undher assumed names'; an' he wint out, followed be Morgan Dooley with a chair in each hand.

"Well, they wasn't two Dooleys in th' hall'd speak whin th' meetin' broke up; an' th' Lord knows, but I don't to this day, who's th' head iv th' Dooley fam'ly. All I know is that I had wan th' nex' mornin'." (August 24, 1895)

11. New Year's Resolutions

Mike Scanlan, mentioned here in the same breath with Shake-speare, was a Chicago writer of Mr. Dooley's day known for his Irish nationalist verse.

Mr. Hennessy looked out at the rain dripping down in Archey Road, and sighed. "A-ha, 'tis a bad spell iv weather we're havin'."

"Faith, it is," said Mr. Dooley, "or else we mind it more thin we did. I can't remimber wan day fr'm another. Whin I was young, I niver thought iv rain or snow, cold or heat. But now th' heat stings an' th' cold wrenches me bones; an', if I go out in th' rain with less on me thin a ton iv rubber, I'll pay dear f'r it in achin' j'ints, so I will. That's what old age means; an' now another year has been put on to what we had befure, an' we're expected to be gay. 'Ring out th' old,' says a guy at th' Brothers' School. 'Ring out th' old, ring in th' new,' he says. 'Ring out th' false, ring in th' thrue,' says he. It's a pretty sintimint, Hinnissy; but how ar-re we goin' to do it? Nawthin'd please me betther thin to turn me back on th' wicked an' ingloryous past, rayform me life, an' live at peace with th' wurruld to th' end iv me days. But how th' divvle can I do it? As th' fellow says, 'Can th' leopard change his spots,' or can't he?

"You know Dorsey, iv coorse, th' cross-eyed May-o man that come to this counthry about wan day in advance iv a warrant f'r sheep-stealin'? Ye know what he done to me, tellin' people I was caught in me cellar poorin' wather into a bar'l? Well, last night says I to mesilf, thinkin' iv Dorsey, I says: 'I swear that henceforth I'll keep me temper with me fellow-men. I'll not let anger or jealousy get th' betther iv me,' I says. 'I'll lave off all me old feuds; an' if I meet me inimy goin' down th' sthreet, I'll go up an' shake him be th' hand, if I'm sure he hasn't a brick in th' other hand.' Oh, I was mighty compliminthry to mesilf. I set be th' stove dhrinkin' hot wans, an' ivry wan I dhrunk made me more iv a pote. 'Tis th' way with th' stuff. Whin I'm in dhrink, I have manny a fine thought; an', if I wasn't too comfortable to go an' look f'r th' inkbottle, I cud write pomes that'd make Shakespeare an' Mike Scanlan think they were wur-rkin' on a dredge. 'Why,' says I, 'carry into th' new year th' hathreds iv th' old?' I says. 'Let th' dead past bury its dead,' says I. 'Tur-rn ye'er lamps up to th' blue sky,' I says. (It was rainin' like th' divvle, an' th' hour was midnight; but I give no heed to that, bein' comfortable with th' hot wans.) An' I wint to th' dure, an', whin Mike Duffy come by on number wan hundherd an' five, ringin' th' gong iv th' ca-ar, I hollered to him: 'Ring out th' old, ring in th' new.' 'Go back into ye'er stall,' he says, 'an' wring ye-ersilf out,' he says. 'Ye'er wet through,' he says.

"Whin I woke up this mornin', th' pothry had all disappeared, an' I begun to think th' las' hot wan I took had somethin' wrong with it. Besides, th' lumbago was grippin' me till I cud hardly put wan foot befure th' other. But I remimbered me promises to me-silf, an' I wint out on th' sthreet, intindin' to wish ivry wan a 'Happy New Year,' an' hopin' in me hear-rt that th' first wan I wished it to'd tell me to go to th' divvle, so I cud hit him in th' eye. I hadn't gone half a block befure I spied Dorsey acrost th' sthreet. I picked up a half a brick an' put it in me pocket, an' Dorsey done th' same. Thin we wint up to each other. 'A Happy New Year,' says I. 'Th' same to you,' says he, 'an' manny iv thim,' he says. 'Ye have a brick in ye'er hand,' says I. 'I was thinkin' iv givin' ye a New Year's gift,' says he. 'Th' same to you, an' manny iv thim,' says I, fondlin' me own ammunition. ''Tis even all around,' says he. 'It is,' says I. 'I was thinkin' las' night I'd give up me gredge again ye,' says he. 'I had th' same thought mesilf,' says I. 'But, since I seen ye'er face,' he says, 'I've concluded that I'd be more comfortable hatin' ye thin havin' ye f'r a frind,' says he. 'Ye're a man iv taste,' says I. An' we backed away fr'm each other. He's a Tip, an' can throw a stone like a rifleman; an', Hinnissy, I'm some-thin' iv an amachoor shot with a half-brick mesilf.

"Well, I've been thinkin' it over, an' I've argied it out that life'd not be worth livin' if we didn't keep our inimies. I can have all th' frinds I need. Anny man can that keeps a liquor sthore. But a rale sthrong inimy, specially a May-o inimy—wan that hates ye ha-ard, an' that ye'd take th' coat off yer back to do a bad tur-rn to—is a luxury that I can't go without in me ol' days. Dorsey is th' right sort. I can't go by his house without bein' in fear he'll spill th' chimbly down on me head; an', whin he passes my place, he walks in th' middle iv th' sthreet, an' crosses himself. I'll swear off on anny-thing but Dorsey. He's a good man, an' I despise him. Here's long life to him." (January 2, 1897)

12. Football on the Road

The competing Bridgeport teams in this piece are named for Irish nationalists: Patrick Sarsfield, the famous soldier of the 1680s, and Charles Stewart Parnell, leader of the Irish Parliamentary party in the 1880s.

"Jawn," said Mr. Dooley, "whin I played futball 'twas spoort; now futball is war."

"How is that?" asked Mr. McKenna.

"Well, when I was a lad th' way we played futball was this way: Twinty or thirty or wan hundherd min an' boys come together in a vacant lot an' we had a round rubber ball that th' biggest man blowed up, an' so th' air wuddent r-run out iv it he stuffed chewed-up bread in th' hole. Thin a lad be th' name iv McGuire he says: 'Go head now,' an' I give her a kick an' put her over th' fince. Thin they brought it back, th' little la-ads did, an' I kicked it on th' roof iv th' Brothers' school. Brother Alexis fetched it down, an' says he: 'Dooley, don't kick so hard,' he says. So I give it wan low kick with th' broad iv me fut an' catched Hinnissy, who was a young man thin, in th' pit iv th' stomach, an' he kicked young Regan, an' Regan kicked Cassidy, an' Cassidy kicked O'Brien, an' O'Brien kicked Brother Alexis an' had to do th' stations iv th' cross, an' a boy be th' name iv Hogan run off with th' ball.

"That was futball. But las' week young Clancy asked me f'r to go over to th' back iv th' dump an' see a game bechune th' Young Parnells an' th' Young Sarsfields. I took Hinnissy with me, may Gawd f'rgive me. He'd ne'er seen a game befure. Th' la-ads was there whin we come. I luked over th' field an' says I: 'What is this?' says I. 'What're they goin' to do?' I says. Hinnissy made no answer. Th' little Mulcahy kid was done up with wooden shields on his shins an' earmuffs on his ears an' a band around his head an' a carnycopy on his nose. He wore matthresses f'r pants an' he had a head iv hair like cole slaw. Th' others was like him. Ye cud iv tol' no wan iv thim fr'm th' other.

"Well, sir, a man blew a whistle an' with that, little Mulcahy reached over an' give Tom O'Brien's son a punch in th' nose. O'Brien calls out, 'Look there, Mike Mulcahy, what ye'er boy's doin' to mine. I want ye to stop him.' 'Stop nowan,' says Mulcahy acrost th' field. 'But if that rasc'lly son iv ye'ers iver kicks that boy iv mine again,' he says, 'I'll have th' law on him,' says he. 'Look out f'r his feet, little Mike,' he says. 'Now, thin, land him.'

"Well, O'Brien wint right acrost th' field afther Mulcahy an' th' last seen iv thim they was collar-an'-elbowin' down toward th' bridge. Just thin Hogan Cassidy threw his fut into little Malachi Dorney an' ol' man Cassidy wint over an' pulled Tom Dorney's nose. I took thim apart near th' river an' come back just as what th' lads call a scrimmage was on. Tommy O'Leary got hol' iv th' ball an' started to run away with it, whin little Duggan fetched him a puck on th' jaw an' brought him down. He'd no more thin done that whin Teddy Clancy nailed Duggan with a kick on th' back an' rolled him on top iv O'Leary an' fell on him. Thin all th' other lads fell on Duggan an' Clancy an' O'Leary, all but wan. That was Dinny Casey, an' he sthrayed around th' edge an' took a kick at any wan he saw, an' particuley at Pete O'Shea.

"Pete O'Shea was Hinnissy's nivyew, an' th' first thing Hinnissy done whin he see his sisther's son gettin' th' worst iv it was to r-run acrost th' shtreet an' come back with an armful iv bricks. He can throw f'r an' old man, an' he fitched Casey with th' first brick. 'Stick it out,' he says to his nivyew. 'Stick it out,' he says. 'I'll clane all iv thim off ye,' he says. An' sure he'd iv done it, but th' lad comes wrigglin' out iv th' pile smilin' an' says he: 'Uncle, lave go ye'er brickbats,' he says. 'What f'r?' says Hinnissy. 'Don't ye see they're all upbarrin' Mulcahy,' says th' kid. ''Twas on'y a down,' he says. 'A what?' says Hinnissy. 'A down,' says th' lad. 'An' how manny more is there?' says Hinnissy. 'A hundherd or more,' says th' lad. 'Well, thin,' says Hinnissy, 'I'm goin' home,' he says. 'If ye have anny wurrud to lave ye'er mother,' he says, 'tell it to me.'

"I took him be th' ar-rm as we wint home, an', says I, 'Hinnissy,' I says, 'ye made a fool iv ye'ersilf,' I says. 'How's that?' says he. 'How's that? Ye'er an illitherate man,' I says. 'I can read an' write,' he says, 'an' give ye th' wurruks iv Willum Carleton be heart.' 'Thrue,' says I. 'But whin ye intherfered with that game did ye know that you was stoppin' th' iducation iv th' youth iv th' land,' I says. 'I did not,' he says, sadly. 'An' now th' thought comes on me an' makes me heart gray with trouble,' he says. 'Win I intherfered with that man that was poundin' Hoolihan with a baseball bat las' winter,' he says, 'did I keep annywan out iv a proper schoolin'?'

"'Ye may have,' says I." (October 26, 1895)

13. Hennessy Umpires a Baseball Game

Like the football game of the last piece, this baseball vignette is full of references to Irish nationalism. The Sarsfields play baseball too; here they face a team sponsored by Bridgeport alderman William J. O'Brien. John F. Finerty was editor of the weekly Chicago newspaper, The Citizen, *which was dedicated to the fight for Irish freedom. And the Clan-na-Gael Guards were a nationalist-oriented militia company, presumably in training to return to Ireland to fight the British.* One of Dunne's early newspaper jobs was to report the home and away games of the Chicago White Stockings Baseball Club for the* Daily News *in 1887.*

"I've just come over fr'm Hinnissy's," said Mr. Dooley. "He's laid up in bed, covered that thick with bandages a coalminer cudden't get down to him in a day with a pick an' a dhrill."

"What ails him?" asked Mr. McKenna.

"Ah," said Mr. Dooley with unusual disgust, "th' ol' fool's been makin' a goat iv himsilf impirin' a baseball game. May th' good Lord give him since befure he dies, an' be quick about it, for he must be past sixty now.

"Las' week th' Sarsfields wrote a challenge an' stuck it in Fin-

---

* For more on "the Cause" in Chicago, see Chapter Six.

erty's paper that they cud bate anny baseball club iv rivolutionists in th' sixth wa-ard f'r tin dollars a game. The Willum J. O'Brien Lith'ry an' Dhramatic Marchin' Club heerd iv it an' they took it up an' last Sundah th' la-ads come together in Grogan's lot down back iv th' dumps. Near iv'ry wan in th' road wint to see th' game an' Clancy, who wants to be aldherman, bought a kag iv beer an' put it on third base. Such a scrap come up about who ought to play third that th' captains had to order th' kag off th' field.

"But that isn't what I was goin' to tell ye. I was talkin' about Hinnissy, th' ol' gazaboy. Whin they'd tossed up pinnies to see which side 'd go to bat first an' th' Sarsfields won they begun lookin' about f'r an impire. 'Tis no easy job, Jawn. I'd as lave be a German minority judge at a prim'ry as impire a game in th' dumps. An' so would anny wan else that had sinse. Hinnissy has none; no more than Hogan's cow. Whin they offered him th' job he stuck his thumbs in his vist an' says he: 'Oh, well, if no wan else will, I will, la-ads.' He was proud iv it. He hadn't held an office but th' wan iv bridgetinder under Colvin since th' war. 'Is he a good man?' says th' captain iv th' Willum J. O'Briens. 'He was out in "forty-eight,"' says th' captain iv th' Sarsfields. 'He looks too old,' says th' captain iv th' O'Briens. 'What's that?' says Hinnissy. 'What's that?' he says. 'Look here, young man,' he says, tippin' his plug hat back till it hung on wan ear. 'Look here,' he says, 'I lay ye tin dollars that I can outrun ye, outlep ye an' outbox ye,' he says— him, th' deluded ol' freak that had me up all las' month rubbin' his jints with arnica f'r inflammathry rhoomatism.

"Well, they put him in behind th' bat an' he bint over th' way he'd seen other impires do, with his hands undher th' tails iv his coat. 'Wan sthreek,' says he. 'What's that?' says th' man at th' bat—it was big Morty Clancy—turnin' round on him. 'Wan ball, I mane,' says Hinnissy. 'What's that?' says Owen Roe O'Neill Mc-Carthy, who was catchin' f'r th' O'Briens. An' thin both nines come up an' gathers around him. I think that was what th' ol' monkey wanted, f'r he cocked his hat an' made a speech to th' assimbled multitood. 'I want to say,' says he, 'that I'm impire iv this game,' he says. 'An' while,' he says, 'I'm impire iv this game,' he says, 'I'll be impire iv this game,' he says. 'Go to ye'er corners,' he says, 'an' we'll start over again.'

"Well, they was nawthin' else to do, f'r Hinnissy was so old that no wan'd lick him, an' if they wanted younger min th' Clan-na-Gael Ga-ards cud not impire wan iv thim games, I tell ye, Jawn, an' get out iv the hospital in time to tind ba-ar at th' picnic. So they wint on. Morty Clancy made a swipe at th' ball an' knocked it over th' fince. Well, Hinnissy owns th' house nixt to th' fince an' th' minyit he heerd th' ball smashin' through a pane iv glass he started acrost th' field after Clancy, who was tearin' along to'rd first base. 'Come back, ye murdhrin' young vilyan,' he says. 'Come back here, now, an' pay f'r that pane iv glass,' he says, 'or I'll have th' law on ye,' he says. An' away he wint afther Clancy.

"Clancy knew 'twas a home run, an' with his head down he tore along, payin' no attintion to what was goin' on behind him. 'Stop,' says Cassidy, th' first baseman iv th' Willum J. O'Briens. 'Stop,' he says. 'Th' impire is callin' ye back,' he says. 'Get out iv me way,' says Clancy, an' he back-heeled Cassidy as much as twinty feet. But at sicond base Malachi Mulligan ketched him be th' legs, an' they rolled each other as far as th' car thracks.

"Well, be this time, th' captain iv th' O'Briens he'd got hold iv Hinnissy, an' some more iv thim helped him. 'Go in,' says they, 'an' tind to ye'er business,' they says. They pushed him down th' field an' stuck him up on th' home plate just in time to have th' ball thrun in an' hit him on his vin'rable stomach. He give wan look like a sick cat to where I was settin', an' thin he lay down on th' ground an' said no more f'r a matther iv five minyits. Thin we picked him up an' I heerd him mutter something. 'What's that?' says I. He pointed to his face. 'Aha,' says I. 'Ladies an' gintlemin,' I says, 'this here impire, this three-year-old, this thriminjus ath-late,' I says, 'in friskin' around has lost his teeth,' I says. 'Both sets,' I says.

"Well, we took him home, an' though he wanted th' priest we give him linymint instead, an' he ought to be able to get out in a week. I wint over to see him to-night. ''Twas all right,' says he, 'but ye oughtn't to've humilyated me befure th' crowd,' he says. 'Hinnissy,' says I, 'whin a rispicted citizen an' head iv a fam'ly goes around makin' a pink monkey iv himsilf,' I says, ''tis the jooty iv a thrue friend to tip him off,' I says. 'Besides,' I says, 'what'd 've happened if Morty Clancy'd come back?' I says. 'Would ye sooner lose ye'er teeth inside or out?' I says.

"An' 'tis thrue, Jawn. As Shakespeare says: 'Ol' min f'r th' council; young min f'r th' ward.'" (June 22, 1895)

14. The Corbett-Mitchell Fight of 1894

When "Gentleman Jim" Corbett took on England's champion heavyweight Charles Mitchell in January 1894, Mr. Dooley connected the event with the fight for Irish freedom. All Bridgeport rejoiced when Corbett won easily—by a knock-out in the third round. Mr. Dooley also describes a similar match between Mr. and Mrs. Malachi Duggan, during which Mr. Duggan claims that he almost married a niece of William Smith O'Brien, a leader of the abortive 1848 rising against British rule in Ireland.

"By gar," said Mr. Martin Dooley. "That there Corbett—there do be no bugs on him, bedad. Did ye r-read about th' prizefight, Jawn?"

"I did not," said Mr. McKenna. "I never saw the paper."

"Well, sir, 'twas tur-rble, Jawn," said Mr. Dooley. "Ye see Corbett was that sore at Mitchell he says, sez he: 'If I get him in th' ring,' he says, 'I dhrive me hand through his hear-rt,' says Corbett. It seems they'd had wur-rds before, an' Corbett he was did sore at Mitchell, mind ye, on account iv Mitchell sayin' aroun' that Sid C. France was a better actor than what Corbett was. An' whin Corbett an' him gets in th' ring he looks at him an' says he, he says, 'I'll sind ye back to England,' he says, 'f'r th' queen to cry over,' says Corbett, an' with that he eyes him an' Mitchell looks pale. Well, sir, Corbett he didn't go in an' fight in th' beginnin', mind ye. He wint aisy. D'ye mind Malachi Duggan? Well, wan day he had a fallin' out with his wife, f'r th' champeenship iv th' Duggan family an' Malachi was winnin' whin Mrs. Duggan gets th' rowlin' pin an' goes at him with it. By dad, she r-run him into a clothes closet an' shtood ga-ard at th' dure like a sinthry. 'Come out,' says she, 'an' fight,' she says, 'ye Limerick buthermilk,' she says. She come fr'm Waterford an' her father was th' best man with a stick in Ireland till he passed away to his repose iv pnoo-mony iv th' lungs. Th' Lord ha' mercy on his sowl. 'Oh, ye wicked woman, let me out,' says Duggan. 'To think,' he says, 'that a man that had the rayfusal iv a niece iv Smith O'Broyn,' he says, 'should 'v tied up,' he says, 'with this Apache. Let me out,' says he. 'There's a bottle iv liniment spilt on th' shilf an' 'tis drippin' down th' back iv me neck.' 'Stay in there,' says she. 'It isn't Hon-ora O'Broyn ye have to deal with,' she says, 'but Mary Eleanor Duggan,' she says, 'daughter iv Terence Desmond,' she says, 'champeen iv all Ireland,' she says. 'If ye come out, little man,' she says, 'I'll break ye're back.' Well, sir, Duggan was a fox. He said nawthin' f'r a few minutes while he rigged up his big high hat on a walkin' stick, an' thin he said, 'I'm comin' out, avick,' an' he pokes out th' hat an' Mrs. Duggan whales away at it an' thin he clinches her, an' bedad he wins th' fight.

"So be Corbett. He says to himself, he says: 'I'll delude this here Saxon,' says he. 'I'll let him smash me,' he says. 'An' if it don't kill me,' he says, 'I've got him.' So he goes up to Mitchell an' he says: 'There's me face.' 'What of it?' says Mitchell. 'Don't ye like it?' says Corbett. 'Sare a bit,' says Mitchell. 'Thin knock it off me,' says Corbett. Well, sir, Mitchell goes an' takes a r-runnin' jump at Corbett's face. D'ye think he minded it? Why, that big strong joynt, he no more minded it than th' rock iv Cashel'd mind ye throwin' a spitball at it. He tur-rned to Mitchell an' he says: 'Is that th' best ye can do?' says th' bould Corbett. 'Now watch me.' Well, sir, this here paper says he wint at him like a ragin' line. He smashes him on th' eye an' in th' jaw, an' ivry time he hit him he broke a bone. Mitchell lay down on th' stage an' begged f'r mercy.

"'Get up,' says Corbett. 'Get up,' he says. 'Get up till I dhrive me good right arm through ye,' he says. 'Get up till I slay ye,' he says. 'In mim'ry iv what ye done to Robert Immit,' he says, an' whin Mitchell got up he swings that tur-rble right fist — —"

During the narrative, Mr. Dooley became visibly excited. With his left hand extended and his right upon his waistcoat, he danced around the shop until the climax of his story was reached, which he celebrated by hitting Mr. McKenna vigorously upon the nose. Mr. McKenna, of irrascible disposition, promptly kicked his friend in the stomach. Then he clutched the old gentleman around the neck, waltzed him out into the back room, threw him violently on the floor and sat on him.

"Will you give up?" said Mr. McKenna.

"Yes, yes," said Mr. Dooley, plaintively. "Let me up, Jawn. Me collar-bone's broke, and thim keys in ye'er pocket hur-rts me."

Mr. McKenna assisted Mr. Dooley to his feet and led him out.

"And what did they do with Mitchell?" he asked.

"I dinnaw," said Mr. Dooley with a look of anguish, "onless they burrid him." (January 27, 1894)

15. A Fishing Trip

"Th' ma-an Holmes" was an alleged mass murderer, "Doctor" H. H. Holmes, who was then on trial for having kidnapped and killed several women at his 63rd Street "murder castle" in Chicago.

"Jawn," said Mr. Dooley, with suppressed indignation, "if iver ye catch me speakin' a wurrud to that man Hinnissy save an' alone in th' wa-ay iv tellin' him what I think iv th' likes iv him ye can refuse to speak to me on th' sthreet, an' whin ye refuse to speak to me on th' sthreet I'll go an' jump into th' pond back iv th' dump an' dhrownd mesilf, I will that.

"Arrah, don't get excited. I'll tell ye about Hinnissy. He come up here las' Choosdah night an' says he: 'I'm goin' fishin',' he says, 'Th' mills has closed down an' I'm takin' me va-cation,' he says, 'without pay,' he says. 'Will ye come with me?' he says. 'What the divvle d'ye want to go for this time iv th' week?' I says. 'Ye can't eat fish till Fridah,' I says. 'Be a spoort,' says he. 'Come on,' he says. So I hired Dinnihy's kid to mind th' store, business bein' poor, and Hinnissy an' I wint off early in th' mornin' up to Wistconsin, where there's a lake that Hinnissy said was full iv bass an' pickles an' throut an' soord fishes an' eyesthers an' all kinds iv game.

"Him an' me, Hinnissy th' fool an' me, bought a pole an' some minnies, f'r th' fish does be cannybals in thim parts, an' out we wint undher a sun so near to us that ye cud almost catch it in ye'er hat. Sare a fish had I iver caught but a can iv salmon, but Hinnissy, th' crazy wan, he said we'd be all right, so I set in th' ind iv th' boat an' dhropped th' minny overboord an' waited. Jawn, look at th' back iv me neck. Broiled, be hivins, broiled! I cukked there like a doughnut f'r five hours. 'Have ye a bite?' says I to Hinnissy. 'Not yet,' says he, 'but patience,' he says, 'an' pass th' bottle.' Th' blisters begun comin' out on me poor neck like bubbles in a pot iv stirabout. 'Have ye a bite?' says I. 'None but fr'm th' fly on th' ind iv me nose,' he says. 'Hit it, Martin, if ye love me. Hol' on,' he says. 'Here's wan,' he says, 'Oh, 'tis a whale. Come here,' he says, 'come up, me beauty,' he says. 'Come up, feerocious shark,' he says. 'Now, d'ye stand by, Martin,' he says, 'an' kill him with th' oar,' he says. 'I think be th' weight an' fight iv him 'tis th' sea sarpint I have here.' 'Thin,' says I, 'f'r hivins sake lave him be or tow him ashore,' says I. 'I had a cousin wanst that had his feet bit off be a fish.' But Hinnissy wint on pullin' an' swearin', an' what d'ye think he fetched? A hoopskirt, by gar. 'Twas bad enough f'r me to hook a box iv beer an' a mud turtle, but a hoopskirt—dear, oh, dear, he was that mad.

"'What ar-re ye goin' to do with it?' says I. 'Ye can't wear it,' I says, 'an' ye can't ate it,' I says, 'an' ye can't put it in th' poor box,' I says. He didn't bat his eye f'r an hour.

"Be this time I'd larned how to handle th' pole, an' I hooked a monsthrous fish, Jawn. Ye know I wouldn't lie about it, avick, an' 'tis th' truth I tell ye whin I say it was as long as fr'm here to th' ice chist an' a good two feet acrost. It was a whale, niver fear, an' a most feerocious wan, and wanst it near hauled me out iv th' boat.

But says I to mesilf, 'I'll do it if I die,' an' I pulled away like a bridge horse. 'Come up,' I says. 'Come up,' says I to th' big fish, 'or be hivins I'll jump in an' throttle ye with me own hands.' Well now, Jawn, a fish is no wan's fool—lasteways ivry fish is not a sucker—an' this big lad knew dam well whin he met his masther, an' all iv a suddent, as I give a sthrong pull, he thrun up th' fight an' come.

"They was a scream fr'm Hinnissy. 'Let go,' he says. 'Come on,' says I, speakin' to th' fish, 'come on,' I says, 'ye'er mine.' 'Let go, f'r hivins sake,' says Hinnissy. 'Let go nothin',' says I, blind with th' fight in me. ''Tis my fish, an' I'll take him if I have to swim ashore with him. Come on,' I says. 'Fish nothin',' says Hinnissy. 'Ye have hooked me ear,' he says, 'an' ye'er stretchin' it like an ol' hose,' he says. 'Let go or I'll shoot.'

"Well, Jawn, I looked, an' what d'ye suppose that ol' bosthoon had done? He'd gone an' hung his ear on me hook. Where was the fish? Th' Lord on'y knows. Wherever it was ye can bet it was dead. No fish 'd iver go through that fight an' not turn up a corpse. Hinnissy said I'd hooked a soapbox an' thried to murdher him f'r disappointment. He's been up an' down th' road blackenin' me char-acter an' tellin' me frinds I have insurance on his life, like th' ma-an Holmes, an' that he'd as lave cuk his meals in a dynnamite facthry as go annywhere with me. I'll have th' law on him. But I'll tell ye about this fish——"

"How long was it?" asked Mr. McKenna.

"I said to ye it was full as long as that stovepipe an' as broad acrost as an eighth iv beer. But what's th' use iv talkin' about it? I was tellin' Morgan Clancy, an' he says undher th' game laws I had a right to Hinnissy's ear. Th' ga-ame warden lives in ye'er wa-ard, an' I wisht ye'd ask him. I dinnaw if it's th' season f'r ears." (August 3, 1895)

16. Ice Skating and Old Age

Mr. Dooley claims kinship here with James C. Dooley, who was
appointed justice of the peace for West Chicago in 1891.

"Skatin'," said Mr. Dooley, "was intinded f'r th' young an' gay.
'Tis not f'r th' likes iv me, now that age has crept into me bones
an' whitened th' head iv me. Sorra take th' rheumatics! An' to
think iv me twinty years ago cuttin' capers like a bally dancer,
whin th' Desplaines backed up an' th' pee-rairies was covered
with ice fr'm th' mills to Riverside. Manny's th' time I done th'
thrick, Jawn, me an' th' others; but now I break me back broachin'
a kag iv beer, an' th' height iv me daily exercise is to wind th'
clock befure turnin' in, an' count up th' cash. Sorra take th'
rheumatics!"

"You haven't been trying to skate?" Mr. McKenna asked in
tones of alarm.

"Not me," said Mr. Dooley. "Not me, but Hinnissy have. Hinnissy have. Hinnissy, th' gay young man; Hinnissy, th' high-
hearted, divvle-may-care sphread-th'-light,—Hinnissy's been
skatin' again. May th' Lord give that man sinse befure he dies!
An' he needs it right away. He ain't got long to live, if me cousin,
Misther Justice Dooley, don't appoint a garjeen f'r him.

"I had no more thought whin I wint over with him that th' silly
goat 'd thry his pranks thin I have iv flyin' over this here bar mesilf. Hinnissy is—let me see how ol' Hinnissy is. He was a good
foot taller thin me th' St. John's night whin th' comet was in th'
sky. Let me see, let me see! Jawn Dorgan was marrid to th' widdy
Casey (her that was Dora O'Brien) in th' spring iv fifty-two, an'
Mike Callahan wint to Austhreelia in th' winter iv sixty. Hinnissy's oldest brother was too old to inlist in th' army. Six an'
thirty is thirty-six. Twict thirty-six is sivinty-two, less eight is
sixty-four, an' nine, carry wan,—let me see. Well, Hinnissy is ol'
enough to know betther.

"The firemin iv injine twinty-sivin had flooded th' vacant lot
acrost fr'm their house an' all th' la-ads an' girls iv Bridgepoort

knew about it. They come sthreamin' up th' sthreet with their skates on their ar-rms, th' girls altogether an' th' la-ads be thimsilves, too. 'Twas thim turned Hinnissy's head, I have no doubt. But f'r me, I know th' diff'rince between wan an' twinty an' five an' sixty. I larn it over again ivry mornin'.

"We wint to th' pond together, an' passed th' time iv day with our frinds an' watched th' boys an' girls playin' shinny an' skylarkin' hand in hand. They come separate, Jawn; but they go home together, thim young wans. I see be his face Spoort Hinnissy was growin' excited. 'Sure,' says he, 'there's nawthin' like it,' he says. 'Martin,' he says, 'I'll challenge ye to race,' he says. 'So ye will,' says I. 'So ye will,' I says. 'Will ye do it?' says he. 'Hinnissy,' says I, 'come home,' I says, 'an' don't disgrace ye'er gray hairs befure th' whole parish,' says I. 'I'll have ye to know,' says he, 'that 'tis not long since I cud cut a double eight with anny wan in Bridgeport,' he says.

"At that Tom Gallagher's young fly-be-night joined in; an' says he, 'Misther Hinnissy,' he says, 'if ye'll go on,' he says, 'I'll fetch ye a pair iv skates.' 'Bring thim along,' says Hinnissy. An' he put thim on. Well, Jawn, he sthud up an' made wan step, an' wan iv his feet wint that way an' wan this; an' he thrun his hands in th' air, an' come down on his back. I give him th' merry laugh. He wint clear daft, an' thried to sthruggle to his feet; an', th' more he thried, th' more th' skates wint fr'm undher him, till he looked f'r all th' wurruld like wan iv thim little squirrels that goes roun' on th' wheel in Schneider's burrud store.

"Gallagher's lad picked him up an' sthud him on his feet; an' says he, politely, 'Come on,' he says, 'go roun' with me.' Mind ye, he took him out to th' middle iv th' pond, Hinnissy movin' like a bridge horse on a slippery thrack; an' th' lad shook him off, an' skated away. 'Come back!' says Hinnissy. 'Come back!' he says. 'Tom, I'll flay ye alive whin I catch ye on th' sthreet! Come here like a good boy, an' help me off. Dooley,' he roars to me, mind ye, 'ain't ye goin' to do annything?' he says. 'Ne'er a thing,' says I, 'but go home.' 'But how'm I goin' to cross?' he says. 'Go down on ye'er knees an' crawl,' says I. 'Foolish man!' I says. An' he done it,

Jawn. It took him tin minyits to get down in sections, but he done it. An' I sthud there, an' waited f'r him while he crawled wan block over th' ice, mutterin' 'Glory be to Gawd' at ivry fut.

"I wint home with him aftherwards; an' what d'ye think he said? 'Martin,' says he, 'I've been a sinful man in me time; but I niver had th' like iv that f'r a pinance,' he says. 'Think iv doin' th' stations iv th' cross on th' ice,' he says. 'Hinnissy,' I says, 'they'se no crime in th' catalogue akel to bein' old,' I says. 'Th' nearest thing to it,' I says, 'is bein' a fool,' I says; 'an' ye're both,' I says." (January 18, 1896)

17. Old Age and Bicycling

Mr. Dooley urges his own comparative youth with a reference to British statesman, William Ewart Gladstone, who had resigned as prime minister the previous March after sixty-one years in the House of Commons. The subject of the piece, old Cassidy, is criticized for having refused to join Colonel Mulligan's Irish Brigade in the Civil War because of his "copperhead" sympathies with the South.

"Jawn," said Mr. Dooley, interrupting his friend, Mr. Mc-Kenna, "there's no two ways about it, whin old age comes down on a man, he must face it an' take it. I'm not so dam old. Look at Gladstun. I was as good a man at a hurlin' match or a dance whin I was young as anny ye know, an' I was captain iv me precinct whin it took min to be captains, I'll have ye know that, an' at this minyit I'd resk me chances with most iv th' la-ads that comes in here—me an' th' icepick an' th' polisman on th' corner. But I know a thing or two, an' I'll tell ye sthraight that I've no sympathy f'r Cassidy. I sint him a bottle, but I'll do no more f'r him. Th' ol' gazabo!

"How old d'ye think that man is. Ah, gawon! Why, they couldn't dhraft him th' wa-ar! 'Tis thrue. Mulligan wanted him an' he was a copperhead. 'What?' says he. 'Fight with me frinds Aleck Stephens an' Borryga-ard?' he says. 'I should say not,' he says. They

wint afther him hard an' he showed where he'd cut th' finger he'd
have to shoot his gun with on th' dredge in th' canal. 'Niver mind,'
says they, 'we'll put ye on th' cannon,' they says. 'All ye'll have to
do is to scratch a match,' they says. 'Ye have a good leg,' says they,
an' they'd 've had him in th' army, but he proved be th' parish
priest he was over age. How old would that make him? Iv coorse
he's lively f'r his age. Who did he lick? Why, Jawn, if I hadn't
been there! I tell ye, Dorney had him down, man alive!

"But annyhow, ye'll admit he's an ol' man, won't ye? He's too
old to ride wan iv thim bicycles annyhow, an' that's what he's
been doin'. I was over talkin' with him on th' stoop iv his house
whin his boy Hughey come along. He have a good job as shippin'
clerk, an' he rides downtown in th' mornin' an' home at night
with his pants tied to his legs. A betther kid niver lived. He come
along on th' wheel, an' says Cassidy: 'I think I'll buy me a bicycle,'
he says. ''Tis a nice way to get around,' he says. 'I could go out to
th' mills on it flyin',' he says. 'Ye could,' says I. 'If ye could get on,'
I says. 'Sure,' says he, 'what's to prevint me gettin' on,' he says.
'All ye have to do,' he says, 'is to take a hop, skip an' a jump,' he
says, 'an' away ye go,' he says. 'If I had a piece iv chewin' gum,' he
says, 'I'd go at it this minyit.' 'Take care,' says I. 'Mike, take care,'
I says. 'Ye raymimber th' fall ye got off th' handcar,' I says. 'D'ye
mean to dare me?' says he. 'Hughey,' he says, 'fetch her up,' he
says. 'Steady,' he says, 'now leggo,' says he, and befure I could say
a wurrud to stop him he was off.

"Well, he done all right f'r a ya-ard or two though he looked
like a man I seen walk into th' draw at th' rid bridge wanst whin
Casey had it an' I was down helpin' him tur-rn it. Thin he begun
to yell. 'Martin,' says he. 'What?' says I. 'Sind Hughey here,' he
says. 'What d'ye want iv him?' I says. 'Go wan,' says I, 'ye bold
man,' I says. 'Ye'er ridin' as though ye an' th' wheel was made in
th' same factory,' I says. 'I know it,' says he, and his voice was gettin' faint, 'but be hivins I can't stop,' he says. An' no more he
could. He wint down th' sthreet like th' wind an' th' more he
thried to stop th' faster he wint. Th' kids along th' sidewalk
stopped their play to look at him. Min got off th' sthreetca-ars an'

cheered him. Mulligan, th' big copper, was comin' out iv his house an' Cassidy called to him. 'Mulligan,' he says, 'stop me,' he says. 'Stop ye'erself,' says Mulligan. 'Fall off,' he says. 'How th' 'ell can I fall off whin I'm settin' on it,' says Cassidy. 'Tiliphone th' man on th' bridge,' he says. 'An' see that he keeps it closed,' he says. 'If I can on'y get to State sthreet I'm all right,' he says. 'Th' buildings'll stop me,' he says. 'Me, oh my, won't annyone take me off!'

"We followed him up an' took him off a lamppost at th' south-wist corner iv Archey road an' Deerin' sthreet."

"In front of Finucane's Hall?" asked Mr. McKenna.

"In front iv Finucane's Hall," said Mr. Dooley. "Th' old skate." (May 25, 1895)

18. The Game of Golf in Chicago

In the 1890s golf became popular in Chicago society circles. On September 13, 1897, the first national tournament to be held in the West opened at the Chicago Golf Club's new course at Wheaton, Illinois. The most exciting match was the semifinal between Scotsman Finley Douglas of St. Andrews and Chicago journalist Herbert J. Whigham, the reigning American amateur champion. Whigham won the match, and the following day Mr. Dooley took notice of the golfing vogue.

"H'm'm," said Mr. Dooley. "A hot game."

"What?" said Mr. Hennessy.

"Golluf," said Mr. Dooley. "Lave me r-read it to ye. Both men dhruv far, but Douglas' ball fell into th' long grass because iv slicin'. Whigham got a good lie an' made th' green be a long brassy shot in two. Douglas got into a boonker on his second, but dhruv out nately with a-a-in-i-bee-ill-ah-see-kay. Now what in th' name iv hivin' is that? Whigham's puttin' was bad an' he wint over th' hole three times. Douglas come on th' green in four with a fine im-ah-ess-haitch-i-e—mashie shot—with a fine mashie shot, but Whigham put away his p-u-t-t-e-r—put away his putter—his putter—an', takin' a small c-l-e-e-k, cleek, won th' hole fin'lly be wan sthroke."

"Good f'r him," said Mr. Hennessy, "he done well. He ought to used th' what-ye-call-im fr'm th' go-off. But what's it all about?"

"Faith, I dinnaw. Th' more I read th' less I know, an' I've had twinty men in here this week askin' me about it. I've studied th' terms an' I've consulted th' pitchers. Here's wan iv sixty women standin' round in short skirts like th' chorus in that there opera, 'The Mascot,' that th' Bridgeport Amachoor Theatricals done last year. Here's a man with a window pole over his head dancin' a highland fling. Here's another man takin' a high ball all alone on th' stoop. Fr'm this it looks as if th' game was f'r th' la-ad on th' stoop to tuck in r-rum till he'd want to dance, too, whin they'd both dance together. But here's another pitcher that shows th' players gettin' out iv an ominybus, an' fr'm that I guess it must be that th' first wan out wins th' match an' th' last wan knows what he is.

"Dorsey, th' polisman, he can't make it out an' he was th' best hurler in th' county whin he was young. Flannagan, th' fireman, that is th' roughest tosser in a handball coort, has gone crazy thryin' to undherstand it. Carmody, th' captain iv th' Motorman's baseball nine, tells me it has him up a tree. Him an' me r-read it upside down an' inside out an' sint over f'r a dichionary an' ast a man in to take a dhrink because we thought he was a Scotchman, an' divvle a bit betther off ar-re we than whin we started. Th' whole sixth wa-ard is crazy about it. Iverybody talks about it an' no wan knows annything about it. I'll bet ye nex' winter they'll be a nightschool down be Finucane's Hall, with a golluf profissor to teach th' la-ads, an' we'll have examinations. 'What is a mashie? Describe a niblick. If James has three foozles an' gives wan to Charley an' eats wan how manny will he have left?' Something must be done to relieve th' suspinse, an' done at wanst.

"F'r mesilf I don't see that it can iver be a gr-reat naytional game. Look at this raypoort iv a ball game: 'Cassidy hit th' ball in th' eye, knockin' it to left field. He thried to make second, but th' empire called him out. "Y'er a human burglar," says Cassidy, advancin' threateningly with a bat in his hand. "I fine ye twinty," said th' empire. At that Long Tom Collins, th' peerless third baseman, hit him on th' nose, an' soon both teams was engaged in a lively rite with th' audience throwin' chairs an' pop bottles at th' empire. It was tin minyits befure th' polis quited down th' contestants an' th' game was rayshumed.' Now, that's spoort; that's plain fun. Ye can see th' raison f'r that. But can ye see anny raison f'r a game that a man can't begin to undherstand without he knows Gaelic as it's talked in Scotland? Th' on'y gleam iv light I had was whin I see that Douglas landed on th' cop. 'Now,' says I, 'there'll be fun. That Wheaton polisman will roll with him, sure.' But ne'er a wur-rud more was then said about it. Ayether th' officer was afraid iv his job or they have wan kind iv copper in Du Page County an' another in Cook.

"No," said the philosopher. "Fr'm th' ividence at hand, onless there's some horrid manin' in th' wur-ruds that we're not onto yet, golluf can niver be a naytional spoort. It lacks th' wan issintial for a good time, iv homicide." (September 18, 1897)

19. Love Affairs in Ireland and Bridgeport

"Was ye iver in love, Jawn?" said Mr. Dooley. "I sup-pose ye was—befure ye was marrid?"

"Yes," said Mr. McKenna. "And why?"

"Nawthin'," said Mr. Dooley. "On'y I was thinkin' 'tis a dam quare disease. I had it wanst mesilf, but 'tis so long ago that I near forgot it. I sup-pose I had it bad, too, as anny wan. 'Twas over beyant, an' th' colleen was a little black-haired wan that her father kep' th' shtore in town an' was wan iv th' landed gintry. He ownded his house an' lot, he did that. I used to go to th' house whin she was asleep an' sit outside on th' grass an' play 'Th' Connock Man's Rambles' on a tin horn. 'Twas not a suitable chune, Jawn, d'ye mind, but 'twas the only wan me brother Mick cud

larn me. Wan night, whin I was rasslin' with th' horn, her father
come up behind me an' give me a kick in th' ear. 'Well,' says I,
'frindship inds whin kicks begins,' an' I turned in an' took a fall
out iv th' ol' robber. 'I can play th' horn mesilf,' says he, givin' me
a clout on th' nose. 'Bedad,' says I, bein' niver lackin' f'r th' answer in thim days. ''Tis not a horn,' I says, 'but a dhrumstick,' an'
I walloped him over th' head. I win th' fight in wan r-round,
Jawn, but 'twas th' ind iv me courtship. Kerrigan's big lad come
over an' lammed me with a hurlin'-stick th' day afther an' ivry
wan iv th' two families got mixed up an' th' upshot iv it was that
instid iv playin' the hor-rn in front iv Honoria's dure I was layin'
ivry night to soak her with a sod iv turf whin she come out to milk
th' cow. Faith, 'twas a good job f'r me it inded that way. I seen her
two year back. She's marrid to a little shrimp iv a milkman an' she
do look that tough she'd be safe if she cooked in a lumber camp.

"I got to thinkin' iv her to-day fr'm wan iv Casey's kids comin'
in here to tell me he's gawn to be marrid. D'ye mind Malachi
Dorgan, that wanst had a hack stand down be Halsted sthreet? Iv
coorse ye do. 'Tis manny a corpse ye've follied in that same hack
to th' long home in Calv'ry. Well, 'tis his daughter. No, not th' rid-
haired wan. She marrid young Coogan. Ye mind him? He was in
th' rail-estate business, Mrs. Dorgan tould me, an' bydad she was
r-right, f'r I seen him wur-rkin' on a dredge in th' river. No, 'tis
th' little slip that use to play r-round th' cor-rners, 'King Willyum
was King George's son an' on th' rile race he r-run,' an' 'London
bridge do be fa-allin' down' an' all thim pretty games. Sure, it
don't seem no more than last week that I chased her away fr'm in
front iv me place. Well, she's got to be a big woman now an' Casey
is gawn to marry her. I seen it comin'. I seen it, Jawn. Faith, I
know thim things as sure as I know 'tis goin' to r-rain whin me leg
pains me. He use to talk iv her whin he had his r-rollers on. Thin
he begun to wear a white necktie an' wash his hands an' face befure supper. That's wan thing, Jawn, love does f'r a man. It makes
him clane, an' marridge, conthrarywise, makes him dirty. Thin
he let th' polisman on th' bate pass him by without peggin' a

brick—which was onusu'l. Afther awhile he wint to dances, an' wan day I see him pass th' plate at early mass. Thin I knowed 'twas all off.

"He come in here to-day an' says he: 'Mr. Dooley, was ye iver in love?' 'No,' says I, 'nor in jail.' 'Well,' he says, 'was ye iver married?' 'No,' says I; 'I had a proposal wanst fr'm th' Impriss iv Rooshia,' I says, 'but her fam'ly was too low f'r me.' 'Ah,' he says, 'no jokin'! I'm goin' to be marrid.' 'No,' says I. 'Ye'er th' tinth man that's said that same thing this week,' I says. ''Tis an epidemic, like dhrunkenness at Chris'mas time. What in-sane asylum is th' poor thing at?' I says. 'She ain't insane,' says he. 'She's the best girl alive,' he says. 'She's Cecilia Dorgan.' 'Glory be to Gawd,' says I. 'Is that so? Dear, oh, dear,' I says. 'Th' Lord save us, an' what'll we hear next?' 'Ah,' he says. 'Ye ould thramps,' he says, 'livin' around like goats,' he says. 'Yes,' says I, 'an' doin' our own wurruk.' 'Ye ould thramps,' he says, 'doesn't know what it is,' he says, 'to have comfort,' he says; 'to have a nice woman,' he says, 'f'r to bid ye welcome when ye come home fr'm wurruk,' he says.

"'I know it,' says I, 'I know it,' I says, me timper risin' at the idjucy iv th' young fool. 'An' I'm glad ye'er to be marrid. I like ye, Cornelius.' 'I know ye do,' says he. 'An' I like ye'er girl,' I says. 'Ye cudden't help it,' says he. 'An' I tell ye what I'll do f'r ye,' I says. 'An' what's that?' says he. 'Whin ye'er wife begins to take in waashin',' I says, 'I'll sind her mine.' By gar, Jawn, he thrun a bottle at me—him that I've bailed out twinty times or more." (May 5, 1894)

20. The Courtship of Danny Duggan

"Ye wasn't up to Honoriah Nolan's weddin', was ye? No, nayether was I. I'm gettin' beyant thim doin's, but I sint thim a kag, tied in blue ribbons. If iver a girl deserved to have a nice home an' do her own washin' 'tis little Honoriah. Not that I riccomind marridge, Jawn. A man who has his sup iv tay an' his tin cint ceegaar alone be himself is th' thrue philosopher, be hivins. But young

min who spind their money on dhrink and hor-rse races ought to
marry. If they have to waste half their wages they might as well be
wastin' thim on their wives. They might that.

"But they do tell me 'twas th' divvle's own time they had
thryin' f'r to bring Danny Duggan to th' scratch. F'r an impetchoos an' darin' people th' Irish is th' mos' cowardly whin it come
to mathrimony that iver I heerd tell iv. Ye see pitchers iv other
min kneelin' down f'r to ask a girl to cook their meals f'r betther
or f'r worse, as Shakespeare says, an' I mind wanst goin' into th'
Widow Meyer's f'r a tub iv beer an' findin' big Neumeister down
on his knees befure th' widow. What did I do? What would anny
man do? I give him th' toe iv me boot an' th' widow marrid an ice
man. Ye wouldn't get no Irishman to kneel. Why, whin I asked—
oho, niver mind. I was tellin' ye about Honoriah. He'd been coortin' her steady f'r two years, an I knowed it. I've see thim comin'
along th' shtreet together, ridin' in th' ca-ar together, sky-larkin'
fr'm th' ball together, her laughin' an' walkin' proud an' happy an'
with her pretty head up in th' air, an' him slobberin' along lookin'
f'r fight. Ye can always tell whin wan iv us is in love with th'
woman we're with. We look so dam disagreeable. 'Tis thrue.
Why, full a year back Danny was that stuck he'd hardly speak to
her.

"Well, that was all right f'r Danny, but it didn't do f'r th' girl.
She minded well some stories she'd hear-rd iv th' bashfulness iv
th' Archey road lads. There was Dolan's daughter, who was
coorted be Hannigan, th' fireman f'r fifteen years, an' would be
coorted now if she hadn't shamed him be sindin' him a wig f'r his
bald head las' Christmas. Thin there was Dacey, the plumber,
who'd niver 'v marrid if he hadn't got into th' wrong buildin'
whin he wint to take out a license f'r his dog, an' got a marridge
license instid. Honoriah was no belaver in deathbed marridges,
an' she an' her mother come together over th' thing an' decided on
what Father Kelly calls a coop—be which he manes they cooped
Duggan, I suppose.

"He come in wan night to play a game iv forty-fives with th'
fam'ly, an' after th' game they set around an' talked an' smoked.

Thin ol' man Nolan pulled off his shoes an' said he thought he'd go to bed. He'd been readin' th' pa-aper upside down, an' it made him sleepy. Pretty soon Mrs. Nolan said she'd have to turn in. Duggan began to get frightened, an' just thin in come Father Kelly, th' saints bless th' good man's head.

"Betther thin he niver come to earth to lift th' weight fr'm thim that's weary an' heavy laden—an' a powerful pracher. 'Oho,' says he. 'What's this?' he says. 'Am I breakin' in,' he says, 'on ye young people?' 'Not at all,' says Honoriah. 'Ye'er welcome,' she says. 'Set down,' she says. 'Move over, Danny,' says th' soggarth. 'No, move down,' he says. 'I'll set on th' ind iv th' sofy,' he says. An' down he sets. Well, sir, I dinnaw what happened fr'm that on, Jawn, an' Nolan got a crick in his neck fr'm thryin' to hear, but 'tis me firm belief that Father Kelly—Gawd be good to him—proposed himself fr Danny to Honoriah Nolan, fr Cassidy, who wint by at th' time, 'll take his solemn oath that he see th' good man down on his knees befure her. He was goin' to call a polisman. Annyhow, all that Nolan knew was whin th' soggarth come to th' fut iv th' stairs with a tear in th' tail iv his eye, though his lips was laughin', an' calls out: 'Come down. Come down there, ye nigligent parents,' he says. 'I want to show ye something.' An' whin th' ol' man come down there was Duggan lookin' as if he was goin' to kill a Chiney-man, an' th' dear little colleen thrimblin' an' cryin', but holdin' on to him like a pair iv ice tongs. 'Pax vobiscum,' says th' priest. 'Pax vobiscum.' And thin Danny Duggan knelt down fr th' first time. I see him goin' home in Father Kelly's horse and buggy as happy as th' da-ay is long. I niver see a more contented man. He wanted to get out an' whale me because I said: 'Good avnin'.' Th' weddin' was a gr-reat success an' they say Duggan showed fr'm th' sta-art that he'll be a good husband."

"What did he do?" asked Mr. McKenna.

"He walked out to th' hack a ya-ard ahead iv her," said Mr. Dooley. (December 8, 1894)

21. In the Spring, a Young Man's Fancy

Nansen was a Norwegian explorer of the Arctic, which is presumably being compared to Chicago in spring.

"In th' spring," said Mr. Dooley, looking out of the window, "in th' spring, as th' pote Shakespeare says, a livelier Irish glistens on th' burnish dove; in th' spring, he says, a young man's fancy tur-rns to thoughts iv love. There goes Packy Casey now to call on th' oldest Gannon girl. He'll catch his death iv cold without his overcoat."

"He will so," said Mr. Hennessy, shivering at the corner of bleak sky to be seen through the window.

"Th' climate iv Chicago," said Mr. Dooley, "is not iv th' kind that encourages coortship. If a young man's fancy was to lightly tur-rn to thoughts iv love in Chicago spring he'd have his feet froze befure he cud get th' question out. Over in Ireland I've seen thim in swarms, th' lovers, marchin' out together under th' moon, with th' glitter in their hair, an' th' lads firin' bits iv turf at thim, but in Ireland spring is spring. Here it's ayether th' middle iv August or th' first iv February all th' year round, an' whichever it is, 'tis dam bad weather, annyhow.

"Now, there's Packy Casey goin' to call on th' Gannon girl. He has no overcoat because he wants to show her that he don't need none—him bein' quite a warrum person. Well, he goes up an' rings th' bell an' there's a great fluttherin' inside th' house. All th' kids r-runs to th' window gigglin' an' Mary Gannon darts around wavin' her hands. 'Mah, can't ye make th' childher come away fr'm th' window. Come away fr'm there, Mike. Ye'er too big a boy to be actin' like a baby. Pah, f'r goodness sake put on ye'er slippers.' Ol' man Gannon winks at th' wife an' says he: 'Mikey, ye little blaggard, come away fr'm th' window an' run down stairs an' get ye'er pah's dimon pin an' full evenin' dhress coat, so's he'll look right befure th' jood, Casey. His father was a dhrayman an' he ain't used to th' ways of th' dump people.' 'Arrah, be quiet, Tim,' says Mrs. Gannon, whippin' on her apron an' goin' to th' dure, while Mary arranges th' music on the pianny. 'Well, good avenin', Packy,' she says. 'Ye'er half froze, ye poor thing. Where's ye'er overcoat?' 'I don't need none,' says Packy. 'It ain't cold,' he says. 'Good avenin', Misther Gannon,' he says. ''D'avenin', son,' says Gannon. 'Good avenin', Julia,' says Packy. 'Good avenin', Mike. Good avenin', Terry,' he says. 'Good avenin', Miss Gannon,' with a blush. Thin th' ol' man winks again an' goes out f'r his pipe an' all th' kids get behind th' lounge an' snicker in their hands till they're dhruv out.

"But Mrs. Gannon sticks. 'Tis again her judgment that she stays there, f'r well she knows nawthin'll come off while she's around. But she can't lave till she's took a chanst iv hearin' a wurrud. So she asks Packy what he takes f'r a cold. 'Onions an' whisky,' he says. 'Oo-o,' says Mary, 'isn't he turrible,' she says. 'I've heerd iv onions bein' good,' says Mrs. Gannon, 'but I don't go much on whisky.' 'Well,' says Packy, who's a mimber iv th' Father Machew S'ciety, 'I don't care so much f'r th' onions mesilf,' winkin' at th' girl. 'Have ye left off ye'er flannels yet,' says Mrs. Gannon. 'I have not,' says Packy. 'Ye'er right not to,' says Mrs. Gannon. 'No wan can affoord to take anny chances with th' Chicago climate. It's killin',' she says. 'It is so,' says Mary Gannon. 'Ye niver can tell what th' weather is goin' to be. Here las' week it was so hot I put on me muslins, an' to-day I cud wear a sealskin sack,' she says. At this th' ol' man in th' dinin'-room belches up a merry laugh, an' so it goes. They talk weather, an' colds an' undherclothin' an' Doctor Innis Davis' cough cure till 'tis time f'r Packy to go, an' niver a wurrud iv what he come f'r crosses his lips. Now if spring was spring instead iv winter, an' if Janooary didn't come in April, thim two'd be out ar-rm in ar-rm exchangin' sweet nawthin's.''

Mr. Hennessy plucked at Mr. Dooley's sleeve and pointed across the street where a couple were walking slowly with their arms joined and their heads uncommonly close together.

"Well," said Mr. Dooley solemnly. "'Tis so. There they ar-re, afther all. Whin people want to make fools iv thimsilves they go be th' calendar, not be th' thermometer. In th' spring a young man's fancy tur-rns to thoughts iv love. I suppose Nansen seen it, too." (May 1, 1897)

22. Felix's Lost Chord

"By dad, if it wasn't f'r that there Molly Donahue," said Mr. Dooley to Mr. McKenna, "half th' life 'd be gone out iv Bridgeport."

"What has Molly Donahue been doin?" asked Mr. McKenna.

"She have been causin' Felix Pindergasht to be sint to th' Sisters iv Mercy Hospital with inflammathry rhoomatism. Ye know Felix. He is a musical janius. Befure he was tin year old he had me mind disthracted be playin' wan iv thim little mouth organs on th' corner near me bedroom window. Thin he larned to play th' ackcar-jeen, an' cud swing it between his legs an' give an imitation iv th' cathedral bell that 'd make ye dig in ye'er pocket to see if ye had a dime f'r a seat. Thin he used to sit in his window in his shirt-sleeves, blowin' 'Th' Vale iv Avoca' on a cornet. He was wan whole month befure he cud get th' 'shall fade fr'm me heart' right. Half th' neighborhood 'd be out on th' sidewalk yellin' 'Lift it, Felix,—lift an' scatther it. Shall fade fr'm me ha-a-rt,—lift it, ye clumsy piper.'

"A few months back th' stupid gawk begun to be attintive to Molly Donahue, an', like th' wild wan she is, she dhrew him on. Did ye iver see th' wan that wudden't? Faith, they're all alike. If it ain't a sthraight stick, it's a crooked wan; an' th' man was niver yet born, if he had a hump on his back as big as a coal-scuttle an' had a face like th' back iv a hack, that cudden't get th' wink iv th' eye fr'm some woman. They're all alike, all alike. Not that I've annything again thim: 'tis thim that divides our sorrows an' doubles our joys, an' sews chiny buttons on our pa-ants an' mends our shirts with blue yarn. But they'll lead a man to 'ell an' back again, thim same women.

"Well, Felix had no luck coortin' Molly Donahue. Wan night she wasn't in; an' th' nex' night ol' man Donahue come to th' dure, an' says, 'Ye can put in th' coal at th' back dure,' he says, an' near broke th' la-ad's heart. Las' week he pulled himself together, an' wint up th' r-road again. He took his cornet with him in a green bag; an', whin he got in front iv Donahue's house, he outs with th' horn, an' begins to play. Well, sir, at th' first note half th' block was in th' sthreet. Women came fr'm their houses, with their shawls on their heads; an' all th' forty-fives games was broke up be raison iv th' la-ads lavin' f'r to hear the music. Befure Felix had got fairly started f'r to serrynade Molly Donahue, th' crowd was big an' boistherous. He started on th' ol' favor-ite, 'Th' Vale iv Avoca'; an' near ivry man in th' crowd had heerd him practisin' it. He wint along splendid till he come to 'shall fade fr'm me heart,' an' thin he broke. 'Thry again,' says th' crowd; an' he started over. He done no betther on th' second whirl. 'Niver say die, Felix,' says th' crowd. 'Go afther it. We're all with ye.' At that th' poor, deluded loon tackled it again; an' th' crowd yells: 'Hist it up. There ye go. No, be hivens he fell at th' last jump.' An', by dad, though he thried f'r half an hour, he cud not land th' 'shall fade fr'm me heart.' At th' last break th' light in Molly Donahue's window wint out, an' th' crowd dispersed. Felix was discons'late. 'I had it right befure I come up,' he says, 'but I missed me holt whin th' crowd come. Me heart's broke,' he says. 'Th' cornet's not ye'er insthrument,' says Dorsey. 'Ye shud thry to play th' base dhrum. It's asier.'"

"Is that all that's going on?" asked Mr. McKenna.

"That an' th' death iv wan iv Hinnissy's goats,—Marguerite. No, no, not that wan. That's Odalia. Th' wan with th' brown spots. That's her. She thried to ate wan iv thim new theayter posthers, an' perished in great ag'ny. They say th' corpse turned red at th' wake, but ye can't believe all ye hear." (January 26, 1895)

23. An Economical Romance

"Jawn," said Mr. Dooley, "if ye'd been up th' r-road las' night I'd iv took ye out in sassiety."

"Whose dog won?" asked Mr. McKenna in the spirit of levity.

Mr. Dooley gave no heed to the remark. "Do ye know ol' Hinnisy, th' miser?"

"Him that had three wives! To be sure."

"Well, he wint an' got marrid again."

"Well, the old villain. And who did he marry?"

"Mrs. Odalia Ann O'Leary. Yis, yis, Odalia Ann; he marrid Odalia Ann O'Leary." Mr. Dooley's utterance was broken with wild laughter, while Mr. McKenna could only walk up and down the little liquor-shop with his hands pressed on his cambric shirt. When they had quieted down Mr. Dooley resumed:

"Well, 'twas a pair. Ye know they live alongside of ache other. Hinnisy have a brown billy goat and Ann Odalia she have a white nanny goat. So 'twas ivident they was made for ache other, Hinnisy says. Th' other night I sees him comin' out iv his house with a plug hat on his head an' a cane in his hand an' him walkin' on his heels. His big kid Tom tould me th' story. He's cellybrated th' occasion be gettin' dhrunk. Hinnisy wint around th' back way an' knocked at th' kitchin dure. 'Come in,' says Mrs. O'Leary. 'How d'ye do this fine avenin'?' she says. 'I'm well, thanks be to Gawd,' said Hinnisy. 'Come here, nanny,' he says, pattin' th' goat. 'She's a pretty crathur,' he says. 'An' I like her name,' he says. 'Th' young people iv th' r-road is gettin' too gay,' he says, 'with their Lucys an' their Mauds,' he says. 'Ol' names is th' best,' he says. D'ye see th' thrickery iv th' la-ad. He knowed dam well that there goat was th' apple iv Ann Odalia's eye. 'I'll have to keep her in dures,' she says. 'She do be gettin' flirtatious with ye-er Willum.' 'Faith,' says Hinnisy, 'Willum could go further an' fare worse,' he says. 'An' so could manny others,' he says. 'Oho,' he says, walkin' up an' down th' room. ''Tis crool to be alone in th' wurruld,' he says. 'Have ye anny morgedge on this property?' 'No,' says Mrs. O'Leary, softly. 'I heerd ye sold th' house an' lot in Cologne sthreet,' she says. 'No,' says he, 'I bought th' wan nex' dure,' he says. 'How much rints d'ye dhraw fr'm thim flats?' he says. 'Th' same as iver,' she says. 'Wan hundherd a month.' He put his ar-rum around her an' th' la-ad that had been outside threw a rock through th' window an' come over here.

"They had a divvle of a weddin' up wist iv th' bridge. Every chick an' chile in Bridgeport was there. They come up in dhrays fr'm Haley's Slough an' ye cudden't get half iv thim in th' church. Whin anny wan'd come down th' middle aisle th' kids 'd all holler, 'There they come now,' an' Potthoff, th' organist 'd begin f'r to play. Whin they did come fin'lly th' la-ad that pumps th' organ was lanin' over th' railin' shootin' spit balls an' Potthoff an' him got into th' 'ell's own row an' they was no music f'r th' weddin'. I heerd Hinnisy give Fa-ather Kelly about two bits, an' whin th' good man seen it, he says sarcastic: 'Mr. Hinnisy,' he says, 'ye made a mistake,' he says. 'Th' poor box is down back iv th' church.' Hinnisy's la-ad was standin' on th' steps an' whin th' ol' man comes up he give him th' foot an' thrun him.

"Thin we all ma-arched down behind thim to his house. We give him th' finest shivaree was iver known in Bridgeport. 'Twas rale sport till some iv th' la-ads got throwin' couplin' pins an' thin th' loot had to sind out th' resarves. An' what d'ye think? He niver asked us if we had a mouth to our face, av'n whin we built a bon-fire befure his dure an' thrun horseshoes down th' chimney."

"The mean man," said Mr. McKenna. "But what could you ex-pect of the likes of him?"

"Sare a thing," said Mr. Dooley. (July 21, 1894)

24. A Winter Night

This piece followed one of the worst blizzards in Chicago history.

Any of the Archey Road cars that got out of the barns at all were pulled by teams of four horses, and the snow hung over the shoulders of the drivers' big bearskin coats like the eaves of an old-fashioned house on the blizzard night. There was hardly a soul in the road from the red bridge, west, when Mr. McKenna got laboriously off the platform of his car and made for the sign of somebody's celebrated Milwaukee beer over Mr. Dooley's tavern. Mr. Dooley, being a man of sentiment, arranges his drinks to conform with the weather. Now anybody who knows anything at all knows that a drop of "J.J." and a whisper (subdued) of hot water and a lump of sugar and lemon peel (if you care for lemon peel) and nutmeg (if you are a "jood") is a drink calculated to tune a man's heart to the song of the wind slapping a beer-sign upside down and the snow drifting in under the door. Mr. Dooley was drinking this potion behind his big stove when Mr. McKenna came in.

"Bad night, Jawn," said Mr. Dooley.

"It is that," said Mr. McKenna.

"Blowin' an' stormin', yes," said Mr. Dooley. "There hasn' been a can in to-night but wan, an' that was a pop bottle. Is the snowploughs out, I dinnaw?"

"They are," said Mr. McKenna.

"I suppose Doherty is dhrivin'," said Mr. Dooley. "He's a good dhriver. They do say he do be wan iv the best dhrivers on th' road. I've heerd that Yerkuss was dead gawn on him. He's me cousin. Ye can't tell much about what a man 'll be fr'm what th' kid is. That there Doherty was th' worst omadhon iv a boy that iver I knowed. He niver cud larn his a-ah-bee, abs. But see what he made iv himsilf! Th' best dhriver on th' road; an', by dad, 'tis not twinty to wan he won't be stharter befure he dies. 'Tis in th' fam'ly to make their names. There niver was anny fam'ly in th' ol' counthry that turned out more priests than th' Dooleys. By gar, I believe we hol' th' champeenship iv th' wurruld. At M'nooth th' profissor that called th' roll got so fr'm namin' th' Dooley la-ads that he came near bein' tur-rned down on th' cha-arge iv a dirty little Mayo man th't was profissor too that he was whistlin' at vespers. His mouth, d'ye mind, took that there shape fr'm sayin' 'Dooley,' 'Dooley,' that he'd looked as if he was whistlin'. D'ye mind? Dear, oh dear, 'tis th' divvle's own fam'ly f'r religion."

Mr. McKenna was about to make a jeering remark to the effect that the alleged piety of the Dooley family had not penetrated to the Archey Road representative, when a person, evidently of wayfaring habits, entered and asked for alms. Mr. Dooley arose, and, picking a half-dollar from the till, handed it to the visitor with great unconcern. The departure of the wayfarer with profuse thanks was followed by a space of silence.

"Well, Jawn," said Mr. Dooley.

"What did you give the hobo?" asked Mr. McKenna.

"Half a bu-uck," said Mr. Dooley.

"And what for?"

"Binivolence," said Mr. Dooley, with a seraphic smile.

"Well," said Mr. McKenna, "I should say that was benevolence."

"Well," said Mr. Dooley, "'tis a bad night out, an' th' poor divvle looked that mis'rable it brought th' tears to me eyes, an'"—

"But," said Mr. McKenna, "That ain't any reason why you should give half a dollar to every tramp who comes in."

"Jawn," said Mr. Dooley, "I know th' ma-an. He spinds all his money at Schneider's, down th' block."

"What of that?" asked Mr. McKenna.

"Oh, nawthin'," said Mr. Dooley, "on'y I hope Herman won't thry to bite that there coin. If he does —" (February 17, 1894)

25. The Optimist

Most of Chicago's steel mills were located far down on the South Side of the city, but from 1865 to 1896 there was a rolling-mill operation of the Illinois Steel Company in Bridgeport, at the corner of Archer and Ashland avenues. Mr. Dooley frequently uses this mill as a geographical reference point, and little Tim Clancy, "the optimist," probably worked there.

"Aho," said Mr. Dooley, drawing a long, deep breath. "Ah-ho, glory be to th' saints!"

He was sitting out in front of his liquor shop with Mr. Mc-

Kenna, their chairs tilted against the door-posts. If it had been hot elsewhere, what had it been in Archey Road? The street-car horses reeled in the dust from the tracks. The drivers, leaning over the dash-boards, flogged the brutes with the viciousness of weakness. The piles of coke in the gas-house yards sent up waves of heat like smoke. Even the little girls playing on the sidewalks were flaming pink in color. But the night saw Archey Road out in all gayety, its flannel shirt open at the breast to the cooling blast and the cries of its children filling the air. It also saw Mr. Dooley luxuriating like a polar bear, and bowing cordially to all who passed.

"Glory be to th' saints," he said, "but it's been a thryin' five days. I've been mean enough to commit murdher without th' strength even to kill a fly. I expect to have a fight on me hands; f'r I've insulted half th' road, an' th' on'y thing that saved me was that no wan was sthrong enough to come over th' bar. 'I cud lick ye f'r that, if it was not so hot,' said Dorsey, whin I told him I'd change no bill f'r him. 'Ye cud not,' says I, 'if 'twas cooler,' I says. It's cool enough f'r him now. Look, Jawn dear, an' see if there's an ice-pick undher me chair.

"It 'd be more thin th' patience iv Job 'd stand to go through such weather, an' be fit f'r society. They's on'y wan man in all th' wurruld cud do it, an' that man's little Tim Clancy. He wurruks out in th' mills, tin hours a day, runnin' a wheelbarrow loaded with cindhers. He lives down beyant. Wan side iv his house is up again a brewery, an' th' other touches elbows with Twinty-Percint Murphy's flats. A few years back they found out that he didn't own on'y th' front half iv th' lot, an' he can set on his back stoop an' put his feet over th' fince now. He can, faith. Whin he's indures, he breathes up th' chimbley; an' he has a wife an' eight kids. He dhraws wan twinty-five a day—whin he wurruks.

"He come in here th' other night to talk over matthers; an' I was stewin' in me shirt, an' sayin' cross things to all th' wurruld fr'm th' tail iv me eye. ''Tis hot,' says I. ''Tis warrum,' he says. ''Tis dam hot,' says I. 'Well,' he says, ''tis good weather f'r th' crops,' he says. 'Things grows in this weather. I mind wanst,' he says, 'we had days just like these, an' we raised forty bushels iv oats to an acre,' he says. 'Whin Neville, th' landlord, come with wagons to take it off, he was that surprised ye cud iv knocked him down with a sthraw. 'Tis great growin' weather,' he says. An', Jawn, by dad, barrin' where th' brewery horse spilt oats on th' durestep an' th' patches iv grass on th' dump, sare a growin' thing but childher has that little man seen in twinty years.

"'Twas hotter whin I seen him nex', an' I said so. ''Tis war-rum,' he says, laughin'. 'By dad, I think th' ice 'll break up in th' river befure mornin',' he says. 'But look how cold it was last winter,' he says. 'Th' crops need weather like this,' he says. I'd like to have hit him with a chair. Sundah night I wint over to see him. He was sittin' out in front, with a babby on each knee. 'Good avnin',' says I. 'Good avnin',' he says. 'This is th' divvle's own weather,' I says. 'I'm suffocatin'.' ''Tis quite a thaw,' he says. 'How's all th' folks?' says I. 'All well, thank ye kindly,' he says, 'save an' except th' wife an' little Eileen,' he says. 'They're not so well,' he says. 'But what can ye expect? They've had th' best iv health all th' year.' 'It must be har-rd wurrukin' at th' mills this weather,' I says. ''Tis war-rum,' he says; 'but ye can't look f'r snow-storms this time iv th' year,' he says. 'Thin,' says he, 'me mind's taken aff th' heat be me wurruk,' he says. 'Dorsey that had th' big cinder-pile—the wan near th' fence—was sun-struck Fri-dah, an' I've been promoted to his job. 'Tis a most re-sponsible place,' he says; 'an' a man, to fill it rightly an' properly, has little time to think iv th' weather,' he says. 'D'ye think we'll have rain?' he says. 'A good sprinkle now'd be just th' thing f'r th' crops,' he says. An' I wint away lavin' him singin' 'Hush-a-bye-babby on th' three tops' to th' kids on his knees.

"Well, he comes down th' road tonight afther th' wind had turned, with his old caubeen on th' back iv his head, whistlin' 'Th' Rambler fr'm Clare,' and I stopped to talk with him. 'Glory be,' says I, ''tis pleasant to breathe th' cool air,' says I. 'Ah,' he says, ''tis a rale good avnin',' he says. 'It'll make a man sleep,' he says. 'D'ye know,' he says, 'I haven't slept much these nights, f'r wan reason 'r another. But,' he says, 'I'm afraid this here change won't be good f'r th' crops,' he says. 'If we'd had wan or two more warrum days an' thin a sprinkle iv rain,' he says, 'how they would grow, how they would grow!'"

Mr. Dooley sat up in his chair, and looked over at Mr. McKenna.

"Jawn," he said, "d'ye know that, whin I think iv th' thoughts that's been in my head f'r a week, I don't dare to look Tim Clancy in th' face." (June 8, 1895)

26. Shaughnessy

"Jawn," said Mr. Dooley in the course of the conversation, "whin ye come to think iv it, th' heroes iv th' wurruld,—an' be thim I mean th' lads that've buckled on th' gloves, an' gone out to do th' best they cud,—they ain't in it with th' quite people naye-ther you nor me hears tell iv fr'm wan end iv th' year to another."

"I believe it," said Mr. McKenna; "for my mother told me so."

"Sure," said Mr. Dooley, "I know it is an old story. Th' wur-ruld's been full iv it fr'm th' beginnin'; an' 'll be full iv it till, as Father Kelly says, th' pay-roll's closed. But I was thinkin' more iv it th' other night thin iver befure, whin I wint to see Shaughnessy marry off his on'y daughter. You know Shaughnessy,—a quite man that come into th' road befure th' fire. He wurruked f'r Larkin, th' conthractor, f'r near twenty years without skip or break, an' seen th' fam'ly grow up be candle-light. Th' oldest boy was intinded f'r a priest. 'Tis a poor fam'ly that hasn't some wan that's bein' iddycated f'r the priesthood while all th' rest wear thimsilves to skeletons f'r him, an' call him Father Jawn 'r Father Mike whin he comes home wanst a year, light-hearted an' free, to eat with thim.

"Shaughnessy's lad wint wrong in his lungs, an' they fought death f'r him f'r five years, sindin' him out to th' Wist an' havin' masses said f'r him; an', poor divvle, he kept comin' back cross an' crool, with th' fire in his cheeks, till wan day he laid down, an' says he: 'Pah,' he says, 'I'm goin' to give up,' he says. 'An' I on'y ask that ye'll have th' mass sung over me be some man besides Father

Kelly,' he says. An' he wint, an' Shaughnessy come clumpin' down th' aisle like a man in a thrance.

"Well, th' nex' wan was a girl, an' she didn't die; but, th' less said, th' sooner mended. Thin they was Terrence, a big, bould, curly-headed lad that cocked his hat at anny man,—or woman f'r th' matter iv that,—an' that bruk th' back iv a polisman an' swum to th' crib, an' was champeen iv th' South Side at hand ball. An' he wint. Thin th' good woman passed away. An' th' twins they growed to be th' prettiest pair that wint to first communion; an' wan night they was a light in th' window of Shaughnessy's house till three in th' mornin'. I raymimber it; f'r I had quite a crowd iv Willum Joyce's men in, an' we wondhered at it, an' wint home whin th' lamp in Shaughnessy's window was blown out.

"They was th' wan girl left,—Theresa, a big, clean-lookin' child that I see grow up fr'm hello to good avnin'. She thought on'y iv th' ol' man, an' he leaned on her as if she was a crutch. She was out to meet him in th' avnin'; an' in th' mornin' he, th' simple ol' man, 'd stop to blow a kiss at her an' wave his dinner-pail, lookin' up an' down th' r-road to see that no wan was watchin' him.

"I dinnaw what possessed th' young Donahue, fr'm th' Nineteenth. I niver thought much iv him, a stuck-up, aisy-come la-ad that niver had annything but a civil wurrud, an' is prisident iv th' sodality. But he came in, an' married Theresa Shaughnessy las' Thursdah night. Th' ol' man took on twinty years, but he was as brave as a gin'ral iv th' army. He cracked jokes an' he made speeches; an' he took th' pipes fr'm under th' elbow iv Hogan, th' blindman, an' played 'Th' Wind that shakes th' Barley' till ye'd have wore ye'er leg to a smoke f'r wantin' to dance. Thin he wint to th' dure with th' two iv thim; an' says he, 'Well,' he says, 'Jim, be good to her,' he says, an' shook hands with her through th' carredge window.

"Him an' me sat a long time smokin' across th' stove. Fin'lly, says I, 'Well,' I says, 'I must be movin'.' 'What's th' hurry?' says he. 'I've got to go,' says I. 'Wait a moment,' says he. 'Theresa 'll'—

He stopped right there f'r a minyit, holdin' to th' back iv th' chair. 'Well,' says he, 'if ye've got to go, ye must,' he says. 'I'll show ye out,' he says. An' he come with me to th' dure, holdin' th' lamp over his head. I looked back at him as I wint by; an' he was settin' be th' stove, with his elbows on his knees an' th' empty pipe between his teeth." (March 28, 1896)

27. Their Excellencies, the Police

In November 1893 a rash of robberies and lootings swept Chicago, and Police Superintendent Michael Brennan blamed the trouble on criminals from out of town who had been attracted by the World's Fair and stayed on after it closed at the end of October. On November 17, Brennan issued a general order declaring that plainclothes police patrols would begin challenging anyone on the streets after one in the morning. This Dooley response appeared the following day. Besides revealing a prevalent negative attitude toward the police, the piece contains a glimpse of an Irish nationalist meeting, at which a collection is taken up for John F. Finerty, Chicago's most prominent spokesman for Irish freedom, and one of Mr. Dooley's favorite targets.

"Ye'll be goin' home early to-night, Jawn dear," said Mr. Dooley to Mr. McKenna.

"And for why?" said that gentleman, tilting lazily back in the chair.

"Because gin'ral ordher number wan is out," said Mr. Dooley, "directin' th' polis to stop ivry man catched out afther midnight an' make thim give a satisfacthry account iv thimsilves or run thim off to th' booby hatch. Iv coorse, ye'll be pinched, f'r ye won't dare say where ye come fr'm; an' 'tis twinty-eight to wan, the odds again' an Orangeman at a wake, that ye'll not know where ye're goin'."

"Tut, tut," said Mr. McKenna, indifferently.

"Ye may tut-tut till ye lay an egg," said Mr. Dooley, severely, "ye ol' hen; but 'tis so. I read it in th' pa-apers yesterdah afthernoon that Brinnan—'tis queer how thim Germans all get to be polismin, they're bright men, th' Germans, I don't think—Brinnan says, says he, that th' city do be overrun with burglars an' highwaymen, so he ordhers th' polis to stick up ivery pedesthreen they meets afther closin' time. 'Tis good for him he named th' hour, f'r 'tis few pedesthreens save an' except th' little kids with panneckers that most iv th' polis meet befure midnight. Look at that there table, will ye? 'An ax done it,' says ye? No, faith, but th' fist iv a Kerry polisman they put on this here bate last week. He done it ladin' thrumps. 'Thank Gawd,' says I, 'ye didn't have a good hand,' I says, 'or I might have to call in th' wreckin' wagon.' Thim Kerry men shud be made to play forty-fives with boxin'-gloves on.

"But as I was sayin', Jawn, th' maraudin' divils has been to wurruk all over town. They're that audacious they bruk into Jawnny Cullerton's dhry goods store, an' him on'y bate f'r th' central comity be two votes! 'Tis a good thing f'r thim Cullerton wasn't there or thim burglars 'd 've had to apply for a racaver th' nixt day, they would that.

"I read about th' ordher, but it slipped me min' las' night. I was down at a meetin' iv th' Hugh O'Neills, an' a most intherestin' meetin' it was, Jawn. I'd been niglictful iv me jooty to th' cause iv late, an' I was surprised an' shocked to hear how poor ol' Ireland was sufferin'. Th' rayport, fr'm th' Twinty-third Wa-ard, which is in th' County Mayo, showed that th' sthreet clanin' conthract had been give to a Swede be th' name iv Oleson; an' over in th' Nineteenth Wa-ard th' County Watherford is all stirred up because Johnny Powers is filled th' pipe-ya-ard with his own rilitives. I felt dam lonely, an' with raison, too; f'r I was th' on'y man in th' camp that didn't have a job. An' says I, 'Gintlemen,' says I, 'can't I do something f'r Ireland, too?' I says. 'I'd make th' 'ell's own conthroller,' says I, 'if ye've th' job handy,' I says; and at that they give me th' laugh, and we tuk up a subscription for Finerty, an' adjourned.

"Well, sir, I started up Ar-rchey Road afther th' meetin', forgettin' about Brinnan's ordhers, whin a man jumps out fr'm behind a tree near th' gas-house. 'Melia murther!' says I to mesilf. ''Tis a highwayman!' Thin, puttin' on a darin' front an' reachin' f'r me handkerchief, I says, 'Stand back, robber!' I says. 'Stand back!' I says.

"'Excuse me,' says th' la-ad. 'I beg ye'er pardon,' he says.

"'Beg th' pardon iv Hiven,' says I, 'f'r stoppin' a desperate man in th' sthreet,' says I; 'f'r in a holy minyit I'll blow off th' head iv ye,' says I, with me hand on th' handkerchief that niver blew nawthin' but this nose iv mine."

"'I humbly ask your pardon,' he says, showin' a star; 'but I'm a polisman.'

"'Polisman or robber,' says I, 'stand aside!' I says.

"'I'm a polisman,' he says, 'an' I'm undher ordhers to be polite with citizens I stick up,' he says; 'but, if ye don't duck up that road in half a minyit, ye poy-faced, red-eyed, lop-eared, thick-headed ol' bosthoon,' he says, 'I'll take ye be th' scruff iv th' neck an' thrun ye into th' ga-as-house tank,' he says, 'if I'm coort-martialed f'r it tomorrow.'

"Thin I knew 'twas a polisman on th' square, an' I wint away, Jawn." (November 18, 1893)

28. Controlling and Inciting Riots

Here Mr. Dooley is skeptical about the potential for keeping the peace of both the Chicago Police Department and the Illinois National Guard, the "I-inn-gee." The piece was written just after Governor John Peter Altgeld ordered the national guard to Pana, in central Illinois, to prevent rioting among striking coal miners. Mr. Dooley is right in contending that the Seventh Regiment was mostly made up of members of the Clan-na-Gael guards, the Chicago Irish-nationalist militia company. John Shea was a noted Chicago policeman; he came up through the ranks, serving as chief of detectives in

1893, and captain of the Desplaines Street Station from 1894 until his death in 1903. A student of Irish poetry, which he quoted by the yard, he was a good friend of Finley Peter Dunne.

"Jawn," said Mr. Dooley, "there'll be war in this here state befure th' week's over."

"For why?" asked Mr. McKenna.

"For an' because," said Mr. Dooley, "th' Sivinth Rig'mint have been called out f'r to keep th' peace. Thim coalminers down be th' middle iv th' state 'v been cuttin' up didoes an' raisin' th' 'ell an' all with th' comfort iv citizens that don't care a dam what coal cost, so long as th' palm lafe fan mines is wurrukin' an' th' min that cut th' hop hasn't gone on shtrike.

"Well, sir, I see be th' pa-aper th' Huns an' other Boolgahrians does be kickin' up 'ell an' th' Main Guy—whither it do be Grover 'r not, dam'd if I know—sinds down polismin an' scouts an' thim joods iv th' First Rig'mint, I-inn-gee, an' sare a bit iv throuble can they pick up with anny wan. Th' Boolgahrians, a low lot iv furriners, declines to fight an' th' joods, not bein' properly thrained as sojers, can't shtir up no excitement.

"D'ye mind whin they sint Jawnny Shea over to Mitchigan avnoo f'r to be liftnant? He came in wan night, an' says he to the disk sergeant: 'How's things?' he says. 'Quite, loot,' says th' guy behind th' disk. 'Nawthin' gawn on?' says Jawn. 'Ne'er a thing,' says the sergeant. ''Tis as quite as th' da-ay afther th' Fourth iv July.' There was a Swede polisman settin' behind th' shtove, an' th' liftnant tur-rns to him, an' says he: 'Olee'—'tis a common name among thim, Jawn—'Olee,' he says, 'go out an' suppriss th' rite.' 'What rite?' says th' Swede. 'What rite?' says Jawn. 'What rite?' he says. 'What th' divvle do I care,' he says. 'Anny rite,' he says. 'An' if ye can't find wan ready made,' says he, 'ye poor polisman,' he says, 'go an' make wan,' he says, 'or I'll have ye up befure th' thrile bourrd,' he says, 'f'r conduck unbecomin' an officer.'

"So be th' Main Guy. Whin th' joods wint down an' could get on no fight he says to himsilf: 'This'll not do,' he says. 'What's th' use iv sojers,' he says, 'if there's no fight,' he says. 'Ordher out th'

Sivinth.' D'ye know what th' Sivinth is, Jawn? Ye don't? D'ye
mind th' Clan-na-Gael ga-ards? Ye do. Have ye seen annything iv
thim lately? No. For why? They are th' Sivinth Rig'mint, I-inn-
gee, no less. Bould an' undaunted. Ivery man iv thim is fr'm
beyant. They do be or-ganized diff'rint fr'm other rig'mints.
There a-are three brigades iv thim—wan fr'm Munster, wan fr'm
Leinster an' wan fr'm Connock. Th' dhrum corpse is fr'm Ulster
an' it does have to ma-arch behind th' rig'mint, f'r be u-nanimous
vote th' la-ads decided that they'd niver ma-arch behind an Ulster
man. Thin each iv the provinces is divided up into counties an'
each iv th' counties into parishes. Th' liftnant is th' head iv th'
county an' he gives th' ordhers: 'Roscommon, showlder ar-rms,'
he says. 'Fa-ather Hogan's parish,' he says, 'right dress. Ye'er feet
ar-re not mates.' Th' captain is the main guy iv th' brigade, an' he
does have the divvle's own time keepin' Mayo an' Sligo a-part.
Whin they come to ilictin' a colonel there was a candy-date fr'm
ivry parrish an' th' on'y way they got out iv it was be unitin' on a
sojer that was discinded fr'm Brian Boru, though some thought
th' job ought to go to a man be th' name iv O'Donnell on account
iv Rid Hugh iv that name, who was th' last befure Finerty that
bate th' Saxon.

"'Twas thim la-ads they sint down f'r to prod up th' Boolgahrians. It caused more excitement in Bridgeport than whin
Hogan's goat got into th' tub iv holy wather at th' little church
wist iv th' bridge, may heaven f'rgive me f'r mintionin' that. Th'
whole road was out. I spilled near wan gallon iv dhrink f'r th' la-
ads an' I give thim what was that ferocious that be hivins I'll bet
me hat they'll massacree th' whole state. Th' night force iv th'
mills all belongs to th' rig'mint an' at th' ca-all they shtruck in a
body. 'Why d'ye lave me?' says th' foreman. 'We're goin' out to
war,' says Sarsfield McInerny. 'Who ar-re ye goin' to fight?' says
th' foreman. 'Shtrikers,' says Sarsfield."

"Have they done any fighting?" asked Mr. McKenna.

"Not yet," said Mr. Dooley. "Not yet, Jawn. But they will.
They will. But there's wan thing I'm thankful for."

"What's that?"

"That they didn't sind out th' Fa-ather Macchew's Fife an' Dhrum Corpse," said Mr. Dooley. "Or th' rivers 'd r-run r-rid with gore." (June 23, 1894)

29. The Stealing of Hogan's Goat

Colonel Breckinridge was a Kentucky congressman whose involvement in a breach of promise suit scandalized the nation in the spring of 1894. Concurrently with this Dooley piece he was being drummed out of Chicago's exclusive Union League Club, while declaring that he would still be a candidate for reelection.

"Jawn, avick," said Mr. Dooley. "Ye'll excuse me tears."

"What are you crying about?" asked Mr. McKenna scornfully.

"I'm weepin'," said Mr. Dooley, "f'r poor ol' Breckinridge. By dad, since th' time Sarsfield Dugan was arristed f'r stealin' Hogan's goat there ain't been annything so sad. Ye see this here Dugan had th' nex' holdin' to ours in Connock beyant, an' he was th' most rispictable man that ever come over th' hills. 'Twas him that bruck up th' hurlin' games iv a Sundah afthernoon, an' whin th' la-ads wint out f'r to shoot Crosby, th' agent, in th' legs with bur-rd shot he spoiled th' divarsion be insistin' on sayin' a pather'n away befure they could take aim. So a comity waited on him an' tol' him th' counthry was too r-rough f'r so good a man, an' he come over here.

"Well, sir, iv all th' pious la-ads ye iver see! He kep' ivery fast day like as if he was starvin' on a bet, he was th' whole thing in th' Saint Vincent de Pauls, he wint to his jooty with a reg'larity that'd make ye, ye hathen, nervous, an' by gar, he passed th' plate, he did, he did. Now mind ye, Jawn, I'm not th' man f'r to object to rel-igon. 'Tis all r-right in its place. But whin a man goes to his jooty an' thin comes ar-round an' tells all about it an' wears it on his hat, by dad, I says, luk out f'r him, Jawn; luk out an' button up ye'er coat.

"Ol' Hogan had a goat that was th' invy iv th' neighborhood an' th' joy iv Hogan. I'll not sa-ay I liked it, but they was thim in Bridgeport that'd go miles to see it lapin' through a hoop that Hogan held f'r it an' bleatin' in chune with th' 'Shells iv Ocean' pokey that Maria Hogan played on the pianny. Well, sir, this here Dugan was wan iv the mos' frayquint visitors over at Hogan's, an' he thried to have Maria larn th' goat f'r to sing hymns iv a Sundah, maintainin', d'ye mind, Jawn, that pokey's was not in line with rel-igon. Wan day Hogan's goat was missin' an' there was a hue-an'-cry all up an' down Ar-rchey road. Th' ol' man was near distracted an' he offered a reward iv tin dollars f'r th' thafe dead 'r alive. No wan suspected Dugan, but a little lad that was nosin' round on his own account seen th' saint settin' on his back-ya-ard stips with his wife feedin' th' goat with celooloid cuffs. So they grabbed Dugan an' r-run him in, th' polis did.

"Well, sir, first he denied it, an' near all th' women in th' parish come in an' swore they niver was such an outrage. But Jawnny Shea, he fixed him with his eye an' made him confiss with th' tears rollin' down his cheeks. 'I done it,' he says. 'Th' Lord f'rgive me,' he says. 'An' why did ye do it?' says th' loot. 'I couldn't help it,' says Dugan. 'Whin th' goat give wan iv thim looks out iv his eyes,' he says, 'an' bleated wanst,' he says, ''twas more than a christian cud stand,' he says. 'Th' divvle sayjuced me into takin' th' goat home to me family,' he says, 'an' I fell.' 'Ye mean,' says Jawnny, 'th' goat was too sthrong f'r ye.' Faith, I cuddent join in th' laugh an' no more cud Dugan, f'r goat stealin' is gran' larceny up this way. He took a chance an' got fifty dollars or wan hundred days."

"But what about Breckinridge?" asked Mr. McKenna.

"Nothin'," said Mr. Dooley, "on'y there do be but wan way to re-strain such as him from becomin' wicked."

"And what's that?"

"Chain up th' goat," said Mr. Dooley. (April 14, 1894)

30. Fire Chief Swenie in Bridgeport

*A fireman since 1850 and chief since 1879, Denis J. Swenie was
one of Chicago's most admired men. The* Evening Post *editorial on
the occasion of his forty-fifth anniversary as a fireman called him
"the boss fire-fighter of the United States. . . . as resolute, as fearless,
as skillful as ever."*

"Be hivins, Jawn," said Mr. Dooley, "if I had a child iv me own
d'ye know what I'd do with him?"

"I do not," said Mr. McKenna.

"I'd give him th' finest schoolin' th' land 'd affoord an' thin I'd
put him on th' fire depa-artmint. I'd make a fireman out iv him, I
would that. There was a fire down be th' slough las' night. Hogan
come home with his rowlers on 'im an' he see a light in his wife's
windy nex' to th' kitchin, an' says he to himsilf: 'She's settin' up,'
he sa-ays. 'I know I c'd licker if I was all r-right,' he says. 'But I'll
take no cha-ances,' he says. 'F'r if she sh'd win,' says he—he do be
a gr-reat dissaplinarian, that Hogan—'there 'd be no livin' with
her.' So he puts his shoes on th' fince an' ha-angs his coat on th'
close-line, where no wan c'd see it, d'ye mind, Jawn, an' takes off
his shirt an' goes into th' ba-arn on his han's an' knees. He give th'
cow a kick an' climbs up into th' ha-ay loft. Thin he lit a ma-atch
to see where he could lay down, an' havin' found a soft spot he
wint qui'tly to sleep. He tol' me to-day whin he come in with his
whiskers bur-rned off close to his face—I niver see mortal man
look like a cokynut befure—that he dhremt he was in hell an' th'
Ol' Guy come in an' says to wan iv his la-ads: 'What's this here
omadhon been doin'?' like th' loot at th' station. 'He was just sint
in be th' pope f'r blessin' himsilf with his lift hand.' 'Where's he
from?' says th' Ol' Guy. 'F'r'm th' County Clare,' says th' other.
'Put him on th' briler,' says th' Ol' Guy, 'an' do him to a tur-rn,' he
says. With that Hogan lipt through th' loft windy. Th' hay was on
fire, Jawn, an' th' nixt seen iv him he was tearin' down th' r-road
with th' spa-arks flyin' fr'm his whiskers like a pinwheel.

"Well, there was th' divvle's own fire. Th' ingines come rollin' up an' th' hose ca-arts an' thruck-an'-ladder twinty-sivin, an' afther a while up come th' chafe himsilf. Dinnis Swenie 'd not been in Bridgeport f'r near tin year-rs. I'd not set eyes on him since I lived down be St. Pathrick's. I used to see him there at high mass, with a long black coat to his back. I niver knowed how it was, but, by dad, it seemed like it happened ivry Sunday about th' gospel ye'd see th' little dhriver come tear-rin' down th' aisle with his hat in his hand. Thin ivry wan'd lave his devotions an' give an eye an' an ear. Ye cud ha-ardly hould th' althar byes, an' avin th' soggarth himsilf'd take a squint over his shoulder—no more thin a squint, d'ye mind. Th' dhriver'd bind over an' whisper an' thin ye'd see the chafe scrapin' around f'r his hat, an' out they'd go together. 'What box?' ye'd hear th' chafe say. 'Twinty-sicond an' Loomis,' an' they was off. Thin ye'd look around an' all th' la-ads that stood up near th' dure where they could ate peanuts was gone. Divvle th' soul could stop thim. I mind wanst whin Miss O'Toole shtarted to sing th' 'Oh Solutauris' 'twas found th' kid that pumped th' organ had r-run away to th' fire an' she had to go it alone.

"Well, sir, I niver see such a greetin' as th' chafe got las' night. 'Twas 'Good avnin' to ye, Misther Swenie,' an' 'Misther Swenie, will ye have a glass iv beer befure ye go in, f'r th' fire's hot?' an' 'Have ye forgot all ye'er ol' frins that know'd ye whin ye r-run with Avalanche tin?' Well, sir, th' chafe looked that plazed. 'Good avnin', Mrs. Doolan,' he'd say. 'Pla-ay away there sivinteen. How's Mike? I hope ye've brought him up well. Why th' 'ell don't ye come along with that pipe. Pla-ay away there tin, d'ye think ye'er here to make a bonfire? Oh, they're all well, thanks be to Gawd, Mrs. Casey. An' how's ye'er own? That's good. Campeen, get ye'er min to stop playin' croquet an' put a laddher up that there tannery. No, I thank ye kindly, Mrs. Dinnihy, I niver indulge. Dorgan, ye big bosthoon, if ye shtand here a minyit longer I'll hitch me horse to ye. D'ye think that laddher was put up to shave that there house?' An' so he'd go on convarsin' iv social doings an' ordherin' th' min till th' fire was out. Faith, he's a gr-reat ma-an. What county is he from?"

"I don't know," said Mr. McKenna. "But what become of Hogan?"

Mr. Dooley winked. "Don't ask me, Jawn," he said. "Go ask Mrs. Hogan. 'Tis no affair iv mine, but Hogan 'll go to sleep in th' da-ark th' rist iv his life." (August 11, 1894)

31. Images of Policemen vs. Firemen

The day after a grain elevator explosion in which five firemen were killed and fifty-one injured, Dunne wrote this piece, comparing the images of Chicago's police and fire departments. The tragedy occurred during the unpopular governorship of John R. Tanner, and the "Three medal," for which Fireman Shay is recommended, was the Tree medal, given annually to the Chicago fireman performing the most heroic act in the line of duty.

"How is it," asked Mr. Dooley, "that whin a fireman dies th' whole city mourns an' whin a polisman dies all annywan says is: 'Who's th' first iligible on th' list?' How is it?"

"I dinnaw," said Mr. Hennessy, "but 'tis so."

"No doubt iv it," continued Mr. Dooley. "I think th' reason is we're bumpin' too much into th' polis foorce. If we was to see thim on'y goin' by in th' get-ap wagon, with th' horses chargin' along an' the gong ringin' we'd play thim f'r pop'lar heroes. A polisman always looks good whin he's goin' by in a hurry. But whin he gets out iv th' chariot an' goes to bat he's no man's frind, an' anny citizen is entitled to move things fr'm th' roof on his head. He mixes in with th' populace an' familyarity breeds contempt, as Shakespeare says. Now 'tis altogether diffrent with th' fireman. No wan is on really intimate terms with him. We may call him by his first name an' play dominoes with him or pitch horseshoes behind th' barn, but we have a secret feelin' that he's a shuperior person that it's not safe to take liberties with. Ye may be settin' in th' injine-house with a fireman as calm an' frindly as ye plaze, an' it's 'Ye'er move, Tom,' an' 'There goes ye'er king row, Felix,' but lave th' ticker buzz wanst an' the gong ring an' ye've suddenly lost equality. Over goes th' boord, out come th' horses an' it's 'Get out iv th' way, there, blast ye,' an' 'All right, Misther Casey.' I niver see th' day whin I felt just right in th' prisince iv a man in a helmet. Did ye iver know a fireman to be slugged? Or robbed? Niver. Th' toughest thief that iver roamed th' sthreets 'll lave alone a lad with a brown sthraw hat an' silver buttons. If I was Tanner an' wanted to be pop'lar I'd hire a fireman to go around with me.

"How can it be anny other way? There used to be a man up here be th' name iv Duggan, an', havin' a large fam'ly, he lived on th' fifth flure iv th' Flaherty Buildin' near the roof. He was a jealous man whin he was dhrunk, an' that was sometimes, an' he used to roar about th' aisy life iv th' firemen. 'Here,' he says, 'am I, a man with a good hot intilleck condimned to wurruk in th' broilin' sun shovellin' coal f'r wan sivinty-five a day,' he says, 'while th' likes iv ye set in ye'er aisy cheers,' he says, 'smokin' ye'er pipes, with nawthin' to do,' he says, 'but decide who's th' champeen dominoes player,' he says. 'Fr'm morn to night ye don't do a tap iv wurruk, an' I an' th' likes iv me pay ye f'r it,' he says. He talked this way in th' injine house day an' night an' th' lads laughed at him an' wint on playin'. On'y wan man didn't like th' talk. He was a dark man be th' name of Shay with a big horseshoe mustache, an' he used to eat half iv it off ivry time Duggan made his speech. I seen he was achin' f'r Duggan's throat, but it's a rule iv th' departmint that mimbers 'r not allowed f'r to lick civilyans. They can lick polisman, if they're able to, but not citizens.

"Th' Flaherty flats took fire wan night an' bein' consthructed f'r poor people out iv nice varnished pine an' cotton waste they burned up without anny loss iv time. Duggan counted his childher an' found wan missing. He had a good manny—twelve or thirteen, I think—but he needed thim all in his business. He counted again an' again, but there was still wan short, an' afther awhile he figured it was th' baby, be th' name iv Honoria. She's a great big girl now—with red hair. Whin Duggan found he was shy a chip he proceeded to throw fits on th' sthreet an' wanted to go into th' buildin', which wud've been th' end iv him, f'r he was full iv rum and wud've burned like a celluloid collar. Cap Kenny iv thruck twinty-nine heerd his ravin' and wanted to know what ailed him. 'He's short a kid,' said th' polisman that was holdin' him be th' hair. Kenny begun cursin' like a tug captain, an' in less thin a minyit he was shinnin' up a ladder with three or four others, among them bein' our frind Shay. Th' cap wint in first an' stayed in five minyits an' had to be carrid out. Thin two others staggered to th' window an' was dhragged out be th' legs. But Shay stuck. We waited an' waited, with all th' pipes playin on th' wan window, an' fin'lly th' Connemara man come out carryin' something in his ar-rums. Glory be, but he was a sight. He was as black as a lump iv coal an' he had no more hair on him thin a lookin'-glass. He slid out to th' ladder an' climbed down, scornin' assistance. Th' women gathered around him, weepin' an' callin' on all th' saints in th' catalogue to bless him, an' th' men swore an' ran to get dhrinks. But Shay paid no attintion to thim. He pegged th' baby at a sthrange woman an' walked over to Duggan. 'What ye said to me las' Choosdah night,' he roared, 'was a lie, an' I'm goin' to club ye'er head off.' An' he fell on th' weepin' father an' wud've kilt him. Cap Kenny pulled him away, an' Shay, lookin' ashamed to death undher th' soot, saluted. 'Pipeman Shay,' says th' cap, 'I will recomind ye f'r th' Three medal,' he says, 'but I fine ye five days' pay f'r lickin' a civilyan,' he says. 'Lord help us, I hope Swenie won't hear iv this,' he says.

"That man Shay used to come into my place an' play forty-fives with me. But d'ye suppose I cud challenge his count as I do other people's, or ask to cut his ca-ards?"

"Ye'd be afraid he'd lick ye," suggested Mr. Hennessy.

"That was wan reason," said Mr. Dooley. (August 7, 1897)

32. The Popularity of Firemen

Another fire-fighting tragedy prompted this piece, which opens with Mr. Dooley naming the four firemen who had died the day before in a downtown factory and warehouse blaze.

"O'Donnell, Sherrick, Downs, Prendergast," Mr. Dooley repeated slowly. "Poor la-ads. Poor la-ads. Plaze Gawd, they wint to th' long home like thrue min. 'Tis good to read th' names, Jawn. Thanks be, we're not all in th' council.

"I knowed a man be th' name iv Clancy wanst, Jawn. He was fr'm th' County May-o, but a good man f'r all that; an', whin he'd growed to be a big, sthrappin' fellow, he wint on to th' fire departmint. They'se an Irishman 'r two on th' fire departmint an' in th' army, too, Jawn, though ye'd think be hearin' some talk they was all runnin' prim'ries an' thryin' to be cinthral comitymen. So ye wud. Ye niver hear iv thim on'y whin they die; an' thin, murther, what funerals they have!

"Well, this Clancy wint on th' fire departmint, an' they give him a place in thruck twenty-three. All th' r-road was proud iv him, an' faith he was proud iv himsilf. He r-rode free on th' sthreet ca-ars, an' was th' champeen handball player f'r miles around. Ye shud see him goin' down th' sthreet, with his blue shirt an' his blue coat with th' buttons on it, an' his cap on his ear. But ne'er a cap or coat'd he wear whin they was a fire. He might be shiv'rin' be th' stove in th' ingine house with a buffalo robe over his head; but, whin th' gong sthruck, 'twas off with coat an' cap an' buffalo robe, an' out come me brave Clancy, bare-headed an' bare hand, dhrivin' with wan line an' spillin' th' hose cart on wan wheel at ivry jump iv th' horse. Did anny wan iver see a fireman with his coat on or a polisman with his off? Why, wanst, whin Clancy was standin' up f'r Grogan's eighth, his son come runnin' in to tell him they was a fire in Vogel's packin' house. He dhropped th' kid at Father Kelly's feet, an' whipped off his long coat an' wint tearin' f'r th' dure, kickin' over th' poorbox an' buttin' ol' Mis' O'Neill that'd come in to say th' stations. 'Twas lucky 'twas wan iv th' Grogans. They're a fine family f'r falls. Jawn Grogan was wur-rukin' on th' top iv Metzri an' O'Connell's brewery wanst, with a man be th' name iv Dorsey. He slipped an' fell wan hundherd feet. Whin they come to see if he was dead, he got up, an' says he: 'Lave me at him.' 'At who?' says they. 'He's deliryous,' they says. 'At Dorsey,' says Grogan. 'He thripped me.' So it didn't hurt Grogan's eighth to fall four 'r five feet.

"Well, Clancy wint to fires an' fires. Whin th' big organ facthry burnt, he carrid th' hose up to th' fourth story an' was squirtin' whin th' walls fell. They dug him out with pick an' shovel, an' he come up fr'm th' brick an' boards an' saluted th' chief. 'Clancy,' says th' chief, 'ye betther go over an' get a dhrink.' He did so, Jawn. I heerd it. An' Clancy was that proud!

"Whin th' Hogan flats on Halsted Sthreet took fire, they got all th' people out but wan; an' she was a woman asleep on th' fourth flure. 'Who'll go up?' says Bill Musham. 'Sure, sir,' says Clancy, 'I'll go'; an' up he wint. His captain was a man be th' name iv O'Connell, fr'm th' County Kerry; an' he had his fut on th' ladder whin Clancy started. Well, th' good man wint into th' smoke, with his wife faintin' down below. 'He'll be kilt,' says his brother. 'Ye don't know him,' says Bill Musham. An' sure enough, whin ivry wan'd give him up, out comes me brave Clancy, as black as a Turk, with th' girl in his arms. Th' others wint up like monkeys, but he shtud wavin' thim off, an' come down th' ladder face for-ward. 'Where'd ye larn that?' says Bill Musham. 'I seen a man do it at th' Lyceem whin I was a kid,' says Clancy. 'Was it all right?' 'I'll have ye up before th' ol' man,' says Bill Musham. 'I'll teach ye to come down a laddher as if ye was in a quadhrille, ye horse-stealin', ham-sthringin' May-o man,' he says. But he didn't. Clancy wint over to see his wife. 'O Mike,' says she, ''twas fine,' she says. 'But why d'ye take th' risk?' she says. 'Did ye see th' captain?' he says with a scowl. 'He wanted to go. Did ye think I'd follow a Kerry man with all th' ward lukkin' on?' he says.

"Well, so he wint dhrivin' th' hose-cart on wan wheel, an' jump-in' whin he heerd a man so much as hit a glass to make it ring. All th' people looked up to him, an' th' kids followed him down th' sthreet; an' 'twas th' gr-reatest priv'lige f'r anny wan f'r to play dominos with him near th' joker. But about a year ago he come in to see me, an' says he, 'Well, I'm goin' to quit.' 'Why,' says I, 'ye'er a young man yet,' I says. 'Faith,' he says, 'look at me hair,' he says,—'young heart, ol' head. I've been at it these twenty year, an' th' good woman's wantin' to see more iv me thin blowin' into a saucer iv coffee,' he says. 'I'm goin' to quit,' he says, 'on'y I want to see wan more good fire,' he says. 'A rale good ol' hot wan,' he says, 'with th' win' blowin' f'r it an' a good dhraft in th' ilivator-shaft, an' about two stories, with pitcher-frames an' gasoline an' excelsior, an' to hear th' chief yellin': "Play 'way, sivinteen. What th' hell an' damnation are ye standin' aroun' with that pipe f'r? Is this a fire 'r a dam livin' pitcher? I'll break ivry man iv eighteen, four, six, an' chem'cal five to-morrah mornin' befure breakfast." Oh,' he says, bringin' his fist down, 'wan more, an' I'll quit.'

"An' he did, Jawn. Th' day th' Carpenter Brothers' box factory burnt. 'Twas wan iv thim big, fine-lookin' buildings that pious men built out iv celluloid an' plasther iv Paris. An' Clancy was wan iv th' men undher whin th' wall fell. I seen thim bringin' him home; an' th' little woman met him at th' dure, rumplin' her apron in her hands." (November 23, 1895)

Chapter Three
Assimilation and Dissolving Community

For all its distinctive coloration, Bridgeport in the 1890s was far from being a stable community. Many forces for change were operating there, most of them somehow related to the complicated process known to that time as "melting" into American life. The Irish had the great advantage of speaking the language in their new home, but, like the other immigrant peoples, they found themselves caught between two worlds, and forced to make uncomfortable compromises in order to become assimilated. By the nineties, the children of the famine immigrants (those who, as Mr. Dooley remarks, had been "born away from home") were making it into the middle class in large numbers—but not without cost to their sense of identity as individuals and as an ethnic group. The stairway of upward mobility was strewn with cases of swallowed pride and stifled old-world customs, and the Chicago Dooley pieces embody the peculiar mixture of fulfillment and frustration that went along with being Irish in America at the turn of the century.

In the first place, to live in the city was to pay a price. This chapter opens with Mr. Dooley's classic statement of the urban immigrant's ambivalence toward his environment. For another thing, the city would not hold still; the ethnic makeup of Bridgeport was changing rapidly in the nineties. Dunne explained the situation in the 1898 preface to his first Dooley collection:

There was a time when Archey Road was purely Irish. But the Huns, turned back from the Adriatic and the stockyards and overrunning Archey Road, have nearly exhausted the original population,—not driven them out as they drove out less vigorous races, with thick clubs and short spears, but edged them out with the more biting weapons of modern civilization,—overworked and under-eaten them into more languid surroundings remote from the tanks of the gashouse and the blast furnaces of the rolling mill.

As the "new immigrants" from southern and eastern Europe moved in, more and more Bridgeporters were moving out and up—to the middle-class West Side around St. Patrick's Church, and Mr. Dooley records the changing climate of his neighborhood in two pieces for May 1897 (2, 3).

In addition, the American dream of success and social advancement also drove damaging wedges into the immigrant community, as Dooley notes in two stories about hard-hearted Irish landlords (4, 5) and one about a German meat-packing millionaire who denies his own brother (6). Other, less tragic signs of creeping respectability are the changed attitude of many Chicago Irishmen toward the newspapers (7) and the running debate between Mr. and Mrs. Hogan on the subject of naming their children (8).

Signs of dissolving cultural unity naturally appeared early among Bridgeport's young people, and Dunne created a group of characters to illustrate the compounded problems of a generation/immigration gap. Most visible here is Molly Donahue, a lively, fad-conscious Bridgeport teenager who squares off against her Irish father some half-dozen times in the Dooley pieces. Molly first scandalizes the neighborhood by riding a bicycle down Archer Avenue at rush hour on a Friday evening—in bloomers (9). In succeeding appearances, she campaigns for the vote, for Elizabeth Cady Stanton's revised Woman's Bible, and for the liberation of "the new woman" (10, 13, 12). Her piano lessons cause a cultural disagreement in the family about the relative merits of "Bootoven's" symphonies and "The Rambler from Clare" (11), and her "home vaudeville show" in retaliation for Hogan's "progressive spoil-five party" nearly drives her father away for good (14).

As for Bridgeport's young men, Mr. Dooley charts two diverging roads toward assimilation, one high and one low, but both causing pain and bewilderment among the neighborhood elders. College had begun to be possible for this generation of Irish-Americans, and

*Bridgeport boys come trooping home from Notre Dame with bicycles,
long hair, pretensions, and the game of football (15, 16). The low
road leads to a life in crime for Jack Carey and Petey Scanlan, Bridgeport natives who turn against their own people in the saddest of Mr.
Dooley's examples of the dissolution of his community (17, 18).*

1. Life in the City

[In September 1897 Dunne returned to the Post *with fresh perspective after a three-week vacation and wrote this piece, a tour-de-
force of linguistic invention and exuberance that James Joyce would
have appreciated. In it, Mr. Dooley mentions Philip Armour, the
founder of one of Chicago's largest meat-packing houses, which stood
in the stockyards to the south of Bridgeport, and Adolph Luetgert, a
German-American sausage manufacturer, who was at this time on
trial for having murdered his wife and ground up her body in his
sausage-making apparatus.]*

"Ye shud take a vacation," said Mr. Hennessy when the philosopher complained of a slight headache. "Ye ought to go away an'
have a few weeks' fishin' or r-run down to Westbaden an' be biled
out, or indulge in some other form iv spoort."

"I shud not," retorted Mr. Dooley firmly. "I'm well enough off
where I am. They'se no disease that afflicts th' American people
akel to th' vacation habit. Ye take a big, sthrong man that's lived
in Chicago all his life, an' if he stays on here he'll niver know a day
iv ill health. He goes out in th' mornin' and dhrinks in th' impure
an' healthy air, filled with mickrobes an' soot an' iron filin's, an' his
chest expands. He ates onwholesome, rich an' appetizin' food. His
muscles is kept firm be dodgin' cable cars an' express wagons.
His mind is rooned an' made ca-am be readin' th' newspapers. His
happy home is infested with sewer gas, an' if he survives he's th'
sthrongest thing that iver was made. But ye take that man out iv
his parnicious an' agreeable atmosphere an' sind him to th' country. He ates wholesome food that his stomach, bein' used to th'

best Luetgert society, rayfuses to intertain. His lungs cave in fr'm consumin' pure air that, like ivrything pure, is too thin. He misses his daily sewer gas an' he finds cow's milk a poor substitute for docthered whisky an' beer with aloes in it. Th' man suffers. He does so. He rayturns to Chicago a shattered invalid an' it takes months iv livin' in onsanitary tinimints an' a steady dite iv cigaroots an' bakin' powdher biscuits to restore him to his proper condition iv robust bad health.

"Now, look at ol' Duggan. There was th' healthiest man in th' wa-ard f'r his age. He was bor-rn an' raised on th' banks iv th' slip where ye can hear th' water poppin' fr'm wan year's ind to another like a shelf iv catsup bottles on a hot night. Th' air was so thick with poisonous gases that a wagon loaded with scrap iron wud float at an ilivation iv tin feet. He lived below th' grade an' th' rain backed into his bedroom. He wurrked in a white lead facthry at night an' had to cross twinty-five railroad thracks an' an ilictric switch on his way to wurruk. He lived mos'ly on canned goods an' fried pork an' drank his beer at an Irish saloon an' his whisky at a German's. Not bein' a corpse befure he was twinty-five, it was a sure thing he'd be a joynt at fifty. An' so he was. A sthronger man niver breathed. But some wan put it in his head he ought to go off to th' counthry f'r his vacation, an' he wint dhrivin' a canal boat mule or cuttin' hay. Whin he come back he was that weak a child cud go to th' flure with him. 'Where have ye been?' says I. 'On me vacation,' says he. 'Well,' I says, 'ye'er pretty near vacated,' I says. 'Yis,' he says, 'I'm glad to get back,' he says. 'I need tinder care,' he says. They nursed him back to life, but 'twas not till his house'd been declared unfit f'r habitation be th' health departmint an' he'd been ejicted afther a free fight be his landlord an' r-run in wanst be th' polis an' over twict be a mail wagon an' was back to wurruk breathin' lead dust be th' quart that he raycovered his ol' sperrits.

"I niver leave town mesilf. I take a vacation be settin' here at me front dure lookin' up at Gawd's an' th' Illinye Steel Company's black-an'-blue sky. Th' ilictric ca-ars go singin' by an' th' air is filled with th' melody iv goats an' cur dogs. Ivry breeze that blows fr'm th' south brings th' welcome tidings that me frind Phil Armour is still stickin' to th' glue business. I cannot see th' river, but I know that it's rollin' grandly backward tord its sewerce laden with lumber hookers an' ol' vigitables. Occasion'lly I hear a tugboat cooin' to its mate an' now an' thin a pathrol wagon flits by on its errand iv love. At night th' tired but unhappy lab'rers rayturns fr'm their tile an' th' air is laden with th' sound iv fryin' liver an' th' cheery perfume iv bilin' cabbage. Whin I want more active amusemint I go in an' start a bung or angle with a fork f'r a sardine. So whin me vacation is over I rayturn rayfrished an' eager f'r th' battle iv life. I don't have to get th' taste iv good butter out iv me mouth.

"They'se no use f'r a Chicago man thryin' to take his vacation out iv town till they put a summer hotel in th' crather iv Mount Vasuvyous. Ayether he ought niver to go away, or——"

"He ought niver to come back," suggested Mr. Hennessy.

"Ye'er r-right," said Mr. Dooley. (September 4, 1897)

2. The Decadence of Greece and the Tenth Precinct

Here Mr. Dooley sees the changing ethnic character of Bridgeport in the context of the Greco-Turkish War of 1897. On May 6, it was reported that the Greeks had won a great battle at Pharsalos, only to retreat immediately, leaving the town to the Moslems.

"That young Hogan is a smart la-ad," said Mr. Dooley. "A smart la-ad an' a good wan, too."

"None betther," said Mr. Hennessy.

"None betther in th' ward," said Mr. Dooley, which was a high appreciation. "But there ar-re things about human nature an' histhry that ain't taught at Saint Ignateeus'. I tell thim to Hogan's la-ad.

"He was walkin' be th' store wan day las' week, an' I ast him how th' wa-ar wint. 'Tis sthrange, with churches two in a block, an' public schools as thick as lamp-posts, that, whin a man stops ye on th' sthreet, he'll ayether ast ye th' scoor iv th' base-ball game or talk iv th' Greek war with ye. I ain't seen annything that happened since Parnell's day that's aroused so much enthusyasm on th' Ar-rchey Road as th' Greek war. 'How goes th' war?' says I to young Hogan. 'How goes the war between th' ac-cursed infidel an' th' dog iv a Christian?' I says. 'It goes bad,' he says. 'Th' Greeks won a thremenjous battle, killin' manny millions iv th' Moslem murdherers, but was obliged to retreat thirty-two miles in a gallop.' 'Is that so?' says I. 'Sure that seems to be their luck,' I says. 'Whiniver they win, they lose; an', whin they lose, they lose,' I says. 'What ails thim?' I says. 'Is th' riferee again thim?' 'I can't make it out,' he says, while a tear sthud in his eye. 'Whin I think iv Leonidas at th' pass iv Thermometer,' he says, 'an' So-an'-so on th' field iv Marathon an' This-or-that th' Spartan hero,' he says, 'I cannot undherstand f'r th' life iv me why th' Greeks shud have been dhruv fr'm pillar to post be an ar-rmy iv slaves. Didn't Leonidas, with hardly as manny men as there are Raypublicans in this precinct, hold th' pass again a savage horde?' he says. 'He did,' says I. 'He did.' 'An' didn't What's-his-name on th' field iv Marathon overcome an' desthroy th' ravagin' armies iv Persia?' he says. 'Thrue f'r ye,' says I. 'There's no doubt in th' wurruld about it,' I says. 'An' look at Alexander th' Great,' he says. 'Aleck was a turror, an' no mistake,' says I. 'An' Miltiades,' he says. 'I on'y know what I hear iv him,' says I. 'But fr'm all accounts he must have been consid'rable iv a fellow,' says I. 'An' in later days Marco Boozaris,' he says. 'He was th' man that come in con-sumption's dreaded form,' says I, 'an' he was afraid iv no man.' 'Well, thin,' says he, 'how ar-re we to account f'r this disgrace?' he says.

"'Well,' says I, 'd'ye raymimber th' fightin' tenth precinct? Ye must've heerd ye'er father tell about it. It was famous f'r th' quality an' quantity iv th' warfare put up in it. Ivry man in th' tenth precinct cud fight his weight in scrap-iron. Most iv thim come fr'm th' ancient Hellenic province iv May-o; but they was a fair sprinklin' iv Greek heroes fr'm Roscommon an' Tipperary, an' a few from th' historic spot where th' Head iv Kinsale looks out on th' sea, an' th' sea looks up at th' Head iv Kinsale. Th' little boys cud box befure they was out iv skirts. Far an' wide, th' tenth precint was th' turror iv its inimies. Ye talk about Leonidas an' th' pass iv Thermometer. Ye ought to've seen Mike Riordan an' his fam'ly defindin' th' pollin'-place whin Eddie Burke's brigade charged it wan fine day. That hero sthud f'r four hours in th' dureway, arrmed on'y with a monkey-wrinch, an' built a wall iv invaders in frint iv him till th' judges cud dig their way out through th' cellar, an' escape to th' polis station.

"'F'r manny years th' tenth precint was th' banner precint iv th' Sixth Wa-ard, an' its gallant heroes repelled all attacks by land or Healey's slough. But, as time wint by, changes come over it. Th' Hannigans an' Leonidases an' Caseys moved out, havin' made their pile. Some iv th' grandest iv th' heroes died, an' their fam'lies were broke up. Polish Jews an' Swedes an' Germans an' Hollanders swarmed in, settlin' down on th' sacred sites,' I says. 'Wan night three years ago, a band iv rovin' Bohemians fr'm th' Eighth Ward come acrost th' river, kickin' over bar'ls an' ash-boxes, an' swooped down on th' tenth precint. Mike Riordan, him that kept th' pollin'-place in th' good days iv old, was th' on'y wan iv th' race iv ancient heroes on earth. He thried to rally th' ingloryous descindants iv a proud people. F'r a while they made a stand in Halsted Sthreet, an' shouted bad but difficult names at th' infidel hordes, an' threw bricks that laid out their own people. But it was on'y f'r a moment. In another they tur-rned an' r-run, lavin' Mike Riordan standin' alone in th' mist iv th' fray. If it wasn't f'r th' intervintion iv th' powers in th' shape iv th' loot an' a wagon-load iv polismin, th' Bohemians'd have devastated as far as th' ruins iv th' gas-house, which is th' same as that there Acropulist ye talk about,' says I.

"'No, my son,' says I. 'On account iv th' fluctuations in rint an' throuble with th' landlord it's not safe to presoom that th' same fam'ly always lives in th' wan house. Th' very thing happened to Greece that has happened to th' tenth precint iv th' Sixth Ward. Th' Greeks have moved out, an' th' Swedes come in. Ye yet may live to see th' day,' says I, 'whin what is thrue iv Athens an' th' tenth precint will be thrue iv th' whole Sixth Wa-ard.'"

"Ye don't mean that," said Mr. Hennessy, gasping.

"I do," said Mr. Dooley, with solemnity. "'Tis histhry." (May 8, 1897)

3. A Polacker on the Red Bridge

"Th' Whole Thing" in Chicago in May 1897 was newly elected Mayor Carter Harrison, Jr. ("young Carther" to Mr. Hennessy), and his newly appointed public works commissioner was Irish immigrant and old-line Democrat Lawrence E. McGann. The notoriously unstrenuous job of bridgetender was a traditional political sinecure in Chicago, a city of many bridges and much water traffic, and the bridge at issue here probably spanned the South Branch of the Chicago River at Halsted Street. (The list of the mayor's new appointments for May included that of "W. Punchek" to the bridge at "S. Halsted Street.") Before the expressways, this bridge was the main entrance to Bridgeport and the entire South Side.

"Change an' decay in all around I see," said Mr. Dooley sadly.

"What's that?" demanded his friend.

"They have put a Polacker on th' r-red bridge," said Mr. Dooley.

"A what?" gasped Mr. Hennessy.

"A Polacker," repeated Mr. Dooley. "A Polacker be th' name iv Kazminski. Th' boys was down there las' night practicin' on him fr'm th' coalyard."

"Dear, oh dear," said Mr. Hennessy, "an' is this what Lawrence McGann an' young Carther have done f'r us? A Polacker on th' r-red bridge! 'Tis but a step fr'm that to a Swede loot at Deerin' sthreet an' a Bohemian aldherman. I niver thought I'd live to see th' day."

In Archer road the command of the "red bridge" is a matter of infinite concern. There are aldermen and members of the legislature in Archer road, clerks of the courts and deputy sheriffs, but their duties do not affect the daily life of the road. Whereas the commander of the bridge is a person of much consideration, for every citizen sees him day by day; it is part of his routine to chat loftily with the wayfarer, and the children help him to turn the bridge.

"'Tis all part iv what I tol' ye th' other day iv th' decay iv this ward," said Mr. Dooley. "We'll always be riprisinted in th' council an' the legis-lathure be people iv our own kind, f'r if ye put wan Irishman among twinty thousand Polackers, Bohemians, Rooshians, Germans an' Boolgaharians he'll be th' leader iv thim all. I wanst knew a man be th' name iv O'Donnell that was prisidint iv th' Zwiasek Nanowdowney Polaki, an' that's th' Polacker National Society. But th' foreign ilimints have to get some reconition nowadays. They're too sthrong to be left out, on'y I wish th' Whole Thing had begun somewheres but on th' bridge. It seems a shame to re-pose that sacred thrust in th' hands iv a man that no wan in th' creek can swear at an' be answered dacintly."

"They've been some fine men on that bridge in its day," said Mr. Hennessy.

"There has so," said Mr. Dooley, kindling. "D'ye ray-mimber Dorsey th' Reaper—him that used to stand be th' hour leanin' over th' rail watchin' f'r th' remains iv Germans that had missed a thrain an' drownded thimsilves to come along. He was a fine man. Thin there was little Clancy. D'ye mind th' time whin the lads fr'm th' mills was r-runnin' down th' road with the little boy sodjers iv th' First Rigimint chasin' thim. Whin th' last iv th' la-ads got acrost Clancy tur-rned th' bridge. 'In th' name iv th' State iv Illinye,' says th' colonel, 'I command ye to close that bridge,' he says. 'Wait till I light me pipe,' says Clancy. 'Close th' bridge, foolish man,' says th' colonel. 'Dam thim matches,' says Clancy, 'they won't stay lit,' he says. 'If ye don't close th' bridge,' says th' colonel, 'I'll fire,' he says. 'Sure, colonel,' says Clancy, 'ye wuddent deprive a poor wur-rkin' man iv th' right to his pipeful iv baccy,' he says. ''Tis against th' articles iv war,' he says. 'Dam th' matches.' Th' colonel ordhered th' little boy sodjers to point their guns at th' man on th' bridge. 'Colonel, oh colonel,' says Clancy. 'What is it?' says th' colonel. 'Ye'er vest is open in front, showin' ye'er shirt, naughty man,' he says. 'There's ladies on th' other side iv th' bridge an' I'd blush to have thim see ye in such a con-dition,' he says. Ye shud've seen th' colonel; he roared an' swore an' told Clancy he'd have his life. But Clancy wint on blowin' out matches till he seen th' last iv th' la-ads disappear in th' distance. Thin he went to wur-ruk on his lever like a man with th' rheumatism, an' whin th' colonel come up he saluted him. 'I've a mind to put ye in irons,' says th' colonel. 'Faith, that's th' reward iv virtue,' says Clancy. 'I thought ye'd make me at least a loot f'r savin' ye fr'm an ondacint exhibition iv ye'ersilf,' he says. 'Goowan now, or I'll tur-rn th' bridge on ye!'

"He was a great man, was Clancy," continued Mr. Dooley. "But a greater was me Uncle Mike, that was on th' bridge some twenty years ago. He had a lifelong gredge again' a man be th' name iv Doherty, th' master iv th' scow Wolfe Tone, an' 'twas in ordher to even up th' scoor with him that he took th' job, for he was be no means partial to wurruk, me Uncle Mike. Doherty knowed he was on th' bridge an' done his best to keep away, but wan day he had to r-run his stanch boat up th' creek an' come whistlin' to th' bridge. Me Uncle Mike seen him comin' an' give no sign f'r half an hour. Thin he crawled out iv his little gazebo, with his pipe in his mouth, an' says he: 'What ahoy?' he says. 'Th' scow Wolfe Tone,' says Doherty, black as coal. 'Whither away?' says me Uncle Mike. 'Niver mind whither away,' says Doherty. 'But open that there bridge or I'll come ashore an' grind ye to powdher,' says he. 'So ye say,' says me Uncle Mike, throwin' a chunk iv coal at him. 'So ye say,' he says. 'But ye can't go through, nivertheless. This here pellucid sthream,' he says (he was a man iv fine language), 'was niver intinded to be sailed be th' likes iv ye,' he says. 'I'm here to lave th' navies iv th' wurruld go by,' he says. 'An' I have special ordhers fr'm th' mayor that if an old sthreet car with th' wheels off comes swimmin' along undher command iv a mullet-headed Mayo man, I'm to close it f'r th' day.' An' with that he put on his coat, locked up th' pole an' wint home. All that day th' creek was jammed with scows an' tugs an' iron ore boats, an' no wan cud find me Uncle Mike. Th' captains come aboard th' Wolfe Tone an' cursed Doherty, the superintindint iv th' rollin' mills pleaded with

him an' th' polis sarched f'r me Uncle Mike. They found him as
dhrunk as a king down th' road. He finally consinted to tur-rn th'
bridge if Doherty would stand on th' top iv his cabin and say
three times, 'Hurrah f'r Mike Dooley, the king iv Connock.' Doherty, bein' a good-natured soul at bottom, done it, me Uncle
Mike swung th' bridge an' with such a tootin' iv whistles as ye
niver heerd, all th' fleet wint through.

"Me Uncle Mike resigned th' nex' day. An' now they have a
Polacker in th' place. Dear, oh dear!" (May 15, 1897)

4. The Soft Spot in a Landlord's Hard Heart

*On May 27, 1896, St. Louis was hit by a cyclone and fire that left
more than one thousand dead. The swiftness with which Chicagoans
offered help to their archrival among American cities prompted Mr.
Dooley's recollection of the one shining deed in the life of a tight-fisted
Bridgeport landlord.*

"Anny more cyclone news?" Mr. Dooley asked Mr. McKenna,
as he came in with a copy of an extra paper in his hand.

"Nothing much," Mr. McKenna responded. "This paper says
the angel of death has give up riding on the whirlwind."

"'Tis betther so," said Mr. Dooley: "a bicycle is more satisfac-
tory f'r a steady thing. But, faith, 'tis no jokin' matter. May th'
Lord forgive me f'r makin' light iv it! Jawn, whin I read about
thim poor people down in St. Looey, shtruck be th' wrath iv Hivin
without more warnin' thin a man gets in a Polock church fight an'
swept to their graves be th' hundhreds, me heart ached in me.

"But they'se always some compinsation in th' likes iv this. To
see th' wurruld as it r-runs along in its ordinrey coorse, with ivry
man seemin' to be lookin' f'r th' best iv it an' carryin' a little hammer f'r his fellow-suff'rers, ye'd think what Hinnissy calls th'
springs iv human sympathy was as dhry in th' breast as a bricklayer's boot in a box iv mortar. But let annything happen like this,
an' men ye'd suspect iv goin' round with a cold chisel liftin' name-

plates off iv coffins comes to th' front with their lips full iv comfort an' kindliness an', what's more to th' point, their hands full iv coin.

"Years ago there used to be a man be th' name of O'Brien—no relation iv th' sinitor—lived down be th' dumps. He was well off, an' had quit wur-rkin' f'r a living. Well, whether he'd been disappointed in love or just naturally had a kick up to him again th' wurruld I niver knew; but this here ol' la-ad put in his time from morn till night handin' out contimpt an' hathred to all mankind. No wan was harder to rent fr'm. He had some houses near Halsted Sthreet, an' I've see him servin' five days' notices on his tenants whin th' weather was that cold ye cudden't see th' inside iv th' furnace-rooms at th' mill f'r th' frost on th' window. Of all th' landlords on earth, th' Lord deliver me fr'm an' Irish wan. Whether 'tis that fr'm niver holdin' anny land in th' ol' counthry they put too high a fondness on their places whin they get a lot or two over here, I don't know; but they're quicker with th' constable thin anny others. I've seen men, that 'd divide their last cint with ye pay night, as hard, whin it come to gather in th' rent f'r two rooms in th' rear, as if they was Lord Leitrim's own agents; an' O'Brien had no such start iv binivolence to go on. He niver seemed to pass th' poorbox in church without wantin' to break into it. He charged tin per cint whin Casey, th' plumber, buried his wife an' borrid money f'r th' funeral expenses. I see him wanst chasin' th' agent iv th' Saint Vincent de Pauls down th' road f'r darin' to ask him f'r a contribution. To look at his har-rsh red face, as he sat at his window markin' up his accounts, ye'd know he was hard in th' bit an' heavy in th' hand. An' so he was,—as hard an' heavy as anny man I iver seen in all me born days.

"Well, Peter O'Brien had lived on long enough to have th' pious curses iv th' entire parish, whin th' fire broke out, th' second fire iv sivinty-four, whin th' damage was tin or twinty millions iv dollars an' I lost a bull terrier be th' name iv Robert Immitt, r-runnin' afther th' ingines. O'Brien disappeared fr'm th' r-road durin' th' fire,—he had some property on th' South Side,—an' wasn't seen or heerd tell iv f'r a day. Th' nex' mornin' the rayport come in that he was seen walkin' over th' red bridge with a baby in his arms. 'Glory be!' says I: 'is th' man goin' to add canniballing to his other crimes?' Sure enough, as I sthud in th' dureway, along come O'Brien, with his hands scalded, his eyebrows gone, an' most iv his clothes tore fr'm his back, but silent an' grim as iver, with a mite iv a girl held tight to his breast, an' her fast asleep.

"He had a house back iv my place,—he ownded th' fifty feet frontin' on Grove Sthreet, bought it fr'm a man named Grogan,—an' 'twas rinted be a widow woman be th' name iv Sullivan, wife iv a bricklayer iv th' same name. He come sthridin' into th' Widow Sullivan's house; an' says he, 'Mistress Sullivan,' he says. 'Yes,' says she, in a thremble, knottin' her apron in her hands an' standin' in front iv her own little wans, 'what can I do f'r ye?' she says. 'Th' rent's not due till to-morrow.' 'I very well know that,' he says; 'an' 'twas not about th' rent I come,' says he. 'But,' he says, 'I've heerd ye spoke iv as a kind woman an' wan that'd had to do with th' bringin' up iv childher,' he says, 'an' I want ye to take care iv this wan,' he says. 'An' I'll pay ye f'r ye'er throuble,' he says.

"We niver knew where he got th' child: he niver told annywan. Docthor Casey said he was badly burnt about th' head an' hands. He testified to it in a suit he brought again O'Brien f'r curin' him. F'r th' man O'Brien, instead iv rayformin' like they do in th' play, was a long sight meaner afther he done this wan thing thin iver befure. If he was tight-fisted wanst, he was as close now as calcimine on a rough-finished wall. He put his tinints out in th' cold without mercy, he kicked blind beggars fr'm th' dure, an' on his dyin'-bed he come as near bein' left be raison iv his thryin' to bargain with th' good man f'r th' rayqueems as annywan ye iver see. But he raised th' little girl; an' I sometimes think that, whin they count up th' cash, they'll let O'Brien off with a character f'r that wan thing, though there's some pretty hard tabs again him.

"They ain't much point in what I've told ye more thin this,—that beneath ivry man's outside coat there lies some sort iv good feelin'. We ain't as bad as we make ourselves out. We've been stringin' ropes across th' sthreet f'r th' people iv Saint Looey f'r thirty years an' handin' thim bricks fr'm th' chimbleys whiniver we got a chance, but we've on'y got wurruds an' loose change f'r thim whin th' hard times comes."

"Yes," said Mr. McKenna, "I see even the aldhermen has come to the front, offering relief."

"Well," said Mr. Dooley, thoughtfully, "I on'y hope they won't go to Saint Looey to disthri-bute it thimsilves. That would be a long sight worse thin th' cyclone." (May 30, 1896)

5. Paternal Duty and Rackrenting Landlord Ahearn

Here Dunne combines the themes of Irish-American avarice and child-rearing difficulty. Mr. Dooley marks his father's age from the poorly organized Rebellion of 1798, when farmers armed only with pikes faced British soldiers in several encounters. Miser Ahearn in the piece names his son for Daniel O'Connell the Liberator, the Irish politician most responsible for Catholic Emancipation in 1829 and the father of modern Irish nationalism.

"I'm havin' a time iv it with Terence," said Mr. Hennessy, despondently.

"What's th' la-ad been doin'?" asked Mr. Dooley.

"It ain't so much what he's doin'," Mr. Hennessy explained, "as what he ain't doin'. He ain't stayin' home iv nights, an' he ain't wurrukin'; but he does be out on th' corner with th' Cromleys an' th' rest, dancin' jig steps an' whistlin' th' 'Rogue's March' whin a polisman goes by. Sure, I can do nawthin' with him, f'r he's that kind an' good at home that he'd melt th' heart iv a man iv stone. But it's gray me life is, thinkin' iv what's to become iv him whin he gets to be a man grown. Ye're lucky, Martin, that ye're childless."

"Sure, I cudden't be anny other way, an' hold me good name," said Mr. Dooley. "An', whin I look about me sometimes, it's glad I am. They'se been times, perhaps—But lave that go. Is there somethin' in th' air or is it in oursilves that makes th' childher nowadays turn out to curse th' lives iv thim that give thim life? It may be in th' thrainin'. Whin I was a kid, they were brought up to love, honor, an' respect th' ol' folks, that their days might be long in th' land. Amen. If they didn't, th' best they cud do was to say nawthin' about it. 'Twas th' back iv th' hand an' th' sowl iv th' fut to th' la-ad that put his spoon first into th' stirabout. Between th' whalin's we got at school h'isted on th' back iv th' big boy that was bein' thrained to be a Christyan brother an' th' thumpin's we got at home, we was kept sore an' sthraight fr'm wan year's end to another. 'Twas no mild doses they give us, ayether. I mind wanst, whin I was near as big as I am now, I handed back some onkind ree-marks to me poor father that's dead. May he rest in peace, per Dominum! He must iv been a small man, an' bent with wurruk an' worry. But did he take me jaw? He did not. He hauled off, an' give me a r-right hook where th' bad wurruds come fr'm. I put up a pretty fight, f'r me years; but th' man doesn't live that can lick his own father. He rowled me acrost an oat-field, an' I give up. I didn't love him anny too well f'r that lickin', but I respected him; an', if he'd come into this place to-night,—an' he'd be near a hundherd: he was born in th' year '98, an' pikes was hid in his cradle,—if he come in here to-night an' pulled me ear, I'd fear to go again him. I wud so.

"'Tis th' other way about now. Did ye iver know a man be th' name iv Ahearn? Ye did not? Well, maybe he was befure yer time. He was a cobbler be thrade; but he picked up money be livin' off iv leather findings an' wooden pegs, an' bought pieces iv th' prairie, an' starved an' bought more, an' starved an' starved till his heart was shrivelled up like a washerwoman's hand. But he made money. An' th' more he made, th' more he wanted, an', wantin' nawthin' more, it come to him fr'm th' divvle, who kept th' curse f'r his own time. This man Ahearn, whin he had acres an' acres on Halsted Sthreet, an' tinants be th' scoor that prayed at nights f'r him that he might live long an' taste sorrow, he marrid a girl. Her name was Ryan, a little, scared, foolish woman; an' she died whin a boy was bor-rn. Ahearn give her a solemn rayqueem high mass an' a monument at Calv'ry that ye can see fr'm th' fun'ral thrain. An' he come fr'm th' fun'ral with th' first smile on his face that anny man iver see there, an' th' baby in his ar-rms.

"I'll not say Ahearn was a changed man. Th' love iv money was knitted into his heart; an', afther th' la-ad come, th' way he ground th' people that lived in his houses was death an' destruction. 'I must provide f'r me own,' he said. But thim that was kind to th' kid cud break th' crust, an' all th' r-rough, hard-wurrkin' tenants paid f'r th' favors he give to th' ol' frauds an' beguilin' women that petted Dan'l O'Connell Ahearn. Nawthin' was too good f'r th' kid. He had nurses an' servants to wait on him. He had clothes that'd stock this ba-ar f'r a year. Whin he was old enough, he was sint to Saint Ignatyous. An' th' ol' man'd take him walkin' on a Sundah, an' pint out th' rows an' rows iv houses, with th' childher in front gazin' in awe at th' great man, an' their fathers glowerin' fr'm the windows, an' say, 'Thim will all be yours whin ye grow up, Dan'l O'Connell, avick.'

"Well, it didn't take an eye iv a witch to see that Dan'l O'Connell was a bor-rn idjet. They was no rale harm in th' poor la-ad, on'y he was lazy an' foolish an' sort iv tired like. To make a long story short, Hinnissy, his father thried iverything f'r him, an' got nawthin'. He didn't dhrink much, he cared little f'r women, he liked to play ca-ards, but not f'r money. He did nawthin' that was bad; an' yet he was no good at all, at all,—just a slow, tired, aisy-goin', shamblin' la-ad,—th' sort that'd wrench th' heart iv a father like Ahearn. I dinnaw what he did fin'lly, but wan night he come into my place an' said he'd been turned out be his father an' wanted a place f'r to sleep. 'Ye'll sleep at home,' says I. 'Ye'er father sh'd take shame to himsilf,—him a rich man.' An' I put on me coat, an' wint over to Ahearn's. I was a power in th' wa-ard in thim days, an' feared no man alive. Th' ol' la-ad met us at th' dure. Whin I started to speak, he blazed up. 'Misther Dooley,' says he, 'my sor-rows are me own. I'll keep thim here. As f'r ye,' he says, an' tur-rned like a tiger on th' boy an' shtruck him with his ol' leathery hand. Th' boy stood f'r a minnyit, an' thin walked out, me with him. I niver see him since. We left Ahearn standin' there, as we used to say iv th' fox in th' ol' counthry, cornered between th' river an' th' wall."

"Ye're lucky to be alone," said Mr. Hennessy as he left.

"I think so," said Mr. Dooley. But there was no content upon his face as he watched a lounging oaf of a boy catch up with Mr. Hennessy, exchange a curtly affectionate greeting, and walk over to where Mrs. Hennessy could be seen reading the "Key of Heaven" beside the parlor stove. (November 13, 1897)

6. An Immigrant Millionaire Denies His Brother

In September 1895 a scandal hit Chicago with the discovery that the water supply was being secretly and illegally tapped by the city's leading meat packers, Armour, Swift, and Nelson Morris. An estimated 38 million gallons were being stolen per day. Of the three, only Morris fits Mr. Dooley's description in this piece. A German immigrant from the Black Forest, he came penniless to America in 1848 and worked first as a watchman in the Chicago stockyards for five dollars a month. He began buying and selling cattle on a small scale, and got his first large contract during the Civil War, supplying beef to Union troops. By the nineties he had built up a worldwide packing operation with over $100 million in annual business.

"Jawn," said Mr. Dooley, "why sh'd annywan want to steal wather?"

"I give it up," replied Mr. McKenna.

"It seems sthrange, doesn't it," Mr. Dooley went on. "They ought to be enough to go 'round. I'll bet ye tin no wan in Archey road 'll iver be cha-arged with what Hinnissy calls this hanyous offince.

"I suppose 'tis because they wasn't annything else they cud take. They'se wan man in th' lot that'd steal even wather. Th' pa-apers says 'tis exthrordinrey that ladin' citizens sh'd hook th' dhrink, but I know a thing or two about this ladin' citizen. I heerd it fr'm Schwartzmeister whin him an' me was frinds, befure he put in th' pool table. This here wan came over fr'm Germany a long time ago, befure th' fire. Well, he was a smart la-ad, an' he done well dhrivin' cattle an' sellin' thim, an' he changed his name an' wint into th' packin' business.

"Whin he wint away fr'm Germany he lift behind a brother, an' niver heerd tell iv him f'r twenty-five or thirty years. Th' man lived though, f'r all iv that, a quite, dacint ol' lad. He had a little holdin' an' a cow an' a pig an' th' use iv th' neighbor's horse, an' he'd have gone peaceful an' continted to his grave but f'r wan thing. He was sick an' he heerd how well th' other was doin' and he wrote to him. Th' rich wan answered, told him to come over an' that he'd look out f'r him. An' he sint him a steerage ticket.

"Th' ol' man's name was Max. Well, ivery wan all over th' parish heerd iv Max's luck an' they wint to see him off on th' thrain an' to cheer him. Th' las' wurruds he said befure he wint was to his wife. 'I'm goin',' he says, 'far away,' he says. 'Aber,' he says, 'avick, I'll come back whin I've got settled an' bring ye an' the kids over,' he says.

"Jawn, it ain't nice in th' steerage iv an immigrant ship. I know. It smells an' it's hot be night an' cold be day. But Max he bore up an' thought iv th' good brother, d'ye mind, waitin' f'r him with a carridge an' four horses. He got to Chicago in th' smokin'-ca-ar. They was no wan at th' deepo to meet him. 'They must be some mistake,' he says to himself, he says. 'I'll go up to his house,' he says. He got a German polisman to tell him where th' brother lived an' trudged up there with his kit on his back. Th' servant tol' him to raypoort at th' office th' nex' day. An' whin he raypoorted what job d'ye think they give him, Jawn? They put him in th' shovel gang at th' salt house.

"Ye niver wurruked in a salt house? Did ye iver mow away clover hay in a counthry barn iv a hot afthernoon? Did ye iver tind a blast in July? Well, nayther iv thim is as near to wurrkin' in a salt house as holy wather is to hell.

"Fr'm sivin o'clock in the mornin' till six at night this here Max shovelled away. All th' wather that's been stolen fr'm th' city be his brother wudden't kill th' thirst that lay like fever on his lips

nor aise his poor, tired, ol' back. But there was th' wife an' childher at home an' he pegged away, makin' no kick an' lettin' on to
no man who he was.

"Salt shovellin' ain't crochayin', Jawn, an' it ain't tindin' a cow,
be a dam sight. An' Max wint fr'm bad to worse till he cud bare
raise his shovel, he was that weak. Th' foreman cursed him an' th'
other min crowded him till wan day th' boss wint to his brother
an' says he: 'That there man Max ye sint me is no good,' he says.
'What's th' matther iv him?' says th' millionaire. 'He's not sthrong
enough,' says th' boss. 'Thin fire him,' says th' brother. An' th' nix'
mornin' whin Max come around with his dinner pail on his arrum
th' boss says: 'Ye can go up an' get ye'er time. We've no further use
f'r ye.'

"Max stayed around town f'r a week. Thin he put what money
he'd saved into a steerage ticket an' wint away. He niver set eyes
but wanst on th' rich wan. An' he's back there in Germany now.
Th' county is takin' care iv him."

"Maybe," said Mr. McKenna, "that accounts for one man steal-
ing water."

"Yis," said Mr. Dooley, "but it'd take more thin an eight-inch
tap to wash away that sin." (September 7, 1895)

7. Changing Attitudes toward the Press

*Mr. Dooley reminisces here about one of the most colorful figures
in Chicago newspaper history, the fire-breathing Wilbur F. Storey,
who edited the* Times *in the 1860s and '70s, and "wore no man's
collar, by Gawd, sir!" He reveled in opportunities to expose hypocrisy and scandal among "prominent citizens," and was famous for
his sensational headlines—for example, "Jerked to Jesus," announc-
ing the hanging of four murderers in 1875.*

"I don't think," said Mr. Dooley, "that th' pa-apers is as good
now as they used to be whin I was a young man."

"I don't see much diff'rence in thim," said Mr. Hennessy. "Except they're all full iv pitchers iv th' prisidint an' secrity iv th' Milwaukee Avnoo Fife an' Dhrum E-lite Society. They give ye th' same advice to vote th' mugwump ticket between ilictions an' th' sthraight ticket at ilictions, an' how th' business in pig-iron is slowly but surely pickin' up, an' how to make las' year's dhress look like next year's be addin' a few jet beads an' an accorjeen pleat. They're as bad now as they iver were an' I've quit readin' thim."

"Ah, but sure," said Mr. Dooley, "ye don't raymimber th' ol' days. Ye don't raymimber Storey's *Times*. That was th' paper f'r ye. What th' divvle did ol' man Storey care f'r th' thrade in pig iron? 'Twas no more to him thin th' thrade in pool checks. He set up in his office with his whiskers thrailin' in an ink pot an' wrote venomious attacks on th' characters iv th' leaders iv high society an' good-natured jests about his esteemed contimprary havin' had to leave Ohio because he stole a cukstove. He didn't have no use f'r prominent citizens except be way iv heavin' scandal at thim. He knowed what th' people wanted. They wanted crime, an' he give it to thim. If they wasn't a hangin' on th' front page some little lad iv a rayporther'd lose his job. They was murdher an' arson till ye cudden't rest, robbery an' burglary f'r page afther page, with anny quantity iv scandal f'r th' woman's page an' a fair assortment iv larceny an' assault an' batthery f'r th' little wans. 'Twas a paper no wan took into his house—f'r th' other mimbers iv th' fam'ly—but 'twas a well-run paper, so it was.

"Ye can hardly find anny crimes nowadays. To look at th' paapers ye'd think they was not wan bit iv rale spoortin' blood left in th' people iv this city. Instead iv it I have to pay to know that Mrs. Dofunny iv Englewood has induced her husband to stay away fr'm home while she gives a function—an' what a function is I dinnaw—an' among thim that'll be prisint, if they can get their laundhry out, 'll be Messers. an' Mesdames What-Dye-Call-Thim an' Messers. an' Mesdames This-an'-That an' Miss What-Dye-Call-Her Now, an' so on. What do I care about thim? Now, if Misther Dofunny had come home with a load on an' found his wife r-runnin' up bills f'r tea an' broke up th' function with his dinner pail it'd be worth readin' about. But none iv th' papers'd say anything about it, now that Storey's gone. Why, mind ye, las' week th' Willum J. O'Brien Lithry and Marchin' Club give a dance, an' befure it got through th' chairman iv th' flure comity fell out with the German man that led th' band an' ivery wan in th' place took a wallup at some wan else with a wind insthrumint. I looked f'r it in th' paper th' nex' day. All they had was: 'Th' Willum J. O'Brien Lithry an' Marchin' Club, includin' th' mos' prominent mimbers iv society in th' sixth ward, give a function at Finucane's Hall las' night. O'Rafferty sarved an' music was furnished be Weinstein's orchesthry. Among those prisint was so-an'-so.' Th' rayporter must've copied th' names off th' blotter at the polis station. An' there was not wan wurrud about th' fight—not wan wurrud!

"Now, if it had been in ol' Storey's day this is th' way it'd read: 'Bill O'Brien, th' tough aldherman fr'm th' sixth ward, has a club named after him, most iv thim bein' well known to th' polis. It is a disgrace to th' decent people iv Bridgepoort. Las' night th' neighbors complained to th' polis iv th' noise an' Lift'nant Murphy responded with a wagon-load iv bluecoats. On entherin' th' hall th' gallant officers found a free fight in progress, wan iv th' rowdies havin' hit th' leader iv th' band, who responded be knockin' his assailant down with a b-flat cornet. Th' disturbers iv th' peace were taken to Deerin' shtreet station an'll be thried befure Judge Scully in th' mornin'.' That's th' way ol' Storey'd give it to thim. He didn't know much about functions, but he was blue blazes on polis news.

"I dinnaw what's comin' over th' people. Whin I was young, if a rayporther wint rubberin' around a dance we might give him a dhrink an' we might throw him in th' canal. It depinded on how we felt tord him. It wasn't rispictable in thim days to have ye'er name in th' paper. It niver got in except whin ye was undher arrest. Now I see har-rd wurkin' men thrampin' down to th' newspaper offices with little items about a christenin' or a wake an' havin' it read to thim in th' mornin' at breakfuss befure they start to th' mills. On'y th' other day th' Bohemian woman that r-runs th' cabbage patch up be Main shtreet come in an' says she: 'We have a party at th' house to-night,' she says. 'Have ye?' says I. 'What for?' I says. 'Me daughter is comin' out,' says she. 'Is she?' says I. 'That's nice iv th' mayor,' I says. 'How long was she in f'r?' says I. An' she wint away mad. What's worse, this here society don't stop afther death. Here's a notice in th' paper: 'Ann Hochheimer'—she marrid a German—'nee O'Toole.' Nee O'Toole! Nee O'Toole! What does that mean? Nee nawthin'! Her name was O'Toole befure she was marrid, f'r twinty-odd years. I knowed her well."

"Well," said Mr. Hennessy, with a sheepish smile. "I must be goin'. We have a progressive euchre party at my house an' I must be there to r-ring th' bell."

"Ye'd betther stay here an' play me forty-fives, f'r th' dhrinks," said Mr. Dooley with compassion.

"No," said Mr. Hennessy, in hollow tones, "me name's in th' pa-aper an' I must riprisint."

And Mr. Dooley, the untainted one, stood alone—the solitary green spot in a desert of "society." (June 26, 1897)

8. Naming the Hogan Baby

One of the Hogan children mentioned here was probably born between January and March 1880 while Charles Stewart Parnell was touring America to raise funds for the Irish Land League. The powerful agitation of this group against landlords and land agents, including a Captain Boycott of County Mayo, brought a new word into the language.

Mr. Dooley yawned. "You look tired." said Mr. McKenna.

"I am that," said Mr. Dooley. "I was at Hogan's christenin' las' night an' 'twas 2 o'clock befure me an' Kelly come down th' road singin': 'Iv a-hall th' towns in I-er-land, Kil-a-kinny f'r me-e-e-e.'"

"Have Hogan another?"

"He have; th' tinth. An' 'twas near to breakin' up th' family. Ye know th' time we seen Hogan comin' out iv th' sicond story window in his shir-rtsleeves. That was whin he said they was no such a saint in th' catalogue as Aloysius. He wanted f'r to na-ame th' kid befure this wan Michael. 'Twas named Aloysius an' th' family calls it Toodles, I belave. Be hivins, Hogan have growed gray haired an' bald thryin' f'r to inthrodjooce th' name iv Michael or Bridget in th' family. Michael was his father's name an' Bridget was his mother's, an' good names they ar-re; none better. Th' first wan was a boy an' afther Mrs. Hogan had th' polis in 'twas called Sarsfield. Th' second was a girl an' 'twas called Lucy, d'ye mind? Lucy! Yes, by dad, Lucy Hogan. Thin they was Honoria an' Ve-ronica an' Arthur an' Charles Stewart Parnell, bor-rn durin' the land lague, an' Paul an' Madge an' William Joyce Hogan, an' th' ol' ma-an all this time tryin' f'r to edge in Michael or Bridget.

"Well, Hogan does be gettin' on in years now an' whin th' last come an' th' good woman was sthrong enough f'r to walk around, says he: 'Whin ar-re ye goin' to christen little Mike,' he says. 'Little who?' says she. 'Little Mike,' he says. 'Little Mike Hogan,' he says, 'th' kid.' 'There'll be no little Mikes around this house,' says she, 'unless they walk over me dead body,' she says. Jawn, she's County May-o to th' backbone. 'D'ye think I'm goin' to sind th' child out into th' wurruld,' she says, 'with a name,' she says, 'that'll keep him from anny employmint,' she says, 'but goin' on th' polis for-rce,' she says. 'Mike is a good name,' says Hogan. ''Twas me fa-ather's,' he says, 'an' he was as good as anny.' 'Don't tell me about ye'er father,' says she. 'Didn't I know him,' she says, 'carryin' around a piece iv ol' chalk,' she says, 'atin' wan ind iv it f'r heartburn an' usin' th' other ind iv it to chalk up for-rty-fives scores on th' table,' she says. 'I had a cousin a priest,' says Hogan. 'Match that if ye dahr.' 'Ye had wan a lamplighter,' says she. 'Me mother's brother kep' a cow,' he says. 'Not afther th' polis found it out,' says Mrs. Hogan. ''Twas me aunt Ayleonara's.' That thrun Hogan, but he come back sthrong. 'Ye'll be namin' no more chil-dren iv mine out iv dime novels,' he says. 'An' ye'll name no more iv mine out iv th' payroll iv th' bridge depar-rtmint,' says she. Thin Hogan wakened. 'What ar-re ye goin' to call it?' he says.

'Augustus,' says she. An' be hivins 'twas Augustus th' priest give it. Th' poor, poor child!

"We had th' divvle's own time gettin' it anny name, bedad. Terence Kelly was th' god fa-ather, an' he insisted on carryin' th' kid to th' church. He lost his prisince iv mind whin he come to where O'Connor is puttin' up a house an' started f'r to climb th' ladder with th' kid over his chowlder. Thin whin he was standin' at th' rail he put th' big hand iv him out an' says, 'Hello, Mick; how's thricks?' to th' good man. They're cousins, d'ye mind. Ye should've seen th' look th' soggarth give him. He got aven though. Kelly couldn't f'r th' life iv him say the confeetjoor. 'Ye hathen,' says th' soggarth. 'Ye standin' up f'r an innocent baby,' he says, 'whin ye don't know ye'er prayers,' he says. 'Take this book,' he says, 'an' go over in th' cor-rner an' larn it,' he says. 'Twas scand'lous. Kelly delayed th' game near an hour an' forty minutes."

"And where was Hogan all this time?" asked Mr. McKenna.

"He didn't come an' no wan seen him at th' house. I wint into th' Dutchman's on me way home f'r to tell him th' election was over an' I found Hogan there thryin' to tell Schmittberger that they had a new kid at th' house an' that they called him Angostura Bitthers Hogan." (November 17, 1894)

9. Molly Donahue and the Divided Skirt

This is the first appearance of Molly Donahue in a starring role. Bridgeport's reaction to her bicycle ride is not all that implausible: in May 1894 Alderman "Bathhouse John" Coughlin had introduced to the city council an ordinance banning women bicycle riders "in bloomers, knickerbockers, baseball attire or trousers." His motion failed to pass, however.

"Jawn," said Mr. Dooley, "did ye iver hear th' puzzle whin a woman's not a woman?"

"Faith, I have," said Mr. McKenna. "When I was a kid, I knew the answer."

"Ye didn't know this answer," said Mr. Dooley. "Whin is a woman not a woman? 'Twas give to me las' Satthurdah night be young Callaghan, th' sthreet-car man that have all th' latest jokes that does be out. Whin is a woman not a woman? mind ye. Whin she's on a bicycle, by dad. Yes, yes. Whin she's on a bicycle, Jawn. D'ye know Molly Donahue?"

"I know her father," said Mr. McKenna. "He run for alderman once and lost an ear."

"Well, well, the dacint man sint his daughter Molly to have a convint schoolin'; an' she larned to pass th' butther in Frinch an' to paint all th' chiny dishes in th' cubb'rd, so that, whin Donahue come home wan night an' et his supper, he ate a green paint ha-arp along with his cabbage, an' they had to sind f'r Docthor Hin-nissy f'r to pump th' a-art work out iv him. So they did. But Donahue, bein' a quite man, niver minded that, but let her go on with her do-se-does an' bought her a bicycle. All th' bicycles th' poor man had himsilf whin he was her age was th' dhray he used to dhrive f'r Comiskey; but he says, ''Tis all th' thing,' he says. 'Let th' poor child go her way,' he says to his wife, he says. 'Honoria,' he says, 'she'll get over it.'

"No wan knowed she had th' bicycle, because she wint out afther dark an' practised on it down be th' dump. But las' Friday evnin', lo an' behold, whin th' r-road was crowded with people fr'm th' brick-yards an' th' gas-house an' th' mills, who shud come ridin' along be th' thracks, bumpin' an' holdin' on, but Molly Donahue? An' dhressed! How d'ye suppose she was dhressed? In pa-ants, Jawn avick. In pa-ants. Oh, th' shame iv it! Ivry wan on th' sthreet stopped f'r to yell. Little Julia Dorgan called out, 'Who stole Molly's dhress?' Ol' man Murphy was settin' asleep on his stoop. He heerd th' noise, an' woke up an' set his bull tarrier be Parnell out iv Lydia Pinkham on her. Malachi Dorsey, vice-prisident iv th' St. Aloysius Society, was comin' out iv th' Ger-man's, an' see her. He put his hands to his face, an' wint back to th' ba-ar.

"But she wint bumpin' on, Jawn, till she come up be th' house. Father Kelly was standin' out in front, an' ol' man Donahue was layin' down th' law to him about th' tariff, whin along come th' poor foolish girl with all th' kids in Bridgeport afther her. Donahue turned white. 'Say a pather an' avy quick,' he says to the priest. Thin he called out to his wife. 'Honoria,' he says, 'bring a bar'l,' he says. 'Molly has come away without annything on,' he says, 'but Sarsfield's pa-ants.' Thin he turned on his daughter. 'May th' Lord forgive ye, Molly Donahue,' he says, 'this night!' he says. 'Child, where is ye'er dhress?' 'Tut, tut!' says th' good man. 'Molly,' he says, 'ye look well on that there bicycle,' he says. 'But 'tis th' first time I ever knowed ye was bow-legged,' he says, says th' soggarth aroon.

"Well, sir, she wint into th' house as if she'd been shot fr'm a gun, an' th' nex' mornin' I see Doheny's express wagon haulin' th' bicycle away."

"Didn't Father Kelly do anything about it?" asked Mr. McKenna.

"No," replied Mr. Dooley. "There was some expicted she'd be read fr'm th' altar at high mass, but she wasn't. Mrs. Hinnissy seen her doin' th' stations f'r a pinance las' Choosdah mornin'." (September 22, 1894)

10. Molly Tries to Vote

In the fall of 1894 Illinois took its first step toward woman suffrage when the legislature passed a law allowing women to vote for statewide school trustees. The law was upheld despite protests from Illinois Attorney General Maloney, and 25,000 women registered on October 16. Four days later, Mr. Dooley reported Molly's attempt. The Australian, or secret, ballot only came into wide use in America in the 1892 elections. The "growler" that Molly reluctantly carries for her father was a bucket of beer, filled up at the corner saloon for home consumption.

"If that Mary Donahue lives long enough she'll bring her poor fa-ather's head in sorrow to the gr-rave," said Mr. Dooley.

"What's the girl been doing?" asked Mr. McKenna.

"Doin', is it?" said Mr. Dooley. "Doin'? She's been to raygisther an' be hivins she swears she'll vote."

Mr. Dooley watched the effect of this on the blasé McKenna and when that citizen of the world showed some interest he resumed:

"Th' girl always had a quare sthreak in her. I mind whin she was a little wan an' th' ol' la-ad'd sind her over f'r his avenin' pint, she'd carry th' growler in a workbasket, she was that pr-roud. 'Twas her that injooced Donahue f'r to buy the plug hat started th' row bechune him an' his brother. Whin she come back fr'm boordin' school she wanted to chase th' goat. Her mother objected. 'F'r why don't ye like Ophalia?'—'twas th' goat's name—says Mrs. Donahue. 'He does be a great help to me in me wur-ruck.' 'His smill,' says th' stuck-up piece, 'is odjoos.' Th' ol' woman hung out, though. She kep' th' goat, by dad, till wan day Mary thried to wash it in coloogne an' thin it r-run away, and was niver seen again. Mrs. Donahue says th' poor baste was so mortified that it lept into th' slough, she did, she did.

"I tould ye about th' bicycle, Jawn. Well, sir, she got a pinance f'r that th' like iv which ain't been knowed in Bridgeport since Cassidy said Char-les Stewart Parnell was a bigger man thin th' pope. Ivry wan thought she was rayformed till las' Sundah, whin she wint to th' sodality meetin' an' give it out cold an' flat that she was goin' to vote. 'Twas all up an' down th' road, but no wan told Donahue, f'r th' man have lived a dacint life an' 'twas knowed 'twould break his heart. He niver heerd iv it till Choosdah. He was wan iv th' judges iv election f'r th' precint, an' he was in th' act iv whalin' 'ell out iv th' raypooblican judge accordin' to th' Australian law that Fitzsimmons made, whin in come his daughter. 'Did ye want to see me?' he says, lavin' go iv th' raypooblican, who was a German man that wurruks at th' dumps. 'Yis,' says Mary. 'I want to raygisther me vote.' 'Ye'er what?' he says. 'Me vote,' she says. 'What d'ye mane, avick?' he says. 'Shure ye have no

vote.' 'I have,' says she. 'I can vote f'r thrustees.' 'Ye can not,' said
Donahue. 'I'll not take ye'er vote.' 'I will,' says th' Dutchman. 'I'll
raygisther ye,' he says. 'If ye do,' says Donahue, 'I'll give ye a puck
in th' eye.' Well, sir, it took two polismen f'r to hould him, an' th'
girl wint home without raygisth'ring. She swears she'll go again
nex' Choosdah."

"D'you think she will?" asked Mr. McKenna.

"I dinnaw, I dinnaw. She's got a spirit iv her own, but I seen
Donahue walkin' up an' down in front iv his dure las' night with
his pipe tur-rned upside down an' his thumbs in his vist. 'Macchew,' I says, 'I hear ye'er daughter is goin' to vote,' I says. 'Misther Dooley,' says he, as mad as a hornet. 'It's dam little th' likes iv
me cares f'r what th' likes iv ye hears,' he says. 'But if anny wan
asks ye,' he says sarcastic, 'f'r free information,' he says, 'with their
booze,' he says, 'ye tell thim that Mattchew Xavier Donahue'll do
all th' votin' f'r th' Donahue family in this here precint.' I heerd he
had her chained to th' bed an' was makin' preparations f'r to have
a noveeney said f'r her recov'ry." (October 20, 1894.)

11. The Piano in the Parlor

In 1890 Edward Harrigan produced a popular musical, Reilly
and the Four Hundred, *about the social pretensions of the "lace-
curtain" Irish. The hit song of the show contained a chorus that ap-
plies to this Dooley piece: "There's an organ in the parlor, to give the
house a tone/ And you're welcome every evening at Maggie Murphy's home."*

"Ol' man Donahue bought Molly a pianny las' week," Mr.
Dooley said in the course of his conversation with Mr. McKenna.
"She'd been takin' lessons fr'm a Dutchman down th' sthreet, an'
they say she can play as aisy with her hands crossed as she can
with wan finger. She's been whalin' away iver since, an' Donahue
is dhrinkin' again.

"Ye see th' other night some iv th' la-ads wint over f'r to see whether they cud smash his table in a frindly game iv forty-fives. I don't know what possessed Donahue. He niver asked his frinds into the parlor befure. They used to set in th' dining-room; an', whin Mrs. Donahue coughed at iliven o'clock, they'd toddle out th' side dure with their hats in their hands. But this here night, whether 'twas that Donahue had taken on a tub or two too much or not, he asked thim all in th' front room, where Mrs. Donahue was settin' with Molly. 'T've brought me frinds,' he says, 'f'r to hear Molly take a fall out iv th' music-box,' he says. 'Let me have ye'er hat, Mike,' he says. 'Ye'll not feel it whin ye go out,' he says.

"At anny other time Mrs. Donahue'd give him th' marble heart. But they wasn't a man in th' party that had a pianny to his name, an' she knew they'd be throuble whin they wint home an' tould about it. ''Tis a mel-odjious insthrument,' says she. 'I cud sit here be the hour an' listen to Bootoven and Choochooski,' she says.

"'What did thim write?' says Cassidy. 'Chunes,' says Donahue, 'chunes. Molly,' he says, 'fetch 'er th' wallop to make th' gintlemen feel good,' he says. 'What'll it be, la-ads?' 'D'ye know "The Rambler fr'm Clare"?' says Slavin. 'No,' says Molly. 'It goes like this,' says Slavin. 'A-ah, din yadden, yooden a-yadden, arrah yadden ay-a.' 'I dinnaw it,' says th' girl. ''Tis a low chune, annyhow,' says Mrs. Donahue. 'Misther Slavin ividintly thinks he's at a polis picnic,' she says. 'I'll have no come-all-ye's in this house,' she says. 'Molly, give us a few ba-ars fr'm Wagner.' 'What Wagner's that?' says Flanagan. 'No wan ye know,' says Donahue; 'he's a German musician.' 'Thim Germans is hot people f'r music,' says Cassidy. 'I knowed wan that cud play th' "Wacht am Rhine" on a pair iv cymbals,' he says. 'Whisht!' says Donahue. 'Give th' girl a chanst.'

"Slavin tol' me about it. He says he niver heerd th' like in his born days. He says she fetched th' pianny two or three wallops that made Cassidy jump out iv his chair, an' Cassidy has charge iv th' steam whistle at th' quarry at that. She wint at it as though she had a gredge at it. First 'twas wan hand an' thin th' other, thin both hands, knuckles down; an' it looked, says Slavin, as if she was goin' to leap into th' middle iv it with both feet, whin Donahue jumps up. 'Hol' on!' he says. 'That's not a rented pianny, ye daft girl,' he says. 'Why, pap-pah,' says Molly, 'what d'ye mean?' she says. 'That's Wagner,' she says. ''Tis th' music iv th' future,' she says. 'Yes,' says Donahue, 'but I don't want me hell on earth. I can wait f'r it,' he says, 'with th' kind permission iv Mrs. Donahue,' he says. 'Play us th' "Wicklow Mountaineer,"' he says, 'an' threat th' masheen kindly,' he says. 'She'll play no "Wicklow Mountaineer,"' says Mrs. Donahue. 'If ye want to hear that kind iv chune, ye can go down to Finucane's Hall,' she says, 'an' call in Crowley, th' blind piper,' she says. 'Molly,' she says, 'give us wan iv thim Choochooski things,' she says. 'They're so ginteel.'

"With that Donahue rose up. 'Come on,' says he. 'This is no place f'r us,' he says. Slavin, with th' politeness iv a man who's gettin' even, turns at th' dure. 'I'm sorry I can't remain,' he says. 'I think th' wurruld an' all iv Choochooski,' he says. 'Me brother used to play his chunes,' he says,—'me brother Mike, that run th' grip ca-ar,' he says. 'But there's wan thing missin' fr'm Molly's playin',' he says. 'And what may that be?' says Mrs. Donahue. 'An ax,' says Slavin, backin' out.

"So Donahue has took to dhrink." (April 20, 1895)

12. The New Woman

Suffrage was one of many planks in the platform of the woman's movement of the nineties, whose overall aim was the emergence of a "New Woman." Molly Donahue joins up in this piece, which opens with another reference to Washington Hesing's German-language paper, the Illinois Staats-Zeitung.

"Well, what's new?" Mr. McKenna asked when he dropped into Mr. Dooley's little store Friday night.

"Dam little I get out iv th' pa-apers," said Mr. Dooley. "They's on'y wan iv thim now printin' good dimocratic news. That's th' Stazseitoong. I've been takin' it f'r two weeks, but I think I'll lave off. I don't like thim cracks iv Wash's about 'Inland' an' 'Ausland.'

But as f'r th' road, why glory be, we've had throuble an' excitement enough. Molly Donahue have up an' become a new woman!

"It's been a good thing f'r ol' man Donahue, though, Jawn. He shtud ivrything that mortal man cud stand. He seen her appearin' in th' road wearin' clothes that no lady shud wear an' ridin' a bicycle; he was humiliated whin she demanded to vote; he put his pride under his ar-rm an' ma-arched out iv th' house whin she committed assault-an'-batthry on th' piannah. But he's got to th' end iv th' rope now. He was in here las' night, how-come-ye-so, with his hat cocked over his eye an' a look iv risolution on his face; an' whin he left me, he says, says he, 'Dooley,' he says, 'I'll conquir, or I'll die,' he says.

"It's been comin' f'r months, but it on'y bust on Donahue las' week. He'd come home at night tired out, an' afther supper he was pullin' off his boots, whin Mollie an' th' mother begun talkin' about th' rights iv females. ''Tis th' era iv th' new woman,' says Mollie. 'Ye're right,' says th' mother. 'What d'ye mean be the new woman?' says Donahue, holdin' his boot in his hand. 'Th' new woman,' says Mollie, ''ll be free fr'm th' opprision iv man,' she says. 'She'll wurruk out her own way, without help or hinderance,' she says. 'She'll wear what clothes she wants,' she says, 'an' she'll be no man's slave,' she says. 'They'll be no such thing as givin' a girl in marredge to a clown an' makin' her dipindant on his whims,' she says. 'Th' women'll earn their own livin',' she says; 'an' mebbe,' she says, 'th' men'll stay at home an' dredge in th' house wurruk,' she says. 'A-ho,' says Donahue. 'An' that's th' new woman, is it?' he says. An' he said no more that night.

"But th' nex' mornin' Mrs. Donahue an' Mollie come to his dure. 'Get up,' says Mrs. Donahue, 'an' bring in some coal,' she says. 'Ye drowsy man, ye'll be late f'r ye'er wurruk.' 'Divvle th' bit iv coal I'll fetch,' says Donahue. 'Go away an' lave me alone,' he says. 'Ye're inthruptin' me dreams.' 'What ails ye, man alive?' says Mrs. Donahue. 'Get up.' 'Go away,' says Donahue, 'an' lave me slumber,' he says. 'Th' idee iv a couple iv big strong women like you makin' me wurruk f'r ye,' he says. 'Mollie 'll bring in th' coal,' he says. 'An' as f'r you, Honoria, ye'd best see what there is in th' cupboord an' put it in ye'er dinner-pail,' he says. 'I heerd th' first whistle blow a minyit ago,' he says; 'an' there's a pile iv slag at th' mills that has to be wheeled off befure th' sup'rintindint comes around,' he says. 'Ye know ye can't afford to lose ye'er job with me in this dilicate condition,' he says. 'I'm going to sleep now,' he says. 'An', Mollie, do ye bring me in a cup iv cocoa an' a pooched igg at tin,' he says. 'I ixpect me music-teacher about that time. We have to take a wallop out iv Wagner an' Bootoven befure noon.' 'Th' Lord save us fr'm harm,' says Mrs. Donahue. 'Th' man's clean crazy.' 'Divvle's th' bit,' says Donahue, wavin' his red flannel undhershirt in th' air. 'I'm the new man,' he says.

"Well, sir, Donahue said it flured thim complete. They didn't know what to say. Mollie was game, an' she fetched in th' coal; but Mrs. Donahue got nervous as eight o'clock come around. 'Ye're not goin' to stay in bed all day an' lose ye'er job,' she says. 'Th' 'ell with me job,' says Donahue. 'I'm not th' man to take wurruk whin they'se industhrees women with nawthin' to do,' he says. 'Show me th' pa-apers,' he says. 'I want to see where I can get an eighty-cint bonnet f'r two and a half.' He's that stubborn he'd 've stayed in bed all day, but th' good woman weakened. 'Come,' she says, 'don't be foolish,' she says. 'Ye wudden't have th' ol' woman wurrukin' in th' mills,' she says. ' 'Twas all a joke,' she says. 'Oh-ho, th' ol' woman!' he says. 'Th' ol' woman! Well, that's a horse iv another color,' he says. 'An' I don't mind tellin' ye th' mills is closed down to-day, Honoria.' So he dhressed himsilf an' wint out; an' says he to Mollie, he says: 'Miss Newwoman,' says he, 'ye may find wurruk enough around th' house,' he says. 'An' if ye have time, ye might paint th' stoop,' he says. 'Th' ol' man is goin' to take th' ol' woman down be Halsted Sthreet an' blow himsilf f'r a new shawl f'r her.'

"An' he's been that proud iv th' victhry that he's been a reg'lar customer f'r a week." (May 4, 1895)

13. The Woman's Bible

In May 1895 Mrs. Elizabeth Cady Stanton and the Sisterhood of
Advanced Women announced that they were preparing a new edition
of the Bible. A contemporary newspaper account stated that "the
Book of Genesis is now ready, and in it Eve is praised rather than
blamed for eating the apple. It is pointed out that Satan did not tempt
her with silks or satins, pearls or diamonds, but with the offer of
knowledge."

"Th' Lord save us fr'm harm," said Mr. Dooley. "Th' Lord save
us fr'm harm. Have ye seen what they're goin' to do downtown?
They're goin' to get up a new Bible."

"What's that? What's that?" Mr. McKenna demanded in great
excitement.

"'Tis thrue I'm tellin' ye. They're goin' to get up a new Bible
f'r women. A woman's Bible, d'ye mind, with annything in th' ol'
Bible that's considered be th' female bicycle club to be a knock f'r
women cut out."

"What good would that do them?" asked Mr. McKenna,
puzzled.

"What good 'd that do them? Why all th' good in th' wurruld.
Donahue's heerd of it iv coorse an' he's wurruked up over it. He
says they'll start out in th' beginnin' an' prove an alibi f'r Eve.
That's goin' back a long way, but Donahue says they lay it all to
th' beginnin', an' his daughter Molly she says that all th' throuble
come because Adam wint around fr'm pillar to post talkin' to polismen an' raypoorters an' tellin' thim that she put him up to
it. 'An' I'll admit,' Donahue says to me, 'I'll admit that they have
got th' worst iv it in th' Bible,' he says. 'Sure,' says I, 'th' Bible
is thrue,' I says. 'Ye'll not deny that, man?' I says. 'Glory be,' says
he. 'Th' Lord save us, no,' he says. 'What would ye make iv me,'
he says. 'A Jew man?' he says. 'Thin,' says I, ''tis thrue. Well,
thin,' I says, 'what's to be done about it?' I says. ''Tis th' statues
that keeps women fr'm comin' into their rights,' I says. 'An' ye
wouldn't find a Bible in th' legislachoor if ye'd stand thim on their

heads,' I says. 'Ye might find ma-arked cards, but ye'd find no Bible,' I says.

"''Tis thrue,' he says. 'Ye have that right,' he says. 'An' I told Molly so,' he says. 'I told her if she wanted annything done she'd best go an' see Billy O'Broyn, I said, for, says I, he's all right at Springfield, an', I says, if ye go into this thing, I says, Father Kelly'll get down on ye, I says. 'But,' says he, 'she wint on f'r to say that it was th' inflooence iv th' Bible. It seems that whin her brother Darcey asked her to go out to th' ball of the Young Man's Sodality, an' she refused, he ups an' quotes th' Bible to her. "Oh, woman, in our hours iv ease, uncertain eye an' ha-ard to get along with in th' house." An' she says that iverywhere women meet th' same roast, an' she's tired iv it. So her an' th' rist iv thim is goin' to rayform it. They are that. They're goin' to lave out annything that rayflicts on th' six. They'll attimpt to show that they was a combination again Eve iv th' snake an' her husband, an' fr'm that come all th' throuble. Iverybody afther that thought it was his jooty to roast, an' th' raysult is ye may search through fr'm ind to ind an' ye won't see wan word about woman suffrage. Iv coorse I know nawthin' about it, f'r whin I was a la-ad an' done me readin', th' Caddychism was good enough f'r me. We had a Bible, though. It fell on me wanst an' was like to break me neck. But we didn't read it. Still,' he says, 'I've no doubt there may be some thruth in what they say, an' if there is,' he says, 'though I'd not be th' first to say th' wurrud, it ought to be rayformed,' he says. 'But iver since it come up I've been dodgin' th' Good Man,' he says, 'an' I don't dare to go to me jooty till 'tis sittled wan way or th' other,' he says.

"That's where Donahue stands, an' I'm with him. I'd as lave as not believe Adam was to blame, though he's dead, poor soul, may he rest, per omnia, an' I'd be th' last to put in a wurrud again th' dead. I want ivry man to have a fair show, an' if fixin' th' Bible'll help thim to vote, thin I say fix it, may th' Lord forgive me. On'y I'll tell thim this, that I've lived in Bridgeport f'r forty years backed be th' Bible an' second papers signed be Judge Kercheval an' a pull at th' polis station, an' I've niver had me vote counted but th' wanst an' that was whin I was captain iv me precint an' a power in th' wa-ard. That's right, Jawn."

"Are they going to have the new woman I hear tell of in that?" Mr. McKenna asked.

"Jawn," said Mr. Dooley severely, "this ain't goin' to be an almanac. It's a Bible I've been tellin' ye about." (May 18, 1895)

14. Molly's Home Vaudeville Show

"They'se another scandal in th' Donahue family," said Mr. Dooley.

"What about?" asked Mr. McKenna, eagerly.

"Molly give a vowdyvill," replied Mr. Dooley.

"A what?"

"A-a vowdyvill."

"What?"

"I tol' ye twict she give a v'riety show," said Mr. Dooley angrily. "Now d'ye know? She's been th' leader iv society so long in th' sixth wa-ard that she was not to be downed be th' Hogans. They give a progressive spoil-five par-rty an' she med up her mind she'd toss thim over th' gashouse—socially, I mane—be havin' a v'riety show. An' she done it. Wait till I get th' Bridgepoort Tin Thousand. Where'd I lave it? Ah! Here it is! Among those prisint was, let's see—Missers an' Misdams Flaherty, Dorsey, Shwartzmeister, Cassidy, Pug Sheehan, Cohen iv Blue Island; Misdams O'Rourke, Danehy; Misses Donahue, Clancy, Flaherty, M. Flaherty, B. Flaherty, J. Flaherty, C. Flaherty, K. Flaherty, O'Donnell, Sheehan, an' Missers Dorsey, Hogan—th' big slob, he come with a kag iv nails aboord—Gallagher, Shaughnessy, an' Dooley. That was me, Jawn. They put me in last, but I was there first—a good head befure Father Kelly.

"Molly Donahue was beamin' an' brimmin' over with wilcome. She met th' people at th' dure an' says she: 'Come in,' she says, 'I'm glad to see ye,' says she, takin' each man iv us be th' hook. I luked around f'r Donahue an' found him settin' out before th' kitchen stove, with his toes turned in an' his elbows on his knees, smokin' a pipe. He ducked whin th' dure opened, but seein' it was me he put the pipe back in his mouth an' says he: 'This is 'ell,' he says. 'I haven't had a shmoke th' livelong night an' I et me supper on th' back stoop,' he says. 'Is there manny in there?' he says. 'Tin,' says I. 'Glory be,' says he, 'an' more comin'? Ye don't mind,' he says, 'if I loosen up me boots,' he says. 'I haven't had thim off th' livelong day,' he says. 'An',' he says, tuggin' at th' nick iv him, 'this here collar's chokin' me be degrees,' he says. 'I feel as though I had th' croup,' he says. 'I'm tired out,' he says, 'but be dad, we've got to throw th' Hogans. They wurked f'r me father on th' ol' sod an' I'd be th' poor stick iv a man f'r to let thim put th' comether over Molly,' he says. 'Not,' he says, 'while I've got a cint in me pocket,' he says.

"I lift him there, Jawn, an' wint in where Sarsfield Dorsey was playin' on th' pianny befure th' dure ladin' into th' settin' room. Th' settin' room was th' stage an' th' dinin' room was f'r th' audjeence. Wan iv th' Immitt la-ads come out an' give us a song an' dance. 'I met her,' says th' lad, 'while sthrollin' be th' brook, an',' says he, ''twas in th' month iv June,' he says; 'th' hivinly stars was overhead,' he says, 'an' silver was th' moon.' Thin he done a step I'd see him practice on th' cor-rner with th' other lads playin' mouth organs f'r him. Miss Molly Donahue sung a song an' Gallagher sung another. Gallagher, ye know him, he spinds most iv his days an' nights hangin' around th' stage dure iv th' Lyceem, an' they say he does be intindin' f'r to be a play acthor himsilf wan iv these days. He was th' stage manager, an' whin he'd got through tellin' us that they was on'y wan gurl in th' wur-ruld f'r him, he come out on th' stage an' says he: 'Ladies an' gintlemin,' says he, 'I have to announce that we have secured th' services iv the distinguished soubrette Mademizelle Goolah Turee, iv th' Halsted Sthreet Opera House,' he says, 'who will kindly oblige us with a skirt dance if me frind Mr. Hogan'll oblige us be closin' his face,' he says. 'Ladies an' gintlemin, let me inthrojooce Mademizelle Goolah Turee,' he says.

"With that out thripped a heifer, Jawn, that ye niver see th' likes of. I'll not tell ye what she had on, though I cud without detainin' ye. She was pretty, I'll say that, with an eye in her head that'd coax a hedge priest, an' th' rosiest cheeks I iver see out iv a book. But th' carryin's on iv her. She give me a wink that sint th' blood to me ears, an' she threw a kick at th' good man an' I seen him make th' sign an' turn pale an' squirm down in his seat. What she done next I won't say. I didn't see all iv it, f'r I was lukin' through me fingers, but jist as she turned a back somerset Mrs. Flaherty rose up. 'Mike,' she says. 'Don't bother me,' says Flaherty, who was crouched down like a man startin' f'r a hundherd ya-ard dash, with his hands clutchin' th' ar-rms iv th' chair. 'Don't ye see I'm busy.' 'Michael,' says she, 'come with me. Childher,' she says, 'this is no place f'r us.' An' out they wint, Flaherty lukin' back till th' dure closed on him.

"At that moment Donahue come down th' stage, with wan shoe an' his collar in his hand. He had his big hand on Mademizelle Goolah Turee's showlder an' says he: 'Woman, lave me house,' he says. 'Go,' he says, 'an' sin no more,' he says. 'As f'r th' rist iv ye,' he says, 'if ye think th' house iv Donahue is th' Lyceem or th' dime museem ye've made th' mistake iv ye'er life,' he says. 'If ye're not all out on th' sthreet within th' minyit Monseer Terence Donahue'll give ye an imitation iv a poor, tired assistant night foreman at th' mills inthrojoocin' a novelty in society be clanin' out his guests with th' leg iv a stove.' An' we lift, all but th' good man, an' he stayed f'r to comfort th' fam'ly."

"Have you seen Donahue since?" asked Mr. McKenna.

"Yis," said Mr. Dooley. "He come in las' night to talk it over. He says: 'I'm havin' no more variety at th' house,' he says. 'How's that?' says I. 'I'm runnin' things me own way this week,' he says, 'an' th' social season's closed f'r repair,' he says." (February 22, 1896)

15. The Dennehy Boy Back from Notre Dame

"There's wan thing with all me faults I niver done," said Mr. Dooley.

"And what's that?" asked Mr. McKenna.

"I niver r-rode a bicycle," replied the philosopher. "I've been a rough man in me day an' I seen th' wurruld an' got me skates upon me, an' whin I was a la-ad manny's th' timptation I let come between me an' me jooty, but so help me hivins, Jawn, I niver done nothin' th' like iv that. An' I'll say this here f'r Bridgeport, that takin' it all an' all fr'm th' slip to Brighton I niver seen a bicycle here but th' wan, an' that wan, praise be to th' saints, is over in Mathias Dennehy's woodshed this blissed moment waitin' f'r Marcella Dennehy, who have an injaynious mind, f'r to schame some way iv makin' ayether a bustle or a coal-scuttle out iv it.

"'Twas young Sarsfield Dennehy ownded it. He come back fr'm Nother Da-ame Collidge las' summer with his head so full iv quare notions that his poor ol' man, as simple a soul, Jawn, d'ye mind, as iver put a pick on his showlder, was afraid to open his mouth f'r fear he'd say something that'd affind th' dam jood. He got Dennehy that there scared, d'ye mind, that he wore his shoes afther supper an' had to r-roll th' growler f'r a pint in a handbag. He'd larned to ride a bicycle—th' la-ad had—an' all winter he's been tellin' me he was gawn to get a wheel. 'Ye'd betther be gettin' a wheelbarrow,' I says. ''Tis more in th' line iv yer fam'ly,' I says. They're not much, Jawn. Not a priest belongin' to thim.

"Well, sir, last Mundah avnin' th' fam'ly was settin' out on th' front stoop, Mrs. Dennehy in her Sundah shawl an' th' ol' man tortured in a coat an' th' brogans he'd wore all day an' glarin' acrost th' sthreet at Mat Dorney, who'd come out iv th' saloon like th' mane divvle he is wipin' his lips f'r to tantalize Dennehy— they was settin' there whin up driv an expriss wagon an' th' driver hauls out a bicycle. 'Glory be to Gawd, who's that f'r?' says Dennehy. ''Tis me new wheel,' says th' la-ad. 'Ye'er not a gawn to r-ride it,' says th' ol' man. 'I am that,' says th' la-ad. 'I am that,' he says. An' up he gets on it an' goes hell bent down th' road. Well, sir, there was th' divvle's own excitement. Th' people all come to the windows f'r to see th' bicycle, an' all th' little lads goes lammin' after it an' cheerin'. Th' wimmen come out wipin' th' dish wather off their hands on their aprons, an' th' young girls stood on th' sidewalk an' giggled. Ol' Desmond, the shoemaker that ain't been east iv Halsted street since some wan tol' him he was dhrafted f'r th' war, seen th' bicycle comin' an' ducked in his shop an' closed th' dure.

"Well, sir, th' la-ad gaws up an' down th' road till th' polis had to turn out f'r to kape th' sidewalk clear. In the manetime ol' Dennehy had ducked acrost to the Dutchman's an' h'isted in a tub 'r two, an' whin he wint out he was walkin' wide an' mutterin' to himsilf. Th' la-ad was through his r-ride, an' was standin' tellin' th' crowd about th' bicycle. 'Ye can't ride it,' says Dorney to th' ol' man. 'By dad,' says Dennehy, 'I cud,' he says, 'if I wanted to.' 'I dahr ye to,' says Dorney. 'I'll take naw dahr,' says Dennehy, 'fr'm any Roscommon hor-rse thief,' he says. 'Give me that there masheen,' he says. Well, sir, he makes a r-runnin' jump at it, an' by gar he goes dam well f'r about a r-rod till he turns to give Dorney th' laugh, whin bang he goes again a path-rol box an' falls like as if he was dhropped fr'm th' top iv th' shot-tower.

"Thin, what d'ye think he does? Oh, 'twas th' Irish iv him. He r-runs into th' cellar an' comes out with th' ax an' goes at th' bicycle like a man choppin' wood. They had th' 'ell's own time with him, an' whin he got through th' bicycle looked like a burrud cage that'd been r-run over be a dhray. Th' next night I seen him settin' on th' stoop with his coat an' shoes off dhrinkin' his beer out iv—what d'ye suppose? Out iv a sprinklin' pot, no less." (May 19, 1894)

16. College Football and Dissension in Bridgeport

Harlow N. Higinbotham and Lyman J. Gage were prominent Chicago financiers. Their luncheon date with Bridgeport's king-making politician William Joyce is unlikely.

"I've got to close up early to-night," said Mr. Dooley. "I'm gawn down to th' polis station f'r to bail out Grogan. They sint f'r me cousin, Judge Dooley, th' lord chafe justice iv th' high court iv Halsted street, but he was takin' tay with Ha-arlow Inn Higinbotham an' Loyman Jay Gage an' Willum Joyce at th' Ritchaloo Hot-el, d'ye mind, an' he sint back wurrud that he was not to be disturbed till tin o'clock."

"What's the matter with Grogan?" asked Mr. McKenna. "Drunk again?"

"Faith, no; they have him put away in th' booby hatch f'r assault with intint to dhrive a pickax into Sarsfield Casey's back. Didn't ye hear th' throuble, Jawn? Dear, oh dear, th' whole r-road is talkin' about it. Ye see 'twas this here way: Sarsfield Casey is captain iv th' football team iv th' Saint Aloysius society iv th' church iv th' Immaculate Conciption, an' Grogan's boy, Hugh O'Neill Grogan, he's captain iv th' football team iv our church. 'Twas Casey invinted th' game in Archey r-road. He was th' main finger iv th' team iv Nothre Da-ame an' whin he come back his hair was that long ye cud lose a sthreet ca-ar in it. Befure he'd been back a week he had half th' la-ads iv Bridgeport playin' football or givin' what th' likes iv him calls a 'college yell.' Wan night big Shaughnessy, ye know th' wan I mane, the bum iv that name, he come into me place por-lyzed and screamin', ' 'rah, 'rah, 'rah, Pontiac.' 'What's atin' ye?' says I. 'What ails ye, man alive?' I says. 'I'm givin' me college yell,' he says. 'I done five years in Pontiac,' he says. 'Whin I was a kid,' he says, 'f'r stealin' a ham,' he says.

"Well, sir, th' first we knowed there was a match game between th' Immaculate Conciption an' Fa-ather Kelly's church wist iv th' bridge. Th' la-ads practiced on th' prairies an' half th' ward's been limpin' about with bandages over their eyes. Th' ol' people thought th' la-ads 'd on'y been fightin' among thimsilves an' paid no attintion to it an' ivry father iv thim tur-rned out to th' game up be th' rollin' mills Thanksgivin' day. 'Tis a prowtestant holiday, annyhow. I didn't go, Jawn, avick. I seen wan game, Jawn, an' I give ye me wurrud whin I feel th' desire to see football I goes out an' makes a call on me nivview Malachi, who's chief sticker f'r Armour and wan iv his most thrusted imployaze. He is that.

"But Grogan wint. He ma-arched out ear-rly with his long coat on his back an' his shtovepipe hat tipped over on wan side iv his head, ma-arkin' time with his feet whin he walked—a Clare man fr'm th' crown to th' sole. He had a front seat an' he cheered like th' divvle, they tell me. Well, th' game began, an' th' first thing Grogan see was Casey reachin' over an' givin' Hugh O'Neill a poke in th' eye. 'Oh, ye thafe,' he says, lanin' over th' r-ropes, 'I'll have th' law on ye,' he says. 'Smash him, Hughey,' he says. 'Ain't ye goin' to smash him, ye disgrace to ye'er family?' 'Set down,' says th' audjence. 'Set down,' they says, 'ye'er interruptin' th' game.' At th' moment there was a r-rush an' Hugh come r-runnin' down th' field with th' ball under his ar-rm an' young Casey runnin' afther him. 'Stand ye'er groun',' yells Grogan. 'Stand ye'er groun',' he says. 'Ar-re ye to be th' first iv th' Grogans to r-run,' he says, 'fr'm a r-red-headed May-o man?' he says. 'Oh me, oh my, what'll I tell his poor mother?' Thin whin Casey grabbed his lad be th' legs an' thrun him like a steer an' all th' rist iv th' la-ads jumped on him, Grogan called: 'Polis! Is there no polisman here will privint murder. Officer Hinnissy,' he says, 'if ye don't save me boy fr'm bein' kilt I'll have ye'er star.'

"Well, they hauled him back an' he wint away. Th' game continued an' just whin our church was whackin' th' divvle out iv th' Immaculates, down th' field come Grogan with his whiskers flyin' in th' air an' a pickax in his hands. He made straight f'r Casey an' 'twud've been all th' la-ad's life was worth if he'd reached him. It took two polismen to hold him till th' hurry-up wagon come."

"I don't suppose they'll prosecute," ventured Mr. McKenna.

"Naw," said Mr. Dooley. "But that ain't th' worst. Father Kelly is mad through. He says he'll excommunicate Grogan. He broke up th' game befure his la-ads could scoor again the Immaculates, an' since thin Father Gallagher have put on such airs that no priest in th' diocese can talk to him." (December 1, 1894.)

17. The Idle Apprentice

On October 11, 1895, Henry "Butch" Lyons, a twenty-seven-year-old Chicagoan of Irish descent, was hanged at the county jail for a murder committed during a robbery attempt the previous February. The crowd around the jail was reported to be the largest since the execution of the Haymarket anarchists in 1887. A Times-Herald *editorial claimed that Lyons, the son of "a drunkard" and "a poverty-stricken working woman," was first sent to the bridewell (city jail) at the age of nine, and that his subsequent criminal career included two hundred arrests, twenty-one terms in the bridewell, and one term in the state penitentiary. The editorial concluded with the question, "Did he have a fair chance?" The day after the hanging, this Dooley piece appeared.*

"They scragged a man to-day," said Mr. Dooley.

"They did so," said Mr. McKenna.

"Did he die game?"

"They say he did."

"Well, he did," said Mr. Dooley. "I read it all in th' pa-apers. He died as game as if he was wan iv th' Christyan martyrs instead iv a thief that'd hit his man wan crack too much. Saint or murdherer, 'tis little difference whin death comes up face front.

"I read th' story iv this man through, Jawn; an', barrin' th' hangin', 'tis th' story iv tin thousan' like him. D'ye raymimber th' Carey kid? Ye do. Well, I knowed his grandfather; an' a dacinter ol' man niver wint to his jooty wanst a month. Whin he come over to live down be th' slip, 'twas as good a place as iver ye see. Th' honest men an' honest women wint an' come as they pleased, an' laid hands on no wan. His boy Jim was as straight as th' r-roads in

Kildare, but he took to dhrink; an', whin Jack Carey was born, he was a thramp on th' sthreets an' th' good woman was wurrukin' down-town, scrubbin' away at th' flures in th' city hall, where Dennehy got her.

"Be that time around th' slip was rough-an'-tumble. It was dhrink an' fight ivry night an' all day Sundah. Th' little la-ads come together under sidewalks, an' rushed th' can over to Burke's on th' corner an' listened to what th' big lads tol' thim. Th' first instruction that Jack Carey had was how to take a man's pocket handkerchief without his feelin' it, an' th' nex' he had was larnin' how to get over th' fence iv th' Reform School at Halsted Sthreet in his stockin' feet.

"He was a thief at tin year, an' th' polis'd run f'r him if he'd showed his head. At twelve they sint him to th' bridewell f'r breakin' into a freight car. He come out, up to anny game. I see him whin he was a lad hardly to me waist stand on th' roof iv Finucane's Hall an' throw bricks at th' polisman.

"He hated th' polis, an' good reason he had f'r it. They pulled him out iv bed be night to search him. If he turned a corner, they ran him f'r blocks down th' sthreet. Whin he got older, they begun shootin' at him th' minyit they see him; an' it wasn't manny years befure he begun to shoot back. He was right enough whin he was in here. I cud conthrol him. But manny th' night whin he had his full iv liquor I've see him go out with his gun in his out-side pocket; an' thin I'd hear shot after shot down th' sthreet, an' I'd know him an' his ol' inimy Clancy 'd met an' was exchangin' compliments. He put wan man on th' polis pension fund with a bullet through his thigh.

"They got him afther a while. He'd kept undher cover f'r months, livin' in freight cars an' hidin' undher viadocks with th' pistol in his hand. Wan night he come out, an' broke into Schwartzmeister's place. He sneaked through th' alley with th' German man's damper in his arms, an' Clancy leaped on him fr'm th' fence. Th' kid was tough, but Clancy played fut-ball with th' Finerty's on Sundah, an' was tougher; an', whin th' men on th' other beats come up, Carey was hammered so they had to carry him to th' station an' nurse him f'r trile.

"He wint over th' road, an' come back gray an' stooped. I was afraid iv th' boy with his black eyes; an' wan night he see me watchin' him, an' he says: 'Ye needn't be afraid,' he says. 'I won't hurt ye. Ye're not Clancy,' he says.

"I tol' Clancy about it, but he was a brave man; an' says he: ''Tis wan an' wan, an' a thief again an' honest man. If he gets me, he must get me quick.' Th' nex' night about dusk he come saunterin' up th' sthreet, swingin' his club an' jokin' with his frind, whin some wan shouted, 'Look out, Clancy.' He was not quick enough. He died face forward, with his hands on his belt; an' befure all th' wurruld Jack Carey come across th' sthreet, an' put another ball in his head.

"They got him within twinty yards iv me store. He was down in th' shadow iv th' house, an' they was shootin' at him fr'm roofs an' behind barns. Whin he see it was all up, he come out with his eyes closed, firin' straight ahead; an' they filled him so full iv lead he broke th' hub iv th' pathrol wagon takin' him to th' morgue."

"It served him right," said Mr. McKenna.

"Who?" said Mr. Dooley. "Carey or Clancy?" (October 12, 1895)

18. On Criminals: Petey Scanlan

Like Jack Carey, the young Irish-American in this piece is related to a real Chicago criminal—one Daniel Carroll. A Times-Herald *editorial a week after his arrest for murder claimed that "from his earliest childhood he has lived a hunted life, like the dogs and cats of the alleys. When he committed some petty offense he was sent to the bridewell, and when released was watched as a suspect. The wonder is that he ever tried to earn an honest living." This Dooley piece appeared a day or two after Carroll's arrest. It may have been the most popular of Dunne's pieces in Chicago in the nineties; one Catholic priest used it as the text for a yearly sermon, and Studs Lonigan's father recalled it in the front-porch revery near the beginning of James T. Farrell's trilogy.*

"Lord bless my sowl," said Mr. Dooley, "childher is a gr-reat risponsibility,—a gr-reat risponsibility. Whin I think iv it, I praise th' saints I niver was married, though I had opporchunities enough whin I was a young man; an' even now I have to wear me hat low whin I go down be Cologne Sthreet on account iv th' Widow Grogan. Jawn, that woman'll take me dead or alive. I wake up in a col' chill in th' middle iv th' night, dhreamin' iv her havin' me in her clutches.

"But that's not here or there, avick. I was r-readin' in th' pa-apers iv a lad be th' name iv Scanlan bein' sint down th' short r-road f'r near a lifetime; an' I minded th' first time I iver see him,—a bit iv a curly-haired boy that played tag around me place, an' 'd sing 'Blest Saint Joseph' with a smile on his face like an angel's. Who'll tell what makes wan man a thief an' another man a saint? I dinnaw. This here boy's father wurrked f'r'm morn till night in th' mills, was at early mass Sundah mornin' befure th' alkalis lit th' candles, an' niver knowed a month whin he failed his jooty. An' his mother was a sweet-faced little woman, though f'r'm th' County Kerry, that nursed th' sick an' waked th' dead, an' niver had a hard thought in her simple mind f'r anny iv Gawd's creatures. Poor sowl, she's dead now. May she rest in peace!

"He didn't git th' shtreak fr'm his father or fr'm his mother. His brothers an' sisters was as fine a lot as iver lived. But this la-ad Petey Scanlan growed up fr'm bein' a curly-haired angel f'r to be th' toughest villyun in th' r-road. What was it at all, at all? Sometimes I think they'se poison in th' life iv a big city. Th' flowers won't grow here no more thin they wud in a tannery, an' th' bur-rds have no song; an' th' childher iv dacint men an' women come up hard in th' mouth an' with their hands raised again their kind.

"Th' la-ad was th' scoorge iv th' polis. He was as quick as a cat an' as fierce as a tiger, an' I well raymimber him havin' laid out big

Kelly that used to thravel this post,—'Whistlin'' Kelly that kep' us awake with imitations iv a mockin' bur-rd,—I well raymimber him scuttlin' up th' alley with a score iv polismin laborin' afther him, thryin' f'r a shot at him as he wint around th' bar-rns or un-dher th' thrucks. He slep' in th' coal-sheds afther that until th' poor ol' man cud square it with th' loot. But, whin he come out, ye cud see how his face had hardened an' his ways changed. He was as silent as an animal, with a sideways manner that watched ivrything. Right here in this place I seen him stand f'r a quarther iv an hour, not seemin' to hear a dhrunk man abusin' him, an' thin lep out like a snake. We had to pry him loose.

"Th' ol' folks done th' best they cud with him. They hauled him out iv station an' jail an' bridewell. Wanst in a long while they'd dhrag him off to church with his head down: that was al-ways afther he'd been sloughed up f'r wan thing or another. Be-tween times th' polis give him his own side iv th' sthreet, an' on'y took him whin his back was tur-rned. Thin he'd go in the wagon with a mountain iv thim on top iv him, swayin' an' swearin' an' sthrikin' each other in their hurry to put him to sleep with their clubs.

"I mind well th' time he was first took to be settled f'r good. I heerd a noise in th' ya-ard, an' thin he come through th' place with his face dead gray an' his lips just a turn grayer. 'Where ar-re ye goin', Petey?' says I. 'I was jus' takin' a short cut home,' he says. In three minyits th' r-road was full iv polismin. They'd been a robbery down in Halsted Sthreet. A man that had a grocery sthore was stuck up, an' whin he fought was clubbed near to death; an' they'd r-run Scanlan through th' alleys to his father's house. That was as far as they'd go. They was enough iv thim to've kicked down th' little cottage with their heavy boots, but they knew he was standin' behind th' dure with th' big gun in his hand; an', though they was manny a good lad there, they was none that cared f'r that short odds.

"They talked an' palavered outside, an' telephoned th' chief iv polis, an' more pathrol wagons come up. Some was f'r settin' fire to th' buildin', but no wan moved ahead. Thin th' fr-ront dure opened, an' who shud come out but th' little mother. She was thin an' pale, an' she had her apron in her hands, pluckin' at it. 'Gintle-min,' she says, 'what is it ye want iv me?' she says. 'Liftinant Cas-sidy,' she says, ''tis sthrange f'r ye that I've knowed so long to make scandal iv me befure me neighbors,' she says. 'Mrs. Scan-lan,' says he, 'we want th' boy. I'm sorry, ma'am, but he's mixed up in a bad scrape, an' we must have him,' he says. She made a curtsy to thim, an' wint indures. 'Twas less than a minyit befure she come out, clingin' to th' la-ad's ar-rm. 'He'll go,' she says. 'Thanks be, though he's wild, they'se no crime on his head. Is there, dear?' 'No,' says he, like th' game kid he is. Wan iv th' po-lismin stharted to take hold iv him, but th' la-ad pushed him back; an' he wint to th' wagon on his mother's ar-rm."

"And was he really innocent?" Mr. McKenna asked.

"No," said Mr. Dooley. "But she niver knowed it. Th' ol' man come home an' found her: she was settin' in a big chair with her apron in her hands an' th' picture iv th' la-ad th' day he made his first c'munion in her lap." (June 13, 1896)

Chapter Four
Bridgeport as a Culture of Poverty

Perhaps the greatest force for the dissolution of the Bridgeport community in the nineties was poverty, which hung over the neighborhood like a fixed black cloud all through the decade. In Chicago, the national economic depression of 1893–1898 was aggravated by an exploding immigrant population, labor unrest, and bitter-cold winters. At the same time, the living and working conditions of poor people there were becoming more visible because of the settlement movement, ushered into the city with the opening of Hull-House in 1889. The very first Dooley piece appeared in the Evening Post *at the onset of the "Black Winter" of 1893–1894, when the panic that the rest of the country had begun to feel the previous summer caught up to Chicago in the wake of the temporary prosperity brought by the World's Fair. And times were still hard when Dunne turned his commentary from local to national affairs at the outbreak of the Spanish-American War of 1898. During the intervening years, the suffering of Bridgeport's poor was one of Mr. Dooley's most frequent subjects of conversation. And he faced the issue, not with the detachment of a social scientist or political reformer, but with the mingled anger, frustration, compassion, and bewilderment of a member of the afflicted culture. The result is a chunk of living social history available nowhere else in American writing.*

An important theme of many pieces is the difference between heartless, humiliating organized relief and personal charity, dispensed with consideration for the recipients' pride. Out-of-work laborer Callaghan tells the St. Vincent de Paul Society to "take ye'er charity . . . an' shove it down ye'er throats," in the first piece of this chapter. Also, Mrs. Hagan, the wife of a blacklisted railroad worker, drives the Ladies' Aid Society from her door, while her husband keeps the family together with a series of back-breaking odd jobs until he is re-instated (2). On the other hand, Mr. Dooley, himself, provides an example of the tactful practice of personal charity when the little Grady girl comes into his saloon in a snow storm to fetch beer for her alcoholic father (3). Moreover, on other occasions, John McKenna finds his friend taking care of a baby in the back room and buying Christmas presents for a mother and children who have just been deserted (4, 5).

Several pieces underscore the contrast, at its most obvious in American cities in the nineties, between the lives of the rich and the poor. Mrs. Mulligan takes her sick baby to the lake for a change of air, but is refused passage through the Illinois Central Railroad's toll fence (6). While discussing the institution of marriage, Mr. Dooley generalizes that "people that can't afford it always have marrid an' always will. 'Tis on'y th' rich that don't" (7). Noticing different styles at the funerals of wealthy "Gran'pah Grogan" and a poor "Connock man up back iv th' dumps" leads Dooley to a meditation on the effects of price fixing by the Beef Trust on the Connock man's children (8).

Two extreme confrontations between poverty and power in Chicago led to extended responses by Dunne through Mr. Dooley. The first was the famous Chicago railway strike of 1894, which spread from a local protest by workers in the employ of George Pullman's Palace Car Company to a nationwide boycott by tens of thousands of railroad workers. Dunne dealt with this strike several times in the summer of 1894. In one piece, Mr. Dooley describes a humorous family quarrel between a labor agitator and his national-guardsman son, who has been called out against his father (10). But the issue is also treated seriously, in two pieces where Mr. Dooley strongly criticizes the callous irresponsibility of Pullman, himself (9, 11). In fact, the climactic piece contains an analogy between the Chicago area during the strike and Ireland in the famine years.

The second Dooley series on poverty was written in the winter of 1896–1897, the fourth of hard times in a row, and the worst. As unemployment increased, the temperature plummeted, and the city's relief bureaucracy foundered in red tape. Dunne responded with his

*most tragic Dooley pieces. The Galway woman, Mother Clancy,
holds out proudly against the shame of going on welfare until it is too
late, and the man sent to investigate her case meets the priest and the
undertaker at her door (12). Banks fail through dishonest deals,
sending people whose savings are gone to the icebox for a suicidal
"light lunch of paris green" (13). A starving Pole named Sobieski is
shot to death by a watchman for picking up bits of coal along the
tracks (14). And Clancy the Infidel, a notorious Bridgeport atheist,
is saved from starvation only through an ironic personal sacrifice by
Father Kelly (15). The series concludes with two Dooley commen-
taries on the unconscionably extravagant masked ball given in February 1897 by the Bradley-Martins of New York. One of these is
printed in Chapter One; the second, written after the ball, is here (16).*

*All told, this group of vignettes constitutes a moving testament of
concern for the urban poor, as well as our only firsthand record of a
crisis potentially as destructive to the Chicago Irish community as
the famine had been to the peasants of Ireland.*

1. Poverty and Pride in the Callaghan Family

*The St. Vincent de Paul Society is an important Catholic chari-
table organization. The Chicago chapter was founded in 1857 by
Peter Dunne's uncle, the Reverend Dennis Dunne, of St. Patrick's
Church.*

"Have you seen Callaghan to-day?" asked Mr. McKenna.

"No," said Mr. Dooley.

"It's too bad about him," said Mr. McKenna.

"It is that, it is that. Th' poor man. Th' hear-rt iv me is gray
with thinkin' iv him over there alone. D'ye know, Jawn, I was th'
last to see him whin he wint away an' th' first whin he come back.
'Twas early last summer he left. They'd had th' divvle's own
winter an' spring iv it—Callaghan out iv wurruk an' th' good
woman down with pnoomony iv th' lungs an' ne'er a dollar in th'
house but what he picked up wanst in a while doin' odd jobs

around. An' him as proud as a pr-rince an' patient as a nun! I mind whin th' Saint Vincent de Pauls wint out f'r to investigate his case. Well, Jawn, ye know what th' Irish is whin they have money. Head and tail up. Give me thim that haven't enough to ate iv their own to help their neighbors. I've seen th' stirabout divided whin th' eyes iv th' childher was poppin' out iv their heads. Well, the chairman iv th' comity that wint to investigate Callaghan's case was old Peter Coogan—an' ye know him—big hear-rt enough but desp'rate r-rough. Mrs. Callaghan was up whin they called an' 'twas 'me good woman this' an' 'me good woman that' an' 'th' mimbers is always r-ready f'r to help th' desarvin' poor.' Con Hogan who was in th' comity tol' me Mrs. Callaghan answered niver a wur-rud, but th' tears come to her big, gray eyes an' she held on to th' table. Coogan's father was wan iv her fa-ather's farmhands in Roscommon, d'ye mind.

"That night th' Saint Vincent de Pauls met in th' basemint iv th' church an' just as th' meetin' begun Callaghan stamped in, big an' fierce. 'Gintlemen,' says he, 'I've been given to undherstand,' he says, 'that some iv ye,' he says, 'has been around to me house,' he says, 'offerin' charity on th' tips iv ye'er muddy boots to me sick woman,' he says. 'Now,' says he, 'I'm no ora-thor,' he says, 'an' I'm f'r peace,' he says, 'but if anny iv ye is minded f'r to offer charity to me wife,' he says, 'I wisht ye'd let me know first,' he says, 'so that I can take ye'er charity,' he says, 'an' shove it down ye'er throats,' he says. 'An' that manes you, Coogan!' With that he thramped out an' no more charity was offered to Mrs. Callaghan.

"Whin summer come he got a job in Kansas an' he come to see me befure he wint away. Be nature he was a light-hear-rted man an' this night ye cud hardly hold him f'r pure joy. Be this an' be that he was goin' to make his fortune an' live like th' gintleman th' husband iv Nora Deane sh'd be—him tur-rned iv fifty an' goin' out to Topeka at wan-sivinty-five a day! I seen him off on th' thrain. I heerd he was doin' well an' th' good woman took a pew in th' church, though she'd been kneeling in the dhraft fr'm th' dure manny's th' Sundah. 'Twas th' sicond wan fr'm Doheny's near th' confissional. That's it, that's it. Th' wan McCarthy, th' plumber, rinted. I niver knowed she was in a bad way till two weeks ago Sundah whin she missed mass. Thin little Mrs. Doherty tol' me she'd found her in bed singin' th' vispers to herself.

"Thursdah night I was walkin' down th' r-road whin who should I meet but Callaghan, walkin' with his chin on his chest, an' white as a sheeted cor-rpse. I called to him but he made no answer. He walked wist a block or two an' thin come back at a tearin' gait an' wint acrost th' street. I niver guessed what ailed him till I looked an' seen that th' fr-ront windows iv th' house was wide open though th' night was could. An' as he opened th' dure I heerd th' keening. 'Tis a har-rd, har-rd wurruld." (November 24, 1894.)

2. A Blacklisted Worker Refuses Relief

The "Apeea's" mentioned here were the members of the American Protective Association, the most prominent anti-Catholic, anti-Irish nativist organization around the turn of the century.

"Th' minyit Thanksgivin' Day's over," said Mr. Dooley, "'tis forgotten; lasteways ye begin thinkin' iv th' next wan. They'se no day afther with us. Sure, th' min that made it must've been Apeea's, f'r puttin' it on a Thursdah. To fall fr'm turkey with crambry sauce to codfish is enough to kill th' faith of anny Christyan. 'Tis so; I always count th' day inded whin Hinnissy takes th' leg. All day long that man was dhrivin' away at th' bur-rd on th' table. He had th' first cut iv th' brist at noon an' at 8 o'clock th' pope's nose fell to him. He took th' las' leg at iliven o'clock in th' night and thin, says he, 'Thanks be,' he says, 'they'se no more turkey.' 'Thanks be,' says I f'r th' turkey, 'they'se no more Hinnissy,' I says. 'Ye've lift enough iv it,' I says, 'to answer to th' thrumpet on th' last day,' I says.

"Well, Jawn, they'se wor-rse things to be thankful f'r thin havin' nothin' more to eat. D'ye know th' Hagans, down be Main sthreet? Ye do, iv coorse. Well, d'ye know that there Macchew

Hagan has been out iv steady wurruk f'r near a year? A proud, black man, Hagan. A Kilkenny man, his father was a school masther near where Dan'l O'Connell come fr'm, but Macchew left away young and wint to wurruk on a railroad.

"I dinnaw how he come to lose his job. Faith, I niver knew he'd lost it till las' week. Th' childher was jus' as clane. Th' good woman wint to her jooties jus' th' same. An' whin ye met Hagan 'twas always: 'Macchew, how d'ye do?' 'Plaze Gawd, well, thank ye.' ''Tis a fine day intirely.' ''Tis so, plaze Gawd.'

"He'd niver let on. But f'r days an' days, Jawn, he thramped th' sthreets—out early, out late. Hinnissy says he's seen him comin' home in th' dark, staggerin' like a dhrunken man an' with his gray face down in his chist. But whin Hinnissy said: 'Good avinin', Misther Hagan; 'tis fine weather we're havin',' he'd come back with a smile on his white lips. 'Fine weather, plaze Gawd,' he'd say. 'Ye'er home late?' 'Ah-h, sure,' says he, 'I like th' walk,' he says. ''Tis gran' to be out loosenin' me ol' bones such a night as th' like.'

"Well, Jawn, d'ye know th' man'd been downtown walkin' fr'm house to house, carryin' coal an' poundin' with a hose at carpets, thin thrampin' home to save th' nickel or, more like, without enough money in his pocket to pay ca-ar fare. He had so! But he'd have a smile an' a proud bow f'r th' bist iv thim. Ye'd niver know fr'm th' face iv him that he wasn't a man ar-rnin' his tin per an' without a care on his mind fr'm six in th' avnin' to five in th' mor-rnin'.

"But the neighbors heerd iv him not bein' well off an' begun to talk iv keepin' him. A comity iv th' Ladies' Aid Society wint to th' house to see th' wife. She looked thim over through th' side iv th' dure. She knew they was comin'. 'What will ye have with me?' she says. 'We hear ye are in disthress,' says Mrs. Cassidy, 'an' we've been diligated,' she says, 'f'r to invistigate ye'er case duly,' she says, 'an' raypoort thereon,' she says. 'Is that all?' says th' little woman. 'That is sufficient,' says Mrs. Cassidy—ye know her, that pompious little fat ol' washerwoman that talks like an advertisement iv bakin' powdher. 'Well, thin,' says th' little woman, 'I thank ye kindly,' she says, an' closed th' dure on thim. Some iv thim was f'r foorcin' their way in an' takin' an invinthry, but they didn't do it.

"Well, las' week I was standin' in front iv Hagan's talkin' with a Kerry man be th' name iv O'Donnell, whin along came Hagan, r-runnin', with his hat in his hand. Whin he seen us he stopped an' put on th' caubeen. 'Good avenin',' says he. 'Fine night,' says I. ''Tis so, plaze Gawd,' says he. Th' little woman met him at th' dure. He caught her in his ar-rms. 'Peggy,' says he. 'Is it thrue?' she says. 'Tell me, 'tis thrue, acushla.' An' he carrid her in, closin' th' dure behind him.

"Well, d'ye know what it was, Jawn? They'd taken th' black list off him an' he'd gone to wurruk. That was it. An' to think iv a man givin' thanks to Hivin f'r bein' allowed to wurruk!" (November 30, 1895)

3. The Grady Girl Rushing the Can

Up in Archey road the streetcar wheels squeaked along the tracks and the men coming down from the rolling-mills hit themselves on their big chests and wiped their noses on their leather gloves with a peculiar back-handed stroke at which they are most adept. The little girls coming out of the bakeshops with loaves done up in brown paper under their arms had to keep a tight clutch on their thin shawls lest those garments should be caught up by the bitter wind blowing from Brighton Park way and carried down to the gashouse. The frost was so thick on the windows of Mr. Martin Dooley's shop that you could just see the crownless harp on the McCormick's Hall Parnell meeting sheet above it, and you could not see any of the pyramid of Medford rum bottles founded contemporaneously with that celebrated meeting.

Still, signs of warmth and good cheer were not lacking about the Dooley establishment. One sign in particular, a faded one and time worn, bearing a legend touching upon Tom and Jerry, hung from the door. It met the eye of the Hon. John McKenna standing on the streetcar platform and conversing with the driver upon the benefits to civilization only possible under the mayoralty of George Brains Swift. Mr. McKenna hopped from the car and went in to find Mr. Dooley sitting comfortably behind the tall stove which was steaming from the reservoir atop. Mr. Dooley was partaking contentedly of an aromatic mixture of a golden color, slightly flecked with Vandyke brown, in which a bit of lemon peel was floating.

"Is it cold out, I dinnaw?" said Mr. Dooley, laying down his glass.

"Oh, no," said Mr. McKenna, rubbing his ear; "it isn't cold. I dropped in to get an umbrella. I'm afraid I'll get sunstruck if I go along without one."

"I didn't know," said Mr. Dooley, calmly chasing the lemon peel around with the spoon. "It isn't cold in here, Jawn, and by gar as long as it isn't, 'tis not mesilf 'd poke me nose out to learn th' timphrature. Some idjuts iv me acquaintance kapes a thermomter about to tell how cold it is, but f'r me, Jawn, I'd as soon have a mad dog in th' house. There was a man be th' name iv Denny that kep' th' block below Finucane's, an' he bought a thermomter f'r to tell how cold it was, an', by gar, th' poor, deluded man 'd be r-runnin' out fr'm morn till night to take a pike at th' thermomter, an' him in his shirt sleeves. Wan day he tuk noomony in th' lungs and died, Gawd rest him, in three days. I wint to his wake. They waked him in beer, but annyhow thim Dennys was always low people. Wan iv thim is a polisman now. It's dam'd little I care how cold it is so long as I have this here fire baychune me an' th' frost. Zaro or twinty daygrees below zaro an' wan lump iv coal in that there shtove, and it's all akel to Dooley. I can plant mesilf in this chair an' say to mesilf: 'Come on winter; I'm here before ye.' Thin to think iv th' poor divvles out in th' night, tortured an' sufferin' with th' cold an' nothin' to cover thim an' protect thim fr'm th' frost—Jawn, there's no divarsion more cheerin'.

Bedad, half th' philo-sophy iv life is in knowin' that some wan is sufferin' whin ye're on aisy street. It is, so it is."

A rattle at the door and a short cry caused Mr. Dooley to pause and listen and finally to toddle out grumbling complaints about the Donohue goat, whose only divarsion was to batter down the tenements of dacint people. As he opened the door his grumbling ceased, and presently he came in carrying something that looked like a rather large parcel of rags, but on close inspection turned out to be a very small girl carrying a very big can.

"Glory be to Gawd," said Mr. Dooley, setting the little girl down in the chair. "Glory be to Gawd, an' did ye iver see th' likes iv that? Luk at her, Jawn, th' unfortunate chick, lyin' out there froze in this murdhrin' night with a can in her hand. Who are ye, poor thing? Let me take a luk at ye. By gar, I thought so. 'Tis Grady's kid—Grady, th' villain, th' black-hearted thafe, to send th' poor choild out to her death. Don't stand there, ye big numb-skull, like a cigar store injun starin'. Go over an' fetch that can iv milk. Musha, musha, ye poor dear. Naw, naw, don't wipe ye'er nose on me apron, ye unmannerly crather. Give me a towl, Jawn, fr'm in under th' shilf where thim Angyostooria bitthers stands. There ye are. Don't cry, dear. Does ye'er—what th' 'ell's baby talk f'r feet, Jawn?"

"Tootsy-wootsies," said Mr. McKenna proudly.

"Does ye'er tootsy-wootsies hurt ye, avick? Dhrink that an' ye'll be as warm as two in a bed."

Mr. Dooley stood with hands on his hips and saw the little Grady girl laving her purple nose in the warm milk. Meantime he narrated the history of her father in forcible language, touching upon his failure to work and provide, his bibulous habits and his tendency toward riotous misconduct. Finally, he walked behind the bar and set out the glasses, as his custom was for closing time. He placed the cash drawer in the small iron safe in the corner and tucked a $5 bill in his vest pocket. Then he turned out the lights in the window and put on his overcoat.

"Where are you going?" asked Mr. McKenna.

"I'm goin' over to lick Grady," said Mr. Dooley.

"Then," said Mr. McKenna, "by heavens," he said, "I'll go with you."

And they marched out together, with the little Grady girl between them. (November 25, 1893)

4. On Charity: A Lost Child

"Br-r-r!" cried Mr. McKenna, entering stiffly and spreading his hands over the pot-bellied stove. "It's cold."

"Where?" asked Mr. Dooley. "Not here."

"It's cold outside," said Mr. McKenna. "It was ten below at Shannahan's grocery when I went by, and the wind blowing like all possessed. Lord love us, but I pity them that's got to be out tonight."

"Save ye'er pity," said Mr. Dooley, comfortably. "It ain't cowld in here. There's frost on th' window, 'tis thrue for ye; an' th' wheels has been singin' th' livelong day. But what's that to us? Here I am, an' there ye are, th' stove between us an' th' kettle hummin'. In a minyit it'll bile, an' thin I'll give ye a taste iv what'll make a king iv ye.

"Well, tubby sure, 'tis thryin' to be dhrivin' a coal wagon or a sthreet-car; but 'tis all in a lifetime. Th' diff'rence between me an' th' man that sets up in th' seat thumpin' his chest with his hands is no more than th' diff'rence between him an' th' poor divvle that walks along behind th' wagon with his shovel on his shoulder, an' 'll thank th' saints f'r th' first chanst to put tin ton iv ha-ard coal into a cellar f'r a quarther iv a dollar. Th' lad afoot invies th' dhriver, an' th' dhriver invies me; an' I might invy big Cleveland if it wasn't f'r th' hivinly smell iv this here noggin. An' who does Cleveland invy? Sure, it'd be sacrelige f'r me to say.

"Me ol' father, who was as full iv sayin's as an almanac, used to sink his spoon into th' stirabout, an' say, 'Well, lads, this ain't bacon an' greens an' porther; but it'll be annything ye like if ye'll on'y think iv th' Cassidys.' Th' Cassidys was th' poorest fam'ly in

th' parish. They waked th' oldest son in small beer, an' was little
thought of. Did me father iver ask thim in to share th' stirabout?
Not him. An' he was the kindest man in th' wurruld. He had a
heart in him as big as a kish iv turf, but he'd say, 'Whin ye grow
up, take no wan's sorrows to ye'ersilf,' he says. '"Tis th' wise man
that goes through life thinkin' iv himsilf, fills his own stomach, an'
takes away what he can't ate in his pocket.' An' he was r-right,
Jawn. We have throubles enough iv our own. Th' wurruld goes
on just th' same, an' ye can find fifty men to say th' lit'ny f'r ye to
wan that'll give ye what'll relieve a fastin' spit. Th' dead ar-re always pop'lar. I knowed th' St. Vincent de Pauls wanst to vote a
monyment to a man an' refuse to help his fam'ly, all in wan night.
'Tis cowld outside th' dure, ye say, but 'tis war-rum in here; an'
I'm gettin' in me ol' age to think that the diff'rence between hivin
an' hell is no broader"—

Mr. Dooley's remarks were cut short by a cry from the back
room. It was unmistakably a baby's cry. Mr. McKenna turned
suddenly in amazement as Mr. Dooley bolted.

"Well, in the name of the saints, what's all this?" he cried, following his friend into the back room. He found the philosopher,
with an expression of the utmost sternness, sitting on the side of
his bed, with a little girl of two or three in his arms. The philosopher was singing:—

> Ar-rah rock-a-bye, babby, on th' three top:
> Whin th' wind blo-ows, th' cradle ull r-rock;
> An', a-whin th' bough breaks, th' cradle ull fa-a-a-ll,
> An' a-down ull come babby, cradle, an' all.

Then he sang:—

> In th' town iv Kilkinny there du-wilt a fair ma-aid,
> In th' town iv Kilkinny there du-wilt a fair ma-aid.
> She had cheeks like th' roses, an' hair iv th' same,
> An' a mouth like ripe sthrawburries burrid in crame.

He rocked the child to and fro, and its crying ceased while
he sang:—

Chip, chip, a little horse;
   Chip, chip, again, sir.
How manny miles to Dublin?
   Threescure an' tin, sir.

The little girl went to sleep on Mr. Dooley's white apron. He lifted her tenderly, and carried her over to his bed. Then he tip-toed out with an apprehensive face, and whispered: "It's Jawn Donahue's kid that wandhered away fr'm home, an' wint to sleep on me dure-step. I sint th' Dorsey boy to tell th' mother, but he's a long time gone. 'Twas me blatherin' waked her. Do ye run over, Jawn, an' lave thim know. I'm near th' ind iv me repertory." (January 4, 1896)

5. Christmas Charity on the Road

"What have ye in ye'er pockets there, Jawn?" asked Mr. Dooley.

"Some Christmas things for the kids," said Mr. McKenna.

Mr. Dooley chuckled, sighed and mopped the bar. Therefore Mr. Dooley was sad. He poured some hot water and a jigger of whisky on a lump of sugar. He poked the fire slowly. He lit a cigar and he blew his nose upon his apron. Each of which actions was a symptom of melancholy.

"Thrue, 'tis thrue," he said. "Christmas an' kids; Christmas an' kids. 'Tis little th' wan 'r th' other is to me this manny's th' year. Christmas is on'y a pathrol box f'r me where th' polisman calls up another lap iv th' beat through wid, an' th' mornin' comin' on. 'Tis well enough f'r thim that has their own. Over beyant I set an' watched th' peat crackin' in th' grate manny's th' Christmas, f'r thim was days an' thim was times. But not now, Jawn avick.

"I knowed Christmas was comin' on. I seen it in th' faces iv th' kids an' in th' bakery windies. I met Cassidy goin' to do an extry shift at th' mills; him, poor la-ad, whose back does be bint like a hoop, that wanst was as straight as a pole. 'Where ar-re ye goin', ye foolish man,' I says, 'at this time iv night with ye'er dinner pail?' 'I'm wurrkin' overtime f'r a week or two,' he says. 'Well, glory be to Gawd,' says I. 'Don't ye wurruk enough be day,' says I, 'without stayin' up all night lookin' f'r a wheelbarrow to r-run?' 'Ah, well,' says he, 'I've got to get some few things f'r Christmas,' he says. An', Jawn, he wint off thryin' to whistle 'Down be th' Tanya-ard Side' through his pipe. He did so.

"Nex' week 'twill be nothin' but Christmas up an' down th' r-road. Whin ye go by look in th' little houses. Look in at Malachi Hinnissy's. Th' fr-ront r-room is locked up as tight as a dhrum an' Hinnissy has to smoke his pipe in th' kitchin. If ye go by afther th' kids 'v been washed an' sint off to school ye'll see th' Christmas three standin' in th' windy, a dam little thing that Hinnissy's ould woman has to kneel down f'r to dhress. Hinnissy himsilf was near laid off las' week. His hands had got that bad fr'm sthringin' pop-corn that he cuddent handle th' thruck. 'Hinnissy,' says th' boss. 'If ye take in fancy sewin' whin ye get home iv nights,' says th' boss, 'ye ought to make money enough to lave th' freighthouse,' he says. Hinnissy said nawthin', but may th' Lord help that there boss whin Malachi takes him at his wurrud an' dhraws his time.

"Christmas mornin' Hinnissy'll have his r-revenge on th' gang boss whither he whales him later 'r not. Th' kids 'll niver give him a chanst to put on a white shir-rt till time f'r high mass. Th' woman 'll be off early to 4 o'clock mass whin th' chur-rch is full iv light an' incense and Molly Donohue's singin' th' Adestee Fydalis up above. Jawn, iv all th' chunes that iver mortal man heerd, give me th' Adestee Fydalis iv a cold Christmas mornin'. An' iv all th' singers that iver sung it I'll lay me money on Molly Donohue, white 'r black, give or take tin pounds. I will that.

"But what th' 'ell? I'm old an' all alone. No, thank ye, Jawn, I'll set here all day. Thank ye kindly, me la-ad. It has no more in it f'r me, without chick or child iv me own. An' 'tis well it hasn't. 'Tis f'r th' childher, an' th' childher alone 'twas made, an' thim that has none 'd betther sup with a lone spoon an' lave their noses out iv other people's porridge. At th' same time, Jawn, mind ye, if I r-run acrost that big loafer iv a Maloney I'll kill him. I'll kill him, I will that. I'll call th' polis f'r him."

"What has Maloney done?" ventured Mr. McKenna.

"What has he done?" roared Mr. Dooley. "What hasn't he done? Hasn't he gone off on a dhrunk? Hasn't he deserted his fam'ly? Hasn't he thrun up his job, with Christmas not two weeks off? D'ye ask me what he's done, him with five childher? I seen thim this mornin', an' I swore be th' hivins above me that if I meet him I'd break his back f'r a Christmas present."

"But what have you got to do with it?" asked Mr. McKenna.

"What've I got to do with it? D'ye hear th' limon-headed jood ta-alk? Come her-re!" roared Mr. Dooley, dragging Mr. McKenna to the rear of the shop and throwing open the door. "D'ye see that there sled? D'ye think that cost me nawthin'? D'ye suppose I made that there doll an' thim choo-choo ca-ars? D'ye think that there expriss wagon was give to me be me constitoo-ents f'r to ride around in an' make calls?"

"Who are they for?" asked Mr. McKenna feebly.

"They're f'r Maloney's childher," said Mr. Dooley with supreme pride. "An' if ye'll ask th' good woman to make some clothes f'r that doll I'll thank ye kindly. 'Twud be immodest in me an'—I—don't—know—what—oh, what th' 'ell!" (December 15, 1894)

6. Mrs. Mulligan and the Illinois Central Railroad

This piece was prompted by the refusal of President Fish of the Illinois Central to have pedestrian crossings installed over his railroad's lakeside tracks.

"Jawn," said Mr. Dooley, "I had Hinnissy in with me las' night. He's a smart ol' buck wanst in awhile. He tol' me he's goin' to get up a new caddychism. It'll go like this: 'Who made ye?' 'Th' Il-linye Cinthral made me.' 'An' why did it make ye?' 'That I might know it, love it, an' serve it all me days.' Be hivins, 'twould be a good thing. They's naw use teachin' th' childher what ain't thrue. What's th' good iv tellin' thim that th' Lord made th' wurruld whin they'll grow up an' find it in th' possission iv th' Illinye Cinthral?

"Th' ma-an that does be at th' head iv th' r-road is a man be th' name iv Fish. I don't know what Fish he is, but he's no sucker. He was a jood down in th' City iv New York an' th' Frindly Sons iv Saint Pathrick or th' Ivy Leaf Plisure Club or some other organization give a party an' this here Fish he wanted f'r to be th' whole thing in it—wanted f'r to take th' tickets an' have th' ba-ar privilege an' lade th' gr-rand ma-arch, d'ye mind. 'Naw,' says they. 'Naw. Ye can't be th' whole thing.' 'Thin,' says th' man-Fish, 'I quit ye.' An' he come out here to run th' Illinye Cinthral.

"Well, he's runnin' it. He's runnin' th' Illinye Cinthral, an' he's runnin' th' earth, an' he's got an irne fince around th' lake, an' if he has his way he'll be puttin' th' stars in a cage an' chargin' ye two bits f'r a look at thim—Show ye'er ticket to th' ma-an at th' gate.

"Jawn, I don't care no more f'r Lake Michigan than th' likes iv you cares f'r th' tin commandments. They're all right, but ye don't use thim. In tin years I've set me eyes on it but twict, an' I on'y see it now as it comes out iv that there faucet. Whin I want what Hinnissy calls eequathic spoorts I goes over here to th' r-red bridge an' takes a ride with Brinnan. But there's thim that uses it an' they say 'tis good f'r babies.

"Ye mind th' Mulligans—thim that lives over beyant Casey's—th' little quite man with th' r-red whiskers. He wurruks hard, but all he's been able to lay up is throuble an' childher. He has tin iv thim old an' young, an' th' last come is sick an' feverish. I seen th' good woman rockin' it wan day on th' stoop, an' says I: 'How's th' kid?' 'Poorly, thank ye,' says she. 'He seems throubled be th' heat. 'Tis mortial hot,' she says. 'Why don't ye take him where 'tis cool?' I says. 'I'm goin' to to-morrah, praise Gawd,' she says. 'I'm goin' to take him down an' give him a r-ride around on th' steamboat. Th' doctor tells me th' lake air'll make him right,' she says. ''Tis ixpinsive,' she says. 'Five cints on th' boat, but 'tis betther than to have th' poor chick sufferin' an' I'm goin' to do it.'

"Ye see, she'd been brought up on th' ol' caddychism an'

thought Gawd ownded th' wurruld, an' she'd niver heerd tell iv th' man-Fish. So I see her goin' off downtown with th' baby in her arms, shieldin' its face fr'm th' blazin' sun, bright an' early. How she found her way acrost th' city I dinnaw. F'r mesilf, I'd as lave attimpt to cross hell as State sthreet. I was r-run over be a gripca-ar th' last time I was there. But annyhow she got acrost to where she cud see th' blue wather iv th' la-ake an' th' crib that Tom Gahan built. 'Twas there she found who ownded th' wurruld. She wint along th' irne fince lookin' f'r a gate an' they was no gate. Thin she wint into th' little deepo an' says she: 'I want to go over to thim boats,' she says. 'Ye'll have to buy a ticket beyant,' says th' man. 'An' how much is it?' says she. 'Tin cints,' says th' man. 'But,' says she, 'I've on'y th' fifteen left,' she says, 'an' th' boat costs tin cints,' she says. 'Lave me in,' she says. 'I can't help it,' says th' man. ''Tis me ordhers,' he says. Ye see, th' man-Fish had tol' thim not to let annywan go to his lake, th' wan he made, d'ye mind, on th' sicond day. An' there she stood, peerin' through th' irne fince an' lookin' out at th' lake—at th' Illinye Cinthral's lake—an' glory be, I suppose she didn't undherstand it, but no more does she undherstand why it is f'r some to live off th' fat iv th' land an' f'r her on'y to bear childher an' see thim die or go to th' bad.

"She come home afther awhile whin th' baby got cross again. I seen her that night. 'Did ye like th' lake?' I says. 'I didn't go,' she says. 'F'r why?' says I. 'Th' Illinye Cinthral wudden' let me,' she says. 'I think it'd done th' baby good,' she says. 'He's onaisy to-night. Maria,' says she, 'will ye take Tiddy while I cuk ye'er father's supper?'

"So I think with Hinnissy they'll have to make a new caddy-chism, Jawn. I hope th' Illinye Cinthral'll be kinder to Mulligan's baby in th' nix' wurruld than it's been in this, f'r unless me eyes have gone back on me, they'll be another sthring iv crape on Mulligan's dure tomo-rah mornin'." (August 10, 1895)

7. Only the Poor Marry

Here Mr. Dooley places Chicago's financial power in the down-town area, "east iv State sthreet," a major north-south thoroughfare just a few blocks from the lake. A "sound-money" democratic news-paper would have been unpopular because of the party's allegiance to William Jennings Bryan and the movement to repeal the gold standard.

"I seen in th' pa-aper th' other day," said Mr. Dooley, "that a woman asked: 'Why don't more young men marry?' Why don't more young men marry?"

"They do," said Mr. Hennessy. "They do. That woman niver r-read th' papers in th' spring iv th' year. Lave her look at th' marredge licenses th' day afther Easther. 'Twud seem as though all th' la-ads an' girls was doin' nawthin' all Lent but cukkin' eggs an' sparkin'. Th' minyit th' bars is let down afther th' holy season they r-rush to th' county clerk's office as though they was on'y wan day left f'r takin' out a license an' if they didn't get it befure night they'd be took up as dhrunk an' disord'ly bachelors an' ol' maids."

"Not at all," said Mr. Dooley. "Not at all. Thim ar-re not rale people. They're Swedes or Bohamians or Germans or Boolgah-rians. Thim foreigners believe in increasin' an' multiplyin', while we native-bor-rn Americans go in f'r addin' an' dividin'—as th' divorce coort records show. In a few years it'll be impossible to find annywan west iv State sthreet that speaks English. People'll laugh at th' sthrange language, th' way we do now at Chinese, an' there'll be a German mayor iv Chicago. I hope not.

"It usen't to be so," the philosopher went on. "Whin I was a young man—an' a gr-reat flirt I was—a girl had to be mighty spry to help bein' marrid. Manny iv thim didn't want to be mar-rid. They had all they cud do to support thimsilves. But whether they wanted to or not, they was dhragged off to th' church in spite iv their protests an' marrid to some wan—it didn't make no differ-ence who it was. Money cut no figure at all. A poor girl was as lible to be marrid as a rich, an' most anny night ye'd see a line iv young men standin' in front iv th' houses where iligible young ladies lived waitin' f'r a chance to propose. They was no ol' maids or bachelors in thim days. Th' polis locked up all unmarrid people found roamin' in th' streets.

"Now, as this bright an' intilligint lady says, young men don't marry no more. They have too much comfort, too much money an' they have their clubs to go to. I see that all around me. In th' ol' days a young man whin he got through his wurruk f'r th' day had no place to go to an' nawthin' to do but to coort some girl. Now look at him! Whin he comes back fr'm th' mill an' washes up an' has his supper what does he do? He goes to some sumchous club an' lolls in th' rich an' ixpinsive r-red plush chairs smokin' his fine 10-cint Havana seegars an' dhrinkin' his bottle iv wine with ne'er a care in th' wurruld. There's no inducemint f'r him to change his lot f'r th' throuble iv rearing a family an' th' grocers' bills an' havin' to wind th' clock an' get up in th' middle iv th' night f'r to see if burglars have got into th' cellar an' are beatin' gongs while they wurruk. None at all. He scorns marredge. It makes no differ to him whether his childher has shoes f'r he has no childher. Burglars may break into th' cellar, but his own thrunk is under th' bed. He lolls at ease on th' plush furniture iv his club an' spinds his tin or twelve dollars a week like a lord."

"In ye'er mind he does," said Mr. Hennessy.

"That's what I was comin' to," said the philosopher. "These people that talk about young men not marryin' are th' same that addhress th' Sons iv th' Revolution as th' American public. They think this large an' haughty republic is bounded be that section iv New England an' Jerusalem lyin' east iv State sthreet. They learn diff'rent ivry iliction night, but they forget what they learn th' nex' day. Th' fact is, Hinnissy, that young men do marry. What I said was sarcastic. People that can't afford it always have marrid an' always will. 'Tis on'y th' rich that don't. They niver did. That's wan reason why they're rich, too. But whin a young man is so poor that he can't afford to keep a dog an' has no more prospects thin a sound-money dimmycratic newspaper, he finds a girl who's got less an' proposes to her an' they're marrid at th' expinse iv th' grocers iv th' neighborhood an' they live unhappy iver after, bringin' up a large fam'ly to go an' do likewise. There've been more people marrid since hard times set in thin iver befure in th' histhry iv th' wurruld. This here wave iv prosperity that's comin', if it's on th' square, will rejooce th' income of the marredge license department fifty per cint. Still, there'll be plenty. All th' wurruld can't get rich in a minyit, and so long as there's broken people on earth there'll be marredges. I tell ye that f'r th' truth. They may fall off in Mitchigan avenoo. They always do whin stocks go up. But over on this side iv th' thracks there niver has been enough prosperity to keep anny man's front stoop clear iv poor an' hopeless bridegrooms. Th' fewer th' jobs in Archey road th' bigger th' vote iv th' sixth wa-ard. That's an ipigram, too."

"But why don't old men marry?" Mr. Hennessy asked.

"If ye mean me be that," returned Mr. Dooley, "I'm doin' a good thrade here as it is. Besides, it's none iv ye'er business." (July 31, 1897)

8. The Beef Trust and the Connock Man's Children

Here the smell from the stockyards of Armour and Brinnock, Chicago meat-packers, starts Mr. Dooley thinking about the effects of the Beef Trust on the poor of Bridgeport.

"Which d'ye think makes th' best fun'ral turnout, th' A-hoaitches or th' Saint Vincent de Pauls, Jawn?" asked Mr. Dooley.

"I don't know," said Mr. McKenna. "Are you thinking of leaving us?"

"Faith, I am not," said Mr. Dooley. "Since th' warm weather's come an' th' wind's in th' south, so that I can tell at night that A-armoor an' me ol' frind, Jawn Brinnock, are attindin' to business, I have a grip on life like th' wan ye have on th' shank iv that shell iv malt. Whether 'tis these soft days, with th' childher beginnin' to play barefutted in th' sthreet an' th' good women out to palaver over th' fence without their shawls, or whether 'tis th' wan wurrud Easter Sundah that comes on me, an' jolts me ol' nut with th' thoughts iv th' la-ads goin' to mass an' th' blackthorn turnin' green beyant, I dinnaw. But annyhow I'm as gay as a babby an' as fresh as a lark. I am so.

"I was on'y thinkin'. Ol' Gran'pah Grogan died las' Mondah,— as good a man as e'er counted his beads or passed th' plate. A thrue man. Choosdah a Connock man up back iv th' dumps laid down his chuvvle. Misther Grogan had a grand notice in th' pa-apers: 'Grogan, at his late risidence, 279 A-archoor Avnoo, Timothy Alexander, beloved husband iv th' late Mary Grogan, fa-ther iv Maurice, Michael, Timothy, Edward, James, Peter, Paul, an' Officer Andrew Grogan, iv Cologne Sthreet station, an' iv Mrs. Willum Sarsfield Cassidy, nee Grogan' (which manes that was her name befure she marrid Cassidy, who wurruks down be Haley's packin'-house). 'Fun'ral be carriages fr'm his late risi-dence to Calv'ry cimithry. Virginia City, Nivada; St. Joseph, Mitchigan; an' Clonmel Tipp'rary pa-apers please copy.'

"I didn't see e'er a nee about th' fam'ly iv th' little man back iv th' dumps, though maybe he had wan to set aroun' th' fire in th' dark an' start at th' tap iv a heel on th' dure-step. Mebbe he had a fam'ly, poor things. A fun'ral is great la-arks f'r th' neighbors, an' mebbe 'tis not so bad f'r th' corpse. But in these times, Jawn dear, a-ho th' gray hearts left behind an' th' hungry mouths to feed. They done th' best they cud f'r th' Connock man back iv th' dumps,—give him all th' honors, th' A-ho-aitches ma-archin' be-hind th' hearse an' th' band playin' th' Dead March. 'Twas almost as good a turnout as Grogan had, though th' Saint Vincents had betther hats an' looked more like their fam'lies kept a cow.

"But they was two hacks back iv th' pall-bearers. I wondhered what was passin' behind th' faces I seen again their windys. 'Twas well f'r himself, too. Little odds to him, afther th' last screw was twisted be Gavin's ol' yellow hooks, whether beef was wan cint or a hundherd dollars th' pound. But there's comin' home as well as goin' out. There's more to a fun'ral thin th' lucks parpitua, an' th' clod iv sullen earth on th' top iv th' crate. Sare a pax vobiscum is there f'r thim that's huddled in th' ol' hack, sthragglin' home in th' dust to th' empty panthry an' th' fireless grate.

"Mind ye, Jawn, I've no wurrud to say again thim that sets back in their own house an' lot an' makes th' food iv th' people dear. They're good men, good men. Whin they tilt th' price iv beef to where wan pound iv it costs as much as manny th' man in this Ar-rchey Road 'd wurruk fr'm th' risin' to th' settin' iv th' sun to get, they have no thought iv th' likes iv you an' me. 'Tis aisy come, aisy go with thim; an' ivry cint a pound manes a new art musoom or a new church, to take th' edge off hunger. They're all right, thim la-ads, with their own porkchops delivered free at th' door. 'Tis, 'Will ye have a new spring dhress, me dear? Willum, ring thim up, an' tell thim to hist th' price iv beef. If we had a few more pitchers an' statoos in th' musoom, 'twud ilivate th' people a sthory or two. Willum, afther this, steak 'll be twinty cints a pound.' Oh, they're all right, on'y I was thinkin' iv th' Connock man's fam'ly back iv th' dumps."

"For a man that was gay a little while ago, it looks to me as if you'd grown mighty solemn-like," said Mr. McKenna.

"Mebbe so," said Mr. Dooley. "Mebbe so. What th' 'ell, anny-how. Mebbe 'tis as bad to take champagne out iv wan man's mouth as round steak out iv another's. Lent is near over. I seen Doherty out shinin' up his pipe that's been behind th' clock since Ash Winsdah. Th' girls 'll be layin' lilies on th' altar in a day or two. Th' spring's come on. Th' grass is growin' good; an', if th' Connock man's children back iv th' dumps can't get meat, they can eat hay." (April 13, 1895)

9. The Pullman Strike: Lemons and Liberty

Because of the successful strike by employees of George Pullman's railroad car manufacturing company and other sympathetic team-sters and carriers, the city of Chicago was deprived of much produce and merchandise in late June of 1894. On July 3, President Grover Cleveland ordered federal troops under General Miles into Chicago to break the strike by getting the mail trains moving again. For the next several days there were many confrontations, some of them bloody, between soldiers and striking workers. Through all of this trouble, Pullman himself was away from the city; the Evening Post *reported that he was "resting" in New York, "too tired" to be interviewed. On July 6, two strikers were killed and several wounded when soldiers fired into a mob that was obstructing passage of a train in South Chicago, some twenty blocks below Bridgeport. On the following day this Dooley piece appeared. This was actually Mr. Dooley's second mention of the Pullman troubles: in the first, quoted in part in Chapter One, piece 6, the sympathy strike by transportation workers outside Chicago is compared to a strike on "Dorgan's section" of the Illinois and Michigan Canal construction job.*

"Th' counthry," said Mr. Dooley, "do be goin' to wrack an' roon. I have nayether limons n'r ice in th' house. Th' laws is defied an' th' constitootion is vilated. Th' rights iv citizens is thrampled upon an' ye can get nayether ice n'r limons f'r love 'r money. Ordher out th' sojers, says I, an' tache th' miscrents what th' 'ell. For why did George Wash'nton an' Andhrew Jackson an' Jeremiah Houlihan fight an' die if a band iv thraitors can come along an' wrinch from an American citizen his limons an' his ice? Am I right? Am I right, Jawn? Am I right? Am I right? I am.

"This ain't no sthrike. A sthrike is where th' la-ads lave off wurruk an' bate Germans and thin go back to wurruk f'r rajooced wages an' thank hivin f'r it. This here is a rivolution again constitooted authority. I seen it in th' pa-aper, an' by gar it must be thrue. I niver r-read th' constitootion an' I niver seen anny wan that r-read it; but it must be all r-right, for an' because 'twas made wan hundhred years ago or more be min that is now dead an' in their graves. God r-rest their sowls, especially Jawn Carroll iv Carrolton, that was a grandfa-ather iv Carroll, th' stove docther. He was, he was. Carroll said so. Could thim patriots do wrong? Didn't they know what was best f'r us afther fightin' f'r our liberties? I should smoke a ham.

"Th' constitootion, Jawn, provides f'r Pullman. I don't know th' ma-an; but I wint in wan iv his ca-ars to th' convintion at Peeory with th' lith'ry club, an' I must say th' convayniences is nice. All ye have to do is to lave ye'er shoes on th' flure an' ye git some wan's else's in th' mor-rnin'. Thin ye crawl into th' side iv th' ca-ar an' whin ye'er removin' ye'er pa-ants a dhrunk man fr'm th' eighth wa-ard comes an' climbs on ye'er neck f'r to get into the hole above ye. 'Tis nice an' quite, an' th' smill iv it is not ba-ad. Ye have some excitement findin' ye'er shirt in th' mornin', but 'tis all a matther iv sport.

"This here Pullman makes th' sleepin'-ca-ars an' th' constitoo-tion looks afther Pullman. He have a good time iv it. He don't need to look afther himsilf. He have limons an' ice to give to his neighbors if he wanted to. He owns towns an' min. He makes princes iv th' rile blood iv Boolgahria go around to th' kitchen dure. He is stiffer thin wan iv his own towels. Whin he has throuble ivry wan on earth excipt thim that rides in smokin' ca-ars whin they rides at all r-runs to fight f'r him. He calls out George Wash'nton an' Abraham Lincoln an' Gin'ral Miles an' Mike Brinnan an' ivry human bein' that rayquires limons an' ice an' thin he puts on his hat an' lams away. 'Gintlemin,' says he, 'I must be off,' he says. 'Go an' kill each other,' he says. 'Fight it out,' he says. 'Defind the constitootion,' he says. 'Me own is not of th' best,' he says, 'an' I think I'll help it be spindin' th' summer,' he says, 'piously,' he says, 'on th' shores iv th' Atlantic ocean.'

"That's Pullman. He slips out as aizely as a ba-ar iv his own soap. An' th' whole wurruld turns in an' shoots an' stabs an' throws couplin'-pins, an' sojers ma-arch out an' Gin'ral Miles looks up the sthreet for some man, to show that he can kill min too. Ye take Abraham Lincoln, but give me Pullman."

Mr. Dooley paused for a while after this deliverance. Then he said, "Jawn, are ye goin' home?"

"Yes," said Mr. McKenna.

"Then dhrop off at Willum Joyce's," said Mr. Dooley, "an' get th' constitootion an' (whisper) look at th' siction about sleepin'-

ca-ars an' see if it don't say something about limons an' ice, too."
(July 7, 1894.)

10. The Pullman Strike: The Tragedy of the Agitator

*During the next week the Pullman strike was broken. However,
rioting and altercations between soldiers and strikers continued, as
Mr. Dooley illustrates with this story of family dissension fostered by
the sympathy strike of Bridgeport longshoremen.*

"Whin he come up, did ye see Dorgan?" asked Mr. Dooley.

"Which Dorgan?" asked Mr. McKenna.

"Why, to be sure, Hugh O'Neill Dorgan, him that was sicrety
iv Deerin' Sthreet branch number wan hundred an' eight iv th'
Ancient Ordher iv Scow Unloaders, him that has th' red dill-dalls
on his throat, that married th' second time to Dinnihy's aunt an'
we give a shivaree to him. Hivins on earth, don't ye know him?"

"I don't," said Mr. McKenna; "and, if I know him, I haven't
seen him."

"Thin ye missed a sight," said Mr. Dooley. "He's ragin' an'
tearin'. He have been a great union man. He'd sthrike on th' moment's provocation. I seen him wanst, whin some scow unloaders
sthruck in Lemont or some other distant place, put on his coat,
lay down his shovel, an' go out, be hivins, alone. Well, his son
goes an' jines th' Sivinth Rig'mint; an', by gar, th' ol' man, not
knowin' about th' army, he's that proud that he sthruts up an'
down th' sthreet with his thumb in th' vest iv him an' give his son
a new shovel, for they was wurrukin' together on th' scow 'Odelia
Ann.' Well, whin th' sthrike come along, iv coorse th' scow unloaders quits; an' Dorgan an' th' la-ad goes out together, because
they're dhrawin' good wages an' th' crick do be full iv men r-ready
f'r to take their places.

"Well, Dorgan had th' divvle's own time paradin' up an' down
an' sindin' out ordhers to sthrike to ivry man he knowed of till
th' la-ad comes over las' Choosdah avenin', dhressed in his rigi-

mintals with a gun as long as a clothes-pole over his shoulder. 'Hughey,' said th' father, 'you look very gran' to-night,' he says. 'Whose fun'ral ar-re ye goin' to at this hour?' 'None but thim I makes mesilf,' says he. 'What d'ye mean?' says th' ol' man. 'I'm goin' over f'r to stand guard in th' thracks,' says th' la-ad. Well, with that th' ol' man leaps up, an' makes a smash at th' kid. 'Po-lisman' he says. 'Polisman,' he says. 'Copper,' he says. 'Twas on'y be Mrs. Dorgan comin' in an' quitein' th' ol' man with a chair that hostilities was averted—as th' pa-apers says—right there an' thin.

"Well, sir, will ye believe me, whin Dorgan wint over with th' mimbers iv th' union that night f'r to bur-rn something, there was me brave Hughey thrampin' up an' down like a polisman on bate. Dorgan goes up an' shakes his fist at him, an' th' la-ad gives him a jab with his bayonet that makes th' poor ol' man roar like a bull. 'In th' name,' he says, 'iv th' people iv th' State iv Illinye,' he says, 'disperse,' he says, 'ye riter,' he says; 'an', if ye don't go home,' he says, 'ye ol' omadhon,' he says, 'I'll have ye thrun into jail,' he says.

"Dorgan haven't got over it yet. It dhruv him to a sick-bed." (July 14, 1894)

11. The Pullman Strike: What Does He Care?

*George Pullman's employees had walked out in the first place because prices in company stores and rents on their company-owned houses at Pullman, Illinois, had not been reduced after lay-offs and salary cuts were announced in May. After the strike was over, these policies remained unchanged, and reports began to come back from the company town of widespread destitution, even starvation, among the workers and their families. As the situation grew worse, and Pullman still refused to capitulate, Dunne responded with this powerful personal attack. In his biography of Dunne (*Mr. Dooley's America [1941], p. 86), Elmer Ellis recounts the reaction to this piece at the Post: "When the typesetter ran off his proof . . . he passed it about the composing room, and later when Dunne stepped*

*into the room for a moment, the typesetters started to drum their
sticks on their cases, and then broke into the more customary applause of handclapping. . . . Dunne remembered it as one of the
great thrills of his life."*

"Jawn," said Mr. Dooley, "I said it wanst an' I sa-ay it again, I'd
liefer be George M. Pullman thin anny man this side iv Michigan
City. I wud so. Not, Jawn, d'ye mind, that I invy him his job
iv runnin' all th' push-cart lodgin'-houses iv th' counthry or in
dayvilopin' th' whiskers iv a goat without displayin' anny other
iv th' good qualities iv th' craythur or in savin' his taxlist fr'm
th' assissor with th' intintion iv layin' it befure a mathrimonyal
agency. Sare a bit does I care f'r thim honors. But, Jawn, th' la-ad
that can go his way with his nose in th' air an' pay no attintion to
th' sufferin' iv women an' childher—dear, oh, dear, but his life
must be as happy as th' da-ay is long.

"It seems to me, Jawn, that half th' throuble we have in this
vale iv tears, as Dohenny calls Bridgeport, is seein' th' sufferin' iv
women an' little childhren. Th' men can take care iv thimselves,
says I. If they can't wurruk let them go on th' polis foorce an'
if they can't go on th' polis foorce let thim follow th' advice big
Pether Hinnissy give th' Dutchman. 'I dinnaw vat to do,' sa-ays
th' Dutchman. 'I have no money and I can get no wurruk.' 'Foolish man,' says Hinnissy. 'D'ye know what th' good book says? To
those that has nawthin' something will be given,' he sa-ays; 'an'
those that has a lot,' he sa-ays, 'some wan'll come along with a
piece iv lead pipe,' he sa-ays, 'in a stockin',' he sa-ays, 'an' take
what they got away,' he sa-ays. 'D'ye see that big man over there?'
he sa-ays, pointin' to Dorgan, the rale estate man. 'Go over an'
take him be th' neck an' make him give up.' Well, sir, th' German,
bein' like all iv th' ra-ace but Hesing, was a foolish la-ad, an' what
does he do but follow the joker's advice. Sure Dorgan give him a
kick in th' stummick, an' whin he got out iv th' hospital he wint to
th' bridewell, an', by dad, I'm thinkin' he was betther off there
than most poor divvles out iv it, f'r they get three meals a da-ay,
av'n if there ain't no toothbrushes in th' cells.

"But as I said, Jawn, 'tis not th' min, ye mind; 'tis th' women an' childhren. Glory be to Gawd, I can scarce go out f'r a wa-alk f'r pity at seein' th' little wans settin' on th' stoops an' th' women with thim lines in th' fa-ace that I seen but wanst befure, an' that in our parish over beyant, whin th' potatoes was all kilt be th' frost an' th' oats rotted with th' dhrivin' rain. Go into wan iv th' side sthreets about supper time an' see thim, Jawn—thim women sittin' at th' windies with th' babies at their breasts an' waitin' f'r th' ol' man to come home. Thin watch thim as he comes up th' sthreet, with his hat over his eyes an' th' shoulders iv him bint like a hoop an' dhraggin' his feet as if he carried ball an' chain. Musha, but 'tis a sound to dhrive ye'er heart cold whin a woman sobs an' th' young wans cries, an' both because there's no bread in th' house. Betther off thim that lies in Gavin's crates out in Calv'ry, with th' grass over thim an' th' stars lookin' down on thim, quite at last. An' betther f'r us that sees an' hears an' can do nawthin' but give a crust now an' thin. I seen Tim Dorsey's little woman carryin' in a loaf iv bread an' a ham to th' Polack's this noon. Dorsey have been out iv wurruk f'r six months, but he made a sthrike carryin' th' hod yistherday an' th' good woman pinched out some vittles f'r th' Polacks."

Mr. Dooley swabbed the bar in a melancholy manner and turned again with the remark:

"But what's it all to Pullman? Whin Gawd quarried his heart a happy man was made. He cares no more f'r thim little matthers iv life an' death thin I do f'r O'Connor's tab. 'Th' women an' childhren is dyin' iv hunger,' they says. 'Will ye not put out ye'er hand to help thim?' they says. 'Ah, what th' 'ell,' says George. 'What th' 'ell,' he says. 'What th' 'ell,' he says. 'James,' he says, 'a bottle iv champagne an' a piece iv crambree pie. What th' 'ell, what th' 'ell, what th' 'ell."

"I heard two died yesterday," said Mr. McKenna. "Two women."

"Poor things, poor things. But," said Mr. Dooley, once more swabbing the bar, "what th' 'ell." (August 25, 1894)

12. Organized Charity and the Galway Woman

The winter of 1896–1897 was the worst in recent memory for the poor of Chicago. On November 30, the Bureau of Associated Charities estimated that 8000 families were destitute. As that figure grew larger, the situation was aggravated by a cold wave that struck in early December and held on until February. Accelerating demands for food and fuel soon swamped the city's relief bureaucracy, and Chicago faced a life-and-death crisis. The remaining Dooley pieces in this chapter were written during that hard winter. In the first, Dunne attacks the self-defeating regulations of the city's Relief and Aid Society with a grim vignette set in another hard winter, 1874.

"Whin th' col' spell comes along about Chris'mas time," said Mr. Hennessy, opening the stove door and lighting a small piece of paper which he conveyed to the bowl of his pipe with much dexterity, just snaring the last flicker with his first noisy inhalation, "whin th' col' weather comes on I wish thim Grogans down in th' alley'd move out. I have no peace at all with th' ol' woman. She has me r-runnin' in night an' day with a pound of tay or a flannel shirt or a this-or-that-or-th'-other thing, an' 'tis on'y two weeks ago, whin th' weather was warrum, she tol' me Mrs. Grogan was as ongrateful as a cow an' smelled so iv gin ye cud have th' deleeryum thremens if ye sat with her f'r an hour."

"What ye shud do," said Mr. Dooley, "is to get ye'er wife to join an organized charity. Th' throuble with her is she gives to onworthy people an' in a haphazard way that tinds to make paupers. If they'se annything will make a person ongrateful an' depindent it's to give thim something to eat whin they're hungry without knowin' whether they are desarvin' iv th' delicate attintion. A man, or a woman ayether, has to have what ye may call peculiar qualifications f'r to gain th' lump iv coal or th' pound iv steak that an organized charity gives out. He must be honest an' sober an' industhrious. He must have a frind in th' organization. He must have arned th' right to beg his bread be th' sweat iv his brow. He must be able to comport himself like a gintleman in fair society an' play a good hand at whist. He must have a marridge license over th' pianny an' a goold-edged Bible on th' marble-topped table. A pauper that wud disbelieve there was a God afther thrampin' th' sthreets in search iv food an' calmin' an onreasonable stomach with th' east wind is no object iv charity. What he needs is th' attintion iv a polisman. I've aften wondhered why a man that was fit to dhraw a ton iv slate coal an' a gob iv liver fr'm th' relief an' aid society didn't apply f'r a cabinet position or a place in a bank. He'd be sthrong f'r ayether.

"I mind wanst there was a woman lived down near Main sthreet be th' name iv Clancy, Mother Clancy th' kids called her. She come fr'm away off to th' wist, a Galway woman fr'm bechune mountain an' sea. Ye know what they ar-re whin they're black, an' she was worse an' blacker. She was tall an' thin, with a face white th' way a corpse is white, an' she had wan child, a lame la-ad that used to play be himsilf in th' sthreet, th' lawn bein' limited. I niver heerd tell iv her havin' a husband, poor thing, an' what she'd need wan f'r, but to dhrag out her misery f'r her in th' gray year sivinty-foor, I cudden't say. She talked to hersilf in Gaelic whin she walked an' 'twas Gaelic she an' th' kid used whin they wint out together. Th' kids thought she was a witch an' broke th' windows iv her house an' ivry wan was afraid iv her but th' little priest. He shook his head whin she was mintioned an' wint to see her wanst in awhile an' come away with a throubled face.

"Sivinty-foor was a hard winter f'r th' r-road. Th' mills was shut down an' ye cud've stood half th' population iv some iv th' precints on their heads an' got nothin' but five days' notices out iv thim. Th' nights came cold, an' bechune relievin' th' sick an' givin' extremunction to th' dyin' an' comfortin' th' widows an' orphans th' little priest was sore pressed fr'm week's end to week's end. They was smallpox in wan part iv th' wa-ard an' diphtheria in another an' bechune th' two there was starvation an' cold an' not enough blankets on th' bed.

"Th' Galway woman was th' las' to complain. How she iver stud it as long as she did I lave f'r others to say. Annyhow, whin she come down to Halsted sthreet to make application f'r help to th' Society f'r th' Relief iv th' Desarvin' Poor she looked tin feet tall an' all white cheek bones an' burnin' black eyes. It took her a long time to make up her mind to go in, but she done it an' stepped up to where th' reel-estate man Dougherty, cheerman iv th' comity, was standin' with his back to th' stove an' his hands undher his coat tails. They was those that said Dougherty was a big-hear-rted man an' give freely to th' poor, but I'd rather take rough-on-rats fr'm you, Hinnissy, thin sponge cake fr'm him or th' likes iv him. He looked at her, finished a discoorse on th' folly iv givin' to persons with a bad moral charackter an' thin turned suddenly an' said: 'What can we do f'r ye?' She told him in her own way. 'Well, me good woman,' says he, 'ye'll undherstand that th' comity is much besieged be th' imporchunities iv th' poor,' he says, 'an' we're obliged to limit our alms to thim that desarves thim,' he says. 'We can't do anything f'r ye on ye're own say so, but we'll sind a man to invistigate ye're case, an',' he says, 'if th' raypoort on ye'er moral charackter is satisfacthry,' he says, 'we'll attind to ye.'

"I dinnaw what it was, but th' matther popped out iv Dougherty's head an' nayether that day nor th' nex' nor th' nex' afther that was annything done f'r th' Galway woman. I'll say this f'r Dougherty, that whin th' thing come back to his mind again he put on his coat an' hurried over to Main sthreet. They was a wagon in th' sthreet, but Dougherty took no notice iv it. He walked up an' rapped on th' dure, an' th' little priest stepped out, th' breast iv his overcoat bulgin'. 'Why, father,' he says, 'ar-re ye here? I jus' come f'r to see——' 'Peace,' said th' little priest, closin' th' dure behind him an' takin' Dougherty be th' ar-rm. 'We were both late.' But 'twas not till they got to th' foot iv th' stairs that Dougherty noticed that th' wagon come fr'm th' county undertaker, an' that 'twas th' chalice made th' little priest's coat to bulge." (December 5, 1896)

13. A Bank Failure at Christmas Time

An adjunct of the continuing local and national depression was the failure of the Bank of Illinois on Monday, December 21, 1896. An unfavorable report by national bank examiners had blamed "injudicious loans" for destroying the bank's capital, and the Clearing-House Association of Chicago had responded by suspending it from membership. At the end of the week, Mr. Dooley commented on the relationship between bankers and depositors.

"It's a quite Chris'mas," said Mr. Hennessy.

"Yes," said Mr. Dooley, "with nawthin' to break th' silence but now an' thin a busting bank. It's a green Chris'mas f'r all th' wur-ruld, but a gray wan f'r thim that has their money put away in th' sthrong boxes. Whin Sandy Kloss comes in th' shape iv a naytional bank examiner it's time to take down ye'er stockin's fr'm th' hearth. Ye'll need thim f'r ye'er feet."

"Well, I'm glad to see thim go," said Mr. Hennessy, the embittered one. "I've been in charge iv a naytional bank examiner mesilf f'r twenty-five years. Me assets is twenty-eight cints, two pool checks an' a pair iv imbridered slippers that I dhrew this mornin' an' me libilities is somewhat in excess. I'm goin' to get out a statement iv me condition. Capital stock, wan million; surplus, wan million; cash on hand, twenty-eight cints; nee-gotyable securities, tin cints; due fr'm other Hinnissys, thirty dollars. Dooley, there's five hundhred thousan' naytional banks iv Illinye in Chicago today, on'y most iv thim was bor-rn with their libilities in excess iv their assets."

"Thrue f'r ye," said Mr. Dooley, "but th' conthroller iv th' currency hasn't annything to do with thim. We have polismen to look after those lads. A nay-tional bank is diff'rent. Some day a bank examiner dhrops in on wan iv thim an' looks over th' books. He raypoorts th' situation to his boss in Wash'nton an' th' boss writes down to th' prisidint iv th' bank. 'Dear sir an' brother,' he says, 'excuse me f'r intrudin' mesilf in ye'er affairs, but I'm tould ye have been lendin' other people's money to ye'erself an' frinds, an' there's some kickin',' he says. 'I thrust ye'll not take it too much to hear-rt if I suggest that this is conthrary to th' laws iv th' United States. Don't think me intrusive if I ask ye to put on a betther front f'r to quite suspicion,' he says. 'I wudden't f'r th' wurruld hurt ye'er feelings, but I have a jooty to perform an' that is to see that public confidence is maintained. If ye will give th' matther a little attintion, without too great inconvenience, an' make good some iv th' markers, ye'll be conferrin' a gr-reat personal favor on me. With best wishes f'r a merry Christmas an' a happy New Year, I am, yours thruly.' Well, th' boys come together an' they look over th' markers an' decide that they can't take thim up at wanst. Now, naytional banks always stand by each other, f'r th' purpose iv sustainin' that confidence so essential to—to—to confidencing th' public. That's th' point. Confidence, to inspire confidence. Th' la-ads with th' markers goes to their brothers an' frinds an' says they, 'We've got a note fr'm th' conthroller iv th' currency sayin' we've broke th' law. Thrue, we've broke oursilves too, but he takes it so much to hear-rt that we feel like doin' a good tur-rn f'r him. We've got our markers here an' we'd like to have money enough on thim to make good.' 'F'r why,' says their frinds. 'To keep up confidence,' says th' la-ads. Well, their brethren rubs their chins an' fin'lly wan iv thim up an' says: 'Th' foundation iv confidence is th' belief iv th' confidenced in th' integrity iv th' operator. This here bank has been conducted on th' wrong lines. Its methods have been unbusinesslike an' it has advanced money on markers that wudden't go across my layout. I don't believe in lindin' sanction or coin to anny entherprise r-run so carelessly. Th' time has come whin th' best way to restore confidince in th' public that's been so often up agin th' game that it can r-read th' ca-ards be th' backs, is to dhrive fr'm business th' careless, th' incompetent an' th' dishonest. Besides,' he says, 'if these markers are med good, a lot that I have become bad,' he says. 'I vote "no."' So th' nex' day early th' bank examiner tacks a ca-ard on th' dure an' the la-ads begin to r-roast each other in the pa-apers, an' th' German man, not having enough money to pay his quarterly license, crawls into th' icebox, takes a light lunch of paris green an' goes into liquidation.

"There's wan Chris'mas story f'r ye, Hinnissy. It ain't what it might be f'r gayety, but it's the divvle f'r facts. Whin I see th' bank examiner playin' Sandy Kloss I want to board up th' chimbley an' put me dough in th' stove. The best a bank can git whin he's around is a r-run f'r its money." (December 26, 1896)

14. Charity and Education: An Immigrant Shot for Stealing Coal

On January 21, 1897, the Times-Herald *claimed that "Chicago's poor are starving within sight of relief," while political red tape was holding up the dispensation of supplies. Two days later, amid rumors that Mayor George Swift was about to issue a proclamation on the relief crisis, a* Times-Herald *editorial described the city in these terms:*

> *. . . when ill-clad, half-famished shapes confront us on the streets; when the cold pinches the denizens of hovels and tenements, when the children in a thousand squalid homes cry for sustenance, when women fight for bread at the county agent's door, and able-bodied men swarm on the railway tracks, eagerly bagging fragments of coal—this crisis is not to be met with perfunctory measures.*

That night, Mr. Dooley told the story of one of those coal-pickers, a Polish immigrant named Sobieski. In the piece he alludes to Mayor Swift's association with a company that manufactured axle grease.

Mr. Dooley put a huge lump of soft coal into the gaping stove and whacked it to pieces with a little iron poker. Then he composed himself luxuriously before the blaze and said "Slanthu" to his friend Mr. Hennessy.

"How low did ye say th' glass was?" he asked.

"Four below," said Mr. Hennessy. "I near froze me ears comin' over here."

"R-rum," said Mr. Dooley. "R-rum'll be th' death iv ye, Hinnissy. 'Tis nat'ral f'r me to dhrink. I have it at me elbow. But 'tis a vice with you, an' anny man that'd lave a comfortable home an' th' society iv his fam'ly on a night like this f'r to put that into his face that steals away his feet is a sot, an' no mistake."

"Well, annyhow," said Mr. Hennessy, not at all abashed by the sarcasm, "I'm betther off than manny a man that has nayether home nor rum."

"Faith ye ar-re," said Mr. Dooley. "They'se no wan had to get out a rile proclamation f'r ye. They'se manny ways iv dealin' with th' poor. Wan is th' ol' fashioned way that prevails among th' poor thimsilves iv packin' away some potatoes an' a pound iv tay an' a side iv bacon in a basket an' takin' it around to th' poorer an' rayturnin' to tell what furniture they had in th' house. Another is th' organized charity that on'y helps thim that can prove that whin they had money they didn't spind it f'r food an' other luxuries but put it by f'r a rainy day. Th' new way is f'r to have th' mayor issue a proclamation callin' upon people f'r to give freely to th' destitute. I haven't heard that th' Whole Thing has donated a bar'l iv axle grease f'r to comfort th' afflicted. Mebbe he has a betther scheme. I shudden't be surprised if he'd set aside th' income fr'm th' Union loop to keep wan fam'ly each year. They'd hardly be enough; but ivry little bit helps, ye know.

"Me own scheme iv charity, Hinnissy, d'ye mind, is to duck whin I can, but whin a case comes up in front iv me eyes so that it hur-rts, d'ye mind, to give what I got an' ask no questions. I look on th' thing th' way an' ol' frind iv mine be th' name iv Hogan did. He was comin' up on th' late car wan night an' th' on'y other passenger was a big, r-rough-lookin' man. As th' conducter passed through th' car he dhropped a nickel. He didn't notice it, but Hogan an' th' other did, an' whin th' conductor got out on th' platform th' big man an' Hogan med a grab f'r it. They reached th' flure together, clinched an' rolled around, an' finally th' big man got on top an' thried to put Hogan's head in th' fire. Hogan hollered quits. 'Do I get it?' says th' big man. 'Sure,' says Hogan.

'If ye want it that bad ye ought to have it.' So be me with th' la-ads on th' street. Anny man that's so far gone that he'll ask ought to have. Besides, I feel this way about it, Hinnissy: Supposin' I was in that fix, wud I r-run up on a man in th' sthreet an' stick out a blue hand an' say: 'Can't ye help another young feller to get a meal?' Not on ye'er life. I'd steal a sock an' a small piece iv lead pipe somewhere, an' I'd not be particular about th' sock, an' I'd stand in th' corner iv an alley an' when a man come along that looked more thin 38 cints I'd tap him wanst if 'twas th' last act iv me degraded career, I wud so. I regard it as th' hite iv civility whin a man asks me f'r money instead iv takin' it away fr'm me. Th' money most people pay in charity is no more thin six per cint on what they steal, annyhow.

"But iv coorse ye can't get people to look at it that way. Ye didn't know a man named Sobieski, that lived down be Grove sthreet, did ye? Ah-ha! Well, he was not so bad, afther all. He's dead, ye know. Last week. Ye see, this here Sobieski had no more sinse thin a grasshopper. He arned enormous wages f'r a man with eight childher—wan twinty-five a day, half a week in good times, sidintary imploymint carryin' pigs iv steel at th' mills. Bimeby th' saviors iv their counthry, believin' th' market was overstocked, shut down an' left time and grocers' bills heavy on Sobieski's hands. Th' col' weather come on, an' Sobieski grew tired iv inaction. Also th' childher were freezin' to death. So he put a bag on his shoulder an' wint over to th' railway thracks to pick up some coal. Wan man can't pick up much coal on th' railway thracks, Hinnissy, but it is an unpardonable crime, just th' same. 'Tis far worse thin breakin' th' intherstate commerce act. Anny offense again' a railway company is high threason, but pickin' up coal is so villainous that they'se no forgiveness f'r th' hidyous wretch that commits it.

"Sobieski walked along th' thracks, gettin' a chunk here an' there, till a watchman seen him, an' pintin' a revolver at him, called 'Halt!' Sobieski didn't know th' English language very well. 'Dam Pole' was about his limit, an' he had that thrained into him be th' foreman at th' mills. But he knew what a revolver meant, an' th' ignorant fool tur-rned an' run with his three cints' worth iv coal rattlin' at his back. Th' watchman was a good shot, an' a Pole with heavy boots is no tin-second man in a fut race. Sobieski pitched over on his face, thried to further injure th' comp'ny be pullin' up th' rails with his hands, an' thin passed to where—him bein' a Pole, an' dyin' in such a horrible sin—they'se no need iv coal iv anny kind.

"That shows wan iv th' evils iv a lack iv idyacation," Mr. Dooley continued. "If Sobieski had known th' language——"

"He'd a halted," said Mr. Hennessy.

"He wud not," said the Philosopher. "He'd niver been there at all. While th' watchman was walkin' knee-deep in snow, Sobie-ski'd been comfortably joltin' th' watchman's boss in a dark alley downtown. Idyacation is a gr-reat thing." (January 23, 1897)

15. Clancy the Infidel, Saved by Father Kelly

At noon on Sunday, January 24, the Chicago temperature was thirteen below zero. That night Mayor Swift proclaimed that instant relief would be provided to all who were in need, regardless of their qualifications. The police, who were to act as relief agents, were in-structed to "feed and warm them first. Inquire about it afterwards." The following weekend, as a rejoinder to the mayor's solution, Mr. Dooley provided this exemplum of personal charity in Bridgeport.

"I suppose I'm a har-rd hear-rted man," Mr. Dooley began.

"Pooh!" said Mr. Hennessy. "Ye're as soft as a babby."

"I suppose," Mr. Dooley repeated sternly, "I'm a har-rd hear-rt-ed man. A man don't come to be six an' fifty years iv age——"

"How many?" Mr. Hennessy demanded.

"Five an' sixty years iv age, I said, without some iv th' mushy sides iv his nature becomin' pethrified. But f'r th' life iv me I can't stay in this here place an' see what's goin' on around me without

wishin' I had me two arrums up to th' elbows in the Bank iv England an' th' strenth in me shoulders to hurl th' coin as far as a
Tipperary man cud peg a rock at a polisman.

"Yis, I know th' wur-ruk iv relief is goin' on, but what th' la-ads
need is th' relief iv wur-ruk. I'm not much iv a believer in wur-ruk
personally, but that's because I was raised a pet. Annyhow, it's
ruinin' th' temper iv th' human race. But manny a man doesn't
known anny betther thin to think he's servin' Gawd best be
poundin' slag fr'm daybreak to sunset an' thin goin' home too
tired to stand or set or lay down. We've hammered it into their
heads that they'se some connection between a pickax an' a dish iv
ham an' eggs, an' bedad they can't be made to believe that wan
ain't th' fruit iv th' other. Givin' thim food don't seem to be anny
use, much less dhress suits, that won't fit anny man in th' polis
station. I niver see th' fam'lies iv th' polis department so well
dhressed as they've been f'r a week.

"I've no kick comin' again th' r-rich men that thrust their hands
down in their pockets an' dhraw out f'r th' poor. They're all right.
Thank heaven f'r weather cold enough so that th' steam pipes
won't heat their bedrooms an' a hot-water bag won't make a carredge warrum enough f'r comfort. 'Tis on'y thin they think iv th'
poor. Wan iv thim says to himsilf: 'Lord, if me hooks are frost-
bitten in these sealskin gloves what must th' poor divvles feel that
have nothin' on their hands but dirt an' chaps?' An' he throws a
thousand into th' pot at th' city hall an' has his name put in th'
paper an' gets Donovan to print his picture an' wondhers whin th'
Lord'll sind f'r him in a motocycle iv fire. But barrin' me joy at
separatin' annywan that r-runs a gashouse or a sthreetcar line fr'm
his overcharges, I have no rel-ligous feelin' about that man. Does
he give to th' poor? Faith, he does not. He gives to himsilf—to the
magnate with th' frost-bitten hands an' th' cold legs. If that sort iv
givin' to th' poor is lindin' to th' Lord, some day whin stocks go
down th' loan'll be called an' th' Commercial Club'll hold a gold
morgedge on paradise. It will so. To think that a man can square
himsilf with his conscience be givin' wan thousan' dollars to a po-

lisman an' tellin' him to disthribute it! Why don't they get the poor up in a cage in Lincoln Park an' hand thim food on th' ind iv a window-pole, if they're afraid they'll bite?

"Afther all 'tis th' poor that keeps th' poor. They ain't wan shrugglin' fam'ly in this war-rd that ain't carryin' three others on its back. A pound iv tay in ye'er house means a hot cup f'r thim poor Schwartzs' and ye'er encouragin' petty larceny be lavin' ye'er soft coal out—I seen ye do it, ye miserable man—so that th' Dugan boys cud steal it because ye don't speak to their father. Th' man Clancy down th' sthreet that nobody likes, him bein' a notoryous infidel, 'd be dead if it wasn't f'r th' poor iv a poor par-ish. He was set down f'r relief out iv th' mayor's fund. He was short coal an' wood, bread an' meat, dhrink an' th' grace iv Gawd, an' some wan put in an application f'r him. That afthernoon a pa-throl wagon dhrew up in front iv his dure an' th' whole neighbor-hood wint over expectin' him to be arrested f'r blasphemyous lan-guage. Th' polisman fooled around in a pile iv stuff an' brought out a parcel. It contained a sprinklin' pot, a pair iv corsets, a bar iv soap, an' ax an' a hammick. Clancy wept tears iv joy. 'But, gintlemin,' he says, 'ye've forgot th' pepper an' salt.' 'What d'ye want pepper an' salt f'r?' says th' polisman. 'How in 'ell can I make a salad out iv this hammick without pepper an' salt?' says Clancy.

"Father Kelly heerd iv th' case that night. He's wan iv th' poor iv th' parish; th' saint got an appetite f'r thruffles at colledge, an' has been satisfyin' it on oatmeal iver since. He'd saved up tin dol-lars f'r to buy th' 'Life iv Saint Jerome,' but whin he heerd iv Clancy he give a sigh an' says he, 'Martin,' he says, 'Jerome'll have to wait,' he says, an' we wint down th' sthreet an' rough-an'-tumbled ivery coal dealer, butcher, grocer an' baker—most iv thim broke thimselves—till we had a wagonload iv stuff. We dumped it at Clancy's, an' th' pagan came out an' wanted Father Kelly f'r to set on th' coal while he proved that th' Bible was nawthin' more nor less thin a book of anecdotes an' that if histori-cal tistimony was believed Queen Victoria'd be pope in Rome to-day. I was f'r feedin' him a piece iv coal, but th' good man says,

'What talk have ye? Go an' starve no more,' an' come away with a grin on his face. He behaved most crazy all th' way up, runnin' behind his parishoners an' hollerin' in their ears or makin' snow balls an' throwin' thim at th' sthreetcar dhrivers whin they touched their hats to him. Near Ashland avenoo we met Keough. Ye know him. He passes th' plate at th' church. I niver cud. It's more thin me relligion 'll stand to put th' conthribution-box under th' nose of a man I don't like. But Keough does it an' he's rich. 'Keough,' says th' good man, 'I want ye to put that crazy Galway man, Clancy, to wurruk,' he says. 'But he's a heathen,' says Keough. 'So he is,' says th' good man. 'He don't go to his jooty,' says Keough. 'I wouldn't lave him,' says th' good man. 'But there me jooty ends. I have no jurisdiction in anny other parish,' he says. 'Much less is it me privilege f'r to visit tormint upon th' sinful,' he says. 'Clancy is a wicked man, a miserable sinner an' a vile pagan but he'll be a long time dead,' he says. 'I'll sind him to ye to-morrah; an' if ye've listened to me attintively f'r th' las' tin years,' he says, 'ye ought to have theological argyments enough to shake his onbelief,' he says. 'Meanwhile,' he says, 'I'll race anny man to th' corner,' an' he won be tin yards.

"He's a good man, that little priest."

"Man?" said Mr. Hennessy, "he's a saint!"

"Mebbe so," said Mr. Dooley. "But ye'd betther not let him hear ye say so." (January 30, 1897)

16. After the Bradley-Martin Ball

Newspapers in February 1897 were full of opinions about the masked ball to be given by the Bradley-Martins of New York. Their own Episcopal pastor publically denounced the family for callously flaunting wealth in a time of general destitution, and Mr. Bradley-Martin argued back that actually he was performing a service, in sending so much money into circulation among designers, artisans, and shopkeepers. Mr. Dooley discussed the ball twice. Because it contains a reminiscence about his youth in Ireland, the first piece ap-

*pears in Chapter One. In this followup piece, Father Kelly compares
America in 1897 with prerevolutionary France.*

"Whin people dhraw f'r to make fools iv thimsilves," said Mr.
Dooley, "they gin'rally fill their hands."

"They do," said Mr. Hennessy. "They do."

"I was thinkin' more par-ticklurly," Mr. Dooley went on, "iv
thim Bradley Martins an' their frinds. Th' pa-apers said it was a
sight, long to be raymimbered, an' I dinnaw that it wasn't. But as
I r-read it over I cudn't help but feelin' sorry that th' human r-race
had taken a flop backward acrost th' cinturies, an' here was min,
an' women, too, carryin' on like th' ring-tailed apes iv commerce.
What possessed thim, Hinnissy? F'r mesilf I can't see no difference between th' likes iv thim an' th' foolish an' daffy savage man
that tatooes himsilf an' goes around with nawthin' on but a blue
undhershirt an' a pink an' green murmaid. Th' savage has th' best
iv it, at that. I knowed wan be th' name iv Simpson that looked
like he'd been weaved f'r a Turkish r-rug, an' he earned his good
ol' twinty-five per at th' dime museem. Him an' th' ossified man
come into my place wanst. He was all right, but his frind was stiff.
What's that?

"I talked it over with th' good man th' other night. They'se few
things livin' or dead, in or out iv books, that he don't know or
can't give a good guess at. Fr'm th' rules iv hurlin' to th' theeries
iv th' ancient Greeks he'll give ye anny hould ye want an' lay ye
down. He's specially sthrong on histhry; he knows it backward
to th' time whin Malachi wore th' collar iv goold that he won fr'm
th' proud invader, as th' song says. I'd been r-readin' about th'
Bradley Martin ball an' I wanted to know who th' people was
they riprisinted. 'Who was Madame Maintainon?' says I. 'She
was a little betther thin she should be,' says he. 'An',' says I, 'who
was Madame Pompydore?' I says. 'She had her faults,' says he.
'An' d'ye mean to say,' says I, 'that decent women bringin' up their
childher in th' fear iv Tammany wint out to imitate th' ——'
'Ladies iv th' coort,' he says. 'Ladies iv th' coort?' says I.

"'Well,' he said, 'perhaps th' poor things knew no betther. But,' he says, 'I'll not tell ye,' he says, 'I was not surprised to see so manny iv thim takin' on th' charackters iv thim that in their life had no charackters, or playin' like childhren at a pasteboard ripri-sintation iv th' days befure th' Frinch rivolution,' he says. 'If ye have r-read in histhry,' says he, 'an' know th' min an' women whose sins, may th' good Lord f'rgive thim, brought on th' guillo-tine,' he says, 'ye'll see all their names in th' list iv disgeeses put on be these sons iv American candle-makers an' grocers an' dhry good merchants.

"'I don't suppose they know, poor things, but no more did th' lads that danced an' sung an' spint their money free in th' ol' days. Ye don't imagine, do ye, that all th' r-rich people in France were ha-ard an' crool, an' that they cut th' poor down with their soords in th' sthreet? Not at all, Martin. Th' poor was no worse off thin those ye see around ye, an' th' r-rich was no more proud an' no less sure they were safe an' doin' th' r-right thing. They wint to mass an' they dhropped their coin into th' plate an' they give to th' poor an' visited th' sick an' had souphouses where a man cud feed his hatred on hot bean soup, which has this advantage, it warms th' stomach an' encourages a rivolutionary thirst f'r champagne. They had their parties an' their dances an' they made business good an' they flaunted their finery befure th' people an' were happy an' gay an' continted as th' day is long. Wanst in awhile some crusty ol' divvle wud tell a rayporter th' public be damned, an' they'd be a vilent denunciation iv this man as unpathriotic. Thin a parson 'd preach timidly about wealth, an' th' Bradley Martins 'd say: "What does he want? We give our money to th' dhressmakers an' th' shoemakers an' th' hackmin. We put it in cir-culation. Ain't we betther to spind it at home thin if we carrid it abroad with us?" An' th' pa-apers 'd say: "Sure, ye ar-re." An' the fancy dhress ball 'd go on an' th' polismin 'd belt th' people cranin' their necks over th' railin' an' wishin' they cud tear th' clothes off with an icepick.

"'These here things wur-ruk slow an' it took two or three hun-dhred years befure th' people—I mean th' poor wans an', what's more important, th' politicians that not bein' able to get through th' front dure wint through th' back—took it into their heads to do business. Meantime I have no doubt they was congrissional comities appinted an' judeecial invistigations started an' th' ball wint on. If a man has time enough to get used to it he can live in th' crather iv a volcano. I used to know a watchman named Casey in a dinnymite magazine out in Brighton that used to set on a kag iv dinnymite smokin' a pipe an' playin' solitaire on another kag. Wan day he yawned an' knocked th' ashes out iv his pipe into th' kag an' th' coroner had to hold th' inquest on a bone collar-button. So 'twas in France. Wan day th' people begun pushin' each other an' ivirybody that didn't lose their head in wan way lost it in another, an' thin Napoleon Bonnypart came into town an' that was th' end iv it all.'

"'Glory be,' says I. 'Is that what we're comin' to?' 'I didn't say so, foolish man,' said he. 'This here ain't France. We have no king here an' no nobility an' th' best-dhressed people ar-re not always th' worst. Afther all 'tis on'y wanst in iviry two or three months th' r-rich cut loose an' thin they ain't really bad. They haven't got that far in their eddycation. 'Twas on'y an imitation Madame Maintainon an' an imitation Looey that pranced through th' New York hotel. Th' nex' day Madame Maintainon was atin' fish balls at breakfast an' Looey th' Foorteenth was downtown with a dinky little hat on th' back iv his head thryin' to guess what sugar certyficates 'd cost th' nex' minyit. That's th' salvation iv th' republic. Looey wurruks f'r a livin' an' Madame Maintainon is reglarly marrid. On'y whin they give a ball they ought to put smoked glasses on th' people that can't tell a real king fr'm a sivin spot.'"
(February 13, 1897)

Chapter Five

Chicago Politics: The View from Archey Road

Political life provided the most visible and controversial career oppor-
tunities for the Irish in American cities in the late nineteenth century.
Between the great famine of the late 1840s and the turn of the cen-
tury, over three million Irishmen had come to America; the 1890
census showed an all-time high of 1,872,000 Americans of Irish
birth. The combination of numbers, linguistic talents, and a cohesive
ghetto community produced the urban political machine, a tightly
woven network of single-minded men, from the boss at the top to the
precinct captain at the bottom, through which few votes were allowed
to slip. The aim, of course, was to get power.

The classic example of Irish boss rule was New York's Tammany
Hall, which became synonymous with corruption when the Tweed
Ring was exposed in 1871. But a similar organization flourished in
Chicago in Mr. Dooley's time. The mayor and city council of two
aldermen from each of thirty-odd wards presided over the dispensa-
tion of a seemingly endless supply of franchises and ordinances nec-
essary to the continued expansion of the fastest growing city in
America. Every new road or building, every railroad, streetcar, and
telegraph line, every installation of gas and water was a potential
source of graft (or "boodle") to the council's "gray wolves."

In all of this, the contribution of the Irish was considerable.
The Cook County Democratic machine was firmly entrenched, and
Irish-dominated. Much of its strength came from the alliance be-
tween King Mike McDonald, Irish political boss, and Carter H. Har-
rison, a popular Yankee, who, by throwing in with the Irish, had been
elected mayor of Chicago an unprecedented five times between 1879

and 1893. McDonald went into semiretirement after 1890, and Harrison was murdered in October 1893, but the machine rolled on through the decade in the hands of a small group of Irish bosses and aldermen, including Michael "Hinky Dink" Kenna, "Bathhouse John" Coughlin, "Johnny de Pow" Powers, and Bridgeport's own William J. O'Brien.

As an experienced political reporter who had been close to the action in Chicago since the 1880s, Peter Dunne was well qualified to describe his city's governmental processes. And the Dooley political pieces do not disappoint. They constitute a valuable inside narrative of the Irish-American preoccupation with power and a vivid microcosm of the urban political machine in America at the turn of the century. Also, because machine politicians made poor or reluctant historians, Mr. Dooley gives us much otherwise unavailable information—about the electoral process, the business of city government, and the people involved in both.

The first group of pieces in this chapter deals with that yearly tribal rite, the aldermanic election, beginning with Mr. Dooley's memory of an energetic contest between Irish and German candidates to represent Bridgeport (Ward Six) in the city council. (Because he served as precinct captain in his corner of the ward in 1873–1875, Mr. Dooley was also well qualified to observe the political animal, and many of his anecdotes are nostalgic laments for the passing of the old "rough-an'-tumble" days—although the Chicago style of politics was still very lively in the nineties.) The second piece contains the analysis of a model campaign waged by the most prominent figure in the political pieces, William J. O'Brien, a real Bridgeport alderman who seems to have been the quintessential ward politician. Next, Mr. Dooley measures the role of women in politics; although they cannot vote, Bridgeport's wives and daughters influence elections by exerting considerable pressure on their franchise-wielding male kin (3). In two more pieces, Mr. Dooley recalls an election during his precinct captaincy when Dorsey's goat, Monica, was involved in a questionable vote-counting incident (4), and a bone-bruising primary at Finucane's Hall, which convinces him once and for all that "politics ain't bean-bag. 'Tis a man's game, an' women, childer, cripples an' prohybitionists 'd do well to keep out iv it" (5).

In the second group of pieces, Mr. Dooley describes Chicago government in action, through glimpses of the inner workings of the mayor's office and the council. To dissuade Hogan from training his son for the clergy, Dooley lists the advantages of being an alderman, not the least of which is license to be "as dhrunk as he pleases an' fight as much as he wants" (6). To illustrate how the mayor and aldermen cooperate to pass bills, Dooley recalls an exchange between Mayor Harrison and Bill O'Brien on the issue of installing a garbage dump in Bridgeport (7). The quality of appointments made by the spoils system is questioned in the story of Hannigan, the water inspector, who avoided his job to the extent that "he used beer as th' chaser" (8). The mechanics of dispensing boodle become clear in the career of Alderman Dochney, who "was expelled fr'm th' St. Vincent de Pauls, an' ilicted a director iv a bank th' same day" (9). And Mr. Dooley's suspicion of self-proclaimed reformers is the theme of a piece in which he exposes a Bridgeport reform committee as being comprised of the community's richest and least compassionate citizens, including a rackrenting landlord who "reforms" his tenants into the cemetery (10).

The third group contains capsule biographies of Chicago Irish politicians, in which sympathy for the hardships of deprived childhood is tempered by the conclusion that nothing so qualifies a man for political life as a talent for rough-house bullying. A young tough with "th' smell iv Castle Garden on him" rises by means of his reputation as a fighter to become boss of the ward, then commits the unpardonable sin of betraying the men who put him there (11). In other pieces, political aspiration ruins the lives and livelihoods of decent people. Convinced by self-serving friends that he can win a seat in the state legislature, little Flanagan throws away his savings, job, and house, then loses the election and slinks home in the fog, hunched over and ruined (12). A similar fate confronts Slattery, "a dacint, quiet little lad," who parlays a successful saloon into an aldermanic seat, then sacrifices his reputation to the lure of easy money. Defeated for reelection and deserted by his steady customers, "all he had left was his champagne thirst" (13). The last biographical sketch is a sympathetic portrayal of the rise of colorful, nineteen-term alderman, Johnny Powers, from grocery boy in the city's toughest neighborhood to acknowledged "prince of boodle" in Chicago (14).

This chapter ends with an extended treatment of the aldermanic election of April 1897, about which Dunne wrote four Dooley pieces in a row (15–18). Together, they contain all of the major themes of Dunne's political musings over the years: corruption in politics, the difficulties of trying to change the system, the dishonest methods by which elections are actually won, and the attraction of unsavory characters to political life. In the election, itself, a safe majority of known boodlers was returned to the council, and the Dooley series ends on a note of skepticism about the possibility of political reform in Chicago.

1. Memories of the O'Reilly-Schultze Election

The candidates for mayor of Chicago in April 1895 were George B. Swift (Republican) and Frank Wenter (a Democrat of Bohemian extraction). Swift won. A "head center of the Fenians" was a cell leader in the Irish-American secret organization, the Fenian Brotherhood, the goal of which was to overthrow the British in Ireland. William Joyce was a Bridgeport political boss who never ran for office himself but wielded power from behind the scenes.

"'Tis warm," said Mr. Dooley. "The spring have come. Th' bur-rds is warblin' in th' bur-rd cages an' th' grass'll be growin' alongside th' grain ca-ars in th' freightyards befure long. It will that. An' Choosdah is iliction day, an' that makes it sthronger. Afther th' returns is all in we'll have th' rale article iv spring an' th' peddlers'll be singin' down th' sthreet.

"Swift? Winter? What diff'rence does it make? Ilictions ain't what they was, Jawn. Runnin' a Bohemian f'r office! Why, whin I was takin' a hand in politics an' captain iv me precinct, with conthrol iv two shut-off min an' half th' r-rid bridge, 'twas th' proud boast iv th' pa-arty that th' Bohemian vote cud be got to a man be promisin' wan Bohemian to let him go downtown an' look at th' lake. 'Twas so. They'll be runnin' Chinamin next. Faith, there's wan wantin' to be mayor iv a place out in Kansas now. Think iv it, Jawn, votin' a laundhry ticket! 'Twould be a great ca-ard f'r th' haythin if he'd tell his audgeences that if they ilicted him he'd wear no man's collar. 'Twas that Tim Dorsey said whin he was runnin' f'r constable. 'Fellow citizens,' says he, 'ilict me to that there office,' he says, 'an' I'll promise ye that I will perform th' jooties,' he says, 'f'r th' inthrest iv me constitooncy,' he says. 'Ye'er wearin' my shirt now,' says Grogan that he used to board with. It bate Dorsey f'r th' job. It did so.

"Thin this here little bald-headed duck iv a Swift. Who th' 'ell's he? No wan cares f'r him—th' little, foolish gazabo goin' around with his head naked. 'Tis ondacint f'r him to be seen in th' sthreet, let alone be runnin' f'r th' Whole Thing. He ought to be locked up with Winter an' all th' other la-ads. 'Tis no time iv year to be talkin' politics, an' annyhow politics ain't what they was, Jawn. I've sold nothin' all day but a bottle iv pop, an' I've had so manny pictures iv candydates in th' window that I've had to light th' gas at noon.

"D'ye suppose in th' old days I cud've hung thim posters without a rite? I sh'd say not. I mind whin Eddie O'Reilly an' Schultze was runnin'. Torchlight procission iv'ry night. O'Reilly'd 've won if they hadn't let th' Dutchman's lads vote fr'm th' 'ospital. But annyhow, I had up a picture iv O'Reilly in th' window, whin in come little Slatthery. D'ye mind him? He was a nervous little la-ad fr'm th' County Kerry. He used to be conductor iv a sthreet-ca-ar. Wan day they was two big hoboes an' a lady in th' ca-ar, an' th' hoboes was chewin' tobacco. 'Conductor,' says th' lady to Slatthery, 'D'ye allow spittin' in this ca-ar?' 'Sure, ma'am,' says Slatthery, 'Annywhere ye like,' he says. They give him th' run f'r that, an' he wint into politics. He come in here wan day an' he seen O'Reilly's picture in th' window. 'What have ye th' face iv that man frightenin' away custom f'r?' he says. 'Who?' says I. 'O'Reilly,' says he. 'What's th' matther with O'Reilly?' says I. 'He's no good,' says he. 'He throws down all his frinds,' says he. 'But th' other man's Dutch,' says I. 'Naw he ain't,' says he. 'He's marrid wan iv Doherty's daughters,' he says. 'An' if Prince Bismark was to marry an Irish girl,' says he, 'he'd be th' head cinter iv th' fanians within wan month.' 'I guess ye'er right,' says I. So I took down O'Reilly an' put up Schultze. I'd no more thin turned be back whin bang! come a brick through th' window. I wint out, an' there was th' prisident, secrity, an' thre-asurer iv th' Eddie O'Reilly Lith'ry Club thryin' to pry up th' sthreet f'r ammunition.

"Now look at it. I aven put up a picture iv th' prohibition can-dydate an' no one set fire to th' house. Little Cassidy come in here yesterday, an', says he, 'Who's all thim ye have in th' window?' he says. 'Thim befure-an'-afther-takin' pictures?' says he. 'Thim 'r th' candydates f'r mayor,' I says. 'Are they?' says he. 'They's al-ways some wan runnin' f'r something,' he says. 'Ain't they?' he says. 'Give me a glass iv beer—a high wan,' he says. An' I've seen that man r-run fr'm th' bridge to th' mills with a ballot-box under his ar-rm fr'm th' pure love iv th' thing.

"Why on'y this afthernoon I met Willum Joyce walkin' down th' sthreet, doin' what? R-readin' a book, no less. D'ye think he'd 've done that tin years ago three days befure iliction? I've seen him goin' downtown settin' on th' flure iv th' car."

Mr. Dooley brushed away a tear and counted up. (March 30, 1895)

2. A Model Campaign for Alderman

William Jennings Bryan had just made his "Cross of Gold" speech and been nominated for president when Dunne wrote this piece in July 1896. William J. O'Brien represented Bridgeport in the city council from 1889 to 1893 and again from 1897 to 1899. Mr. Dooley is his only biographer.

"D'ye know," said Mr. Dooley, "that histhry repeats itself, as th' good book says. An' th' more I hear iv th' young man Bryan th' more I wish he was bor-rn a dumby, though if he had been he'd 've wore his ar-rms down to a stump befure now thryin' to make himsilf undherstud.

"I mind th' first time Willum J. O'Brien r-run f'r office, th' Raypublicans an' th' Indypindants an' th' Socialists an' th' Pro-hybitionist (he's dead now, his name was Larkin) nommynated a young man be th' name iv Dorgan that was in th' law business in Halsted Sthreet, near Cologne, to r-run again' him. Smith O'Brien Dorgan was his name, an' he was wan iv th' most ilo-quint young la-ads that iver made a speakin' thrumpet iv his face. He cud holler like th' impire iv a base-ball game; an', whin he de-livered th' sintimints iv his hear-rt, ye'd think he was thryin' to confide thim to a man on top iv th' Audiotorium tower. He was prisidint iv th' lithry club at th' church; an' Father Kelly tol' me that, th' day afther he won th' debate on th' pen an' th' soord in favor iv th' pen, they had to hire a carpenter to mend th' windows, they'd sagged so. They called him th' boy or-rator iv Healey's slough.

"He planned th' campaign himsilf. 'I'll not re-sort,' says he, 'to th' ordin'ry methods,' he says. 'Th' thing to do,' he says, 'is to pri-sint th' issues iv th' day to th' voters,' he says. 'I'll burn up ivry precin't in th' ward with me iloquince,' he says. An' he bought a long black coat, an' wint out to spread th' light.

"He talked ivrywhere. Th' people jammed Finucane's Hall, an' he tol' thim th' time had come f'r th' masses to r-rise. 'Ray-mimber,' says he, 'th' idees iv Novimb'r,' he says. 'Raymimber Demosthens an' Cicero an' Oak Park,' he says. 'Raymimber th' thraditions iv ye'er fathers, iv Washin'ton an' Jefferson an' An-dhrew Jackson an' John L. Sullivan,' he says. 'Ye shall not, Billy O'Brien,' he says, 'crucify th' voters iv th' Sixth Ward on th' double cross,' he says. He spoke to a meetin' in Deerin' Sthreet in th' same wurruds. He had th' Sthreet-car stopped while he coughed up reemarks about th' Constitution until th' bar-rn boss sint down an' threatened to discharge Mike Dwyer that was dhrivin' wan hundherd an' eight in thim days, though thrans-ferred to Wintworth Avnoo later on. He made speeches to polismin in th' squadroom an' to good la-ads hoistin' mud out iv th' dhraw at th' red bridge. People'd be settin' quite in th' back room playin' forty-fives whin Smith O'Brien Dorgan'd burst in, an' addhress thim on th' issues iv th' day.

"Now all this time Bill O'Brien was campaignin' in his own way. He niver med wan speech. No wan knew whether he was f'r a tariff or again wan, or whether he sthud be Jefferson or was knockin' him, or whether he had th' inthrests iv th' toilin' masses at hear-rt or whether he wint to mass at all, at all. But he got th' superintindint iv th' rollin'-mills with him; an' he put three or four good fam'lies to wurruk in th' gas-house, where he knew th' main guy, an' he made reg'lar calls on th' bar-rn boss iv th' sthreet-ca-ars. He wint to th' picnics, an' hired th' or-chesthry f'r th' dances, an' voted himsilf th' most pop'lar man at th' church fair at an expinse iv at laste five hundherd dollars. No wan that come near him wanted f'r money. He had headquarthers in ivry saloon fr'm wan end iv th' ward to th' other. All th' pa-apers printed his pitcher, an' sthud by him as th' frind iv th' poor.

"Well, people liked to hear Dorgan at first, but afther a few months they got onaisy. He had a way iv breakin' into festive gatherin's that was enough to thry a saint. He delayed wan prize fight two hours, encouragin' th' voters prisint to stand be their principles, while th' principles sat shiverin' in their cor-rners until th' polis r-run him out. It got so that men'd bound into alleys whin he come up th' sthreet. People in th' liquor business ray-fused to let him come into their places. His fam'ly et in th' coal-shed f'r fear iv his speeches at supper. He wint on talkin', and Willum J. O'Brien wint on handin' out th' dough that he got fr'm th' gas company an' con-ciliatin' th' masses; an', whin iliction day come, th' judges an' clerks was all f'r O'Brien, an' Dorgan didn't get votes enough to wad a gun. He sat up near all night in his long coat, makin' speeches to himsilf; but tord mornin' he come over to my place where O'Brien sat with his la-ads. 'Well,' says O'Brien, 'how does it suit ye?' he says. 'It's sthrange,' says Dorgan. 'Not sthrange at all,' says Willum J. O'Brien. 'Whin ye've been in poli-tics as long as I have, ye'll know,' he says, 'that th' roly-boly is th' gr-reatest or-rator on earth,' he says. 'Th' American nation in th' Sixth Ward is a fine people,' he says. 'They love th' eagle,' he says, 'on th' back iv a dollar,' he says. 'Well,' says Dorgan, 'I can't un-dherstand it,' he says. 'I med as manny as three thousan' speeches,' he says. 'Well,' says Willum J. O'Brien, 'that was my majority,' he says. 'Have a dhrink,' he says." (July 18, 1896)

3. The Role of Women in Bridgeport Politics

The assassination of Mayor Carter Harrison prompted a special election in December 1893 in which Democrat John P. Hopkins defeated Republican George Swift. Mr. Dooley picked the winner two weeks before the election in this piece. Father Maurice J. Dorney was a well-known figure in Irish nationalist circles in Chicago.

"Well, Jawn," said Mr. Dooley, "who's goin' to be elected?"

"Swift," said Mr. McKenna, who is a republican.

"Ye'er a liar," said Mr. Dooley, who is a democrat. "Swift has no more chanst iv bein' mayor than Father Dorney has iv bein' elected gran' master iv th' orangemen—Gawd f'rgive me f'r sayin' it. Niver mind, McKinna. Don't tell me, by gar; I know. Ye can't beat that there Hopkins no more than ye cud bate a polisman playin' forty-five. He have th' ca-ards up his sleeve, he have, he have.

"For why, says ye? Listen to me, Jawn, ye poor, deluded gom, that's been in politics since ye got out iv short clothes an' knows no more about it than ye know about th' catechism, an' ye know dam little iv that beyant 'Why did he make me?' Listen to me, avick, an' I'll give ye a pointher or two. Did ye niver know I was in politics wanst? I was that. I was captain in me precint whin we carrid it f'r O'Broyn be more votes than they was min, women, childhern an' goats in th' whole sixth wa-ard. I was in politics thin, captain iv me precint, an' they was no man in Bridgeport wist iv Finucane's that cud throw me down. Sare a wan. I shtud like Willum Joyce an' Bill O'Broyn an' Stuckart rolled in wan, f'r

I was as gr-reat a han' at visitin' round an' quotin' th' pothry iv little Mike Scanlan as Joyce, an' I could whale hell out iv anny man fr'm Haley's to th' bridge, an' I shtud like a king among th' Dutch. I cud ate a manger full iv cole slaw. I was a pollytician wanst, though I've braced up an' rayformed since, Jawn, an' I'll tell ye no lie, the man that gets th' women with him can shtay at home an' write his message. He can that.

"Now, Jawn, mind ye, women don't vote, but women r-runs thim that does vote, as Brady said at th' raffle. It don't make no diff'rence what th' man is. He takes his ordhers fr'm th' captain at home in wan way or th' other, an' though he may be as big as a grain elevator an' whin it comes to an argyment about gettin' in th' coal though he may be able to give her th' shovel an' win out, he does what she wants done, divvle th' liss. An' a woman, if she had th' brains iv Daniel O'Connell, still she'd be a woman all th' same an' f'r th' best-lukin' guy in th' race. A man says to himself: 'What's th' qualifications iv th' candidate? Will he clane th' sthreets, will he lower taxes, will he put me brother on th' polis force?' he says. He asks himself thim quistions. But with a woman 'tis diff'rent. Says she: 'Ain't he a nice-lukin' man?' says she. ''Tis a shame to bate such a nice-lukin' man,' she says. 'Mike,' she says, 'ye'er goin' to vote for Hopkins,' she says. 'No,' says he, 'I was thinkin' iv votin' f'r Swift,' he says. 'What!' says she. 'F'r that little baldheaded duck?' says his wife. 'Why, Mike, f'r shame,' says she. 'Why,' she says, 'he ain't got no hair,' says she. Ye can bank, Jawn, that a woman 'll niver like a baldheaded man. Whether 'tis because iv th' old sayin' that a man loses his hair f'r his sins or whether because whin a man is bald no woman has anny hold upon him, 'tis not f'r me to say. Now, a man can stand off thim little dodgers they sends around before election day. He can stand thim off. An' he can take a long chance with a frind who grabs him be th' buttonhole in th' sthreet, f'r he can call a copper if he wants to get away. But how th' 'ell is a man goin' to dodge an argyment that he gets in th' mornin' an' night an' at meal times, whin he's sober an' whin he has his rollers upon him? There's no escape unliss he'll ate his meals on th' front stoop an' sleep in th' ba-arn. None at all, Jawn.

"I seen it wur-rk whin Tom Sinnott was a candidate f'r something or another. Donovan had him bate blind in the sixth whin Sinnott came up to a party. They hadn't seen Donovan, but some wan had it around that he came fr'm Connock an' was a dashin' boy, but whin Sinnott appeared 'twas all off with me brave Harry. Sinnott wint to all th' balls and christenin's fr'm wan ind iv th' wa-ard to th' other, makin' luv to th' daughters iv th' precint commitymen. Dam near all iv thim accipted him, too, at that, f'r th' rollin' mills was shut down. Well, sir, they say whin he'd propose to a girl he'd say: 'Molly,' he'd say, 'don't say nothin' about this till afther th' 'lection,' he'd say. 'Thin we'll announce it,' he'd say. 'Is ye'er father a sthrong democrat?' 'Th' sthrongest that iver lived.' 'Thin he wouldn't vote th' raypublican ticket?' 'I sh'd say not.' 'Thin give him these here pasters,' he'd say. 'Maybe ye cud get him to use thim,' he'd say. 'Here's some f'r his friends. Will ye rassle through th' nex' waltz with me, Julia?' Well, sir, whin it come election day Donovan wasn't in it. They say Sinnott lived in his cellar f'r a month an' it cost him th' first year's salary squarin' breach iv promise suits.

"An' there ye are, Jawn." (December 9, 1893)

4. An Old Style Election Day in the Ward

The Civic Federation was a group of citizens supporting clean government, most of whom were well-to-do Republicans. It had been formed in time to sponsor a slate of candidates in the aldermanic election of April 1894.

Mr. McKenna, looking very warm and tired, came in to Mr. Dooley's tavern one night last week, and smote the bar with his fist.

"What's the matter with Hogan?" he said.

"What Hogan?" asked Mr. Dooley. "Malachy or Matt? Dinnis or Mike? Sarsfield or William Hogan? There's a Hogan f'r ivry block in th' Ar-rchey Road, an' wan to spare. There's nawthin' th' matter with anny iv thim; but, if ye mean Hogan, th' liquor dealer, that r-run f'r aldherman, I'll say to ye he's all right. Mind ye, Jawn, I'm doin' this because ye're me frind; but, by gar, if anny wan else comes in an' asks me that question, I'll kill him, if I have to go to th' bridewell f'r it. I'm no dam'd health officer."

Having delivered himself of this tirade, Mr. Dooley scrutinized Mr. McKenna sharply, and continued: "Ye've been out ilictin' some man, Jawn, an' ye needn't deny it. I seen it th' minyit ye come in. Ye'er hat's dinted, an' ye have ye'er necktie over ye'er ear; an' I see be ye'er hand ye've hit a Dutchman on th' teeth. Jawn, ye know no more about politics thin a mimber iv this here Civic Featheration. Didn't ye have a beer bottle or an ice-pick? Ayether iv thim is good, though, whin I was a young man an' precinct captain an' intherested in th' welfare iv th' counthry, I found a couplin' pin in a stockin' about as handy as annything.

"Thim days is over, though, Jawn, an' between us politics don't intherest me no more. They ain't no liveliness in thim. Whin Andy Duggan r-run f'r aldherman against Schwartzmeister, th' big Dutchman,—I was precinct captain then, Jawn,—there was an iliction f'r ye. 'Twas on our precinct they relied to ilict Duggan; f'r the Dutch was sthrong down be th' thrack, an' Schwartzmeister had a band out playin' 'Th' Watch on th' Rhine.' Well, sir, we opened th' polls at six o'clock, an' there was tin Schwartzmeister men there to protect his intherests. At sivin o'clock there was only three, an' wan iv thim was goin' up th' sthreet with Hinnissy kickin' at him. At eight o'clock, be dad, there was on'y wan; an' he was sittin' on th' roof iv Gavin's blacksmith shop, an' th' la-ads was thryin' to borrow a laddher fr'm th' injine-house f'r to get at him. 'Twas thruck eighteen; an' Hogan, that was captain, wudden't let thim have it. Not ye'er Hogan, Jawn, but th' meanest fireman in Bridgeport. He got kilt aftherwards. He wudden't let th' la-ads have a laddher, an' th' Dutchman stayed up there; an', whin there was nawthin' to do, we wint over an' thrun bricks at him. 'Twas gr-reat sport.

"About four in th' afthernoon Schwartzmeister's band come up Ar-rchey Road, playin' 'Th' Watch on th' Rhine.' Whin it got near Gavin's, big Peter Nolan tuk a runnin' jump, an' landed feet first in th' big bass dhrum. Th' man with th' dhrum walloped him over th' head with th' dhrumstick, an' Dorsey Quinn wint over an' tuk a slide trombone away fr'm the musician an' clubbed th' bass dhrum man with it. Thin we all wint over, an' ye niver see th' like in ye'er born days. Th' las' I see iv th' band it was goin' down th' road towards th' slough with a mob behind it, an' all th' polis foorce fr'm Deerin' Sthreet afther th' mob. Th' la-ads collected th' horns an' th' dhrums, an' that started th' Ar-rchey Road brass band. Little Mike Doyle larned to play 'Th' Rambler fr'm Clare' beautifully on what they call a pickle-e-o befure they sarved a rayplivin writ on him.

"We cast twenty-wan hundherd votes f'r Duggan, an' they was on'y five hundherd votes in th' precinct. We'd cast more, but th' tickets give out. They was tin votes in th' box f'r Schwartzmeister whin we counted up; an' I felt that mortified I near died, me bein' precinct captain, an' ree-sponsible. 'What'll we do with thim?' says Dorsey th' plumber. 'Throw thim out th' window,' says I. Just thin Dorsey's nanny-goat that died next year put her head through th' dure. 'Monica,' says Dorsey (he had pretty names for all his goats), 'Monica, are ye hungry,' he says, 'ye poor dear?' Th' goat give him a pleadin' look out iv her big brown eyes. 'Can't I make ye up a nice supper?' says Dorsey. 'Do ye like paper?' he says. 'Would ye like to help desthroy a Dutchman,' he says, 'an' perform a sarvice f'r ye'er counthry?' he says. Thin he wint out in th' next room, an' come back with a bottle iv catsup; an' he poured it on th' Schwartzmeister ballots, an' Monica et thim without winkin'.

"Well, sir, we ilicted Duggan; an' what come iv it? Th' week befure iliction he was in me house ivry night, an' 'twas 'Misther Dooley, this,' an' 'Mr. Dooley, that,' an' 'What 'll ye have, boys?'

an' 'Niver mind about th' change.' I niver see hide nor hair iv him f'r a week afther iliction. Thin he come in with a plug hat on, an' says he: 'Dooley,' he says, 'give me a shell iv beer,' he says: 'give me a shell iv beer,' he says, layin' down a nickel. 'I suppose ye're on th' sub-scription,' he says. 'What for?' says I. 'F'r to buy me a goold star,' says he. With that I eyes him, an' says I: 'Duggan,' I says, 'I knowed ye whin ye didn't have a coat to ye'er back,' I says, 'an' I'll buy no star f'r ye,' I says. 'But I'll tell ye what I'll buy f'r ye,' I says. 'I'll buy rayqueem masses f'r th' raypose iv ye'er sowl, if ye don't duck out iv this in a minyit.' Whin I seen him last, he was back dhrivin' a dhray an' atin' his dinner out iv a tin can." (April 7, 1894)

5. A Republican Primary at Finucane's Hall

This pessimistic report on the liveliness of Chicago's Republicans was corroborated when Cook County went Republican by 35,000 votes in the following month's election for county officials.

"D'ye know, Jawn," said Mr. Dooley, "I believe if th' raypublicans keep up their luck they'll carry th' sixth wa-ard."

"I hope so," said Mr. McKenna, who became a republican under the delusion that Mr. Blaine would free Ireland. "But it's a long time coming."

"So it is, so it is," said Mr. Dooley, democrat. "An' may it niver come till I'm in me grave. Wanst th' road goes raypublican I'll move into Tixas an' niver come back. But if th' dimocrats don't stir thimsilves an' show they've as much spirit as they had whin I was a young man an' captain iv me precinct, they'll be no place f'r thim bechune th' rid bridge an' Brighton Park.

"Th' people up here likes spirit. How did Billy O'Brien hol' his own all these years but because he done dumb-bell exercise with a beer kag in wan hand an' a German polisman in th' other? How come Eddie Burke—may he rest in peace—to have th' ward f'r so long but because, bit iv a man that he was, with on'y th' leg iv a cuk stove in his hand, he wint thru a roomful iv his innimies, back an' forward twict? Sure, politics ain't bean-bag. 'Tis a man's game, an' women, childer, cripples an' prohybitionists 'd do well to keep out iv it.

"I mind wanst whin ye could spot a raypublican a mile away be his eyeglasses an' side-whiskers. 'Tis sthrange, Jawn, how many raypublicans wore side whiskers. 'Twas not till th' dam mug-wumps come into th' pa-arty that anny dimocrat wint around with thrailers on his chops. As I said, ye could spot thim a block away, an' most iv th' time they was a block away—ispicially on th' day iv iliction. They was on'y 2 raypublicans out an' out in our precinct an' whin Duffy run f'r alderman I personally attinded to puttin' both iv thim into th' big manhole at Grove sthreet. I did so.

"Th' other day I wint down th' sthreet, an' whin I got near to Finucane's Hall I heerd th' divvil an' all iv a row. It made me heart beat high. 'Glory be,' says I, 'th' ol' times is comin' back,' I says. 'If I on'y knew who was up,' says I, 'I'd take wan punch at th' ol' la-ad over there pryin' up th' pavin' block. But,' I thought, ''tis sthrange they'd be holdin' primaries an' niver let on to me.' So I wint over to where a big polisman was shooin' away some small lads an' says I: 'Who's ahead?' says I. 'No wan,' says he. 'They've just begun,' he says. 'Shannahan has th' crowd, but Hogan has th' judges,' he says, duckin' his head f'r a brick. 'Well,' says I, 'no matter how it comes out,' says I, 'they'll be a good dimocrat ilicted.' 'Th' 'ell they will,' says he. 'It's a raypublican prim'ry.' Well, Jawn, I was that overcome I'd 've lift at wanst, but th' fun was too good an' I stuck. A man come out iv th' crowd without coat or vist an' wint runnin' up th' road with Eddie Gallagher beltin' him over th' head with a picture iv our martyred president, James A. Garfield. Thin I see thim rowlin' a fat German man across th' sthreet, an' ivry minute his brother raypublicans 'd take a runnin' jump in th' air an' come down on him. Th' little man with th' pavin' block was wan iv th' bist politicians an' thru-est shots I iver see. I wint over to him an', says I: 'Good f'r ye, Clonmel.' 'An' how did ye guess it?' says he with a smile. 'Sure, on'y a Tip could throw like that,' says I. 'They're too big,' says he. 'Give me a stone weighin' wan pound an' smooth an' I could stand on th' wather wurruks an' knock a man off th' Audiotoryum tower,' says he. 'Look,' says he, 'while I get that big Kerry man, Kelly—th' wan near th' dure.'

"Th' judges was inside, an' they had th' window built so high that th' voters cuddn't put their tickets in on a clothes pole. Mike Murphy was ladin' th' la-ads on th' outside. He's a dam fine or-rator, an' 'twas a shame we lost him because iv Finerty. 'Fellow raypublicans,' says he, 'will ye permit this here to go on?' he says. 'Will ye see thrampled in th' dust th' principles iv Abraham Lincoln, Uless S. Grant an' James Gee Blaine?' he says. 'Will ye let thim pups iv Hogans do ye up,' he says. 'Shades iv our martyred heroes forbid!' he says. 'If ye'll follow me there 'll be ne'er a one iv ye that won't have a bridge befure nex' Choosdah.'

"Well, it made me ashamed iv th' dimocratic party, the way they wint at it. Befure th' pathriotic sintiments iv Murphy was out iv his mouth, wan iv th' judges come through th' skylight with th' ballot box undher his ar-rm, made a leap like a bridge-jumper, an' wint tearin' towards th' mills. Th' other judges was pulled out feet foremost an' th' last I see iv th' clerk, a little man with red hair had him down an' was whalin' him with a bust iv Wendell Phillips."

"You ought to be republican," said Mr. McKenna.

"Jawn," said Mr. Dooley, "if annywan had said that tin year ago I'd 've rolled him. But 'tis different now. I'd vote th' ticket sthraight—if I was sthrong enough." (October 5, 1895)

6. The Advantages of Being an Alderman

The Infanta Eulalia of Spain (not Bulgaria) visited Chicago during the World's Fair of 1893. Alderman John Powers of the Nineteenth Ward was, in fact, a native of County Waterford.

"By dad," said Mr. Dooley, the other night, "I'm goin' to r-run f'r aldherman, I am so. Hogan was just in here an' he was ta-alkin' about his little kid. He an' th' gossoon's mother can't make up their minds about what the kid'll be. Hogan says, 'The ould woman,' he says, 'wants to make a priest iv him,' he says. 'But I,' he says, 'I think he ought to be a lawyer.' 'Don't ye do it, Hogan,' says I. 'Don't ye do it,' says I. 'There's priests an' lawyers enough,' I says, 'to sind two worlds to hell,' I says, 'an' get thim out again,' I says. 'Make him an aldherman,' I says. An' thin what d'ye think th' big fool asks me? 'Where can I find a school,' he says, 'to sind him to?' School, mind ye, Jawn. 'School?' says I. 'Faith, Hogan, if ye don't sind him to school at all, at all, he's sure,' I says, 'to be wan.'

"But 'tis thrue I've told ye there's no job like it. No work or worry. Nawthin' but to sit down with ye'er hat cocked over ye'er eye an' ye'er feet on a mahogany table, an' watch th' roly boly dhrop into ye'er mit. Th' most wurruk an aldherman has to do is to presint himself with a gold shtar wanst a year so he won't forget he's an aldherman. Whin he has th' shtar upon him he can go annywhere an' divvle th' cint to pay. 'Tis good f'r annything fr'm a ball to a christenin', an' by gar Billy O'Broyn wurrked it on th' church. He wint to mass over at Father Kelly's wan Sundah mornin' to square himsilf, an' whin Dinnis Nugent passed th' plate to him he showed th' shtar. 'Ar-re ye an aldherman?' says Nugent. 'I am that,' says O'Broyn. 'Thin,' says Nugent, stickin' th' plate undher his nose, 'thin,' he says, 'lave half f'r th' parish,' he says. Well, sir, O'Broyn was that mad he waited till afther mass an' he made Nugent ate th' 'Key iv Hiven' and four chapters in 'The Lives iv the Saints' in th' vesthry.

"Whin you an' me, Jawn, wants to go to th' theayter, what do we do? Dig down in th' jeans iv us an' hand out th' dough. What does an aldherman do? He goes up as gr-rand as a lord an' flashes the shtar. 'Good avenin', aldherman,' says th' man on th' dure. 'Good avenin',' says the aldherman. 'Kindly give me a box with yellow satin linin' in it,' he says, 'an' have thim girls,' he says, 'in th' las' act come down to th' fr-ront iv th' stage,' he says. 'F'r me sight is poor to-night,' he says. 'Fr'm duckin' f'r th' worst iv it,' he says. Whin there's a procession, who rides in th' hacks with th' flags an' green boughs on thim? Th' aldherman. Whin there's a bankit at th' Audiotorium who has th' front seat an' th' first grab at th' pie? Th' aldherman. Did ye iver hear iv an aldherman bein' arristed? By gar, I believe th' polisman that 'd arrist an' aldherman wouldn't get off short iv tin years. He can get just as dhrunk as he pleases an' fight as much as he wants an' go home, yellin' at ivery shtep, an' what th' 'ell does a man want more thin that? Whin that there Boolgahrian princess that they called the infant—her that had two childher—was here, who do ye think dhrove around with her but that little shkate iv a Waterford man iv a Jawnny Powers. R-rode around with her with a shtove-pipe hat on his head an' a di-mon as big as a coalscuttle in his shirt. Mike Gallagher was in here an' told me about it, an' he said th' infant was goin' up to th' house to have supper, but Jawnny told her 'twas ironin' day, an' th' women folks 'd be tired out. 'Well,' says I to Gallagher, whin I heerd it, 'I wondher where th' infant borrid money,' I says, 'to get back to Boolgahria on,' I says.

"'Tis an iligant job, Jawn. Ye have nawthin' to worry ye. Whin ye'er hungry ye go to a bankit. Whin ye'er broke all ye have to do is to give something away that don't belong to ye. 'Tis th' only thrade left f'r a young man, an' I'm goin' to have Hogan begin tachin' his boy rough-an'-tumble fightin' to-morrow an' give him th' proper shtart." (February 10, 1894)

7. The Dance of Legislation Through the Council

This recollection of a clash between Mayor Carter Harrison and Bridgeport's Billy O'Brien was prompted by President Grover Cleveland's inability to prevent a filibuster in the U.S. Senate by William Jennings Bryan and other supporters of the free coinage of silver. Frank Lawler, a prominent Democrat and sometime alder-

man, is mentioned near the end because he claimed to have "Big Steve" Cleveland's ear.

"D'ye know, Jawn," said Mr. Martin Dooley when Mr. Mc-Kenna came in Thursday night. "D'ye know what I'd do if I was Cleveland?"

"No, faith," responded Mr. McKenna, facetiously. "Turn down the damper?" this being a current phrase along the Archey road for robbing a cash drawer.

"No, sir," replied Mr. Dooley, haughtily, "I'd not. An' if ye're referrin' with ye'er scand'lous tongue to that little epi-sode iv me an' Mike Hanrahan's game cock ye'll be after movin' out this minyit to Brighton Par-rk, where ye can bandy ye'er rough jokes with th' hoboes iv ye'er own set."

Mr. McKenna made no reply to this pointed rebuke beyond whistling a bar of "The Bowery." And Mr. Dooley resumed: "No, sir, if I was Big Steve I'd call me hackman an' I'd say: 'Dhrive me over to the sinit.' An' whin I got there I'd cock me hat over me ear an' I'd walk in among thim an' I'd say: 'Now, here, mind ye, what is it ye la-ads wants? Ar-re ye lukin' f'r trouble with me? Is it a fight ye're afther? Because if it is they'll be nare a wan iv ye has a man on a bridge or on th' polis force nex' week.' Thim sintiments, Jawn, 'd ind all this divilment that's goin' on in th' sinit. Mind ye, now, I don't know who have th' right iv it. It's dam little I cares whether th' roly-boly that comes across that there bar is in gold or silver or cotton battin' so long as th' Eyetalian man with th' bas-ket'll take it f'r limons an' nutmegs. But 'tis as plain as th' nose on ye'er face, Jawnny, that there's somebody runnin' the game wrong.

"Now, mind ye, old Hahrson niver done it that way. I mind whin th' old geezer was in befure. He wanted a ga-arbage cream-ery put up wist iv th' bridge and Bill O'Brien, that was alderman in thim days, says, 'No,' says he. 'We'll have no garbage creamery up here,' says he. 'I'm lukin' out f'r th' inthrests iv me consti-tooents,' he says, 'an' me constitooents,' he says, 'demands,' says he, 'a dump where th' goats can get a dairy lunch,' he says. A witty lad, that O'Brien. I seen him break a man's jaw at a dance wanse be way iv a joke. 'What time is it?' says the la-ad. 'It's just struck wan,' says O'Brien, givin' him a punch that was near to knockin' his head off.

"Well, th' main guy laughed at th' joke an' th' next night th' creamery was kilt in th' council. Th' day afther that Googin's big kid, Malachi, was fired fr'm th' red bridge. Oh, thin there was blood flowin' in Haley's slough. Googin wint down to see th' ol' geezer. 'What th' 'ell'd ye throw down me boy f'r?' says he. 'Throw him down?' says th' ol' geezer; 'me throw down wan iv ye'er boys—wan iv th' family iv me ol' friend Googin? Tommy,' he says to th' clerk. 'What,' says th' clerk. 'Who thrun young Googin off th' rid bridge?' 'Well,' says th' clerk. 'To tell ye th' truth,' he says, 'Bill O'Brien come in to-day an' says: "I want a new man f'r th' rid bridge." "What's th' matter with Googin?" I says. "Googin," he says. "Googin's no good," he says. "We're tired iv thim big amadhons fr'm Ma-yo," he says. "Throw him off my charge," says he. "I've got a young English lad that's worth tin Googins together."' 'That's an outrage,' says th' Whole Thing. 'Put Mr. Googin's boy back,' he says. 'An' whin O'Brien comes around with his friend fr'm London,' he says, 'call th' polis.'

"Well, sir, ye shud've seen Googin. Ye know him, Jawn. He came out here with tears in his eyes, swearin' vingince. He was a strong man, that Googin. He had eight lads, all iv thim vote get-ters. Four iv thim worked in th' rollin' mills an' wan was conduc-tor iv a street ca-ar. Th' oldest lad was marrid to Mary Haley, an' her father was foreman up in a packin' house an' voted two hun-dred Dutch. Thin Mrs. Googin, she that was O'Donnell, was re-lated to th' Dorneys an' th' Coughlins, an' Tim Coughlin's youn-gest son was prisident iv th' young men's sodality. Ye knew th' Dorneys. They were th' best men that iver captained th' gashouse precinct, an' they had a pull like a bridge horse. Wan iv th' Dorney girls was marrid to th' liftnant at Deering sthreet an' an-other was sparkin' th' paymaster at th' ca-ar barns.

"They was all fr'm th' war part iv Ma-yo, an' whin Googin come home an' rayported what th' Main Guy told him, 'twas like

whin they used to spread th' light over beyant. First they formed
th' Dennis Googin Anti-O'Brien Club an' then they formed th'
County Ma-yo Phalanx, which was christened be Coughlin's kid,
and they had eight hundred mimbers before Sundah. They put
up a Dutchman named Schwartzmeister that kep' a beer cellar
down be Halsted sthreet f'r alderman an' wint up in a body to
burn O'Brien's bar-rn. Whin Billy heard iv it he was pahrlyzed.
He wint down to see the Whole Thing. 'Well,' says th' ol' man,
'ar-re ye in favor iv th' creamery?' 'I am that,' says Bill. 'An' yez
don't care f'r the dumps?' 'I wouldn't give a dam,' says Bill, 'if the
goats kape Fridah th' year round,' he says, 'if ye'll on'y haul th'
Googins off.'

"So Bill he voted f'r th' creamery an' th' Googins turned down
Schwartzmeister. Th' Dutchman didn't settle f'r th' uniforms he
got f'r th' Ma-yo phalanx an' th' shuriff closed him up, an' th' last I
see iv him he was drivin' a pop wagon.

"Now that there's pollytics, Jawn, mind ye, an' if ye meet Lawler
I wish ye'd tell him th' next time Big Steve comes to see him he'd
give him a wurrud iv advice how to land th' sinit. He's a smart
man, Cleveland is, but he wuddent know whether to take th'
elevated train or a freightca-ar to get to Finucane's Hall." (October 21, 1893)

8. Political Appointments by the Spoils System

*After his victory in the special election of December 19, 1893,
Mayor John Patrick Hopkins declared war on inefficiency at city
hall. Singling out the water office as the special dumping ground for
do-nothing political appointees, Hopkins called for longer working
days and fewer employees in city jobs. Ebenezer Wakeley was the
perennial mayoral candidate of the prohibition party.*

"There does be a ma-an out in bleedin' Kansas," said Mr.
Dooley, "an' be hivins he ought to be wur-rkin' in th' city hall."

"Faith," said Mr. McKenna, "there's many like him. I just rode up with the president of the Bismarck Club and he tells me since John Patrick come in it's harder to get a man into the city hall than 'tis to get a camel into the kingdom of heaven."

Mr. Dooley looked gloomy at this remark and continued: "'Twas that I was gettin' at. Th' man in Kansas he says, says he, that labor-savin' machinery like thim auttymatic corkscrews an' th' like have incraysed th' projoocin' power iv th' wurruld to that extint that if ivery man done his shtroke iv wurruk no wan man'd have to put in more thin two hours a day; th' rist iv th' time he'd have f'r goin' to the baseball game or takin' his wife to th' opry— if he wurrked in th' rollin' mills. He says, says he, that th' rayson so many lads is sleepin' undher th' Randolph street viduck, he says, is that some other man, he says, is goin' ahead satisfyin' his greed f'r wurruk by stickin' at it f'r tin hours at a stritch. 'Tis shameful th' appetite f'r har-rd wurruk some min has. Praise be to Gawd, I was niver cur-rsed with it. I can wurruk an' let it alone, an' if I wurruk late to-night I can get up early to-morrah an' do divvle a shtroke.

"Now, says I, what a figure that Kansas man'd cut in th' city hall. Begorra, they'd pick him out f'r a marvel iv industhry. Min 'd pint at him an' say: 'That fellow'll wurruk himsilf into a grave.' Jawn, I knowed a man named Hannigan, Francis Xavier Hannigan, a Wexford man, an' a bum be th' same token. Hahrson give him a job in th' wather office an' he was to be a wather inspector. Well, sir, d'ye suppose that Hannigan iver inspicted wather? Not be a dam sight. He avoided it. He used beer as th' chaser. I seen him hangin' round th' corner playin' forty-fives on th' top iv a bar'l an' dancin' jig stips an' says I: 'Hannigan,' I says, 'why ain't ye down be th' city hall,' I says, 'inspictin' wather,' I says. 'I hear,' says I, 'there's microbes an' th' divvle knows what all in it,' says I. 'It needs to be sieved,' I says. 'Goowan now,' says he, 'an' mix me a proosic acid cocktail,' he says. 'I'm no ga-arden hose.' Well, sir, no wan in th' city hall iver see hide nor hair iv Hannigan excipt whin he'd dhrop in to get his letthers on Choosdahs, Thursdahs an' Saturdahs, an' he become that ins'lint he rayfused to sal-oot Willum Joyce whin he see him. Bedad,

Willum didn't like that an' whin Hannigan fin'ly sint wurrud down to th' mayor to have his letthers fetched out to him they picked him up an' thrun him down, they did so, they did. Th' last I see iv him he was ma-archin' at th' hid iv a pro-cession carryin' a banner f'r 'We wants bread or wurruk.' Faith, Hannigan wanted nayther. What he wanted was jelly cake an' a foldin' bid."

"Can you blame him?" asked Mr. McKenna, the politician.

"Blame him?" responded Mr. Dooley. "Divvle th' bit. I don't blame no man f'r escapin' this here wurruk habit. Laste iv all a man in th' city hall. Take me cousin, Mike Dooley, that runs th' plumbin' shop down be Grove street. That man dam near drunk himsilf into a lunytic asylum to elect Jawn Patrick. He niver cared a rap who was mayor till some man tould him th' dips was thryin' to land Jawn Patrick because iv his name. 'Throw him down because he's a Turk,' says me Cousin Mike, 'not if I have to pawn me sawder pot,' an' bedad he wint out that 'd never drunk a drop in his life before, an' called on ivry saloon-keeper iv th' wa-ard an' come home night after night bilin'. All f'r th' Turk in him. Why, to show ye what Mike Dooley done, he had a job iv wurruk tinkerin' up a waste pipe f'r Dave Shannahan and Dave's a black raypublican, as ye know. While he was wurrkin' Mike talked about th' campaign an' they fell to quarrelin'. Fin'lly Mike he says: 'Will ye vote f'r Hopkins, ye degen'rate tur-rk?' 'I'll not,' says Dave. 'Thin take ye'er ol' waste pipe to the divvle an' have him wipe th' jint,' says me Cousin Mike, gettin' out iv th' hole while th' wather poured out all over th' basement. Well, sir, Dave had to promise to vote f'r Jawn Patrick before me Cousin Mike'd go an-other sthroke. Thin me brave Dave whips aroun' an' says he: 'Whin ye vote f'r Swift I'll pay ye th' bill, Mr. Dooley,' says he. Now Mike is dam close and this made him think. 'If ye give me half I'll vote f'r the arnychist,' he says. 'No, sir,' says Dave. 'If ye give me a quarter iv th' bill I'll vote f'r Ebenezer Wakeley,' says Mike. 'No,' says Dave. 'Thin,' says me Cousin Mike, 'go to Halifax,' he says, an' he tears out. Now, whin he come back fr'm Westbaden, where it took a week to boil th' tea out iv him, don't ye think he deserved a job?"

"Didn't he get one?" asked Mr. McKenna.

Mr. Dooley replied in pantomime. He raised his hands as if lifting a human form, cast them down fiercely and delivered a kick at the empty air that shook his entire frame. Then he returned to washing the glasses and Mr. McKenna went home. (January 6, 1894.)

9. Hanging Aldermen: How Boodle is Dispensed

This piece appeared while a gang of aldermen were trying to pass an ordinance extending the current street-railway franchise for fifty years. It was widely held that the bill's sponsors were being bribed by streetcar magnate, Charles T. Yerkes, and public cries of "hang the aldermen" were reported in the press.

Chicago is always on the point of hanging some one and quartering him and boiling him in hot pitch, and assuring him that he has lost the respect of all honorable men. Rumors of a characteristic agitation had come faintly up Archey Road, and Mr. Hennessy had heard of it.

"I hear they're goin' to hang th' aldhermen," he said. "If they thry it on Willum J. O'Brien, they'd betther bombard him first. I'd hate to be th' man that 'd be called to roll with him to his doom. He cud lick th' whole Civic Featheration."

"I believe ye," said Mr. Dooley. "He's a powerful man. But I hear there is, as ye say, what th' pa-apers 'd call a movement on fut f'r to dec'rate Chris'mas threes with aldhermen, an' 'tis wan that ought to be encouraged. Nawthin' cud be happyer, as Hogan says, thin th' thought iv cillybratin' th' season be sthringin' up some iv th' fathers iv th' city where th' childher cud see thim. But I'm afraid, Hinnissy, that you an' me won't see it. 'Twill all be over soon, an' Willum J. O'Brien'll go by with his head just as near his shoulders as iver. 'Tis har-rd to hang an aldherman, annyhow. Ye'd have to suspind most iv thim be th' waist.

"Man an' boy, I've been in this town forty year an' more; an' divvle th' aldherman have I see hanged yet, though I've sthrained th' eyes out iv me head watchin' f'r wan iv thim to be histed anny pleasant mornin'. They've been goin' to hang thim wan week an' presintin' thim with a dimon' star th' next iver since th' year iv th' big wind, an' there's jus' as manny iv thim an' jus' as big robbers as iver there was.

"An' why shud they hang thim, Hinnissy? Why shud they? I'm an honest man mesilf, as men go. Ye might have ye'er watch, if ye had wan, on that bar f'r a year, an' I'd niver touch it. It wudden't be worth me while. I'm an honest man. I pay me taxes, whin Tim Ryan isn't assessor with Grogan's boy on th' books. I do me jooty; an' I believe in th' polis foorce, though not in polismen. That's diff'rent. But honest as I am, between you an' me, if I was an aldherman, I wudden't say, be hivins, I think I'd stand firm; but— well, if some wan come to me an' said, 'Dooley, here's fifty thousan' dollars f'r ye'er vote to betray th' sacred inthrests iv Chicago,' I'd go to Father Kelly an' ask th' prayers iv th' congregation.

"'Tis not, Hinnissy, that this man Yerkuss goes up to an aldherman an' says out sthraight, 'Here, Bill, take this bundle, an' be an infamyous scoundhrel.' That's th' way th' man in Mitchigan Avnoo sees it, but 'tis not sthraight. D'ye mind Dochney that was wanst aldherman here? Ye don't. Well, I do. He ran a little conthractin' business down be Halsted Sthreet. 'Twas him built th' big shed f'r th' ice comp'ny. He was a fine man an' a sthrong wan. He begun his political career be lickin' a plasth'rer be th' name iv Egan, a man that had th' County Clare thrip an' was thought to be th' akel iv anny man in town. Fr'm that he growed till he bate near ivry man he knew, an' become very pop'lar, so that he was sint to th' council. Now Dochney was an honest an' sober man whin he wint in; but wan day a man come up to him, an' says he, 'Ye know that ordhnance Schwartz inthrajooced?' 'I do,' says Dochney, 'an' I'm again it. 'Tis a swindle,' he says. 'Well,' says th' la-ad, 'they'se five thousan' in it f'r ye,' he says. They had to pry Dochney off iv him. Th' nex' day a man he knowed well come to Dochney, an' says he, 'That's a fine ordhnance iv Schwartz.' 'It is, like hell,' says Dochney. ''Tis a plain swindle,' he says. ''Tis a good thing f'r th' comp'nies,' says this man; 'but look what they've done f'r th' city,' he says, 'an' think,' he says, 'iv th' widdies an' orphans,' he says, 'that has their har-rd-earned coin invisted,' he says. An' a tear rolled down his cheek. 'I'm an orphan mesilf,' says Dochney; 'an' as f'r th' widdies, anny healthy widdy with sthreet-car stock ought to be ashamed iv hersilf if she's a widdy long,' he says. An' th' man wint away.

"Now Dochney thought he'd put th' five thousan' out iv his mind, but he hadn't. He'd on'y laid it by, an' ivry time he closed his eyes he thought iv it. 'Twas a shame to give th' comp'nies what they wanted, but th' five thousan' was a lot iv money. 'Twud lift th' morgedge. 'Twud clane up th' notes on th' new conthract. 'Twud buy a new dhress f'r Mrs. Dochney. He begun to feel sorrowful f'r th' widdies an' orphans. 'Poor things!' says he to himsilf, says he. 'Poor things, how they must suffer!' he says; 'an' I need th' money. Th' sthreet-car comp'nies is robbers,' he says; 'but 'tis thrue they've built up th' city,' he says, 'an' th' money'd come in handy,' he says. 'No wan 'd be hurted, annyhow,' he says; 'an', sure, it ain't a bribe f'r to take money f'r doin' something ye want to do, annyhow,' he says. 'Five thousan' widdies an' orphans,' he says; an' he wint to sleep.

"That was th' way he felt whin he wint down to see ol' Simpson to renew his notes, an' Simpson settled it. 'Dochney,' he says, 'I wisht ye'd pay up,' he says. 'I need th' money,' he says. 'I'm afraid th' council won't pass th' Schwartz ordhnance,' he says; 'an' it manes much to me,' he says. 'Be th' way,' he says, 'how're ye goin' to vote on that ordhnance?' he says. 'I dinnaw,' says Dochney. 'Well,' says Simpson (Dochney tol' me this himsilf), 'whin ye find out, come an' see me about th' notes,' he says. An' Dochney wint to th' meetin'; an', whin his name was called, he hollered 'Aye,' so loud a chunk iv plaster fell out iv th' ceilin' an' stove in th' head iv a rayform aldherman."

"Did they hang him?" asked Mr. Hennessey.

"Faith, they did not," said Mr. Dooley. "He begun missin' his jooty at wanst. Aldhermen always do that after th' first few weeks. 'Ye got ye'er money,' says Father Kelly; 'an' much good may it do ye,' he says. 'Well,' says Dochney, 'I'd be a long time prayin' mesilf into five thousan',' he says. An' he become leader in th' council. Th' las' ordhnance he inthrojooced was wan establishin' a license f'r churches, an' compellin' thim to keep their fr-ront dure closed an' th' blinds drawn on Sundah. He was expelled fr'm th' St. Vincent de Pauls, an' ilicted a director iv a bank th' same day.

"Now, Hinnissy, that there man niver knowed he was bribed—th' first time. Th' second time he knew. He ast f'r it. An' I wudden't hang Dochney. I wudden't if I was sthrong enough. But some day I'm goin' to let me temper r-run away with me, an' get a comity together, an' go out an' hang ivry dam widdy an' orphan between th' rollin' mills an' th' foundlin's' home. If it wasn't f'r thim ray-pechious crathers, they'd be no boodle annywhere."

"Well, don't forget Simpson," said Mr. Hennessy.

"I won't," said Mr. Dooley. "I won't." (December 17, 1898)

10. The Wave of Reform Hits Bridgeport

In 1894 the Lexow Commission had exposed wholesale corruption in the New York City Police Department; Teddy Roosevelt's appointment as police commissioner was one result of the investigation. This Dooley piece appeared in early January 1895 amid public clamoring for a similar reform group to clean up the Chicago police courts.

"This here wave iv rayform," said Mr. Dooley, "this here wave iv rayform, Jawn, mind ye, that's sweepin' over th' counthry, mind ye, now, Jawn, is raisin' th' divvle, I see be th' pa-apers. I've seen waves iv rayform befure, Jawn. Whin th' people iv this counthry gets wurruked up, there's no stoppin' thim. They'll not dhraw breath until ivry man that took a dollar iv a bribe is sent down th' r-road. Thim that takes two goes on th' comity iv th' wave iv rayform.

"It sthruck th' r-road las' week. Darcey, th' new polisman on th' bate, comes in here ivry night f'r to study spellin' an' figgers.

I think they'll throw him down, whin he goes to be examined. Wan iv th' wild la-ads down be th' slough hit him with a brick wanst, an' he ain't been able to do fractions since. Thin he's got inflammathry rheumatism enough to burn a barn, an' he can't turn a page without makin' ye think he's goin' to lose a thumb. He's got wife an' childher, an' he's gettin' on in years; but he's a polisman, an' he's got to be rayformed. I tell him all I can. He didn't know where St. Pethersburg was till I tould him it was th' capital iv Sweden. They'll not give him th' boots on that there question. Ye bet ye'er life they won't, Jawn.

"I seen th' aldherman go by yisterday; an' he'd shook his dimon'stud, an' he looked as poor as a dhrayman. He's rayformed. Th' little Dutchman that was ilicted to th' legislachure says he will stay home this winter. Says I, 'Why?' Says he, 'There's nawthin' in it.' He's rayformed. Th' wather inspictor, that used to take a dhrink an' a segar an' report me two fassets less thin I have, turned me in las' week f'r a garden hose an' a ploonge bath. He's rayformed. Th' wave iv rayform has sthruck, an' we're all goin' around now with rubbers on.

"They've organized th' Ar-rchey Road Lexow Sodality, an' 'tis th' wan institootion that Father Kelly up west iv th' bridge 'll duck his head to. All th' best citizens is in it. Th' best citizens is thim that th' statue iv limitations was made f'r. Barrister Hogan tol' me—an' a dacint man, but given to dhrink—that, whin a man cud hide behind th' statue iv limitations, he was ready money. I niver seen it. Is that th' wan on th' lake front? No, tubby sure, tubby sure. That's Columbus. No wan 'd hide behind that.

"Th' Ar-rchey Road Lexow Sodality is composed iv none but square men. They all have th' coin, Jawn. A man that's broke can't be square. He's got too much to do payin' taxes. If I had a million, divvle a fut would I step to confession. I'd make th' soggarth come an' confess to me. They say that th' sthreets iv Hivin was paved with goold. I'll bet ye tin to wan that with all th' square men that goes there ivry year they have ilecloth down now."

"Oh, go on," said Mr. McKenna.

"I was goin' to tell ye about th' Lexow Sodality. Well, th' chairman iv it is Doherty, th' retired plumber. He sold me a house an' lot wanst, an' skinned me out iv wan hundherd dollars. He got th' house an' lot back an' a morgedge. But did ye iver notice th' scar on his nose? I was r-rough in thim days. Ol' Mike Hogan is another mimber. Ye know him. They say he hires constables be th' day f'r to serve five days' notices. Manny's th' time I see th' little furniture out on th' sthreet, an' th' good woman rockin' her baby under th' open sky. Hogan's tinants. Ol' Dinnis Higgins is another wan. An' Brannigan, th' real estate dealer. He was in th' assissors' office. May Gawd forgive him! An' Clancy, that was bail-bondman at Twelfth Sthreet.

"They appointed comities, an' they held a meetin'. I wint there. So did some iv th' others. 'Twas at Finucane's, an' th' hall was crowded. All th' sodality made speeches. Doherty made a great wan. Th' air was reekin' with corruption, says he. Th' polis foorce was rotten to th' core. Th' rights iv property was threatened. What, says he, was we goin' to do about it?

"Danny Gallagher got up, as good a lad as iver put that in his face to desthroy his intelligence, as th' good book says. 'Gintlemen,' says he, 'wan wurrud befure we lave,' he says. 'I've listened to th' speeches here to-night with satisfaction,' he says. 'I'm proud to see th' rayform wave have sthruck th' road,' he says. 'Th' rascals must be dhriven fr'm th' high places,' he says. 'I see befure me in a chair a gintleman who wud steal a red-hot stove an' freeze th' lid befure he got home. On me right is th' gintleman who advanced th' wave iv rayform tin years ago be puttin' Mrs. Geohegan out on th' sthreet in a snowstorm whin she was roarin' with a cough. Mrs. Geohegan have rayformed, peace be with her undher th' dhrifts iv Calv'ry! I am greeted be th' smile iv me ol' frind Higgins. We are ol' frinds, Dinnis, now, ain't we? D'ye mind th' calls I made on ye, with th' stamps undher me arms, whin I wurruked in th' post-office? I've thought iv thim whin th' lockstep was goin' in to dinner, an' prayed f'r th' day whin I might see ye again. An' you, Misther Brannigan, who knows about vacant lots, an' you Misther Clancy, th' frind iv th' dhrunk an' disordherly, we're proud to have ye here. 'Tis be such as ye that th' polisman who dhrinks on th' sly, an' th' saloon-keeper that keeps open f'r th' la-ads an' th' newsboys that shoots craps, 'll be brought to justice. Down with crime! says I. Fellow-citizens, I thank ye kindly. Th' meetin' is adjourned siney dee; an' I app'int Missers Dooley, O'Brien, Casey, Pug Slattery, an' mesilf to lade out th' Lexow Sodality be th' nose,'"

Mr. McKenna arose sleepily, and walked toward the door.

"Jawn," said Mr. Dooley.

"Yes," responded Mr. McKenna.

"Niver steal a dure-mat," said Mr. Dooley. "If ye do, ye'll be invistigated, hanged, an' maybe rayformed. Steal a bank, me boy, steal a bank." (January 5, 1895)

11. A Brand from the Burning: A Political Biography

In order to avoid prosecution, Tammany Hall leader Richard Croker left New York secretly in May 1894. A month later he turned up in Europe, where he was to spend the next three years. Mr. Dooley responded to the news of Croker's flight with this biographical sketch of a Bridgeport boss.

"I see be th' pa-apers," said Mr. Dooley, "that Croker have flew th' coop. 'Tis too bad, too bad. He wa-as a gr-reat man."

"Is he dead?" asked Mr. McKenna.

"No, faith, worse thin that; he's resigned. He calls th' la-ads about him, an' says he: 'Boys,' he says, 'I'm tired iv politics,' he says. 'I'm goin' to quit it f'r me health,' he says. 'Do ye stay in, an' get ar-rested f'r th' good iv th' party.' Ye see thim mugwumps is afther th' Boss, an' he's gettin' out th' way Hogan got out iv Connock. Wan day he comes over to me fa-ather's house, an' says he, 'Dooley,' he says, 'I'm goin' to lave this hole iv a place,' he says. 'F'r why?' says th' ol' man; 'I thought ye liked it.' 'Faith,' says Hogan, 'I niver liked a blade iv grass in it,' he says. 'I'm sick iv it,' he says. 'I don't want niver to see it no more.' And he wint away.

Th' next mornin' th' polis was lookin' f'r him to lock him up f'r stealin' joo'lry in the fair town. Yes, by dad.

"'Tis th' way iv th' boss, Jawn. I seen it manny's th' time. There was wanst a boss in th' Sixth Wa-ard, an' his name was Flannagan; an' he came fr'm th' County Clare, but so near th' bordher line that no wan challenged his vote, an' he was let walk down Ar-rchey Road just 's though he come fr'm Connock. Well, sir, whin I see him first, he'd th' smell iv Castle Garden on him, an' th' same is no r-rose gyranium, d'ye mind; an' he was goin' out with pick an' shovel f'r to dig in th' canal,—a big, shtrappin', black-haired lad, with a neck like a bull's an' covered with a hide as thick as wan's, fr'm thryin' to get a crop iv oats out iv a Clare farm that growed divvle th' thing but nice, big boldhers.

"He was a de-termined divvle though, an' th' first man that made a face at him he walloped in th' jaw; an' he'd been on th' canal no more thin a month befure he licked ivry man in th' gang but th' section boss, who'd been a Dublin jackeen, an' weighed sixteen stone an' was th' 'ell an' all with a thrip an' a punch. Wan day they had some wurruds, whin me bold Dublin man sails into Flannagan. Well, sir, they fought fr'm wan o'clock till tin in th' night, an' nayther give up; though Flannagan had th' best iv it, bein' young. 'Why don't ye put him out?' says wan iv th' la-ads. 'Whisht,' says Flannagan. 'I'm waitin' f'r th' moon to come up,' he says, 'so's I can hit him right,' he says, 'an' scientific.' Well, sir, his tone was that fierce th' section boss he dhropped right there iv sheer fright; an' Flannagan was cock iv th' walk.

"Afther a while he begun f'r to go out among th' other gangs, lookin' f'r fight; an', whin th' year was over, he was knowed fr'm wan end iv th' canal to th' other as th' man that no wan cud stand befure. He got so pop'lar fr'm lickin' all his frinds that he opened up a liquor store beyant th' bridge, an' wan night he shot some la-ads fr'm th' ya-ards that come over f'r to r-run him. That made him sthronger still. When they got up a prize f'r th' most pop'lar man in th' parish, he loaded th' ballot box an' got th' goold-headed stick, though he was r-runnin' against th' aldherman, an' th' little soggarth thried his best to down him. Thin he give a cock fight in th' liquor shop, an' that atthracted a gang iv bad men; an' he licked thim wan afther another, an' made thim his frinds. An' wan day lo an' behold, whin th' aldherman thried f'r to carry th' prim'ries that'd niver failed him befure, Flannagan wint down with his gang an' ilicted his own dilligate ticket, an' thrun th' aldherman up in th' air!

"Thin he was a boss, an' f'r five years he r-run th' ward. He niver wint to th' council, d'ye mind; but, whin he was gin'rous, he give th' aldhermen tin per cint iv what they made. In a convintion, whin anny iv th' candydates passed roun' th' money, 'twas wan thousand dollars f'r Flannagan an' have a nice see-gar with me f'r th' rest iv thim. Wan year fr'm th' day he done th' aldherman he sold th' liquor shop. Thin he built a brick house in th' place iv th' little frame wan he had befure, an' moved in a pianny f'r his daughter. 'Twas about this time he got a dimon as big as ye'er fist, an' begun to dhrive down town behind a fast horse. No wan knowed what he done, but his wife said he was in th' r-rale estate business. D'ye mind, Jawn, that th' r-rale estate business includes near ivrything fr'm vagrancy to manslaughter.

"Whativer it was he done, he had money to bur-rn; an' th' little soggarth that wanst despised him, but had a hard time payin' th' debt iv th' little church, was glad enough to sit at his table. Wan day without th' wink iv th' eye he moved up in th' avnoo, an' no wan seen him in Bridgeport afther that. 'Twas a month or two later whin a lot iv th' la-ads was thrun into jail f'r a little diviltry they'd done f'r him. A comity iv th' fathers iv th' la-ads wint to see him. He recaved thim in a room as big as wan iv their whole houses, with pitchers on th' walls an' a carpet as deep an' soft as a bog. Th' comity asked him to get th' la-ads out on bail.

"'Gintlemen,' he says, 'ye must excuse me,' he says. 'I am too busy f'r to engage,' he says, 'in such matthers.' 'D'ye mane to say,' says Cassidy, th' plumber, 'that ye won't do annything f'r my son?' 'Do annything,' says Flannagan. (I'll say this f'r him; a more darin' man niver drew breath; an', whin his time come to go sthandin' off th' mob an' defindin' his sthone quarry in th' rites iv

sivinty-siven, he faced death without a wink.) 'Do?' he says, risin'
an' sthandin' within a fut iv Cassidy's big cane. 'Do?' he says.
'Why,' he says, 'yes,' he says; 'I've subscribed wan thousand dollars,' he says, 'to th' citizen's comity,' he says, 'f'r to prosecute him;
an',' he says, 'gintlemen,' he says, 'there's th' dure.'

"I seen Cassidy that night, an' he was as white as a ghost. 'What
ails ye?' says I. 'Have ye seen th' divvle?' 'Yes,' he says, bendin' his
head over th' bar, an' lookin' sivinty years instead iv forty-five."
(May 12, 1894.)

12. A Victim of the Game of Politics

"Eliction day is comin' round," said Mr. Dooley. "I know it be
what th' polisman that dhrinks this beat tol' me. He says there
ain't room in th' station f'r to get a sheet iv blotting paper in. Bill
O'Broyn held a ratification meetin' at Finucane's las' night an'
walloped th' raypublican candidate immedjately afther. I seen Bill
Joyce with th' pa-ants iv him tucked in his boots goin' out be
Brighton Park f'r to talk with th' farmers. Sare a shtove pipe hat'll
Bill wear till th' counthry's saved a week fr'm nex' Choosdah.

"I heerd Grady, th' orator, holdin' out to a crowd th' other
night. He said, be hivins, if th' constitution wasn't rayconstructed
th' counthry 'd go to th' divvle an' all. 'Th' workin' man,' says th'
lazy bum, 'is th' mainstay iv our institutions,' he says. 'On these
here broad chowlders,' he says, 'rists th' future prosperity iv th'
counthry,' he says, fetchin' himself a belt. He hasn't done a lick iv
wurruk in three years an' his wife cooks on a canal-boat. 'Ye'er th'
support iv th' counthry,' I says, 'are ye?' 'Me,' he says, 'an' other
toilers,' he says. 'Well,' says I, 'if ye don't mind, Grady,' says I, 'it's
sthrange ye'er wife's back ain't broke,' I says. 'An' why?' says he.
'Well,' says I, 'ye support th' counthry,' I says, 'an' ye'er wife sup-
ports ye,' I says. 'No wonder she have a cough,' I says. He was
that mad!

"But 'tis all th' game in politics, Jawn, tubby sure. Whin I was
a young man there was no handier in th' precint with anny manes

iv reform, fr'm a piece iv gaspipe in a stockin' to a speech to th' German voters. I was well liked be th' Germans in thim days, though they're again me now. I was always out peddlin' tickets an' bur-rnin' ballots f'r th' good iv th' cause. But the likin' lift me long ago, an' small loss. 'Tis all white stockin' an' no leg inside like th' Kilkenny girls. Bluff an' cheat. 'Good mornin', Casey, an' how's th' good woman' th' da-ay befure iliction an' 'Th' 'ell with Casey' th' da-ay afther. Bad ciss to thim. They're howlin' about th' ol' flag an' th' rights iv workinmin at Finucane's an' down be th' slough th' women goes about with their feet thrippin' wan another an' th' childher's eyes gets bigger an' their faces smaller day be day. Dimmycrat or raypublican—what th' 'ell.

"Did ye know little Flanagan? Naw! But ye'er father did. He seen what politics was in his day. He was a dacint man as iver lived, mass ivry Sundah, to his jooty wanst a month an' put away his pipe behind th' clock Shrove Choosdah night. He wurrked hard, th' little man, an' he had some money in th' bank an' a nice little house with a front yar-rd whin some la-ads fr'm down th' road tol' him he cud bate Dennehy f'r th' legis-lachure. Th' little man was took with th' idee. Glory be to Gawd, he had about as much notion iv what th' legis-lachure was as he had iv what th' King iv Boohlgaria ate f'r breakfas', but he knew it was gran' an' his wife was plazed to death an' all th' girls begged him to r-run. An' he r-run. Th' fam'ly took on gr-reat airs. None iv th' Flanagan girls 'd do more than wink at ye, an' Mrs. Doheny (fr'm Wexford, where all th' backbiters come fr'm) swore she saw Mrs. Flanagan standin' befure a lukin'-glass sayin': 'Ah, good mornin' to ye, Mrs. Legislachure Flanagan, an' how's th' good man?' 'Thank ye kindly, Mrs. Ga-arfield'—'twas in thim da-ays. 'Atin' three squares a day, thanks be to Gawd.' They called her Mrs. Legis-lachure to th' da-ay iv her death, poor soul.

"Night afther night ye'd see th' touchers comin' up to Flanagan's an' goin' away with th' little man, an' him sthruttin' with his mass coat on his back an' his shtovepipe on the side iv his head an' all th' fam'ly peekin' out iv th' window at him. He'd come home sin-gin' later. He dhrew his money out iv th' bank an' he give up his job. I think he wakened whin he had to put a morgedge on th' little house, f'r I see him comin' away fr'm Schwartzheim's shakin' a bit. But they says: 'Tim, ye can't lose,' they says. 'Ye win aisy,' they says. 'What th' 'ell; ye'll get it all back th' first day in th' legis-lachure.'

"He wint to th' station iliction night f'r to hear th' returns. He come away early. 'Twas a raw night with a smother iv fog in th' sthreet but I see him comin' home, crouched down like with his coat wide open an' his hands be his side. They was lights in th' house but he wint around be th' back dure." (October 27, 1894)

13. The Council Ruins a Decent Man

The Municipal Voter's League, founded in Chicago in January 1896, was successful in keeping fourteen "gang aldermen" from being renominated before the April election. After praising the league for this encouraging feat, Mr. Dooley goes on, in this election-eve piece, to name the "Big Three" incumbent boodlers remaining on the ballot: John Colvin, Mike Ryan, and Johnny Powers. Of the three, only Powers was returned to the council the following day.

"Jawn," said Mr. Dooley, "I wondher if th' push'll go back to th' council. They'se some fourteen iv thim that won't, fourteen as good lads as iver swung a lead pipe in a yarn stockin' or shelled an overcoat pocket—fourteen iv thim laid up in rows like th' corpses at th' morgue, as dead as Brian Boru or Julius Caesar.

"But how many more'll break in, d'ye think? How about ye'er ward? Which is it, Bigane or Ackerman? An' how about Jawnny Colvin? There's a nice spit iv a lad. I knowed him years ago whin I was a young man an' had charge iv one precint an' cud carry it, too, again anny man that come up th' road. He lived over on th' North Side and he r-run f'r th' council because he had nawthin' else to do. He was so ragged in thim days that he cuddent wear a short coat with dacincy. They say—Hinnissy says—that op-porchunity makes th' man. Colvin made th' opporchunity. He'd

been in th' council about a year whin I met him on me way to pay
th' dog tax. He'd put on twinty poun's an' he was dhressed as
though he had a window dhresser f'r a vallay. He shook hands
with me, he did, th' gr-reat man, an' he give me a fine seegar an'
says he, 'I don't recall ye'er name,' he says, 'but ye'er face is familiar.' Says I: 'That's quare,' I says. 'Ye haven't seen honest men so
often in ye'er life that ye shud forget wan,' I said. An' with that I
flung him a cold look an' wint me way. I heerd him laugh behind
me back.

"Will Colvin go back, d'ye think, an' little Mike Ryan an'
Jawnny Powers? Oh, there'd be th' crowd iv honest an' upright
min to r-run th' city. Where'd a poor slob iv an aldherman like
John Bigane come in with thim? What'd th' iv'ryday, hard-
wurrukin' aldherman that's busy fr'm morn to night stealin' annything fr'm a milk can to a mile iv paved sthreet, what'd he do with
thim three buckos runnin' th' machine? I tell ye, it'll be a ha-ard
winter f'r th' poor but dishonest gazabo if they break in. I've
heard talk enough iv th' needs iv th' property owners an' th' op-
prission iv the tax-payer, but I view with alarm—as Casey said
whin they asked him to put up $500 an' r-run f'r constable—I
view with alarm th' threatened impoverishmint iv th' fink aldhermin if th' Big Three take hold.

"Bein' in th' council ain't altogether th' good thing some people
seem to suppose, Jawn. I mind wanst we sint in a man be th'
name iv Slattery. He was a dacint, quiet little lad that r-run a saloon over near Grove sthreet, had a nice class iv trade, can an'
glass, an' closed his place regular at midnight. He cudden't tell a
dimon' fr'm a piece of babbitt metal, an' I don't suppose th' poor
man was downtown iver in his life but whin he wint to renew th'
license.

"Well, he got into th' council, an' they needed him, an' whin
they give him a hundhred or two he swallowed his throat an' was
scared half into a fit. Not be th' dishonesty iv th' thransaction. He
had no more notion iv that thin th' goat has nex' dure. 'Twas
th' size iv th' roll. Man an' boy he'd niver seen that much money

pass fr'm wan man to another annywhere but on th' stage iv th' Halsted Sthreet Op'ra House.

"But 'tis an easy game to larn wanst ye r-read th' cards, an' me little man larned it as though th' a, b, ab iv it 'd been taught him at his mother's knee. Jawn, in less than a month he come in here with a plug hat cocked on his head and a lamp in his shirt bosom, whacked th' bar with his hand an' ordhered a bottle iv champagne. 'What's that?' says I. 'A nice bottle iv champagne,' says he. 'Will ye have Budweiser or Pilsener?' says I. 'Look here,' says he, 'I'll dhrink no beer. I want a bottle iv champagne,' he says. I dhrew him a glass iv beer an' laid it on th' bar. 'Now,' says I, 'dhrink that,' I says; 'put down as much as 5 cints,' I says, 'an' thin,' I says, 'chase ye-ersilf in a hurry or I'll give ye throubles iv a rale kind,' I says. An' we niver spoke again.

"But mark what happened. In two years he was thrun down be th' la-ads, f'r to tell th' truth he wasn't much account, poor fool, an' whin he failed to get th' Duggan boy out iv th' bridewell th' day befure th' prim'ries they was such a vilent uprising f'r a more public-spirited ripresintative that he had to withdraw. His saloon business was gone. Th' place was overrun be a gang iv tough boys that lived on him an' r-run out all th' nice, quiet thrade. No man'd think iv sindin' his child afther a pitcher iv beer iv a Saturdah night with thim toughs hangin' around playin' pool. Th' money he got in th' council give out. Th' neighbors'd not speak to him an' the brewery closed his place. All he had left was his champagne thirst. I don't know whether it sticks to him now, whin all th' wurruk he gets th' year around is a month in th' South Town assissor's office."

"Well, what about it?" said Mr. McKenna.

"Nawthin' at all; on'y I was thinkin' iv that sayin': 'Opportunity may make a man in some places, but in th' council it makes a bum.'" (April 4, 1896)

14. The Career of Alderman John Powers

The saloon-keeping partner of Bridgeport's William J. O'Brien, "Johnny de Pow" served a total of thirty-eight years (between 1888 and 1927) as nineteenth-ward alderman. In January 1898, Jane Addams began a serious effort to unseat him from the council: Hull-House was in the nineteenth, and Powers was the city's most visible symbol of municipal corruption. Immediately, the Municipal Voters' League and most of the Chicago press ranged themselves solidly behind the Hull-House campaign. Mr. Dooley, however, registered this dissenting opinion, and in the April election Powers won easily.

Mr. Dooley and Mr. Hennessy had been discussing politics as a business and Mr. Dooley said:

"I'm not settin' up nights wishin' f'r th' desthruction iv Jawnny Powers an' th' likes iv him. I've knowed Jawnny f'r manny years, iver since he come here fr'm Waterford, with a face on him f'r all th' wurruld like th' flap iv a envelope, an' wint to wurruk in th' grocery store down be Jefferson an' Harrison sthreet. He was a smooth little lad an' bimeby he marrid th' lady that ownded th' store an' wint into politics.

"I don't believe they was anny reason in Jawnny Powers' eddication f'r to think that he'd throw away money because iv his conscience throublin' him. Th' place he lived in was th' toughest on earth. They was hardly a house around that didn't shelter a man that was able to go out anny night with half a brick or th' end iv a bullyard cue an' arn his daily bread. Acrost fr'm where he sold groceries was Law avnoo, a sthreet that no polisman iver enthered an' come out with a whole skin. Back iv him was Sebor sthreet, where th' Cashin twins used f'r to burn th' path-rol boxes, an' a few blocks west 'twas a sthrange night whin ye cudden't hear Chick McMillan's big revolever roarin' like a batthry iv artill'ry.

"They raise no saints in that part iv th' nineteenth ward, an' they was nawthin' Jawnny Powers seen afther he got into th' council that'd make him think th' worse iv Alick Swan iv Law avnoo. He didn't meet so manny men that'd steal a ham an' thin shoot a polisman over it. But he met a lot that'd steal th' whole West Side iv Chicago an' thin fix a gr-rand jury to get away with it. It must've been a shock to Jawnny Powers, thim first two years in th' council. Think iv this quite, innocent little groceryman that knew no thieves but thim that lurked along alleys with their hats pulled over their eyes, bein' inthrojooced to bigger thieves that stole in th' light iv day, that paraded their stovepipe hats an' goold watches an' chains in Mitchigan avnoo. Did ye iver see an aldherman go by th' Chicago Club? He looks at it as if he ownded it.

"Whin Jawnny Powers wint into th' council I don't suppose he had anny idee what a gr-reat man he'd make iv himsilf. He thought iv most all th' wurruld except th' nineteenth as honest. He believed that th' la-ads that presided over th' municipyal purity meetin's was on th' square an' he hated th' ladin' mimbers iv churches an' th' boys that gives money to home missions an' thrainin' schools because he thought they were inhumanly honest. It didn't take long f'r to make him see diff'rent. Inside iv his first term he begun to undherstand that they was rale, flesh-an'-blood, bribe-givin' men. They was good fellers, th' same as Chick McMillan, an' betther to dale with because if things didn't go right they'd not be apt to come down an' shoot bullets through th' sawdust ham in front iv a man's grocery store. An' whin wanst he got their measure he knew how to threat thim. He's quick to larn, Jawnny Powers is. None quicker. But I wudden't iv had his expeeryence f'r twict his money. I'd rather set back here an' believe that whin a man dhresses dacint he's respectible an' whin he has money he won't steal."

"Somethin' ought to be done to rayform th' rayformers," suggested Mr. Hennessy.

"Thrue," said Mr. Dooley. "I'm thinkin' iv gettin' up an organization to do th' wurruk. I'd attimpt to put a branch in ivry church an' charitable society in Chicago an' in ivry club. An' whin anny man that abuses Jawnny Powers an' Yerkuss while buyin' th' wan an' guaranteein' th' bonds iv th' other'd come up f'r Main Shepherd or Chief Angel I'd agitate again him. I wudden't let him set by while Jawnny Powers was bein' done up an' purtend he was in on th' play; I'd get afther him.

"Thin I'd put up a social colony like Hull House down town near th' banks an' th' boord iv thrade an' th' stock exchange. I'd have ladin' citizens come in an' larn be contact with poor an' honest people th' advantage iv a life they've on'y heard iv. I think th' Hull House idee is right, but I'd apply it diff'rent. A man wur-rukin' in a bank all day thryin' to get money anny way he can, how's he goin' to know anny diff'rent? What he needs is to be cheered up, have th' pi-anny played to him be nice-lookin' girls, an' find out somethin' iv th' beauties iv honest poverty be con-varsin' with poor an' honest people."

"But where'd ye get th' la-ads to r-run it?" asked Mr. Hennessy.

"That's easy," said Mr. Dooley. "If ye'll get th' bankers I'll get th' others. I know thousands iv poor but honest men that ar-re on'y waitin' f'r th' chanst to get wan crack at a banker." (January 15, 1898)

15. The Campaign of 1897: Dooley for Mayor

In 1897 there were eight candidates for mayor of Chicago; nine if we include Mr. Dooley, who announced his entry into the race in this piece. Two candidates stood out: Carter Harrison, Jr., the regular Democratic nominee, and the son of Chicago's five-time mayor, Carter H. Harrison; and John M. Harlan, a reform alderman, the son of a United States Supreme Court Justice, and the Municipal Voters' League choice, running on a "Citizens' Party" ticket. It was widely held that young Harrison was in league with Chicago street-railway magnate Charles T. Yerkes. J. Irving Pearce was a little-known independent candidate with no chance of winning.

"Where ar-re ye'er pitchers iv th' candydates?" asked Mr. Hennessy. At this season of the year the houses of call along the Archey road are rendered more or less beautiful by the lithographs of the candidates for office. The German proprietors hang up all the pictures that are sent to them, with exact impartiality. The members of the ruling race generally make a severe choice and exclude all others. But Mr. Dooley had none at all.

"I didn't want to hang up wan iv Carther Haitch's," he said, "an' if I hung up wan iv Harlan's O'Brien'd murdher me. I didn't have anny iv me own so I con-cluded I'd lave th' thing alone."

"An' ar-re ye a candydate, ould fool?" demanded Mr. Hennessy, his face breaking into a broad grin.

"Am I a candydate?" replied Mr. Dooley. "Am I a candydate? Iv coorse I am. D'ye suppose that I'm to be denied th' same privilege that's ixtinded to ivry citizen iv Chicago? Am I goin' to stay at home hidin' me lights undher this bar whin a majority iv me fellow citizens is proposin' to emolyate thimsilves on th' althar iv our beloved city? Did ye iver know me to flinch in th' face iv fire or r-run fr'm th' jooties imposed upon me be th' constitution? Iv coorse I'm a candydate, an' like ivry other candydate bedad I'm going to win!

"I studdid th' question a long time befure I consinted to accept th' unanimous demand fr'm mesilf to offer me name f'r th' suffrages iv th' people. It meant f'r me that I wud have to give up me practice at th' bar in exchange f'r sivin thousan' dollars a year salary; an' ye know what that means to a man that's makin' eight hundherd. It meant that I'd have to abandon th' felicities iv domestic life f'r th' hurly-burly iv th' campaign an' desert me wife an' childher, which I have none to speak of, in th' inthrests iv th' common veal. But me counthry called me an' I cud not lay down. I'm a candydate an' I have me platform.

"I med it out iv me own head, an' 'tis wan that will appeal to th' business inthrests iv th' community. I don't mean th' business inthrests in Janooary, whin th' rayform banquets ar-re held, but th' business inthrests in March, just befure th' iliction. In th' first place I'm f'r that gran' old man Yerkuss. I am aware bad things are said about him be people that ride on his sthreet-cars, but ye must admit that he's done manny things f'r th' divilopmint iv this gr-reat an' growin' city. I believe in encouragin' him, f'r he carries th' prosperity iv Chicago on his shoulders, an' 'tis betther to give him more sthreets than to make him take thim away fr'm us with an ax. If I am mayor I pledge mesilf to give Yerkuss anything he wants—at rejooced rates.

"I believe in fair assissmints provided th' rale estate boord an' th' capitalists don't have to pay thim. Th' men that ar-re buildin' up this gr-reat an' growin' city iv ours sh'd not be worrid be havin' to pay taxes. They have throuble enough buildin' steam yachts.

"I am in favor iv th' enfoorcemint iv th' civil sarvice rayform afther I've put me own people in office. 'Tis necessary f'r th' proper pre-sarvation iv th' spirit iv rayform in this great an' growin' city iv ours that th' lad on th' red bridge sh'd be thrun out an' some good man put in his place. Thin if another man wants it we'll give him an examination that'll take his hide off.

"I believe in clean sthreets always, provided no taxes is paid f'r to clean them. Th' business inthrests iv this gr-reat an' growin' city iv ours should not be required to bear a heavier burden thin they now bear. Instead iv hirin' men an' puttin' sweepers to wurruk I'll organize prayer meetin's to pray f'r rain.

"Th' polis sh'd be de-voorced fr'm politics.

"Gamblin' is a gr-reat evil an' I wud rigidly rigulate it to th' downtown sthreets, where it wud help th' business inthrests iv this gr-reat an' growin' city iv ours.

"I am in favor iv th' departmint stores. I riconize thim as a mon-sthrous evil, but they are a sign iv th' gr-reat an' growin' cinthri-lization iv thrade an' cannot be stopped so long as they pay rint an' advertise.

"I denounce th' sale iv opyum as detrimintal to th' morals an' injooryous to th' complexions iv th' race, but owin' to th' lar-rge number iv houses in this gr-reat an' growin' city iv ours that ar-re occupied by opyum j'ints I wud so rigulate th' thraffic that it cud grow without inflictin' injury on th' people.

"Fin'lly, I denounce as criminal, wasteful, extravagant, dam-nable, scand'lous an' low th' prisint administhration an' all ad-ministhrations past an' to come, an' on this platform," said Mr. Dooley, "I appeal to ye, Hinnissy, f'r ye'er suffrages."

"I've on'y wan undher th' Austhrelyan law," said Mr. Hennessy, "an' that's pledged already."

"Very well," said Mr. Dooley, "go on thin an' vote f'r J. Irving Pearce, if ye want to." (March 27, 1897)

16. The Campaign of 1897: The Crow in the Tree

Charles Yerkes had recently made the dramatic gift of a huge telescope and observatory to the city of Chicago, some said to distract attention from his shady business practices and political meddling. Earlier in the week when this piece appeared, Citizen's party candidate Harlan had charged that Yerkes was taking an active part in the campaign; Yerkes had replied that Harlan was "a fraud and an ass." Evangelist Dwight L. Moody was in town for a revival that same week; hence Mr. Dooley's references to him.

"Me poor head is achin' with th' turmoil iv th' campaign," said Mr. Hennessy. "With all th' candydates in th' field I'm crazy. It usen't to be so. In th' good ol' days whin it was allus Charter H. Harrison again Jawn M. Smythe's Unknown we niver had no throuble in pickin' an' choosin'. We ayether voted f'r Charter or some wan else did. I mind goin' to th' polls about noon wan iliction day to deposit me vote. 'What's ye'er name?' says th' clerk. 'Hinnissy,' says I. 'Hinnissy, Hinnissy, Timothy Hinnissy, is it?' he says. 'It is,' says I. 'Well, I'm sorry, Mr. Hinnissy,' says he, 'but there was a man in here an hour ago that voted f'r ye,' he says. 'Ye'll have to pick a name out iv this list,' he says. An' I voted undher th' name iv Olson."

"Ye needn't put ye'erself to throuble choosin'," said Mr. Dooley. "All ye have to do is to vote f'r th' people's choice, th' boy orator iv Haley's slough—an' that's me. There's nawthin' wrong with me platform. I'm f'r civil sarvice rayform that doesn't rayform. I'm f'r compinsation f'r franchises if none iv it iver gets to th' people that wud spind it in exthravagance. I want th' saloons closed afther midnight—th' saloons iv Schwartzmeister an' Ahern, rowdy places. I'll close me own whin I get tired. Why ain't I th' ideel candydate?

"An' I'm f'r th' Sthreet Ca-ar Magnum. I'm th' on'y candydate that comes out fair an' square an' declares that he's th' creature iv that gr-reat an' good man. Some iv me opponents is fightin' him an' some others is sayin' nawthin', but diggin' har-rd into th' pockets where he keeps his change. But I'm a corporation man, a sthreet railway tool, an' if ilicted I promise to deliver over a blanket morgedge on th' town to that saint on earth th' Sthreet Ca-ar Magnum. What he'll be in th' hereafther I dinnaw, but if he didn't put up that tillyscope f'r to survey a route f'r a trolley line in Moodyville I don't know th' frind iv th' people.

"If half th' men on earth did as much good as th' Sthreet Ca-ar Magnum iviry human bein' 'd be a stockholder. I heard a fellow say wanst that th' man that made two shares iv stock grow where on'y wan growed befure was a binifacthor to th' race. Th' Sthreet Ca-ar Magnum makes eight grow. An' if half th' men on earth was as honest as th' Sthreet Ca-ar Magnum they'd have th' other half in th' pinitintiary. They'se no frills on this great an' good philanthropist. He searches out th' hear-rts iv men an' whin he finds thim r-rings thim up. Ye can't deceive a lad that meets Virtue whin it comes f'r a dividend an' that knows where th' rayform ilimint does its bankin'. A man comes along with a fair front concealin' th' divilish purpose iv givin' th' people iv this city a chanst f'r their lives—wan chanst in tin thousand f'r to lift their heads an' thank th' Lord f'r livin'. He wants to make it so a man can go to th' city hall to pay his taxes without havin' his pocket picked. He wants to write acrost th' page, dark with bloodshed an' plunder, wan line iv goold that our childher—ye'ers, not mine, f'r I have none, thank th' Lord—can r-read without shame. An' people believe in him, an' crowd to hear him, an' cheer him, an' bid him good luck. But not th' Sthreet Ca-ar Magnum. Thank th' saints f'r wan man clear-sighted enough to pinithrate human motives. Thank th' Lord f'r th' crooked yardstick. Th' Sthreet Ca-ar Magnum says: 'He's a fraud an' an ass.' A fraud an' an ass!

"An' mebbe he is, too. An ass, annyhow, to think that annything can be done that th' Sthreet Ca-ar Magnum doesn't write "eempreematoor" in, like an archbishop in a caddychism. Th' on'y candydate that has a r-right to live is th' wan that turns in his platform like a thrip-sheet iv a conductor f'r th' Sthreet Ca-ar Magnum to approve. An' th' Sthreet Ca-ar Magnum knows his business. He has what th' pa-apers calls 'th' key iv th' situation.' I butt up again a man on th' sthreet an' he falls again another man an' that man reels again you, Hinnissy, walkin' along th' curb, ca'm an' peaceful, an' out ye go into th' mud. I don't like Schwartzmeister—an' I don't—an' I heave a rock through his window, an' lo! an' behold, I hit me cousin Mike standin' at th' ba-ar takin' his quiet dhrink. I go out to make th' Sthreet Ca-ar Magnum give back part iv what he took, an' th' first thing I know me banker that has his bonds piled up like cordwood in his safe tells me to take th' little account that I'm savin' against license day around th' corner an' lave it in th' ash bar'l. Th' crow is up in th' three, no doubt, black an' ugly, stealin' me potatoes an' makin' me life miserable with his noise, but whin I throw a club at him he's out iv th' way an' it smashes into a nest full iv eggs that some frind of mind has been hatchin' out.

"An' that's why I'm th' sthreetcar candydate. I believe in th' Magnum. I am in favor iv corruption an' bribery, f'r 'tis on'y be means iv thim we can live comfortably, die happy an' dhraw inthrest. Virtue is shovellin' coal at a dollar-an'a-half a day."

"I don't believe it," said Mr. Hennessy, flaring up. "I don't believe wan wur-rud iv it."

"Go wan," said Mr. Dooley. "Ye've been to hear Moody." (April 3, 1897)

17. The Campaign of 1897: Postelection Analysis

In the election of Tuesday, April 6, Carter Harrison, Jr., won a landslide victory, and a safe majority of known boodlers was re-

turned to the city council. These included Bridgeport's Billy O'Brien,
who had been serving as a state senator. The Union League Club
was the bastion of Chicago's WASP business and community leader-
ship. Here, Mr. Dooley explains the election as a product of the com-
bined stupidity of voters and reformers.

"That frind iv ye'ers, Dugan, is an intilligent man," said Mr.
Dooley. "All he needs is an index an' a few illusthrations to make
him a bicyclopedja iv useless information."

"Well," said Mr. Hennessy, judiciously, "he ain't no Soc-rates
an' he ain't no answers-to-questions colum; but he's a good man
that goes to his jooty, an' as handy with a pick as some people are
with a cocktail spoon. What's he been doin' again ye?"

"Nawthin'," said Mr. Dooley, "but he was in her Choosday.
'Did ye vote?' says I. 'I did,' says he. 'Which wan iv th' distinguished bunko steerers got ye'er invalu'ble suffrage?' says I.
'I didn't have none with me,' says he, 'but I voted f'r Charter
Haitch,' says he. 'I've been with him in six ilictions,' says he, 'an'
he's a good man,' he says. 'D'ye think ye're votin' f'r th' best?' says
I. 'Why, man alive,' I says, 'Charter Haitch was assassinated three
years ago,' I says. 'Was he?' says Dugan. 'Ah, well, he's lived that
down be this time. He was a good man,' he says.

"Ye see, that's what thim rayform lads wint up again. If I liked
rayformers, Hinnissy, an' wanted f'r to see thim win out wanst in
their lifetime, I'd buy thim each a suit iv chilled steel, ar-rm thim
with raypeatin' rifles, an' take thim east iv State Sthreet an' south
iv Jackson Bullyvard. At prisint th' opinion that pre-vails in th'
ranks iv th' gloryous ar-rmy iv ray-form is that there ain't annything worth seein' in this lar-rge an' commodyous desert but th'
pest-house an' the bridewell. Me frind Willum J. O'Brien is no
rayformer. But Willum J. undherstands that there's a few hun-
dherds iv thousands iv people livin' in a part iv th' town that looks
like nawthin' but smoke fr'm th' roof iv th' Onion League Club
that have on'y two pleasures in life, to wur-ruk an' to vote, both iv
which they do at th' uniform rate iv wan dollar an' a half a day.
That's why Willum J. O'Brien is now a sinitor an' will be an al-

dherman afther next Thursdah, an' it's why other people are sind-
ing him flowers.

"This is th' way a rayform candydate is ilicted. Th' boys downtown has heerd that things ain't goin' r-right somehow. Franchises
is bein' handed out to none iv thim; an' wanst in a while a mimber
iv th' club, comin' home a little late an' thryin' to riconcile a pair iv
r-round feet with an embroidered sidewalk, meets a sthrong ar-rm
boy that pushes in his face an' takes away all his marbles. It begins
to be talked that th' time has come f'r good citizens f'r to brace up
an' do somethin', an' they agree to nomynate a candydate f'r aldherman. 'Who'll we put up?' says they. 'How's Clarence Doolittle?'
says wan. 'He's laid up with a coupon thumb, an' can't r-run.' 'An'
how about Arthur Doheny?' 'I swore an oath whin I came out iv
colledge I'd niver vote f'r a man that wore a made tie.' 'Well,
thin, let's thry Willie Boye.' 'Good,' says th' comity. 'He's jus' th'
man f'r our money.' An' Willie Boye, after thinkin' it over, goes to
his tailor an' ordhers three dozen pairs iv pants, an' decides f'r
to be th' sthandard-bearer iv th' people. Musin' over his fried
eyesthers an' asparagus an' his champagne booze, he bets a polo
pony again a box of golf-balls he'll be ilicted unanimous; an' all th'
good citizens make a vow f'r to set th' alar-rm clock f'r half-past
three on th' afthernoon iv iliction day, so's to be up in time to vote
f'r th' riprisintitive iv pure gover'mint.

"'Tis some time befure they comprehind that there ar-re other
candydates in th' field. But th' other candydates know it. Th'
sthrongest iv thim—his name is Flannigan, an' he's a re-tail dealer
in wines an' liquors, an' he lives over his establishment. Flannigan
was nomynated enthusyastically at a prim'ry held in his bar-rn;
an' befure Willie Boye had picked out pants that wud match th'
color iv th' Austhreelyan ballot this here Flannigan had put a man
on th' day watch, tol' him to speak gently to anny raygistered
voter that wint to sleep behind th' sthove, an' was out that night
visitin' his frinds. Who was it judged th' cake walk? Flannigan.
Who was it carrid th' pall? Flannigan. Who was it sthud up at th'
christening? Flannigan. Whose ca-ards did th' grievin' widow,
th' blushin' bridegroom, or th' happy father find in th' hack?

Flannigan's. Ye bet ye'er life. Ye see Flannigan wasn't out f'r th' good iv th' community. Flannigan was out f'r Flannigan an' th' stuff.

"Well, iliction day come around; an' all th' imminent frinds iv good gover'mint had special wires sthrung into th' club, an' waited f'r th' returns. Th' first precin't showed 28 votes f'r Willie Boye to 14 f'r Flannigan. 'That's my precin't,' says Willie. 'I wondher who voted thim fourteen?' 'Coachmen,' says Clarence Doolittle. 'There are thirty-five precin'ts in this ward,' says th' leader iv th' rayform ilimint. 'At this rate, I'm sure iv 440 meejority. Gossoon,' he says, 'put a keg iv sherry wine on th' ice,' he says. 'Well,' he says, 'at last th' community is relieved fr'm misrule,' he says. 'To-morrah I will start in arrangin' amindmints to th' tariff schedool an' th' arbitration threety,' he says. 'We must be up an' doin',' he says. 'Hol' on there,' says wan iv th' comity. 'There must be some mistake in this fr'm th' sixth precin't,' he says. 'Where's the sixth precin't?' says Clarence. 'Over be th' dumps,' says Willie. 'I told me futman to see to that. He lives at th' cor-ner iv Desplaines an' Bloo Island Av'noo on Goose's Island,' he says. 'What does it show?' 'Flannigan, three hundherd an' eighty-five; Hansen, forty-eight; Schwartz, twinty; O'Malley, sivinteen; Casey, ten; O'Day, eight; Larsen, five; O'Rourke, three; Mulcahy, two; Schmitt, two; Moloney, two; Riordon, two; O'Malley, two; Willie Boye, wan.' 'Gintlemin,' says Willie Boye, arisin' with a stern look in his eyes, 'th' rascal has bethrayed me. Waither, take th' sherry wine off th' ice. They'se no hope f'r sound financial legislation this year. I'm goin' home.'

"An', as he goes down th' sthreet, he hears a band play an' sees a procission headed be a calceem light; an', in a carredge, with his plug hat in his hand an' his di'mond makin' th' calceem look like a piece iv punk in a smoke-house, is Flannigan, payin' his first visit this side iv th' thracks." (April 10, 1897)

18. The Campaign of 1897: An Alderman's Life

This biographical sketch outlines the typical steps on the road to political success in the Chicago Irish community. It is probably a composite of the careers of several aldermen, including Billy O'Brien (who ran a saloon) and Thomas Reed (the only "Tom" from Bridge-port to serve on the council in the nineties).

"Did I go f'r to see th' new aldhermen inaugerated?" said Mr. Dooley. "Faith, I did not. I did not. I have other ways iv losin' me money thin be goin' to th' council chamber inaugeration night. Th' six hundherd discharged polismen was enough to scare anny square man away. If they'd been real polismen there would've been room f'r a handball game in th' gallery an' young Charter wudn't 've had a quorum on th' flure iv th' council.

"Aldhermen, Hinnissy, have lost their inthrest f'r me. They prisint, as young Duffy says, too few variations. Whin ye see wan ye see thim all. I know th' la-ad fr'm this ward as well as I know you—knowed him since his head was no higher thin me knee. He started good enough. His father was a man fr'm th' wist iv Ireland, a har-rd wur-rkin', quite, stoop-shouldhered man, that slept tin hours a night an' wurrked twelve a day and put in th' other two eatin' food that didn't always agree with him. He wint to his jooty reg'lar an' whin he died had a large an' continted fun'ral.

"Th' la-ad played in th' sthreets night an' day an' was dhragged to school be th' ear iv'ry month or so. He seemed to be a dacint enough little thing as kids go till he begun to dhrift down to'rd Halsted sthreet an' r-run with th' gang iv big boys. Thin th' polis got to layin' hands on him an' 'twas a crool thing to see a big copper comin' up th' sthreet with little Tom be th' coat collar, him cryin' an' screamin' an' bringin' all th' women to th' dure to cur-rse th' polis foorce. They said he was th' lookout f'r th' lads that hung round th' railway thracks waitin' f'r th' Bohemians comin' home with their time in their pockets. Annyhow, th' judge sint him to th' rayform school where he added pickin' pockets to his other accomplishments until wan day he was hoisted over th' fence an' out into th' sthreet. He lived under th' sidewalks afther that f'r a year, comin' out only be night, to lurk along th' sides iv buildin's f'r all th' wurruld like a rat.

"They had him up manny a time f'r annything fr'm dhrunk an' disordley to poundin' in a man's head with a brick, but he kept out iv th' penitentiary be means iv th' pull that was developin' in him, f'r he was bar-rn with a fine taste f'r politics an' long befure he was a voter—I don't mean befure he was twinty-wan, but befure he was a voter—he was con-sidered handy at th' prim'ries.

"They's no doubtin' he's a smart la-ad. Afther awhile he seen th' immorality iv dividin' up th' wages iv a Bohemian laborer with seven other strong ar-rm boys an' havin' to fight f'r his share. He had a change iv hear-rt an' he see a gr-reat light an' he opened a saloon an' gamblin' house. Meantime he'd wur-rked his way up fr'm alternate iv th' aldhermanic con-vintions to diligate to th' city con-vintions an' wanst he was made chairman iv th' diligation. That was th' tur-rnin' point iv his life. They was a rich man wanted to be threasurer iv th' city. 'Tis a job that's always give to rich men because they want it worse thin annywan else an' are willin' to pay f'r a chanst to rob th' public out iv th' money they've stole fr'm private citizens. Well, this here r-rich man coughed up $1,500 f'r th' diligation an' got it—solid. They come together afther th' con-vintion to divide up. 'Gintlemen,' said Tommy, 'ye know what I got. There are thirty iv ye. I propose to be fair with ye. Here's tin dollars a-piece. Go an' spind it as ye like.' Now, this didn't suit th' push, particul'y a la-ad be th' name iv Morrisey that'd been th' whole thing in th' wa-ard befure an' had on'y give Tommy th' place iv chairman iv th' diligation to keep him fr'm fightin'. 'D'ye mean to say that ye'er goin' to hang on to twelve hundherd dollars that we wur-rked so hard f'r?' he says. 'I take that f'r me services as a promoter,' says Tommy. 'The fifth ward got on'y five hundherd.' Iv coorse they was only wan thing f'r Morrisey to do, an' he done it. They were both good chunks iv men an' they had it all over th' flure, undher th' tables, acrost th' shtove an' out in th' sthreet. Whin 'twas over Morrisey lay on th' pavement a bundle iv rags an' blood an' th' new boss iv th' wa-ard strutted back to th' barroom. Th' diligation gathered around him. He wiped th' blood fr'm his face an' turnin' to his constitooents said: 'Gintlemen, what'll ye have? Th' dhrinks are on Morrisey, an' I'll pay f'r thim out iv his share.'

"Ye know his record since. He's got rich an' powerful. He on'y comes in th' ward th' week befure iliction. He gives liberal to th' poor, he keeps his horses, he wears a diamond as big as an ink-stand an' almost anny day ye'er lible to see him an' th' prisidint iv th' sthreet ca-ar comp'ny ar-rm-in-ar-rm. I see Morrisey on th' sthreet ivry day or two. He's wan iv th' la-ads that complains to th' iliction commission iv vilations iv th' prim'ry law."

"Well, ye can't stop a good man," said Mr. Hennessy.

"No," said Mr. Dooley. "Ye can't." (April 17, 1897)

Chapter Six

Cathleen ni Houlihan in Chicago: Irish-American Nationalism

A thorough survey of Mr. Dooley's Chicago accomplishment must include his examinations of the connection between Ireland and Great Britain, a desperately thorny problem, snarled into the Irish identity since Henry II landed near Waterford in 1171 and peculiarly transformed by the journey to Chicago. The American contribution to the movement to free Ireland had always been a confused and confusing, tragicomic business, taken far too grimly by its fanatic adherents, too easily mocked from outside. There was, first of all, the pain of the struggle itself: hundreds of years of bungled conspiracies, abortive or disastrous risings, and repressive reactions from England, all of this sharpened in recent memory by the experience of the famine. Secondly, those involved in the movement in America were immigrants: in a country with strong nativist and Anglophile strains they were exposed to malicious mockery and accusations of subversion and "divided loyalties." Their position was vulnerable; their sensitivity to criticism, razor sharp. On the other hand, there was much that deserved laughter and badly needed changing in the American nationalist organizations, the Fenian Brotherhood and its successor, the Clan na Gael. The trick was to separate unfair and prejudiced from just and well-meaning criticism. Unfortunately, most of the leaders of Irish-American nationalism were incapable of so discriminating—especially in the 1890s amid the frustration and disillusionment that followed the tragic death of Irish parliamentary leader Charles Stewart Parnell, who had been driven from power by an adultery scandal in 1891. Refusing to shirk the sensitive, emotion-laden issue of Irish freedom,

Finley Peter Dunne became, through Mr. Dooley, a most incisive critic of the movement. For his trouble, he was rewarded with several enemies of the "rale sthrong" Mayo variety, the kind "that hates ye ha-ard."

One of these was John F. Finerty, Chicago's most visible Irish nationalist in the 1880s and '90s owing to his editorship of the Citizen, *the weekly newspaper which he had founded in 1882 for the purpose (quoting the opening editorial): "of presenting to the public in a truthful manner the status of the Irish question, and affording Irish-Americans a wider opportunity to express sympathy with the cause of their motherland." Born in Galway City in 1846, Finerty had been deported for revolutionary activities at the age of eighteen. He came straight to Chicago, where he became active in the American branch of the nationalist movement and began a career in journalism. He made a name for himself with exciting coverage for the* Times *of the wars against the Sioux Indians of 1876–1881, and the following year, running as a Republican, he won a seat in Congress. He served only one term—partly because of a notorious preference for Irish rather than Chicago affairs. (Mr. Dooley recalls the time "me frind Jawn Finerty come out iv th' House iv Riprisintitives; an', whin some wan ast him what was goin' on, he says, 'Oh, nawthin' at all but some damned American business.'") He was more successful with the* Citizen, *which became the leading Irish-American journal in the Midwest.*

By the nineties, however, Finerty had become a middle-aged rhetorician—out of touch with Ireland, obsessed by "the Cause," hypersensitive to criticism, and paranoid; in short, a sitting duck for Mr. Dooley. Inevitably, they clashed in an intermittent war of words stretching through the decade. Finerty became one of Dunne's favorite targets. In turn, Dunne was lambasted in a series of Citizen *editorials as a traitor to the Irish race, engaged only in "murdering two languages, by a bad combination of both, in order to make fools and bigots laugh" (*Citizen, *July 2, 1898). The* Citizen *editor's attitude here exemplifies the special blindness of the fanatic heart, for Mr. Dooley did have a salutary trenchant message for the nationalists.*

In these pieces, first of all, there are humorous perspectives on the past history of Irish-American nationalism. Mr. Dooley's memory goes back to the most bizarre of nationalist events, the Fenian invasion of Canada of 1866 (piece 1). He also recalls the printing and dispensation of Irish Republic Bonds in the old days (2), and the talk at meetings of the Clan na Gael in the 1880s about sending dynamiters to England (3). (Dunne often presents Mr. Dooley as a lapsed Clansman, a one-time believer in violent revolution who now espouses a milder view. He takes full advantage of the satiric possibilities of the Clan's alphabetical codes, secret handshakes, and elaborate hierarchy of officers and "camps.") These first three pieces appeared in the context of the 1895 quarrel between England and America about the boundary of Venezuela, and the impending Boer War suggested the fourth, in which Mr. Dooley daydreams about an Irish-German alliance against "th' Sassenach." Similarly, in 1897 the threat of war in Cuba prompts a Dooley history lesson about the flight from Ireland of the Wild Geese in the seventeenth century (5), and another recollection of the dynamite policy in Chicago nationalist circles in the 1880s (6).

Nationalist-oriented events in his own time in the British Isles also evoked responses from Dunne. After Gladstone's Third Home Rule Bill has passed the British House of Commons in the fall of 1893, Mr. Dooley provides a realistic, moving assessment of the moribund revolutionary movement in Ireland (7). In addition, Gladstone's retirement in March 1894 and the British cabinet crisis of June 1895 allow Mr. Dooley to set the lackluster present against the excitement of Parnell's day, when victory seemed close at hand (8, 9). Finally, an abortive plot to blow up Buckingham Palace in 1896 is the occasion for Mr. Dooley's most pointed satiric thrust at the archetypal boastful and blundering Irish-American revolutionary (10).

About the particular contribution of Chicagoans to the fight for Irish freedom, Mr. Dooley had mixed emotions: sympathy for the rank and file nationalists and suspicion for the motives of their leaders. "Did ye iver," he asks in 1895, "see a man that wanted to free Ireland th' day afther to-morrah that didn't run fr aldherman soon or late? Most iv th' great pathriotic orators iv th' day is railroad lawyers. . . . Most iv th' rale pathriots wurruks fr th' railroads too—

tampin' th' thracks!" Dooley carefully scrutinizes the cluster of nationalist commemorative occasions in the Chicago Irish community. These include the annual August 15 picnic of the city's United Irish Societies (11), the St. Patrick's Day parade (12), and the celebration by the Orangemen of the Battle of the Boyne (13). Invariably, Dooley finds these events to be riddled with hypocrisy and self-delusion. As a further indication of the climate, he examines the local tragedy most responsible for turning public opinion against the nationalist cause in Chicago in the 1890s: the brutal murder of popular Clan na Gael figure, Dr. Patrick Henry Cronin (14). This chapter ends with a generalizing Dooley piece of 1899, in which Dunne marks "the decline of national feeling" for Ireland among the American Irish and their fair-weather friends in American political life (15).

When Dunne moved on to a New York-based commentary on the wider world, Irish-American nationalism in Chicago lost a valuable critic. To those who were listening, Mr. Dooley provided many things: perspective on the Clan na Gael and Fenian past, warnings to the nationalists of the threat of internal dissension and venal political aspiration, determined deflation of the excesses and hypocrisy of nationalist rhetoric, and a realistic evaluation of the unpromising status of the movement in Ireland and America. Still, his pieces were misconstrued by the nationalist leaders. In addition to Finerty's opposition, Dunne was periodically accused of affiliation with the American Protective Association, an Anglo-Saxon supremacist, anti-immigration group, and Patrick Ford of the Irish World *(New York's answer to the* Citizen*) even refused to carry advertisements for a collection of Dooley pieces. That these men ignored Mr. Dooley's valid and well-intentioned remarks is one more illustration of William Butler Yeats's sad maxim: "Too long a sacrifice/ Can make a stone of the heart."*

1. The Fenian Invasion of Canada

On St. Patrick's Day, 1858, in Paris, a new secret society was launched, the Irish Republican (or Revolutionary) Brotherhood, the aim of which was "to make Ireland an independent democratic republic." Later that year in New York, an American branch was founded—the Fenian Brotherhood, named for the Fianna, warrior-heroes of Irish legend. The movement in America grew during the Civil War through the formation of the various "Irish Brigades," many of which stayed together after the war, merely transferring their allegiance from Union or Southern to Fenian leadership. At a convention in Philadelphia in October 1865, the Brotherhood founded a provisional government for the Irish Republic in exile and conceived the fantastic scheme of invading Canada, in hopes of provoking an international incident between England and the United States, thereby aiding the Irish cause indirectly. Incredibly, the invasion took place. In June 1866, some eight hundred Fenians under the command of "General" John O'Neil crossed the Niagara River and engaged Canadian troops in several small skirmishes before retreating to Buffalo, New York. The raid produced eighty-odd casualties, but no diplomatic crisis. Later attempts in 1870 and 1871 were similarly unsuccessful. Apparently, some of the returning Fenians had been represented in court by Grover Cleveland, then a young Buffalo lawyer. This Dooley piece appeared as public sentiment was beginning to mount in favor of American intervention in Cuba, which was steadfastly opposed by President Cleveland.

"I see be th' pa-apers," said Mr. Dooley, "that Cleveland have sint out a tip to th' Cuban rivoluters, that if they keep on rivolutin' on th' primises he'll have thim all arristed an' sint to th' bridewell for disorderly conduct. There's an ordinance again rivolutin' in this counthry, though nawthin' has been said about it before. 'Tis like midnight closin'. Wan administhration laves us keep open till we get tired, an' another makes us shut up tight an' on'y let in thim polismin we know well. So be Cleveland an' th' Cuban rivoluters.

"D'ye know, Jawn, 'twas this same Cleveland that definded th' Fenians whin they was took up f'r invadin' Canada. 'Twas so. He was not much in thim days,—a kid iv a lawyer, like Doheny's youngest, with a lot iv hair an' a long coat an' a hungry look. Whin th' Fenians come back fr'm Canada in a boat an' landed in th' city iv Buffalo, New York, they was all run in' an' sare a lawyer cud they get to definnd thim till this here Cleveland come up, an' says he: 'I'll take th' job,' he says. 'I'll go in an' do th' best I can f'r ye.' Me uncle Mike was along with thim, an' he looked Cleveland over; an' says he: 'Ye'll do th' best ye can f'r us,' he says, 'will ye?' he says. 'Well,' he says, 'I'll take no chances,' he says. 'Sind f'r th' desk sergeant,' he says. 'I'm goin' to plead guilty an' turn informer,' he says. 'Tis lucky f'r Cleveland me uncle died befure he r-run f'r President. He'd 've had wan vote less.

"I'll niver forget th' night me uncle Mike come back fr'm Canada. Ye know he was wan iv th' most des'prit Fenians that iver lived; an', whin th' movement begun, he had to thread on no wan's shadow befure he was off f'r th' battle. Ivry wan in town knew he was goin'; an' he wint away with a thrunk full iv bottles an' all th' good wishes iv th' neighborhood, more be reason iv th' fact that he was a boistherous man whin he was th' worse f'r wear, with a bad habit iv throwin' bricks through his neighbors' windys. We cud see him as th' thrain moved out, walkin' up an' down th' aisle, askin' if there was anny Englishman in th' car that 'd like to go out on th' platform an' rowl off with him.

"Well, he got up in New York an' met a lot iv other des'prit men like himsilf, an' they wint across th' bordher singin' songs an' carryin' on, an' all th' militia iv New York was undher ar-rms; f'r it 'd been just like thim to turn round an' do their fightin' in New York. 'Twas little me uncle Mike cared where he fought.

"But, be hook or crook, they got to where th' other Fenians was, an' jined th' army. They come fr'm far an' near; an' they were young an' old, poor lads, some iv thim bent on sthrikin' th' blow that 'd break th' back iv British tyranny an' some jus' crazed f'r fightin'. They had big guns an' little guns an' soord canes an' pitchforks an' scythes, an' wan or two men had come over armed with baseball bats. They had more gin'rals thin ye cud find in a Raypublican West Town convintion, an' ivry private was at laste a colonel. They made me uncle Mike a brigadier gin'ral. 'That'll do f'r a time,' says he; 'but, whin th' fun begins, I'll pull Dorney off his horse, an' be a major gin'ral,' he says. An' he'd 've done it, too, on'y they was no fightin'.

"They marched on, an' th' British run away fr'm thim; an', be hivins, me uncle Mike cud niver get a shot at a redcoat, though he searched high an' low f'r wan. Thin a big rain-storm come, an' they was no tents to protect thim; an' they set aroun', shiverin' an' swearin'. Me uncle Mike was a bit iv a politician; an' he organized a meetin' iv th' lads that had come over with him, an' sint a comity to wait on th' major gin'ral. 'Dorney,' says me uncle Mike, f'r he was chairman iv th' comity, 'Dorney,' he says, 'me an' me associated warriors wants to know what th' 'ell,' he says. 'What d'ye mane?' says Dorney. 'Ye brought us up here,' says me uncle Mike, 'to fight the British,' he says. 'If ye think,' he says, 'that we come over,' he says, 'to engage in a six days' go-as-you-please walkin' match,' he says, 'ye'd betther go an' have ye'er head looked into be a vethrinary surgeon,' he says. 'Have ye anny British around here? Have ye e'er a Sassenach concealed about ye'er clothes?' he says. 'We can't do annything if they won't stand f'r us,' says Dorney. 'Thin,' says me uncle Mike, 'I wash me hands iv th' whole invasion,' he says. 'I'll throuble ye f'r me voucher,' he says. 'I'm goin' back to a counthry where they grow men that 'll stand up an' fight back,' he says; an' he an' his la-ads wint over to Buf-falo, an' was locked up f'r rivolution.

"Me uncle Mike come home on th' bumpers iv a freight car, which is th' way most rivoluters come home, excipt thim that comes home in th' baggage car in crates. 'Uncle Mike,' says I to him, 'what's war like, annyhow?' 'Well,' says he, 'in some rayspicts it is like missin' th' last car,' he says; 'an' in other rayspicts 'tis like gettin' gay in front iv a polis station,' he says. An', by dad, whin I come to think what they call wars nowadays, I believe me uncle Mike was right. 'Twas different whin I was a lad. They had wars in thim days that was wars." (June 15, 1895)

2. The Venezuela Boundary and the Irish Republic

*In 1895, England became embroiled in a dispute with Venezuela
over the boundary of British Guiana. Citing the Monroe Doctrine,
President Cleveland and his secretary of state, Richard Olney, demanded that England accept arbitration of the boundary dispute.
When this Dooley piece appeared in December, England had refused
the arbitration offer, Cleveland had just sent a belligerent message to
Congress on the issue, and war seemed a distinct possibility. Mr.
Dooley is here following the old political saw that "England's misfortune is Ireland's opportunity." By February, cooler heads had pre-
vailed, and a boundary commission was set up.*

Mr. McKenna found Mr. Dooley standing at the end of his bargain counter with the glasses on the tip of his nose. He was in
deep contemplation of a pile of green paper which he was thumb-
ing over.

"Jawn," said he, as Mr. McKenna walked over and looked on
curiously, "d'ye know a good man that I cud thrust to remodel
th' shop?"

"And what's got into you?" asked Mr. McKenna.

"I'm goin' to have two large mirrors put on th' side an' wan
below. Thin I'm goin' to have th' ceilin' painted green, an' a bullyard table put in th' back room. 'Twill be a place to par'lyze ye
whin 'tis through with."

"And what 'll pay for it?" asked Mr. McKenna, in blank
amazement.

"This," said Mr. Dooley, whacking the pile before him. "Here's
twenty thousand dollars iv th' bonds iv th' Irish raypublic. They
bear inthrest at twenty-five per cint, an' they're signed be Xavier
O'Malley, Pagan O'Leary (th' wicked wan), an' O'Brien, th'
threeasurer. Me cousin Mike put thim up with me f'r a loan iv
five. He wurruked in th' threeasurer's office; an', whin th' polis
broke up th' Irish rivolution, he put on his coat an' stuck a month's
bond issue in his pocket. 'They may come in handy wan day,' he
says; f'r he was a philosopher, if he did take a dhrop too much.

Whin he give me th' bonds, he says, says he, 'Hol' on to thim,' he says, 'an' some time or other they'll make a r-rich man iv ye.' Jawn, I feel th' time has come. Big Steve is on th' rampage; an' if Ireland ain't a raypublic within a month, I'll give ye these here documents f'r what I paid on thim.

"I have me information fr'm Hinnissy, an' Hinnissy have it fr'm Willum Joyce, an' ye know how close Joyce is to Finerty. They're as thick as three in a bed. Hinnissy was in las' night. 'Well,' says I, 'what's th' news?' I says. 'News?' says he. 'They'se on'y wan thing talked about,' he says. 'We're goin' to have a war with England,' he says. 'An' th' whole Irish army has inlisted,' he says. 'Has Finerty gone in?' says I. 'He has,' he says. 'Thin,' says I, ''tis all off with th' Sassenach. We'll run thim fr'm th' face iv th' earth,' I says. ''Tis th' prisint intintion iv mesilf to hire a good big tug an' put a hook into Ireland, an' tow it over th' big dhrink, an' anchor it ayether in th' harbor iv New York or in th' lake. There it'd stand and we'd rope it in an' make it th' fightin' ground iv the wurruld. Annywan that wanted f'r to bate annywan else'd go to Ireland. It'd make no difference whether 'twas Corbett an' Fitzsimmons or th' Prince iv Wales and the Czar iv Rooshia. Anny man cud fight there without th' polis comin' in f'r to interfere. It'd be a grand thing f'r Ireland an' a grand thing f'r all th' rist iv th' wurruld. Whin two imminent statesmin come together we cud give a gar'ntee that they'd be no deaths on th' primises.

"Hinnissy didn't take th' idee kindly. He was mad clear through. 'I'll tell ye now,' he says. 'That th' time has come f'r to disthroy th' Saxon. Long years,' he says, 'have we laid quite undher his tyranny an' now,' he says, 'th' opporchunity has arrived f'r to soak him,' he says. 'We'll fight him on land an' sea,' he says. 'We'll show him that, as that duck Olney says, th' United States is th' whole thing on this continent an' its fist is law.'

"'We will, we will,' says I. 'Be th' way, Hinnissy,' I says, 'has ye'er wife thim bonds yet?' I says. 'She has,' says he. 'Well,' says I, 'did ye see what happened to thim?' 'No,' he says. 'They fell tin per cint because iv th' war news,' I says. 'Glory be,' says he, 'is that thrue? 'Tis too bad, too bad. I'll tell ye, Martin,' he says, 'I'm f'r war. I'd do annything f'r to dhrive th' Saxon fr'm th' sacred soil. If 'twas left to me, me arms 'd be red with blood to th' elbows. But,' he says, 'I don't know what me wife 'll think about it. Women are sthrange crathers,' he says."

"Do you think there will be war?" Mr. McKenna asked.

"I don't know," said Mr. Dooley. "But if there is, I'm prepared for to sacrifice th' last dhrop iv Hinnissy's blood an' th' last cint iv Hinnissy's money before surrindhring. Have a bond with me." (December 21, 1895)

3. The Dynamite Campaign in the Clan na Gael

In 1867, the Clan na Gael (or, Brotherhood of the Gaels) had been founded by Irish-American advocates of the violent overthrow of British rule in Ireland. The Clan surfaced on the front pages of the world's newspapers on St. Patrick's Day, 1883, when explosions at Britain's Local Government Board in Whitehall and at the offices of the London Times *opened the so-called Dynamite Campaign, a plan to blow up the major symbols of British nationality. Over the next two years, bombings occurred at Victoria Station, in Scotland Yard, under London Bridge, at Parliament and at the Tower of London. Many of the dynamiters had departed from Chicago "camps" of the Clan, which were solidly in favor of physical force. In fact, the whole campaign may have been masterminded by Alexander Sullivan, an enigmatic Chicago lawyer who was the apex of the ruling "Triangle" of the Clan in the 1880s. Mr. Dooley remembers accurately that a Clan leader was known as a "senior guardian," and the "Apeeas" were the anti-Irish bigots of the American Protective Association. In the context of the Venezuela boundary dispute, this anecdote was meant to assert that there would be no war against England simply because American money interests were against it.*

Mr. McKenna had discoursed of war to his heart's content. He had been to a meeting of the Wolf Tones and the Wolf Tones had been for war and a resolution had been offered by the secretary volunteering to invade Canada the first time they could get a day off at the rolling mills, and it had passed unanimously and amid the wildest applause. Mr. Dooley listened attentively and then he removed his glasses and wiped them on his waistcoat.

"Jawn," he said; "ye may take off ye'er ep'lets an' lay down ye'er double-barl'd shot gun an' hang up ye'er fife an' dhrum. They'll be no war.

"F'r why? They was a man be th' name iv McGuire wanst that lived in th' twinty-sicond ward, but belonged to th' same camp with me. He was th' mos' rarin', tarin' dinnymiter that iver lived. Whiniver I wint to th' lodgeroom f'r to smoke a see-gar an' have a talk with th' la-ads I knew an' hear Tim Darsy sing 'Let Ireland ray-ha-mimber th' da-ays iv old' me ears'd be split with this man McGuire's orathry. 'Ah,' says he, 'Ar-re ye min or ar-re ye slaves?' he says. 'Will ye sit idly here with ye'er hands in ye'er pockets while th' craven flag iv th' Sassenach floats o'er th' green land,' he says, 'an' a brave people is gr-round down beneath th' feet iv tyranny?' he says. 'Or will ye ray-mimber O'Donnell an' O'Neill iv th' r-red hand, an' Sarsfield an' Immit an' Meagher an' Wolf Tone an' John Mitchel an' sthrike wan blow f'r freedom?' he says. 'Oh,' he says, 'if 'twas lift to me not wan shtone'd stand on another in that ac-cursed land,' he says. 'I'd give th' las' cint iv me money an' th' las' dhrop iv me blood f'r th' cause,' he says, 'if I cud die,' he says, 'cryin' Ireland free,' says McGuire, th' cooper iv th' twinty-sicond ward.

"Well, wan night th' camp was more quite whin I wint in, an' afther awhile th' dure was bolted an' th' sanyor garjeen got up. He was white in th' face an' low-spoken, f'r he believed th' way to conquer England was f'r to hoist a church or two an' kill a polisman. An' be th' same token I believed th' same mesilf in thim days. I know diff'rent now. He said they had lads planted in London an' Liverpool, an' at a certain signal 'twas th' intintion f'r to blow up Windsor Castle an' maybe take a leg off th' Prince iv Wales. Th' cinthral exicutive had ordhered an assismint iv five dollars apiece, an' he'd put th' matther to a vote. Thin me bould McGuire he ups an' says 'Wait a minyit,' he says. 'Wait a minyit,' he says. 'Sure, now, ye don't mane we have to give up five?' he says. 'F'r th' cause iv freedom,' says the s. g. 'Well, now,' says McGuire, 'I think 'tis too much,' he says. 'I'm as sthrong f'r th' cause as annywan,' he says, 'but,' says he, 'it looks as though ye was thryin' to crowd this here thing. Five dollars is a lot iv money to spind,' he says. 'I vote no,' says McGuire, the cooper. Th' rist iv us paid down, but th' nix' time I see McGuire he'd jined th' peace movement.

"Now, McGuire, th' cooper, ain't th' prisidint iv a bank an' he ain't th' iditor iv a newspaper an' he ain't profissor iv a college. He might be, but no wan iver asked him an' so he's just McGuire, th' cooper. But McGuire's in th' bist iv comp'ny. F'r months an' months th' papers have been roarin' f'r war, like a dhrunk man with a rock in his hand. 'Come on,' says they. 'Th' back of me hand an' th' sowl iv me fut to ye. We'll have no aggregation on th' sile iv America,' they says. Well, Big Steve he woke up wan mornin' an' took his pin in his hook an' dahred England f'r to fight. Thin th' war was over. Th' first man to declare peace was Profissor von Holstein, th' imminent Boolgahrian. 'Ach du lieber Gott,' says he. 'We can't have war,' he says. 'What th' 'ell,' he says, 'do we want to be fightin' a great power like England?' he says. ''Tis un-American,' he says, him bein' a Puritan father that come over in th' Mayflower or th' Etruria.

"Thin some wan lost a dollar an' a half in Wall sthreet. Maybe 'twas th' same wan that'd been yellin' f'r war f'r tin years an' maybe he took th' dollar an' a half away fr'm th' likes iv you an' me. But f'r all that he declared again war. 'What,' says he, 'fight England,' he says. 'Honor iv th' counthry,' he says. 'An' how about th' visted inthrests?' he says. 'How about that coin iv mine?' he says. 'Wait till I'm short some stock,' he says, 'befure ye talk iv honor,' he says. Ah thin, 'twas all off. Th' Monroe sthreet docthrine was where Hinnissy is whin he takes his summer tour— on th' hog thrain.

"I've been tirin' me poor head out readin' about th' gloryous thraditions iv our common Anglo-Saxon ancisthry an' wondhrin' where I an' Schwartzmeister an' little Angelo, th' fruitman, an' th'

Spaniard that sells me th' seegars an' Swede Bill comes in. I'm daft to know where them Apeeas was that we heerd so much iv. Have they gone home to Canada to inlist? Suppose Big Steve'd give us war annyhow, wud th' Chicago Club an' th' Virginia Hotel secede fr'm th' union? An' if we had war wud th' Civic Featheration solve th' problem iv rayform be sindin' all th' Irish to th' front?"

"I'm for preserving the national honor at any price," said Mr. McKenna, judiciously.

"Have ye th' price?" asked Mr. Dooley. (December 28, 1895)

4. An Irish-German Alliance in Bridgeport

In January 1896, war between Germany and England was being widely predicted. Germany seemed ready to support the independence of the Transvaal Republic, and British troops were preparing to enter South Africa to fight the Boers.

Mr. McKenna was aware that a gentle feud had existed between Mr. Dooley and Mr. Schwartzmeister, the German saloon-keeper down Archey Road, for some years. It was based upon racial differences, but had been accented when Mr. Schwartzmeister put in a pool table. Of course there was no outburst. When the two met on the street, Mr. Dooley saluted his neighbor cordially, in these terms: "Good-nobben, Hair Schwartzmeister, an' vas magst too yet, me Brave bucko!" To which Mr. Schwartzmeister invariably retorted: "Py chapers, Tooley, where you haf been all der time, py chapers?" But this was mere etiquette. In the publicity of their own taverns they entertained no great regard for each other. Mr. Schwartzmeister said a friend of his had been poisoned by Mr. Dooley's beer, and Mr. Dooley confessed that he would rather go to a harness-shop for whiskey than to Mr. Schwartzmeister's. Consequently, Mr. McKenna was amazed to learn that Mr. Schwartzmeister had been entertained by the philosopher, and that they had paraded Archey Road arm-in-arm at a late hour.

"Tubby sure he was," said Mr. Dooley. "Tubby sure he was. Right where ye're standin' at this moment, me dhrinkin' beer an' him callin' f'r hot Irish. 'Make it hot,' he says. 'Make it hot, me frind; an' we'll make it hot f'r the British between us,' says Schwartzmeister.

"It come about this way: Ye see Willum Joyce come in, an' says he, 'We've got thim.' 'Sure,' says I. 'We've the comityman, haven't we?' 'Th' Dutch is with us,' he says. 'I mane the Germans is our frinds.' 'Ye're goin' too far there,' says I. 'Stuckart was again Reed las' spring.' 'No, no,' says Willum Joyce, he says. 'Th' Germans is up in ar-rms again th' Sassenach,' he says. 'Mind ye,' he says, 'mind ye,' he says, ''tis our jooty to be frindly with th' Germans,' he says. 'I'm now on me way f'r to organ-ize a camp iv me Dutch frinds down be th' slough,' he says. An' off he goes.

"'Twas not long afther whin I heerd a man singin' 'Th' Wearin' iv th' Green' down th' sthreet, an' in come Schwartzmeister. 'Faugh a ballagh,' says he, meanin' to be polite. 'Lieb vaterland,' says I. An' we had a dhrink together.

"'Vell,' says he (ye know th' murdhrin' way he has iv speakin'), 'here we are,' he says, 'frinds at las'.' 'Thrue f'r ye,' says I. 'Tooley,' he says, f'r he calls me that, 'we're wan to-night, alretty,' he says. 'We are that,' says I. 'But, glory be, who iver thought th' Irish'd live to see th' day whin they'd be freed be th' Dutch? Schwartz, me lieber frind,' I says, 'here's a health to th' imp'ror, hock,' says I. 'Slanthu,' says he; an' we had wan.

"''Twud be a great combination,' says I. 'We'd carry th' wa-ard be th' biggest majority iver heerd iv,' I says. 'We wud so,' says he. 'I'd be aldherman.' 'Afther me,' says I. ''Tis my turn first,' I says. 'I don't know about that,' says he. 'Now,' says I, 'look here, Schwartzmeister,' I says. 'This here arrangement between Germany an' Ireland has got to be brought down to th' Sixth Wa-ard,' I says. 'Do ye f'rgive th' way we done ye in th' beer rites?' I says. 'I do,' says he. 'They was befure me time.' 'Well,' says I, 'are ye sure ye can get over th' whalin' ye got whin th' Sarsfield Fife an' Dhrum Corpse met th' Frederick Willum Picnic Band?' I says. 'I do,' says he. 'An' ye have no har-rd feelin' about th' way th' bridges has been give out?' 'Not a thrace,' says he. 'Well,' says I, 'Schwartz,' I says, 'they'se wan thing more,' I says. 'We're both pathrites,' I says. 'We have a common cause,' I says. 'Ye're a Dutchman, an' I'm iv th' other sort,' I says. 'But we're both again th' Sassenach,' I says. 'An' in th' inthrests iv th' freedom iv Ireland,' I says, 'I f'rgive ye th' pool table.'

"Well, sir, Jawn, he wept like a child. 'Tooley,' he says, 'we'll march side be side,' he says. 'Both iv us in th' front rank,' he says. 'Aldherman Tooley an' Aldherman Schwartzmeister, to free Ireland,' he says. 'But where does Germany come in?' he says. 'Germany!' says I, 'Germany! Well, we'll take care iv Germany, all right. We'll let Germans into th' prim'ries,' I says. An' there an' thin we formed th' Sarsfield-an'-Gatty camp. Gatty is a German frind iv Schwartzmeister. We shook dice to see which name'd come first. Ireland won. They was my dice.

"I learned Schwartzmeister th' Shan-van-Voght befure we was through; an' I've got th' German naytional chune be heart,—'Ich vice nit wauss allus bay doitan.' What'll ye have to drink, Jawn?"

And, as Mr. McKenna went out, he heard his friend muttering: "Freed be th' Dutch! Freed be the Dutch! An' we niver give thim so much as a dillygate." (January 11, 1896)

5. The Flight of the Wild Geese

On May 18, 1897, U.S. Senator William "Billy" Mason of Illinois made a windy, three-hour speech in support of Cuban independence from Spain. Two days later, the Senate passed a resolution acknowledging the belligerent rights of the Cuban revolutionaries. Meanwhile, it was reported that a Spanish legislative session on the Cuban issue had erupted into a fist fight. All of this belligerence resulted in the following Dooley discussion of the famous Wild Geese, Irish soldiers who fled the homeland after the defeat of James II's Catholic forces at the Battle of the Boyne in 1690. Captain Schaack was a German-American policeman in Chicago, whose pursuit of the Market Street gang seemed to some to reflect anti-Irish prejudice.

James Stephens was the Irish revolutionary leader who, after the collapse of the 1848 rising, escaped to Paris, where he founded the Irish Republican Brotherhood in 1858.

"I see," said Mr. Dooley, "that th' sinit has recognized th' billymasonry iv Cuba."

"Th' divvle take th' sinit," said Mr. Hennessy, "'tis always reconizin' something about Cuba. Th' throuble is that if th' war goes on f'r long, no wan'll be able to reconize Cuba itself. If I was th' Prisidint iv th' United States d'ye know what I'd do? I'd back down a man iv war in Havana harbor an' declare Cuba lieber in a minyit, I wud so."

"I think we cud lick th' Spanyards," said Mr. Dooley, "but f'r th' wan thing. Did ye see about that Jook of Tetchuan that belted his opponent in th' nose afther th' manner iv th' Illinois ligislature?"

"I did," said Mr. Hennessy.

"He's an ornamint to anny deliberative assimbly."

"He is so; he's the Pete Gallagher iv Spain."

"D'ye know what his right name is?"

"I don't," said Mr. Hennessy.

"It's O'Donnell," said Mr. Dooley, striking the bar heavily with his fist. "I tell ye 'tis so. I seen it in Jawn Finerty's paper. Ye've heerd tell iv Red Hugh O'Donnell, th' la-ad that stood th' Sassenach off with an army ar-rmed with pikes an' flails an' pitchforks. Well, whin th' big bosthoon iv an English king r-run away from Boyne wather O'Donnell had to duck, too, an' he wint to Spain an' they give him th' best job they had—superintendent of th' water office or chief of polis or something like that—an' this here sthrong-arm man is his discindant.

"They'se a lot iv prominent Irishmen outside iv Ireland. Th' prisidint iv th' Frinch at wan time was a man be th' name iv Pat McMahon, a brave an' thrue man. Whin he was fightin' f'r th' Imp'ror Looey Napoleon, a man I didn't like, though I shtud up f'r him again th' Germans, Mack wint clean through th' inimy's army an' got up on a hill. Th' imp'ror was afraid har-rm wud befall him an' he sint f'r him to come back. Mack answered: 'Gee soo,' he says. 'Gee rest,' he says, which is th' Frinch f'r 'I've got this far an' I'm goin' to stick.' They were always a gr-reat fam'ly f'r stickin', th' McMahons. Another distinguished Irishman doin' th' best he cud away fr'm home was th' Jook of O'Malley, that died th' other day in Italy. He was a cousin iv Tommy O'Malley, th' plumber that Shaack thried to do up, but he didn't belong to th' Market sthreet gang.

"All over Europe ye'll find mimbers iv th' rulin' race holdin' good places. They are jooks an' gin'rals an' princes, th' best in th' land. Ye talk about th' soft things we pick up in this counthry, but I tell ye th' Irish are ivrything in Europe, except in Garmany, where they refuse to go. Some day whin I get tired iv Chicago I'm goin' to France to look up a second cousin iv mine that is a gr-reat man over there. He was in th' risin' thirty years ago an' he had to lave between days, so he shtruck out f'r France, where Stephens was livin' an' issuin' bonds f'r th' new raypublic. He was as likely a man as ye iver set eyes on—six feet two in his stockins, weighed fifteen stone without as much fat as ye'll see on a brick wall, an' had an eye that was black be nature always an' sometimes be raison iv th' art iv his frinds. He was a killin' man with th' ladies, an' whin he wint to France they appreciated his graces iv manner. He took to th' ar-rmy an' th' imp'ror iv th' Frinch spotted him at wanst an' rushed him to th' front iv all his rigimint. He become bodyguard iv Looey Napoleon an' I heerd that wanst he kicked Monsier Thiers down th' steps iv th' palace f'r making free with th' name iv Dooley. Some day I'm goin' to Paree an' I'll look him up. If he ain't a jook or a earl be this time, I don't know th' man. He was very pushin' an' he cud lick most anny cabinet that sthud in his way. Th' Jook iv Dooley!"

"It's a wondher to me," said Mr. Hennessy, "that these gr-reat men didn't stay in Ireland an' help liberate th' counthry."

"No wondher at all," replied Mr. Dooley. "There wasn't room f'r thim an' they wint where their talents cud shine. Ireland is full iv great men. D'ye suppose this here O'Donnell cud've soaked his frind an' got away with it if it was in th' County May-o an' not in Spain, an' if th' man's name was O'Connor instead iv Comas, an' if they'd been other O'Donnells an' O'Connors standin' by? Faith, in less thin a minyit that jook wud've been undher a pile iv states-men as high as th' roof, an' whin he come out he'd be a belted earl, as Shakespere says. A man has to be a good man to live in Ireland, but a very ordin'ry Irishman 'll do to rule in foreign lands. Why don't ye r-run f'r office, Hinnissy?" (May 22, 1897)

6. Hypocritical Journalism: Jingoes and Nationalists

The Chicago Citizen *had been so vociferously in favor of the Dy-namite Campaign against England that its editor became known in the British press as "Finerty the Dynamitard." Throughout the terror bombings of 1883–1885, the* Citizen *had praised what one of its headlines called "God's Mercy Manifested in Atlas Powder." Thus, John Finerty is the obvious target when Mr. Dooley pointedly distin-guishes rhetoric from action in a piece comparing the war-mongering Chicago press just before the Spanish-American War with the Irish nationalist press in the eighties. Joseph Medill was the editor of the jingoist Chicago* Tribune, *and General Stewart Woodford was President McKinley's Minister to Spain.*

"I wondher what in 'ell ails McKinley," said Mr. Hennessy.

"What about?" demanded Mr. Dooley.

"That he don't open up war again Spain," said Mr. Hennessy.

"I don't know, I'm sure," Mr. Dooley rejoined. "He'd ought to, that's sure. Here is Cuba bein' depop'lated an' rooned an' here ar-re we smokin' cigars made in Wisconsin an' our commerce bein' desthroyed an' all th' big type in th' newspapers wearin' out an' yet no fight. It can't be that he's afeerd. We wud ate Spain up in a day, we wud indeed. Look at our raysoorces! Look at th' men we cud put in th' field: Fitzsimmons, th' Boston baseball nine, th' Clan-na-Gael Gyaards, th' Englewood Cadets an' Joseph Meddle,

th' editor iv th' Thrybune! Cud anny totterin' dy-nasty iv Europe
overcome that mar-rtial array, as th' fellow says. Yes, I know they
have some brave editors in Spain—as gallant a lot iv la-ads as iver
slung a pen. But they're not in the same class with our sojers. Th'
columns iv their pa-apers ain't so long. They can't do th' sthrat-
ee-gee that a good American editor is brought up on.

"McKinley ought to rely upon thim more thin he does. He's
not got th' thrue spirit an' they're th' la-ads to give it to him.
He wastes too much time in palaverin'. He sinds over Gin'ral
Woodford to say to th' Queen iv Spain: 'Madam, th' Prisidint pre-
sints his compliments to ye an' wants to know if ye won't be so
kind as to come to some arrangement in Cuba,' he says. Thin
iv'rybody takes a fresh light an' waits. Bimeby th' queen comes in
an' says she: 'Presint to Misther Mack renewed assurances iv me
mos' distinguished consideration an' tell him to go to blazes,'
she says. 'I'll communicate ye'er majesty's roar at wanst,' says
Woodford. Whin he rayturns he says: 'Th' Prisidint desires me to
convince ye iv his more thin fatherly affection, to assure ye that
ye'er th' on'y girl he iver really cared f'r, but he's sorry f'r to tell ye
in reply to ye'er rayquist iv even date that he has other engage-
mints that'll prevint him fr'm acceptin'.' An' so it goes an' nawthin
is done.

"Now, if we left it to th' newspa-apers they'd be no small talk.
Woodford'd go over to th' widow woman with wan small child,
an' him a king, an' he'd say: 'Look here, we don't want no more
nonsense, see! Will ye give us Cuba or will we take it off ye?' An' if
she rayfused, thin th' Prisidint'd call out th' Mulligan Gya-ards
an' th' Aurora Zouaves an' Father Macchew's Fife an' Dhrum
Corpse an' th' Civic Featheration an' th' Woman's Club an' all th'
r-rest iv our fightin' strength, an' he'd confront th' Spanyard with
solid, warlike columns iv th' Thrybune an' he'd nail Cuba an' in a
few years we'd have th' island prosperous an' happy, an' 'd be
raisin' our own supplies iv yellow fever 'stead iv importhin' thim
fr'm abroad.

"What cud Spain do? Wan good editor cud blow all her hundhred ships into smithereens with a single article on circulation, and th' Spanish ar-rmy iv wan hundhred thousan' men'd crumble befure th' gallant char-rge iv wan American hackman. You bet-cher life.

"When th' movement to free Ireland be freein' quantities iv dinnymite was goin' on, a man be th' name iv Grady had a pa-aper he called 'Th' Explosive' down on Halsted sthreet. It was a pathrite pa-aper an' it advised me an' others f'r to go acrost th' sea an' spoil th' ancient architecsure iv Great Britain. I didn't go. But wan day I got me a small piece iv gas pipe plugged at both inds with a fuse in wan, an' took Dorsey down with me to see Grady. 'Misther Grady,' says I, 'I'm goin' over,' I says. 'Good,' says he. 'That's right,' he says. ''Tis on'y through th' courage an' fidel-ity iv her sons that Ireland can be freed. Ar-re ye fixed with th' stuff?' he says. 'I am,' says I, an' I pulled th' gas pipe. He tur-rned white as his shirt. 'Take that out,' he says. 'Take it away fr'm here or I'll—Oh, merciful powers, that I should have let this loonatic into me office. Take it away, I tell ye.' 'Ye needn't be afraid,' I says. 'I'm very careful. I'll give it to Dorsey. Here, Tim,' an' I tossed th' gas pipe to him. Grady give a scream iv turror an' in two leaps was at th' window. Another wan took him to th' sthreet an' it was a whole day before he cud be injooced to come back. He changed th' pa-aper into an organ iv th' undhertakers' association."

"An' what iv it?" said Mr. Hennessy.

"Nawthin'," said Mr. Dooley. "On'y if we go to war with Spain we don't want to lean too har-rd on th' editors. We may need other assistance." (October 2, 1897)

7. The Irishman Abroad

Mr. Dooley has few illusions about the climate for revolution in Ireland in the 1890s, and he refutes the American rhetoricians con-vincingly with this explanation of the paradox of Irish accomplish-ment abroad and failure at home.

Mr. Dooley laid down his morning paper, and looked thought-fully at the chandeliers.

"Taaffe," he said musingly,—"Taaffe—where th' divvle? Th' name's familiar."

"He lives in the Nineteenth," said Mr. McKenna. "If I remember right, he has a boy on th' force."

"Goowan," said Mr. Dooley, "with ye'er nineteenth wa-ards. Th' Taaffe I mane is in Austhria. Where in all, where in all? No: yes, by gar, I have it. A-ha!

> "But cur-rsed be th' day,
>> Whin Lord Taaffe grew faint-hearted
> An' sthud not n'r cha-arged,
>> But in panic depa-arted."

"D'ye mind it,—th' pome be Joyce? No, ye gom, not Bill Joyce n'r Dan Corkery n'r Tommy Byrnes. Joyce, th' Irish pote that wrote th' pome about th' wa-ars whin me people raysisted Crom-well, while yours was carryin' turf on their backs to make fires for th' crool invader, as Finerty says whin th' sub-scriptions r-runs low. 'Tis th' same name, a good ol' Meath name in th' days gone by; an' be th' same token I have in me head that this here Count Taaffe, whether he's an austrich or a canary bur-rd now, is wan iv th' ol' fam'ly. There's manny iv thim in Europe an' all th' wurruld beside. There was Pat McMahon, th' Frinchman, that bate Looey Napoleon; an' O'Donnell, the Spanish jook; an' O'Dhriscoll an' Lynch, who do be th' whole thing down be South America, not to mention Patsy Bolivar. Ye can't go annywhere fr'm Sweden to Boolgahria without findin' a Turk settin' up beside th' king an' dalin' out th' deck with his own hand. Jawn, our people makes poor Irishmen, but good Dutchmen; an', th' more I see iv thim, th' more I says to mesilf that th' rale boney fide Irishman is no more thin a foreigner born away from home. 'Tis so.

"Look at thim, Jawn," continued Mr. Dooley, becoming elo-quent. "Whin there's battles to be won, who do they sind for? McMahon or Shur'dan or Phil Kearney or Colonel Colby. Whin there's books to be wrote, who writes thim but Char-les Lever or Oliver Goldsmith or Willum Carleton? Whin there's speeches to be made, who makes thim but Edmund Burke or Macchew P. Brady? There's not a land on th' face iv th' wurruld but th' wan where an Irishman doesn't stand with his fellow-man, or above thim. Whin th' King iv Siam wants a plisint evenin', who does he sind f'r but a lively Kerry man that can sing a song or play a good hand at spile-five? Whin th' Sultan iv Boolgahria takes tea, 'tis tin to wan th' man across fr'm him is more to home in a caubeen thin in a turban. There's Mac's an' O's in ivry capital iv Europe atin' off silver plates whin their relations is staggerin' under th' creels iv turf in th' Connaught bogs.

"Wirra, 'tis hard. Ye'd sa-ay off hand, 'Why don't they do as much for their own counthry?' Light-spoken are thim that suggests th' like iv that. 'Tis asier said than done. Ye can't grow flowers in a granite block, Jawn dear, much less whin th' first shoot 'd be thrampled under foot without pity. 'Tis aisy f'r us over here, with our bellies full, to talk iv th' cowardice iv th' Irish; but what would ye have wan man iv thim do again a rig'ment? 'Tis little fightin' th' lad will want that will have to be up before sunrise to keep th' smoke curlin' fr'm th' chimbley or to patch th' rush roof to keep out th' March rain. No, faith, Jawn, there's no soil in Ireland f'r th' greatness iv th' race; an' there has been none since th' wild geese wint across th' say to France, hangin' like flies to th' side iv th' Fr-rinch ship. 'Tis on'y f'r women an' childher now, an' thim that can't get away. Will th' good days ever come again? says ye. Who knows! Who knows!" (November 4, 1893)

8. Gladstone and Parnell

On the day this piece appeared, William Ewart Gladstone retired from the British parliament, sixty-one years after his maiden speech in the commons. He was succeeded as prime minister by young, dandyish Lord Rosebery, whose government was to last only sixteen

months. Mr. Dooley takes the occasion to recall the "union of hearts"
of 1886, when Parnell's Irish party joined with Gladstone's Liberals
to bring down the conservative government led by Lord Salisbury.

"I see be th' pa-aper," said Mr. Dooley, "that Gladstun have
quit his job. He must 've got somethin' betther, for I'm tol' 'tis a
good job, an' pays as much as tin a day with what ye can make on
th' side. Glory be to Gawd, but th' ol' gazabo must be gettin'
foolish. I niver knew but wan man before that iver give up a political job, an' that was Tom Cloonan. By dad, he had th' rights iv
it, too. He was night bridge-tinder at the Halsted sthreet bridge
an' he tol' th' mayor he cuddent sleep, 'f'r,' he says, 'th' tugboats
whistlin'.' 'An' what do they be whistlin' f'r?' says th' Whole
Thing. 'F'r me to open th' bridge an' let thim through,' says me
brave Tom.

"Gladstun has gone," continued Mr. Dooley. "An' he was a
gr-reat man. By gar he must be near a hunderd year ol' an' just as
good up to a year ago as a colt. I r-read in the *Irish Wurrld* where
he gets up in th' mornin' an' Mrs. Gladstun says, says she: 'Bill,
where ar-re ye goin'?' she says, Mrs. Gladstun says. 'Bill,' says
she, 'where ar-re ye goin', I dunno?' says Mrs. Gladstun. 'I'm
goin',' he says, 'acrost th' sthreet,' he says, 'f'r to chop down a tree
or two,' he says, 'f'r to give me an appytite,' he says, 'f'r breakfuss,'
says he. And him, Jawn, by hivins, as ol' as Casey's goat that was
dhropped here be Noah's ar-rk because he was that tumuljous in
th' smill iv him that th' ladies on boord th' boat cudden't shtand
him. An ol' man, by gar, near a hundred. Whin ye'er at th' age iv
him, Jawn, 'tis out in Calv'ry Cimitry ye'll be, in a crate, with
a little shtone above ye ma-arked, 'Here lies Jawn McKinna,
Riquies—cat in passy.' If thim cigareets don't kill ye th' good
Lord'll smite ye f'r thrying to bate me nickel-in-th'-slot mash-een.
Niver mind now. 'Tis gawn. I didn't know but what ye might be
in here while Hogan was on watch."

"Gladstun wouldn't have quit but his lamps gave out," said Mr.
McKenna to change the subject.

"Did his lamps give out? Glory be to Gawd, is tha-at so?

Musha, 'twas a gray day f'r th' ol' home whin thim lamps give out. I don't take much stock in this here Lord Raspberry they're goin' to give the job to. By jays, fr'm th' pictures they print iv him he looks like wan iv thim play-actors. 'Twas so Prindygast's gossoon had his pictures took whin he wint on the sta-age. He sint thim home to his father with 'Yours thruly, Robert Immitt Prindygast' in black ink bayneath it. An' th' ol' la-ad was that stuck up he wore th' armholes out iv his vist fr'm keepin' his thumbs in thim. He tol' us his son was playin' Julius Cayzar with Sarrah Bernhardt. 'I don't like it,' he says. 'F'r th' sake iv th' fam'ly,' he says. 'But the la-ad makes good money,' he says. 'An' 'tis th' coin we're afther.' Well, sir, whin Robert Immitt come here Prindygast invited us down-town to see him, an' where d'ye suppose he was playin'? In a dime museem, by gar. He done th' bearded woman up-stairs an' wan iv th' bloodhounds in 'Uncle Tom's Cabin' downstairs. What's that? 'Tis no lie, I'm tellin' ye. Didn't Prindygast move over to th' Boolgahrian sittlemint in th' ninth wa-ard, where no wan knew him?"

"What's that to do with Gladstone?" suggested Mr. McKenna.

"Well, I was sayin'," said Mr. Dooley, "that Gladstun was a great man. But there was wan gr-reater. 'Twas Charles Stewart Parnell. Mind ye, Jawn, Gladstun wasn't always a frind of Ireland, mind ye that. By dad, he put more dinnymiters in th' booby-hatch thin anny man iv his day. An' he an' Parnell, they had it out an' out at th' prim'ries an' th' convintions. They was just like Billy O'Broyn an' Willum Joyce, d'ye mind. An' though most iv th' time Gladstun'd win out he always knew he had an argymint, f'r Parnell had th' la-ads back iv him, an' whiniver the comity'd give him a judge, by dad, 'twas all day moosh with Gladstun. Well, sir, wan day th' ol' la-ad he goes to Parnell an' says he: 'Parnell, we've had many a scrap,' he says. 'We have that,' says Parnell. 'But there's no ha-ard feelin',' says Gladstun. 'Divvle th' bit,' says Parnell. ''Twas all in the line iv di-varsion f'r me.' 'Well,' says Gladstun, 'we're all good fellows,' he says. 'Let's be good fellows together,' he says. 'An' we can skin Salsbry,' he says, 'Salsbry's a dip'ty.' 'He is,' says Parnell. 'I know it,' says Gladstun. 'I know the ca-amp he belongs to,' says he. 'Thin,' says Parnell, 'I'm right along with ye.' An' they had a frish wan together an' they niver parted till poor Parnell passed away, may his sowl—"

"But—Ireland isn't free yet!" said Mr. McKenna.

"No," said Mr. Dooley. "Th' Prince iv Wales thrun thim down." (March 3, 1894)

9. The British Cabinet Crisis of 1895

Lord Rosebery's Liberal government fell in June 1895, and the Tories under Lord Salisbury took over. The immediate cause of the crisis was a controversy over the purchase of explosives by Rosebery's war secretary, Sir Henry Campbell-Bannerman. Here, John McKenna puts the British trouble in the perspective of the Chicago style of politics. He begins with a reference to the recent appointment of John Finerty as chairman of an upcoming "Irish race convention" in Chicago. Matthew P. Brady and William Joyce were well-known for their oratorical contributions to the fight for Irish freedom: Brady was a lawyer and city prosecutor, and Joyce had been president of Chicago's United Irish Societies in 1891.

Mr. Dooley, much disturbed by the British cabinet crisis, was attempting to get the facts of the situation firmly in mind when his friend, John McKenna, came in.

"Well," he said, "they're havin' th' divvil an' all to pay in England."

"I don't blame them," said Mr. McKenna cordially. "I knew Finerty's appointment would stir up the animals."

"Arrah, thin, now what are ye talkin' about, Jawn?" demanded Mr. Dooley. "'Tis not, Jawn, as if that has disturbed thim, though I'll say this f'r him, he's hit some thunderin' blows at th' Sassenach. 'Dad, there's th' lad to throw th' ink acrost th' pa-aper, an' make thrones an' dy-nasties thremble. Gawd bless him f'r th' good he's done. I use t' think Brady was his akel, but th' captain has wiped up th' earth with him. D'ye know that Macchew P. has give it up f'r good an' all an' has took to writin' come-all-ye's? He have so. Molly Donahue had wan iv his songs—'Walkin' with Looloo in th' Pa-ark'—with ne'er a wurrud about dinnymite in it. They've give him a vote iv censure in th' Wolf Tones. They have so.

"Naw, 'tis another matther, quite, an' to save th' life iv me, I can't make head nor tail iv it. Ye see Gladstun he thought he was all r-right when he thrun down Char-les Stewart Parnell. He thought thin with Char-les Stewart Parnell out iv th' way he was th' whole thing, an' he done a lot iv swellin' around an' revokin' licenses an' gettin' lads on in th' pipe ya-ard an' th' like iv that. Well, he was th' whole thing for a while, an' he fixed it up with some iv our own la-ads an' he had th' station with him an' done as he pleased.

"But there was manny a hammer out again him at that— manny a wan. Th' house iv lords was that sore they thrun out annything he sint to thim without askin' with ye'er love or by ye'er leave. An' they was thim in his own pa-arty that didn't love him over much an' was around givin' him a quite roast now and thin."

"He ought to have gone to the central committee," suggested Mr. McKenna, the practical politician.

"So he ought, so he ought," assented Mr. Dooley. "But mebbe th' centhral comity was again him. Perhaps he'd appinted some man that wasn't right gas inspictor or turned down a good man f'r a bridge. Ye can't tell."

"The way to treat the likes of those fellows," said Mr. McKenna, "is to take and throw them out of the party."

"But mebbe they had a dhrag," said Mr. Dooley. "Ye can't please ivrybody. 'Tis just as Willum J. O'Brien said. No matther what ye do ye'er cursed be wan side or th' other. Gladstun seen it an' he thrun up his job."

"He was crazy," said Mr. McKenna. "If the committee wasn't with him why didn't he revoke their licenses? Anyhow, if he was good he ought to be able to carry the primaries."

"Be that as it may," said Mr. Dooley, "he got tired iv thryin', an' says he to th' la-ads: 'I'm goin' to quit,' he says. 'Ye can take me job an' see how well ye can r-run it ye'ersilves,' he says. 'I quit ye,' he says. 'I'm goin' down to Wes' Baden an' boil out.' So he quit an' wint away, an' they give his book to Lord Rosebery—a young la-ad that ownded race hor-rses—a mere child. It seems they didn't do annything to Rosebery but peg him up in th' air, Jawn. He thought he was th' whole thing, too, but I'm dom if he was ayether. But he wint on with his head in th' air an' handed out th' good things till th' other day, whin he inthrojooced a risolution to increase th' pay iv wan iv his la-ads. This here la-ad had two names, an' he might have gone on another payroll, but Rosebery says, 'No, no,' he says, 'he's a good, hard-wurrkin' man an' he ought to have more money,' he says. Well, sir, divvle th' copper would they give th' poor man. They voted to rejooce th' salary."

"That comes of having a committee on credentials to let in the likes of them," said Mr. McKenna in disgust.

"Mebbe so," said Mr. Dooley. "But they thrun him down annyhow."

"But couldn't he go to the police captain and adjourn the meeting and clean out the hall?" said Mr. McKenna, much puzzled by this extraordinary recital.

"I dinnaw," replied Mr. Dooley. "I dinnaw about that. Annyhow he didn't. Mebbe his nerve quit him. What he done was th' cowardliest thing I iver heerd tell iv. He up an' resigned—thrun up his job—an' they give it to a man be th' name iv Sal'sbury that had quite a big push behind him. Did ye iver hear tell iv th' like iv that in all ye'er born days? Quit his job! Dear, oh dear!"

"Well," said Mr. McKenna sagely, "he may be all right where he is, but he wouldn't do for the sixth ward. I knew a man once that was a candidate for collector of internal revenue and was appointed gauger. Somebody asked him if he was going to take it. 'Take it?' he says. 'I should think so. It was what I was looking for.' How is it all coming out, at all?"

"I dinnaw," said Mr. Dooley. "Willum Joyce come in here las' night an' he said it was a big thing f'r Ireland. 'How is that?' says I. 'Well,' says he, 'they'll be a crool man put in to rule th' counthry,' he says, 'an' he'll burn th' houses an' seize th' cattle an' mebbe kill a lot iv people,' he says, 'an' thin there'll be throuble,' he says. 'Ireland is niver well off,' he says, 'but whin she's unfortunate,' he says. I hear th' mimbers iv th' Wolf Tones is goin' about with so manny dinnymite bombs in th' tails iv their coats they don't dare to set down." (June 29, 1895)

10. The Tynan Plot

In September 1896 a New York Irishman, P. J. P. Tynan, was arrested in France for having fomented a "Fenian-Russian Nihilist" plot to assassinate Queen Victoria and the Czar, who was about to visit England. According to British detectives, Tynan had planned to tunnel under Buckingham Palace and blow it up. He was quickly released after having been identified as the notorious eccentric who had written a 700-page book claiming responsibility for the Dynamite Campaign and the murder of Lord Frederick Cavendish in Dublin's Phoenix Park. It was also reported that Tynan had been publicizing his plot for years in New York saloons. Coincident with the Tynan affair was the return to America of three Irish-Americans who had been imprisoned in England since 1883 for dynamite conspiracy. Dunne responded to all of the publicity with this tour-de-force Dooley piece.

"Well," said Mr. Dooley, "th' European situation is becomin' a little gay."

"It 'tis so," said Mr. Hennessy. "If I was conthrollin' anny iv the gr-reat powers, I'd go down to th' Phosphorus an' take th' sultan be th' back iv th' neck an' give him wan, two, three. 'Tis a shame f'r him to be desthroyin' white people without anny man layin' hands on him. Th' man's no frind iv mine. He ought to be impeached an' thrun out."

"Divvle take th' sultan," said Mr. Dooley. "It's little I care f'r him or th' likes iv him or th' Ar-menyans or th' Phosphorus. I was runnin' over in me mind about th' poor lads they have sloughed up beyant f'r attimptin' to blow up Queen Victorya an' th' cza-ar iv Rooshia. Glory be, but they'se nawthin' in the wide wurruld as aisy to undherstand as a rivoluchonary plot be our own people. You'll see a lad iv th' right sort that'd niver open his head fr'm wan end iv th' year to th' other; but, whin he's picked out to go on a mission to London, he niver laves off talkin' till they put him aboord th' steamer. Here was Tynan. They say he had a hand in sindin' Lord Cavendish down th' toboggan, though I'd not thrust his own tellin' as far as th' len'th iv me ar-rm. Now he figured out that th' thrue way to free Ireland was to go over an' blow th' windows in Winzer Palace, an' incidentally to hist th' queen an' th' Rooshian cza-ar without th' aid iv th' elevator. What this here Tynan had again th' Rooshian cza-ar I niver heerd. But 'twas something awful, ye may be sure.

"Well, th' first thing th' la-ads done was to go to Madison Square Garden an' hold a secret meetin', in which thim that was to hand th' package to th' queen and thim that was to toss a piece iv gas pipe to his cza-ars was told off. Thin a comity was sint around to th' newspaper offices to tell thim th' expedition was about to start. Th' conspirators, heavily disgeesed, was attinded to th' boat be a long procission. First come Tynan ridin' on a wagon-load iv nithroglycerine; thin th' other conspirators, with gas-pipe bombs an' picks an' chuvvels f'r tunnellin' undher Winzer Castle; thin th' Ah-o-haitches; thin th' raypoorthers; thin a brigade iv Scotland Ya-ard spies in th' ga-arb iv polismin. An' so off they wint on their secret mission, with th' band playin' 'Th' Wearing' iv th' Green,' an' Tynan standin' on th' quarther deck, smilin' an' bowin' an' wavin' a bag iv jint powdher over his head.

"No sooner had th' conspirators landed thin th' British gover'mint begun to grow suspicious iv thim. Tynan was shadowed be detictives in citizens' clothes; an', whin he was seen out in his backyard practisin' blowin' up a bar'l that he'd dhressed in a shawl an' a little lace cap, th' suspicions growed. Ivrywhere that Tynan wint he was purshooed be th' minions iv tyranny. Whin he visited th' house nex' dure to th' queen's, an' unloaded a dhray full iv explosives an' chuvvels, the fact was rayported to th' polis, who become exthremely vigilant. Th' detictives followed him to

Scotland Yard, where he wint to inform th' captain iv th' conspiracy, an' overheard much damming ividence iv th' plot until they
become more an' more suspicious that something was on, although what was th' intintions iv th' conspirators it was hard to
make out fr'm their peculiar actions. Whin Tynan gathered his
followers in Hyde Park, an' notified thim iv the positions they was
to take and disthributed th' dinnymite among thim, th' detictives
become decidedly suspicious. Their suspicions was again aroused
whin Tynan asked permission iv th' common council to build a
bay window up close to th' queen's bedroom. But th' time to act
had not come, an' they continted thimselves with thrackin' him
through th' sthreets an' takin' notes iv such suspicious remarks as
'Anny wan that wants mementoes iv th' queen has on'y to be
around this neighborhood nex' week with a shovel an' a basket,'
an' 'Onless ye want ye'er clothes to be spoiled be th' czar, ye'd best
carry umbrellas.' On th' followin' day Tynan took th' step that was
needed f'r to con-vince th' gover'mint that he had designs on the
monarchs. He wint to France. It's always been obsarved that,
whin a dinnymiter had to blow up annything in London, he laves
th' counthry. Th' polis, now thoroughly aroused, acted with com-
mindable promptness. They arristed Tynan in Booloon f'r th'
murdher iv Cavendish.

"Thus," said Mr. Dooley, sadly, "thus is th' vengeance f'r which
our beloved counthry has awaited so long delayed be th' hand iv
onscrupulious tyranny. Sthrive as our heroes may, no secrecy is
secure against th' corruption iv British goold. Oh, Ireland, is this
to be thy fate forever? Ar-re ye niver to escape th' vigilance iv th'
polis, thim cold-eyed sleuths that seem to read th' very thoughts
iv ye'er pathriot sons?"

"There must have been a spy in th' ranks," said Mr. Hennessy.

"Sure thing," said Mr. Dooley, winking at Mr. McKenna.
"Sure thing, Hinnissy. Ayether that or th' accomplished detictives at Scotland Yards keep a close watch iv the newspapers. Or
it may be—who knows?—that Tynan was indiscreet. He may
have dhropped a hint of his intintions." (September 19, 1896)

11. The Annual Freedom Picnic

Every August 15 the Chicago United Irish Societies gathered at Ogden's Grove for a picnic celebration of the anniversary of Red Hugh O'Neill's victory over British forces at the Battle of the Yellow Ford in 1598. Mr. Dooley attended the 1894 picnic, at which Matthew P. Brady, William Joyce, and John Finerty all spoke. John M. Smyth was a successful furniture dealer in Chicago.

"There's wan thing about th' Irish iv this town," said Mr. Dooley.

"The police?" said Mr. McKenna.

"No," said the philosopher. "But they give picnics that does bate all. Be hivins, if Ireland cud be freed be a picnic, it 'd not on'y be free to-day, but an impire, begorra, with Tim Haley, th' Banthry man, evictin' Lord Salisb'ry fr'm his houldin'. 'Twud that.

"Jawn, th' la-ads have got th' thrick iv freein' Ireland down to a sinsible basis. In th' ol' days they wint over with dinnymite bombs in their pockets, an' ayether got their rowlers on thim in Cork an' blew thimsilves up or was arristed in Queenstown f'r disordherly conduct. 'Twas a divvle iv a risky job to be a pathrite in thim days, an' none but those that had no wan dipindint on thim cud affoord it. But what was th' use? Ireland wint on bein' th' same apprissed green oil it had always been, an' th' on'y difference th' rivolutions made was ye sa-aw new faces on th' bridges an' th' Wolfe Tones passed another set iv resolutions.

"'Tis different now. Whin we wants to smash th' Sassenach an' restore th' land iv th' birth iv some iv us to her thrue place among th' nations, we gives a picnic. 'Tis a dam sight asier thin goin' over with a slug iv joynt powder an' blowin' up a polis station with no wan in it. It costs less; an', whin 'tis done, a man can lep aboord a Clyburn Avnoo ca-ar, an' come to his family an' sleep it off.

"I wint out last Choosdah, an' I suppose I must've freed as much as eight counties in Ireland. All th' la-ads was there. Th' first ma-an I see was Dorgan, the sanyor guarjeen in the Wolfe Tone Lithry Society. He's th' la-ad that have made th' Prince iv

Wales thrimble in his moccasins. I heerd him wanst makin' a speech that near injooced me to take a bumb in me hand an' blow up Westminsther Cathedral. 'Ar-re ye,' he says, 'men, or ar-re ye slaves?' he says. 'Will ye,' he says, 'set idly by,' he says, 'while th' Sassenach,' he says, 'has th' counthry iv Immitt an' O'Connell,' he says, 'an' Jawn Im Smyth,' he says, 'undher his heel?' he says. 'Clear th' way!' he says. 'Cowards an' thraitors!' he says. 'Faugh-a-ballagh!' he says. He had th' beer privilege at th' picnic, Jawn.

"Hinnissy, th' plumber, who blew wan iv his fingers off with a bumb intinded f'r some iv th' archytecture iv Liverpool, had th' conthract f'r runnin' th' knock-th'-babby-down-an'-get-a-nice-seegar jint. F'r th' good iv th' cause I knocked th' babby down, Jawn, an' I on'y wish th' Queen iv England 'r th' Prince iv Wales cud be injooced to smoke wan iv th' seegars. Ye might as well go again a Roman candle. Th' wan I got was made iv baled hay, an' 'twas rumored about th' pa-ark that Hinnissy was wurrukin' off his surplus stock iv bumbs on th' pathrites. His cousin Darcey had th' shootin' gallery privilege, an' he done a business th' like iv which was niver knowed be puttin' up th' figure iv an Irish polisman f'r th' la-ads to shoot at. 'Twas bad in th' end though, f'r a gang iv Tipp'rary lads come along behind th' tent an' begun throw'n stones at th' copper. Wan stone hit a Limerick man, an' th' cry 'butthermilk' wint around; an' be hivins, if it hadn't been that Mike Brinnan, th' wise la-ad, sint none but German polismen to th' picnic, there'd not been a man left to tell th' tale."

"What's that all got to do with freeing Ireland?" asked Mr. McKenna.

"Well, 'tis no worse off thin it was befure, annyhow," said Mr. Dooley. (August 18, 1894)

12. St. Patrick's Day

By the 1890s, St. Patrick's Day was well established as the most important Irish-American occasion of the year in Chicago. Mr. Dooley was never enthusiastic about it, and in 1896 he explained

why. The day, he contends, has been transformed from a neighbor-
hood cultural event to a city-wide political sideshow. As proof, he
compares the parade route in the old days, which falls strictly within
Chicago's Irish-American West Side area, and the route in the nine-
ties, which includes the central business district and its major artery,
Michigan Avenue. The 1896 celebration was preceded by a debate in
the city council between Aldermen McCarthy and Lammers on the
issue of whether city hall ought to be closed in honor of St. Patrick.
The McCarthy forces lost, and the hall remained open. The Chicago
Inter-Ocean *was a fairly staid Republican newspaper.*

Mr. Dooley stretched his arms infinitely and yawned until his
glasses slipped from his nose. "Oh, y-a-ah! Dear ah, me! Dear ah,
me! Bad ciss to old age, says I. To hear thim talk ye'd think it
crept on ye. But it don't. It leps at ye whin ye're not prepared, an'
wanst it has ye down ye'er like O'Broyn—not Tim, but a frind iv
mine that wurrked f'r Dorsey, th' conthractor—whin th' machinery broke on wan iv thim laddher chains that they put in f'r
to roon th' hon'rable thrade iv carryin' th' hod. Wan iv th' hods
afther another dumped on th' poor man an' he stood there with th'
bricks pourin' down on him an' breakin' on his head, an' him
fightin' thim off as though they was alive. Whin the last hod was
diposited, O'Broyn—a good man an' well thought iv—wint to
Dorsey an' says he: 'I don't know th' name iv th' la-ad that med
that ma-chine,' says he, 'but if I cud take it to th' prim'ries,' he
says, 'I'd be mayor iv th' town befure th' snow flies,' he says.
'An',' he says, 'if ye charge me f'r th' bricks I'll put in a bill f'r a
hat,' he says.

"But that ain't what I started f'r to tell ye. 'Twas about ol' age.
Jawn, avick, keep young while ye may. I'm not so old mesilf.
Lasteways there's manny a good-lookin' woman up an' down th'
Archey road that has an eye on me. But if I was to take count of
th' minyits be how I feel afther Pathrick's day I'd be too old to do
annything with but print in th' Inter Ocean. I wud so.

"'Twas not th' parade. Th' Lord knows I didn't ma-arch in

that. What business have we in Mitchigan Avenoo? There ain't a vote or a subscriber to th' Citizen there an' they'se twenty-sivin blocks iv unfrindly houses without enough dhrink to start a fight on. Sure, we'd a-done betther if we'd stuck where we belonged. Displaines street, right flank ristin' again Alderman Brinnan's; south to Harr'son, wist to Bloo I'land avnoo, south-wist to Twilfth, where th' procission 'll counthermarch befure th' Jesuit Church an' be reviewed be his grace th' archbishop, be th' clargy an' th' mayor an' th' board iv aldhermin. Attintion! Carry ar-rms. Where's th' band? Officer Mulcahy, go over to Dochney's an' chop that band away fr'm th' bar. Hol' on there, Casey, don't back that big saw horse again me. Ma, look at da-da in Gavin's hack. Ar-re ye ready? Play up th' wearin' iv the green, ye baloon-headed Dutchmin. Hannigan, go an' get th' polis to intherfere—th' Sons iv Saint Patrick an' th' Ancient Order's come together. Glory be, me saddle's slippin'. Ar-re ye ready? For-wa-ard, march!"

Mr. Dooley had grown excited and was dancing around the room and roaring out commands and entreaties.

"Dear me," said Mr. McKenna, "what ails you, entirely?"

The philosopher quieted himself and went on. "I was comparin' th' parades," he said. "The ol' days has gone, an' here are th' joods marchin' up an' down Mitchigan avnoo in new clothes like masons or thrade unions. Sure I'd 've give an eye to be back at th' ol' times befure they put on style an' thried to impriss th' wur-ruld with how many votes we cud tur-rn out rain 'r shine. 'Twas Pathrick's day thin. But now it might as well be th' anni-varsary iv th' openin' iv th' first clothin' store in Chicago."

"But where did you get it?" Mr. McKenna asked, surveying his friend with the discriminating gaze of an expert.

"Well," said Mr. Dooley, "in th' av'nin' I wint to th' banquet iv th' Fr-rindly Ordher iv th' Sons of Roscommon. I responded to th' toast iv 'The Women Gawd Help Thim,' an' afther it was over we got talkin' about th' man Lammers that inthrojooced an ordinance again' closin' th' city hall on th' day. Thin some wan mintioned th' name iv 'Buck' McCarthy an' spoke iv what he'd done to

Lammers. Well, Jawn, if Buck McCarthy uses all th' health we dhrunk to him he'll live to be as old as I feel this blissid minyit." (March 21, 1896)

13. Boyne Water and Bad Blood

On July 12th the Protestant Irish of Chicago marched in celebration of the 1690 Battle of the Boyne, at which the Protestant forces under William of Orange had won a questionable victory over James II's Catholic Irish. (James is said to have bungled the battle by ordering his ablest commander, Patrick Sarsfield, to guard the rear all day long, instead of participating in the fighting.) In 1795 in Ulster, the Protestant Orange Order had been established to support British rule in Ireland: the Boyne parades were their idea. Mr. Dooley reports somewhat ruefully that the 1895 Orange parade took place without incident—one more sign that the nationalist spirit is on the wane. He does not exaggerate the past bloody history of July 12 in America. There had been terrible Orange-Green riots on that day; the worst, in New York City in 1870 and 1871.

"Jawn," said Mr. Dooley to Mr. McKenna, "what did th' Orangeys do to-day?"

"They had a procession," said Mr. McKenna.

"Was it much, I dinnaw?"

"Not much."

"That's good," said Mr. Dooley. "That's good. They don't seem to be gettin' anny sthronger, praise be! Divvle th' sthraw do I care f'r thim. They niver harmed hair nor head iv me; an' they ain't likely to, ayether, so long as th' R-road keeps th' way it is. Faith, 'twud be a fine pot iv porridge th' like iv thim 'd ate if they come up into Bridgepoort. I'm an ol' man, Jawn,—though not so dam ol' at that,—but I'd give tin years iv me life to see an Orange procession west on Ar-rchey Road with th' right flank restin' on Halsthed Sthreet. It'd rest there. Th' Lord knows it wud.

"Jawn, I have no dislike to th' Orangeys. Nawthin' again thim.

I'd not raise me hand to thim, I wud not, though me cousin Tim
was kilt be wan iv thim dhroppin' a bolt on his skull in th' ship-
yards in Belfast. 'Twas lucky f'r that there Orangey he spoke first.
Me cousin Tim had a ship-ax in his hand that'd've evened things
up f'r at laste wan iv th' poor pikemen that Sarsfield had along
with him. But I've nawthin' again thim at that but th' wan that
croaked Tim. I'd like to meet that lad in some quite place like th'
picnic at Ogdin's Grove on th' fifteenth iv August, some place
where we'd have fair play.

"Jawn, live an' let live is me motto. On'y I say this here, that 'tis
a black disgrace to Chicago f'r to let th' likes iv thim thrapze
about th' sthreets with their cheap ol' flags an' ribbons. Oh dear,
oh dear, if Pathrick's Day on'y come some year on' th' twelfth day
iv July! Where'd they be, where'd they be?

"D'ye know things is goin' to th' dogs in this town, Jawn,
avick? Sure they are, faith. I mind th' time well whin an Orangey'd
as lave go through hell in a celluloid suit as march in this here
town on the twelfth iv July. I raymimber wanst they was a man be
th' name iv Morgan Dempsey,—a first cousin iv thim Dempseys
that lives in Cologne Sthreet,—an' he was a Roscommon man,
too, an' wan iv th' cutest divvles that iver breathed th' breath
iv life.

"Well, whin th' day come f'r th' Orangeys to cillybrate th' time
whin King Willum—may th' divvle hould him!—got a stand-
off,—an' 'twas no betther, Jawn, f'r th' Irish'd 've skinned him
alive if th' poor ol' gaby iv an English king hadn't ducked—
What's that? Don't I know it? I have a book at home written be an
impartial historyan, Pathrick Clancy O'Broyn, to prove it. What
was I sayin'? Whin th' twelfth day iv July come around an' th'
Orangeys got ready to cillybrate th' day King Willum, with all his
Gatlin' guns an' cannon, just barely sthud off Sarsfield an' his men
that had on'y pikes an' brickbats an' billyard cues, th' good people
was infuryated. I dinnaw who was th' Whole Thing in thim days.
He was niver ilicted again. But, annyhow, he give it out that
th' Orangeys' procission must not be hurted. An' all th' newspapers asked th' good people to be quite, an' it was announced at

high mass an' low mass that annywan that sthruck a blow 'd be excommunicated.

"Well, ye know how it is whin modheration is counselled, Jawn. Modheration is another name f'r murdheration. So they put two platoons iv polismin in front iv th' Orangeys an' three behind, an' a double column alongside; an' away they wint.

"No wan intherfered with thim; an' that didn't plaze Morgan Dempsey, who'd served his time as calker in a ship-yard. Bein' iv a injaneyous disposition, he made up his mind f'r to do something to show that pathrietism wasn't dead in this counthry. So he got up in a hallway in Washington Sthreet, an' waited. Th' procission come with th' polismen in front an' behind an' along th' sides, an' th' German Band, thryin' to keep wan eye on the house-tops on both sides iv th' sthreet, an' to read th' music iv 'Lillibullero' an' 'Croppies lie down' an' 'Boyne Wather' with th' other. Th' Orangeys didn't look up. They kept their eyes pointed sthraight ahead, I'll say that f'r thim. They're murdherin' vilyans; but they're Irish, iv a sort.

"Whin they come by Dempsey, he pokes his head out iv th' dure; an' says he, 'Th' 'ell with all th' Prowtestant bishops.' Now that same over in Derry'd have had all th' tilin's in town flyin'; but th' Orangeys 'd been warned not to fight, an' they wint sthraight on, on'y they sung 'Lillibullero.' Did ye niver hear it? It goes (*singing*):

'Ho, brother Teigue, dost hear th' decree
That we shall have a new deputy?
  Lillibullero, bullin a la,
  Lero, lero, lillibullero.
There was an ol' prophecy found in a bog,
  Lillibullero, bullin a la,
That Ireland should be ruled be an ass an' a dog,
  Lillibullero, bullin a la.
An' now this same prophecy has come to pass,
  Lillibullero, bullin a la,
For Talbot's th' dog an' James is th' ass,
  Lillibullero, bullin a la.'

"Th' Lord f'rgive me f'r singin' it, Jawn. See if there's anny wan near th' dure.

"Well, whin they got through, Dempsey puts his hands to his mouth, an' yells, 'Th' 'ell with King Willum.' That was more thin th' Orangeys cud stand. They halted as wan man, an' roared out, 'Th' 'ell with th' pope.' 'What's that?' says th' captain iv th' polis foorce. He was a man be th' name of Murphy, an' he was blue with rage f'r havin' to lead th' Orangeys. 'What's that?' he says. 'Th' 'ell with th' pope, ye meal-headed bog-throtter,' says th' main guy iv th' Orangeys. 'Ma-arch on, Brass Money.' Murphy pulled him fr'm his horse; an' they wint at it, club an' club. Be that time th' whole iv th' line was ingaged. Ivry copper belted an Orangey; an' a sergeant named Donahue wint through a whole lodge, armed on'y, Jawn, with a clarinet an' wan cymbal. He did so. An' Morgan Dempsey, th' cute divvle, he sthood by, an' encouraged both sides. F'r, next to an Orangey, he likes to see a polisman kilt. That ended wan Orangey parade.

"Not that I think it was right. I suppose they ought to be left walk about, an' I'm a fair man. If th' blackest iv thim wint by now, I'd not raise me hand"—

"Hello," says Mr. McKenna, "here goes Killen, the Armagh man. They say he digs with his left foot."

"Jawn," said Mr. Dooley, eagerly, "if ye run up on th' roof, ye'll find th' bricks loose in th' top row iv th' chimbley. Ye might hand him a few." (July 13, 1895)

14. A New Verdict in the Cronin Murder Case

Dr. Patrick Henry Cronin had been a well-liked Chicago physician, social singer, and Irish nationalist, known to be connected with Clan na Gael Camp 96, from which much of the planning for the Dynamite Campaign had issued. His public accusations that fellow camp members were embezzling Clan funds led to his murder on the evening of May 4, 1889. The brutal affair (Cronin had been bludgeoned to death and his body was found in a catch-basin) split Chi-

cago's nationalists into "Croninite" and "anti-Croninite" factions,
and the subsequent sensational publicity struck a killing blow to the
nationalist movement in Chicago. As city editor of the Times, *Peter*
Dunne had been intimately involved in the case, which broke shock-
ingly with the indictment of Sergeant Daniel Coughlin, the Chicago
policeman who had been put in charge of the investigation. After a
lengthy trial, marred by jury-tampering, Coughlin and two other
Clansmen were convicted of first-degree murder and given life sen-
tences. The whole mess came to the surface again when Coughlin
was granted a new trial in June 1893. His acquittal on March 9,
1894, once more polarized the Chicago Irish into fighting factions,
as this Dooley piece, written the day after the verdict, illustrates.

"Jawn," said Mr. Dooley when Mr. McKenna came in.

"What is it?" said his friend.

"F'r th' first time since I've knowed ye, an' I've knowed ye since
ye was a little freckle-face kid that thrun stones at me whin I was
dhrivin' dhray, I'm glad to see ye. I've been settin' here since noon
today, by gar, sindin' me sowl to the divvle be lyin'—me that
swore off lyin' durin' lint."

"What have you been lying about?" asked Mr. McKenna.

"Well, sir; ivry man in th' A-archey road has his own opinions
on matthers in gen'ral an' I have me own. Now, if a man keeps a
grocery shop or r-runs a bakery no wan cares a dam about his
opinion. He goes along sellin' choo-choo an' doughnuts an' sare a
bit does he need to moind whither Gladstun have a game eye or
Bisma-arck have made frinds with th' Geezer. No wan asks him
what he thinks iv annything. But th' minyit a man opens a little
licker shtore, be dad, his opinion is as vall'ble as if he was th'
dhriver iv a sthreetcar. By gar, Jawn, I've been supplyin' opinions
to th' r-road f'r tin years. I have that. On'y las' week th' man that
runs that there bum little bank down be Finucane's he come in
here an' says he: 'Well,' he says, 'what d'ye think iv that schame iv
issuin' certificates again th' saynorage,' he says. 'I think' says I, not
knowin' anny more about what th' idjut was dhrivin' at thin you,
Jawn, 'I think' I says, ''tis all r-right.' ''Tis not,' says he. 'Why

d'ye sa-ay 'tis all right?' 'Because,' says I to make good, 'he was beat at th' prim-ries,' says I. 'An' thim Dutch always makes a roar,' I says. 'Well,' he says, 'ye'er a nice man to be a citizen iv this counthry,' says he. 'Ye ought to go back to Ireland,' he says. An', by gar, Jawnny, I—I almost lost a fight.

"Well, sir, whin this here verdict was brought in ivry wan in th' r-road asked me me opinion iv it. Schneider, the low Dutchman what keeps down below, he comes in an' he says, says he, in his German brogue, he says: 'Well, Mr. Dooley, what ye t'ink iv dis here Coughlin peezness,' he says. 'Well,' says I, 'Bisma-ark,' I says (I allways calls him Bisma-ark), 'Bisma-ark,' I says, 'I'm ashamed iv me race,' I says. ''Tis a low outrage,' I says. ''Tis time some wan stopped this here business,' says I. 'F'r,' I says, 'if 'twas wan iv ye'er people he'd be hung,' I says. He bought a dhrink or two an' wint away.

"Pretty soon I hears a r-roar an' in bounds Maloney, th' new sanyer guardjean iv the Wolf Tone Timp'rance an' Beniv'lent Sodality. 'Huroo!' he says. 'Huroo!' says I. 'Who's ilicted?' 'He's acquitted,' says he. 'Huroo! huroo!' says I. 'Huroo!' I says. ''Tis a vindication iv us again th' dips,' says I. ''Tis that,' says he. An' he bought an' wint away. Well, sir, he'd got no further than th' bridge whin in comes Hogan that's wan iv th' other side. 'Give us a dhrink,' he says. 'What d'ye think iv it?' ''Tis a nice clear day,' I says, duckin'. 'I mean th' verdict,' he says, lukin' at me ha-ard. 'What verdict?' says I. 'Haven't ye hear-rd?' he says, brightenin' up. 'They've acquitted him.' 'Acquitted him!' says I. 'Glory be to Gawd,' I says. 'How cud they do it?' says I. ''Tis a disgrace,' I says, an' he bought another wan an' wint away.

"Well, Jawn, I was shtandin' at th' ind iv th' bar talkin' with th' doctor fr'm over th' drugstore an' discussin' matters an' tellin' him that though I sup-posed th' jury was honest, I cudden't understand how they cud acquit, whin Maloney come in an' sagged again th' cheese box. He'd been there no more than a minyit whin in come Hogan an' sagged again the mirror. 'Dooley,' says Hogan. 'Give all the gintlemin in th' house a dhrink,' he says. 'Maloney,' he says, 'can have a ba-ar iv soap.' 'Dooley,' says Maloney, 'I believe in threatin' th' unimployed right,' he says. 'Give Hogan a dhrink.' An' with that they clinched. Bedad, they'd'v masacreed each other if it wasn't f'r me puttin' th' feet into Hogan an' calling f'r a German polisman."

"Oho," said Mr. McKenna, "of course you went for Hogan. You're a Clan all right."

"What's that?" demanded Mr. Dooley, starting up.

"You're in camp ninety-six," said Mr. McKenna, backing toward the door.

"I'll have ye to know," roared Mr. Dooley, rushing out and shaking his fist, "that ye're a liar. I was in it long before they was a ninety-six."

Then he paused and let his hand drop. "Jawn," said he, "ye'er a British spoy." (March 10, 1894)

15. The Decline of National Feeling

Mr. Dooley indicates that Irish nationalism in America has reached a low point in this his last St. Patrick's Day piece in Chicago. He marks the transformation from election-year sympathy toward Ireland to Anglophile and imperialist attitudes on the part of President McKinley, Ambassador to England Joseph Choate, and Senator Henry Cabot Lodge. Michael Davitt and T. P. O'Connor were prominent Irish nationalists in the 1890s.

"What ar-re ye goin' to do Patrick's Day?" asked Mr. Hennessy.

"Patrick's Day?" said Mr. Dooley. "Patrick's Day? It seems to me I've heard th' name befure. Oh, ye mane th' day th' low Irish that hasn't anny votes cillybrates th' birth iv their naytional saint, who was a Fr-rinchman."

"Ye know what I mane," said Mr. Hennessy, with rising wrath. "Don't ye get gay with me now."

"Well," said Mr. Dooley, "I may cillybrate it an' I may not. I'm thinkin' iv savin' me enthusyasm f'r th' queen's birthday, whiniver it is that that blessid holiday comes ar-round. Ye see, Hinnissy, Patrick's Day is out iv fashion now. A few years ago ye'd see the Prisident iv th' United States marchin' down Pinnsylvanya Avnoo, with the green scarf iv th' Ancient Ordher on his shoulders an' a shamrock in his hat. Now what is Mack doin'? He's settin' in his parlor, writin' letthers to th' queen, be hivins, askin' afther her health. He was fr'm th' north iv Ireland two years ago, an' not so far north ayether,—just far enough north f'r to be on good terms with Derry an' not far enough to be bad frinds with Limerick. He was raised on butthermilk an' haggis, an' he dhrank his Irish nate with a dash iv orange bitthers in it. He's been movin' steadily north since; an', if he keeps on movin', he'll go r-round th' globe, an' bring up somewhere in th' south iv England.

"An' Hinnery Cabin Lodge! I used to think that Hinnery would niver die contint till he'd took th' Prince iv Wales be th' hair iv th' head,—an' 'tis little th' poor man's got,—an' dhrag him fr'm th' tower iv London to Kilmainham Jail, an' hand him over to th' tindher mercies, as Hogan says, iv Michael Davitt. Thim was th' days whin ye'd hear Hinnery in th' Sinit, spreadin' fear to th' hear-rts iv th' British aristocracy. 'Gintlemen,' he says, 'an' fellow-sinitors, th' time has come,' he says, 'whin th' eagle burrud iv freedom,' he says, 'lavin',' he says, 'its home in th' mountains,' he says, 'an' circlin',' he says, 'undher th' jool'd hivin,' he says, 'fr'm where,' he says, 'th' Passamaquoddy rushes into Lake Erastus K. Ropes,' he says, 'to where rowls th' Oregon,' he says, 'fr'm th' lakes to th' gulf,' he says, 'fr'm th' Atlantic to th' Passific where rowls th' Oregon,' he says, 'an' fr'm ivry American who has th' blood iv his ancesthors' hathred iv tyranny in his veins,—your ancesthors an' mine, Mr. McAdoo,' he says,—'there goes up a mute prayer that th' nation as wan man, fr'm Bangor, Maine, to where rowls th' Oregon, that,' he says, 'is full iv salmon, which is later put up in cans, but has th' same inthrest as all others in this question,' he says, 'that,' he says, 'th' descindants iv Wash'nton an',' he says, 'iv Immitt,' he says, 'will jine hands f'r to protect,' he says, 'th' cod-fisheries again th' Vandal hand iv th' British line,' he says. 'I therefore move ye, Mr. Prisident, that it is th' sinse iv this house, if anny such there be, that Tay Pay O'Connor is a greater man thin Lord Salisberry,' he says.

"Now where's Hinnery? Where's th' bould Fenian? Where's th' moonlighter? Where's th' pikeman? Faith, he's changed his chune, an' 'tis 'Sthrangers wanst, but brothers now,' with him, an' 'Hands acrost th' sea an' into some wan's pocket,' an' 'Take up th' white man's burden an' hand it to th' coons,' an' 'An open back dure an' a closed fr-ront dure.' 'Tis th' same with all iv thim. They'se me frind Joe Choate. Where'd Joe spind th' night? Whisper, in Windsor Castle, no less, in a night-shirt iv th' Prince iv Wales; an' the nex' mornin', whin he come downstairs, they tol' him th' rile fam'ly was late risers, but, if he wanted a good time, he cud go down an' look at th' cimit'ry! An' he done it. He went out an' wept over th' grave iv th' Father iv his Counthry. Ye'er man, George Washington, Hinnissy, was on'y th' stepfather.

"Well, glory be, th' times has changed since me frind Jawn Finerty come out iv th' House iv Riprisintatives; an', whin some wan ast him what was goin' on, he says, 'Oh, nawthin' at all but some damned American business.' Thim was th' days! An' what's changed thim? Well, I might be sayin' 'twas like wanst whin me cousin Mike an' a Kerry man be th' name iv Sullivan had a gredge again a man named Doherty, that was half a Kerry man himsilf. They kept Doherty indures f'r a day, but by an' by me cousin Mike lost inthrest in th' gredge, havin' others that was newer, an' he wint over to th' ya-ards; an' Doherty an' Sullivan begin to bow to each other, an' afther a while they found that they were blood relations, an', what's closer thin that whin ye're away fr'm home, townies. An' they hooked arms, an' shrutted up an' down th' road, as proud as imp'rors. An' says they, 'We can lick annything in th' ward,' says they. But, befure they injyed th' 'lieance f'r long, around th' corner comes me cousin Mike, with a half-brick in each hand; an' me brave Sullivan gives Doherty th' Kerry man's thrip, an' says he, 'Mike,' he says, 'I was on'y pullin' him on to give ye a crack at him,' he says. An' they desthroyed Doherty, so that he was in bed f'r a week."

"Well, I wondher will Mike come back?" said Mr. Hennessy.

"Me cousin Mike," said Mr. Dooley, "niver missed an iliction. An' whin th' campaign opened, there wasn't a man on th' ticket, fr'm mayor to constable, that didn't claim him f'r a first cousin. There are different kinds iv hands from acrost th' sea. There are pothry hands an' rollin'-mill hands; but on'y wan kind has votes." (March 11, 1899)

Chapter Seven
Mr. Dooley's Philosophy

By 1897, the fifth year of his editorship at the Chicago Evening
Post, *Finley Peter Dunne's inside perspective on the realities of
American city life had brought about a significant darkening of his
world view. Naturally, Mr. Dooley was affected, too. More and more
of his discussions seem designed to prove the constancy of pervasive
suffering and hypocrisy. Many of these fatalistic pieces have appeared in earlier chapters; for example, the bitter vignettes from the
winter poverty crisis of 1896 – 1897 (Chapter 4, pieces 12 – 16) and
the cynical four-part series on the municipal election of April 1897,
in which Mr. Dooley throws his support to robber baron Charles T.
Yerkes (Chapter 5, pieces 15 – 18). Some of the most powerful
dark philosophizing from 1897 does not, however, fit thematically
into the preceding chapters. The odd pieces are thus collected here
chronologically.*

*In the spring of 1897, Dunne began exploring the human propen-
sity for self-delusion more and more frequently. On May 29, Mr.
Dooley declared that suicide is the ultimate delusion, for "th' man
that kills himsilf always has th' thought sthrong in his mind that he
will be prisint at the ceremonies, lookin' on like a man in th' gallery
iv th' Lyceum Theater" (piece 1). Next, Dooley celebrates Queen Victoria's Diamond Jubilee by refuting the prevalent contemporary illu-
sion that western civilization is progressing (2). Then, on the Fourth
of July, he describes Bridgeport laborers who celebrate "th' declaration iv indepindince that they never heerd tell iv. To-morrah they'll be
shovellin' sand or tampin' a thrack with a boss standin' over thim
that riprisints all they know iv th' power iv providince" (3). In ex-
plaining why he refused to attend the dedication of a new statue,
Dooley then advocates willful self-delusion: "If there's annything*

goin' on, I see it in th' pa-apers, an' it reads betther th'n it looks. To me th' Logan monymint is a hundhred miles high an' made iv goold. That's because I niver seed it" (4). In September 1897 comes a parody of "expert testimony" at a murder trial that ends with a cynical judgment of the American criminal justice system (5). In the context of Dunne's other dark pieces, the wild flights of absurdity here are frightening as well as funny. Early December finds Father Kelly convinced of the necessity of self-delusion through reading: "'tis betther to go to th' circus thin to r-read anny book. But 'tis betther to r-read a book thin to want to go to th' circus an' not be able to" (6). Finally, the winter holidays prompt a bleak, three-part meditation on the seemingly inevitable cycle of suffering and self-delusion in which Bridgeport and the world are caught (7, 8, 9).

Shortly after the New Year, Dunne temporarily ended the Dooley venture with a bitter farewell piece in which Mr. Dooley lists several disreputable Chicagoans who have flourished despite his diatribes against them and declares that "all th' histhry an' pothry an' philosophy I've give ye an' th' Archey road fr all these years" has come to "nawthin'" (10). This chapter ends with a second, and milder, farewell piece that Dunne wrote in January 1900, on the eve of his permanent move to New York City (11). His critique of the Spanish-American War and two briskly selling collections had brought Mr. Dooley to the brink of national celebrity. In this final Chicago piece, Dunne looks back fondly over the landmarks and characters that he and Mr. Dooley were about to leave forever.

1. Suicide and Self-Delusion

This discussion was inspired by the suicide in Chicago of a German-American dancing instructor, who shot himself in the head then fell 140 feet from a thirteenth-floor balcony of the Chamber of Commerce building downtown. A note was found, blaming his wife.

"He niver hit annything till he sthruck th' groun'," said Mr. Dooley reading. "Ivry bone in his body was broken."

"An' well it might be," said Mr. Hennessy. "If it hadn't been he'd've gone through th' flure. An' what possessed him to do it?"

"He was a German, that's all," said Mr. Dooley. "Ye see th' Germans have a sort iv fad f'r helpin' thimsilves out iv th' wurruld. Whin wan iv thim fails in his bank or imbizzles fr'm th' public funds, or his wife loses her hair or his coat don't fit him or somebody steals th' Abend Pest fr'm his durestep he goes out an' spoils other people's property with himsilf. To me suicide is a kind iv play actin'. Th' man that kills himsilf always has th' thought sthrong in his mind that he will be prisint at the ceremonies, lookin' on like a man in th' gallery iv th' Lyceum Theater. It's a sort iv pride with him. He'll be standin' back somewhere an' hearin' th' remarks iv th' people as they come upon th' corpse. 'Poor man, why did he do it?' ''Twas a turrible thing, but I suppose he had nawthin' to live f'r.' 'Well, he was a brave man, so he was,' an' there he is lookin' on with a satisfied smile on his face while they carry himsilf tinderly to th' home where his wife is weepin' an' tearin' her hair because she put too much sugar in his coffee that mornin'. If he on'y knew that a man can't be in th' hearse an' march in th' pro-cession too, perhaps he'd think twict befure he jumped wanst.

"But mebbe 'tis as well he can't look on. Instead iv people weepin' over him, th' comment he'd hear would be: 'Another blame fool!' And his wife is sure to marry again. Women don't like suicides. If they did they'd be more iv thim.

"F'r mesilf, even barrin' me belief that whin a man goes out that way he'll wake up in th' big smokehouse, I can't stand f'r th' suicide. 'Tis not that I think a man's a coward f'r r-runnin' away fr'm the evils he knows about to those he don't know about but'll dam soon find out. I can undherstand how a marrid man can look longingly forward to a time whin he will have no wan to talk to him at breakfast th' night after th' meetin' iv th' camp. It ain't cowardly to r-run away fr'm wurruk or shame or debts. 'Tis nathral f'r human bein's to duck such circumstances. On'y I don't believe in r-runnin' too far. I know well a man ain't goin' to r-read his own death notice in bed th' nex' mornin'. They don't deliver the pa-aper in th' place where his ticket is bought f'r. Th' letter he writes will be misspelled annyhow, an' 'tis a thousand to wan th' pitcher th' rayporter digs up to print'll be a tintype that he had took at th' circus whin he was more or less in th' way iv havin' too much pink lemonade aboord, an' that he thought he'd desthroyed. No, sir; I believe in r-runnin' as far as Halsted sthreet, but niver as far as th' lake.

"A fifth ward man named Schwartz had th' right idee. He was throubled be his wife. She was a crool woman—a reg'lar termagant. She took in washin', an' whin he come home fr'm the baseball game nine times out iv tin she had a sick headache. She niver let him alone. She was always in th' house, doin' somethin'. No matther how late he stayed out, his wife'd be settin' up f'r him, or if she wasn't settin' up f'r him she'd be in bed. She niver dhrank or swore or wint out gallivantin' or done annything to vary th' monotony iv his hard life. She took in washin'.

"Well, ye may talk as ye like about th' gr-reat throubles iv life, but 'tis such little worries as this that crushes a man's haughty sperrit. Schwartz ill-threated his wife, but nawthin' he did cud break her obstinate nature. Whin he woke up in th' morning there she was cukkin' breakfast f'r him. Whin he was sick th' neefaryous woman nursed him till he was well. She minded his clothes an' took care iv his shirts, an' even wint to church an' prayed f'r him. At last he cud stand it no longer, an' he come to me. 'Dooley,' he says, 'I'm tired iv life,' he says. 'Ar-re ye?' says I. 'An' how does life feel about you?' I says. 'I'm goin' to commit suicide,' he says. 'Good,' says I. 'If ye wait here a minyit,' I says, 'till I can call a boy to send to th' dhrug store, I'll stand threat f'r a pound iv rough-on-rats,' I says. 'No,' says he, with a sad smile. 'I don't believe in that,' he says, 'but I'm goin' to dhrink mesilf to death,' he says. 'There's no use keepin' up th' sthruggle anny longer,' he says. 'Schwartz,' says I, 'ye'er life has been wan long an' uninterrupted suicide,' I says. 'I don't blame ye,' says I. 'Ye've had great burdens to bear,' I says, 'but I'll inform ye iv this, me man, that if ye don't clear out iv my place an' go to home to ye'er fam'ly, th' nex' time I see ye I'll erase ye with an ice-pick,' I says. 'I don't believe in suicide,' I says, 'but I have sthrong faith in assault-an'-bath'ry,' I says."

"Did he do it?" asked Mr. Hennessy.

"He did not," said Mr. Dooley. "He eloped with a Bohemian woman an' she made him wurruk an' she beat him ivry pay night an' he become quite continted an' happy." (May 29, 1897)

2. Progress in the Victorian Era

Mr. Dooley marks Queen Victoria's Diamond Jubilee in June 1897 with the following attack on the nineteenth century's faith in progress, most notably presented in Herbert Spencer's theories of Social Darwinism. Chicago was divided on the issue of commemorating Victoria's sixtieth year as queen. The United Irish Societies resolved to mourn the event, while the city's British-Americans staged a Jubilee Celebration at the Auditorium. Earlier in the month, several lynchings of black men had been reported, one in Dayton, Ohio.

"Ar-re ye goin' to cillybrate th' queen's jubilee?" asked Mr. Dooley.

"What's that?" demanded Mr. Hennessy, with a violent start.

"To-day," said Mr. Dooley, "her gracious Majesty Victorya, Queen iv Great Britain an' that part iv Ireland north iv Sligo, has reigned f'r sixty long and tiresome years."

"I don't care if she has snowed f'r sixty years," said Mr. Hennessy. "I'll not cillybrate it. She may be a good woman f'r all I know, but dam her pollytics."

"Ye needn't be pro-fane about it," said Mr. Dooley. "I on'y ast ye a civil question. F'r mesilf, I have no feelin' on th' subject. I am not with th' queen an' I'm not again her. I'm rejoiced to see me frinds Jawn R. Walsh an' J. V. Clarke jinin' in th' movement iv her lyal subjects in Chicago to honor th' occasion, an' faith they ought to do something to square thimsilves, f'r they were both outrajous Fenians in th' ol' days an' give her manny a sleepless night. At th' same time I corjally agree with me frind Captain

Finerty, who's put his newspaper in mournin' f'r th' ivint. I won't march in th' parade, an' I won't put anny dinnymite undher thim that does. I don't say th' marchers an' dinnymiters ar-re not both r-right. 'Tis purely a question iv taste, an', as the ixicutive says whin both candydates are mimbers iv th' camp, 'Pathrites will use their own discreetion.'

"Th' good woman niver done me no har-rm; an', beyond throwin' a rock or two into an orangey's procission an' subscribin' to tin dollars' worth iv Fenian bonds, I've threated her like a lady. Anny gredge I iver had again her I burrid long ago. We're both well on in years, an' 'tis no use carrying har-rd feelin's to th' grave. About th' time th' lord chamberlain wint over to tell her she was queen, an' she came out in her nitey to hear th' good news, I was announced into this wurruld iv sin an' sorrow. So ye see we've reigned about th' same lenth iv time, an' I ought to be cillybratin' me di'mon' jubilee. I wud, too, if I had anny di'mon's. Do ye r-run down to Aldherman O'Brien's an' borrow twinty or thirty f'r me.

"Great happenin's have me an' Queen Victorya seen in these sixty years. Durin' our binificent prisince on earth th' nations have grown r-rich an' prosperous. Great Britain has ixtinded her domain until th' sun niver sets on it. No more do th' original owners iv th' sile, they bein' kept movin' be th' polis. While she was lookin' on in England, I was lookin' on in this counthry. I have seen America spread out fr'm th' Atlantic to th' Pacific, with a branch office iv the Standard Ile Comp'ny in ivry hamlet. I've seen th' shackles dropped fr'm th' slave, so's he cud be lynched in Ohio. I've seen this gr-reat city desthroyed be fire fr'm De Koven Sthreet to th' Lake View pumpin' station, and thin rise felix-like fr'm its ashes, all but th' West Side, which was not burned. I've seen Jim Mace beat Mike McCool, an' Tom Allen beat Jim Mace, an' somebody beat Tom Allen, an' Jawn Sullivan beat him, an' Corbett beat Sullivan, an' Fitz beat Corbett; an', if I live to cillybrate me goold-watch-an'-chain jubilee, I may see some wan put it all over Fitz.

"Oh, what things I've seen in me day an' Victorya's! Think iv that gran' procission iv lithry men,—Tinnyson an' Longfellow an'

Bill Nye an' Ella Wheeler Wilcox an' Tim Scanlan an'—an' I can't name thim all: they're too manny. An' th' brave Gin'rals,—Von Molkey an' Bismarck an' U. S. Grant an' gallant Phil Shurdan an' Coxey. Think iv thim durin' me reign. An' th' invintions,—th' steam-injine an' th' printin'-press an' th' cotton-gin an' the gin sour an' th' bicycle an' th' flyin'-machine an' th' nickel-in-th'-slot machine an' th' Croker machine an' th' sody fountain an'—crownin' wur-ruk iv our civilization—th' cash raygisther. What gr-reat advances has science made in my time an' Victorya's! f'r, whin we entered public life, it took three men to watch th' bar-keep, while to-day ye can tell within $8 an hour what he's took in.

"Glory be, whin I look back fr'm this day iv gin'ral rejoicin' in me rhinestone jubilee, an' see what changes has taken place an' how manny people have died an' how much betther off th' wurruld is, I'm proud iv mesilf. War an' pest'lence an' famine have occurred in me time, but I count thim light compared with th' binifits that have fallen to th' race since I come on th' earth."

"What ar-re ye talkin' about?" cried Mr. Hennessy, in deep disgust. "All this time ye've been standin' behind this bar ladlin' out disturbance to th' Sixth Wa-ard, an' ye haven't been as far east as Mitchigan Avnoo in twenty years. What have ye had to do with all these things?"

"Well," said Mr. Dooley, "I had as much to do with thim as th' queen." (June 19, 1897)

3. Freedom and the Fourth of July

A big, foolish-looking youth of 19 or 20 was standing across the street from Mr. Dooley's establishment with an expectant grin on his face. An electric car bustled down the Archey road. As it arrived opposite the point where the foolish-looking youth stood, there was an execrable explosion; the trucks of the car seemed almost to leave the tracks, the women passengers screamed and the sulphurous ante-Fourth atmosphere became still more pungent with the remarks of the motorman. Mr. Dooley emerged from his shop waving an ice-pick at arm's length.

"Timothy Hogan," he shouted, "if ye don't go away from here this minyit I'll tell yer mother an' I'll scrape th' face iv ye with this here comb. G' way, I tell ye, or I'll make ye look like a screendure, ye omnacious ruffyan."

The leering patriot withdrew to carry on his villainous work at the next corner, and Mr. Dooley returned to the bar looking blown and angry.

"Wan iv th' worst mistakes iv th' fathers iv their counthry, Hinnissy," he said, "was signin' th' declaration iv indipindince on th' Fourth iv July. If they'd done it on th' twinty-second iv Febrooary 'twud've been all right. An' if Wash'nton had had himself bor-rn on th' Fourth iv July that wud've been thoughtful. I can cillybrate Wash'nton's birthday an' keep as cool as an iceberg anny day iv th' year. But whin ye give ivry man, boy an' jackeen in town th' privilege iv provin' that he's a pathrite be firin' cannons an' pistols whin th' sun is borin' into a man's neck like a bone collar-button ye do an injury to th' race that I'll not f'rgive, f'r wan."

"It looks to me," he went on in a melancholy tone, "as if they was too much noise an' smoke about pathritism in America f'r th' good iv th' counthry. Th' Fourth iv July stands f'r nawthin' but th' right to carry concealed weapons wanst a year. Whin a man thinks he can square himself with his jooty to th' nation be settin' off a bunch iv firecrackers under his neighbor's window, or buyin' two dollars worth iv roman candles an' shootin' thim in his shirt sleeves with his suspenders hangin' down behind, an' settin' fire to a barn, he's in danger iv forgettin' some items iv personal property whin he makes out his schedule f'r th' tax assessor. It ain't th' man that sets all day on th' dure step, with a piece iv punk in his hand throwin' firecrackers at servant girls on their way to th' park that's to be relied on whin somewan is needed f'r to repil th' foreign invader or th' domistic foe, as Jawn Finerty says in his paper, anny more thin it is th' man who puts a flag in his buttonhole and goes out on th' sthreet corner hollerin' about liberty. That big Hogan bosthoon has made more noise thin anny lad on th' r-road to-day, an' he'd r-run away fr'm a justice coort constable—an' that's th' hite iv cowar-dice.

"I don't mind th' little la-ads, though wan iv thim did throw a bunch iv crackers in here las' night, th' divvle, an' scare me out iv a year's growth. 'Twas th' biggest iv th' Sullivan twins, an' I'll break his back if I lay hands on him. But to see grown, pie-face men spindin' th' day touchin' off crackers f'r th' mere spoort iv hearin' th' noise is enough to make a Christian wish th' declaration iv indipindince had niver been written be Andhrew Jackson. I wondher if these ravin' idjits iver think iv th' misery they make. Do they iver think iv narvous sick people an' little childher sufferin' fr'm th' heat an' poor ol' lads with bad hearts, that stop beatin' ivery time a gun bangs? Iv coorse they don't, or if they do they don't care. They set on th' step, with an expression iv unfurnished rooms to let on their foolish faces an' th' pants iv thim burnin' on their legs, an' bombard quiet people with their crackers an' their torpedoes. May th' undhertaker make a mistake an' decorate thim with Roman candles some day."

"Ye seem hot about it," said Mr. Hennessy.

"I am," said Mr. Dooley. "I didn't sleep wan wink las' night. An' th' little girl nex' dure that's been sick has had a bad turn. If I'd got near that Hogan imp, I'd've engraved him, I wud."

At this instant there came a roar like the fall of a wall, followed by a scattering clatter of small shot.

"There they go," said Mr. Dooley, with an expression of despair. "There they go, th' pathrites, th' loyal sons iv America, th' murdherin' fools. To-day they're cillybratin' th' declaration iv indipindince that they never heerd tell iv. To-morrah they'll be shovelin' sand or tampin' a thrack with a boss standin' over thim that riprisints all they know iv th' power iv providince. An' may they pound sand an' tamp th' thrack to th' end iv their days who think freedom is noise." (July 3, 1897)

4. The Dedication of the Logan Statue

July 22, 1897, was Logan Day in Chicago. St. Gaudens' statue of Civil War General and Illinois Senator John A. Logan was unveiled, and a huge crowd watched the ceremonies and subsequent parade. The statue was accepted for the state by Republican Governor John R. Tanner, who was then under heavy attack for having signed into law a bill granting street-railway franchises to Charles T. Yerkes for up to fifty years.

Mr. Hennessy appeared at Mr. Dooley's establishment Thursday night looking greatly discomposed. He was flushed and dirty and tired. As he buried his nose in a tall glass of beer, from which his friend had considerately removed the "collar" by a dexterous wave of his finger, he conveyed the information that he had been in Michigan Avenue joining in the Logan ceremonies. Whereupon Mr. Dooley lectured him on the beauties of the quiet life.

"Iv coorse," he said, "that's where ye'd be."

"It was gr-rand," said Mr. Hennessy. "They was anny quantity iv sojers fr'm th' reg'lar ar-rmy an' the gov'nor, an' such a crowd as ye niver see th' like iv. I was near cr-rushed to death."

"Sure," said Mr. Dooley. "An' it's a gr-reat pity ye wasn't. F'r th' likes iv you there's no enjoyment this side iv bein' kilt. Why don't ye go out an' have ye'erself r-run over be a steam rowler an' have an 'ell iv a time. I wud if I was you.

"Hinnissy, ye'er an ol' fool. Ye wurruk hard over at th' mills. I see ye off at half-past six in th' mornin' an' whin ye come home ye'er so tired ye walk as though ye had a horse hitched to each leg. Ye get a holiday an' how d'ye enjoy it? Ye'er off downtown with th' sun cukkin' th' back iv ye'er head like a mustard plasther. Ye go where th' crowd is thickest an' ye stand f'r hours where Bohemian women can spill head cheese sandwiches on ye'er good clothes an' polismin shove ye fr'm pillar to post an' pickpockets steal ye'er watch—f'r what? To see a lot iv Swede farmhands, that 've gone into th' ar-rmy because they're afraid to wurruk puttin' in hay, march by in wrong time, bumpin' their muskets into each other, or to plaze ye'er eyes with a squint at John Tanner lookin' like th' man that owns a livery stable an' has just won a tournament pitchin' hor-rse shoes. There might be some use in wantin' to see Yerkuss. I'd go round th' corner to look at him mesilf an' pray heaven he wudden't take such a likin' to me that he'd want to steal me. But I'd as lave go downtown to see wan iv Yerkuss' bridge horses marchin' up th' sthreet as to see John Tanner. He don't stand a divvle iv a lot higher with Yerkuss thin th' bridge horse even if he does live at th' Audiotoroom instead iv havin' a stall with th' other crathers in th' Halsted sthreet bar-rn.

"An' ye didn't know Logan. I did, an' divvle a hair iv his head did I like whin he was alive. I seen him an' heard him talk in a tent wanst down be Main sthreet an' th' things he said about th' dimmycrats, Hinnissy, was enough to make ye want to put a can iv dinnymite undher his statue an' let it go at that. Th' kindest wurrud he had was chicken thief. I followed his carredge f'r a mile to get a shy at him with a piece iv har-rd coal. Sure, half th' men that wint to see him in brass wud've hanged him in life—an' been burned in ile be th' other half. That was because he was a fighter. A man that's a fighter, an' a good fighter, needs inimies, an' it's always a question with him whether he has more frinds or inimies. He wakes up in th' mornin' an' finds that th' balance is in favor iv his frinds an' he says, says he: 'I'll go out an' make a few inimies,' or he sees he's long on inimies an' he goes out an' does a few iv thim up. Logan niver made anny frinds, but he done th' nex' thing to it. He made inimies—an' kilt them off. He liked frinds, but if he had to make a choice he'd prefer inimies. To a good fighter a man's best frind is his worst inimy. That's what young Hogan calls an ipigram, an' I give it to ye free. Ye can take it ayether way ye like.

"I knowed Logan, I tell ye, an' though I'd 've nailed him with a chunk of anthracite twenty years ago, I'd put a wreath on his grave to-day. It on'y takes a little while to smooth out th' char-ackter iv a man that fought long an' hit har-rd. But not f'r Logan nor f'r Char-les Stewart Parn'll wud I thrust mesilf to that crowd downtown. I've been here, man an' boy, forty years, an' it's twinty iv thim most since I see th' lake. I've been in State sthreet foor or five times in all these years. I've been to th' Audiotoroom twict an' wanst I wint by th' Masonic Temple on me way to get a car comin' fr'm th' city hall. What f'r shud I lave quite an' peace to dodge cable cars an' have me pocket picked? If there's annything goin' on I see it in th' pa-apers, an' it reads betther th'n it looks. To me th' Logan monymint is a hundhred miles high an' made iv goold. That's because I niver seed it. If I'd gone with you it'd be no higher than an Injun cigar sign an' built iv ol' melted-down dog tags an' other joolry. Th' crowd was magnificent to read about; if I'd seen it, it wud've been just a million sweatin', badly dhressed people, squallin' babies, faintin' women an' a bad smell. Th' sojers were sojerly an' gr-rand, but if I'd seen thim close by I'd 've picked out more thin wan man that'd r-run away fr'm a cow. The bands played beautiful in th' papers, but if I'd been on th' curb with a man with a tall hat standin' in front iv me an' a woman behind me atin' rock candy in me ear, all th' bands'd stop playin' befure they come by. So I set here in th' cool shade, playin' solitaire with mesilf an' cheatin' outhrageous, an' whin th' pa-apers come up I bought wan an' enjoyed th' gloryous scene f'r two hours. I heard th' oration; ye didn't. It was grand an' th' man that made it knew more about Shakespeare thin Logan did. But I'll bet ye a hat he was a fat man in a black coat an' swabbed his forehead with a wet towel between sintences.

"Glory be, I've often thought I was lucky not bein' prisint at some iv th' grand occasions I've r-read about. I knowed a man wanst that see th' pope iv Rome an' he become a ragin' pagan. 'Why,' he says, 'he was a little bit iv a thin man that didn't weigh more thin wan hundhred pounds,' he says. 'He cudden't carry a bucket iv coal upstairs,' he says."

"He was a liar," said Mr. Hennessy.

"I believe he was," said Mr. Dooley. "But he wint to th' bad just th' same." (July 24, 1897)

5. Expert Testimony at the Luetgert Trial

In May 1897 Adolph Luetgert was arrested in Chicago for the murder of his wife. Scientists were called in to determine the validity of police allegations that Luetgert had ground up his wife's remains and mingled them with the raw materials in his sausage factory. The trial was in progress when Mr. Dooley presented this transcript of a day's debate among the experts. Luetgert was eventually convicted.

"Annything new?" said Mr. Hennessy, who had been waiting patiently for Mr. Dooley to put down his newspaper.

"I've been r-readin' th' tistimony iv th' Lootgert case," said Mr. Dooley.

"What d'ye think iv it?"

"I think so," said Mr. Dooley.

"Think what?"

"How do I know?" said Mr. Dooley. "How do I know what I think? I'm no combi-nation iv chemist, doctor, osteologist, polisman, an' sausage-maker, that I can give ye an opinion right off th' bat. A man needs to be all iv thim things to detarmine annything about a murdher trile in these days. This shows how intilligent our methods is, as Hogan says. A large German man is charged with puttin' his wife away into a breakfas'-dish, an' he says he didn't do it. Th' on'y question, thin, is, Did or did not Alphonse Lootgert stick Mrs. L. into a vat, an' rayjooce her to a quick lunch? Am I right?"

"Ye ar-re," said Mr. Hennessy.

"That's simple enough. What th' coort ought to've done was to call him up, an' say: 'Lootgert, where's ye'er good woman?' If Lootgert cudden't tell, he ought to be hanged on gin'ral principles; f'r a man must keep his wife around th' house, an' whin she isn't there, it shows he's a poor provider. But, if Lootgert says, 'I don't know where me wife is,' the coort shud say: 'Go out, an' find her. If ye can't projooce her in a week, I'll fix ye.' An' let that be th' end iv it.

"But what do they do? They get Lootgert into coort an' stand him up befure a gang iv young rayporthers an' th' likes iv thim to make pitchers iv him. Thin they summon a jury composed iv poor, tired, sleepy expressmen an' tailors an' clerks. Thin they call in a profissor from a colledge. 'Profissor,' says th' lawyer f'r the State, 'I put it to ye if a wooden vat three hundherd an' sixty feet long, twenty-eight feet deep, an' sivinty-five feet wide, an' if three hundherd pounds iv caustic soda boiled, an' if the leg iv a guinea pig, an' ye said yestherdah about bi-carbonate iv soda, an' if it washes up an' washes over, an' th' slimy, slippery stuff, an' if a false tooth or a lock iv hair or a jawbone or a goluf ball across th' cellar eleven feet nine inches—that is, two inches this way an' five gallons that?' 'I agree with ye intirely,' says th' profissor. 'I made lab'ratory experiments in an' ir'n basin, with bichloride iv gool, which I will call soup-stock, an' coal tar, which I will call ir'n filings. I mixed th' two over a hot fire, an' left in a cool place to harden. I thin packed it in ice, which I will call glue, an' rock-salt, which I will call fried eggs, an' obtained a dark, queer solution that is a cure f'r freckles, which I will call antimony or doughnuts or annything I blamed please.'

"'But,' says th' lawyer f'r th' State, 'measurin' th' vat with gas,—an' I lave it to ye whether this is not th' on'y fair test,—an' supposin' that two feet acrost is akel to tin feet sideways, an' supposin' that a thick green an' hard substance, an' I daresay it wud; an' supposin' you may, takin' into account th' measuremints,— twelve be eight,—th' vat bein' wound with twine six inches fr'm th' handle an' a rub iv th' green, thin ar-re not human teeth often found in counthry sausage?' 'In th' winter,' says th' profissor. 'But th' sisymoid bone is sometimes seen in th' fut, sometimes worn as a watch-charm. I took two sisymoid bones, which I will call poker dice, an' shook thim together in a cylinder, which I will call Fido, poored in a can iv milk, which I will call gum arabic, took two pounds iv rough-on-rats, which I rayfuse to call; but th' raysult is th' same.' Question be th' coort: 'Different?' Answer: 'Yis.' Th' coort: 'Th' same.' Be Misther McEwen: 'Whose bones?' Answer:

'Yis.' Be Misther Vincent: 'Will ye go to th' divvle?' Answer: 'It dissolves th' hair.'

"Now what I want to know is where th' jury gets off. What has that collection iv pure-minded pathrites to larn fr'm this here polite discussion, where no wan is so crool as to ask what anny wan else means? Thank th' Lord, whin th' case is all over, the jury'll pitch th' tistimony out iv th' window, an' consider three questions: 'Did Lootgert look as though he'd kill his wife? Did his wife look as though she ought to be kilt? Isn't it time we wint to supper?' An', howiver they answer, they'll be right, an' it'll make little diff'rence wan way or th' other. Th' German vote is too large an' ignorant, annyhow." (September 11, 1897)

6. Reading and Believing

On the day this piece appeared, the Chicago Times-Herald *printed a literary supplement entitled "Good Books for Christmas." Michael L. Ahern's* Political History of Chicago, *published in 1886, boasted coverage of "Local politics from the city's birth; Chicago's mayors, aldermen and other officials; county and federal officers; the fire and police departments; the Haymarket horror; miscellaneous."*

"Ivry time I pick up me mornin' paper to see how th' scrap come out at Batth'ry D," said Mr. Dooley, "th' first thing I r-run acrost is somethin' like this: 'A hot an' handsome gift f'r Christmas is Lucy Ann Patzooni's "Jims iv Englewood Thought"'; or, 'If ye wud delight th' hear-rt iv yer child, ye'll give him Dr. Harper's monymental histhry iv th' Jewish thribes fr'm Moses to Dhryfuss'; or 'Ivrybody is r-readin' Roodyard Kiplin's "Busy Pomes f'r Busy People."' Th' idee iv givin' books f'r Christmas prisints whin th' stores are full iv tin hor-rns an' dhrums an' boxin' gloves an' choo-choo ca-ars! People must be crazy."

"They ar-re," said Mr. Hennessy. "My house is so full iv books ye cudden't tur-rn around without stumblin' over thim. I found th' life iv an ex-convict, the 'Prisoner iv Zinders,' in me high hat th' other day, where Mary Ann was hidin' it fr'm her sister. Instead iv th' childher fightin' an' skylarkin' in th' evenin', they're settin' around th' table with their noses glued into books. Th' ol' woman doesn't read, but she picks up what's goin' on. 'Tis 'Honoria, did Lor-rd What's-his-name marry th' fair Aminta?' or 'But that Lady Jane was a case.' An' so it goes. There's no injymint in th' house, an' they're usin' me cravats f'r bookmarks."

"'Tis all wrong," said Mr. Dooley. "They're on'y three books in th' wurruld worth readin',—Shakespeare, th' Bible, an' Mike Ahearn's histhry iv Chicago. I have Shakespeare on thrust, Father Kelly r-reads th' Bible f'r me, an' I didn't buy Mike Ahearn's histhry because I seen more thin he cud put into it. Books is th' roon iv people, specially novels. Whin I was a young man, th' parish priest used to preach again thim; but nobody knowed what he meant. At that time Willum Joyce had th' on'y library in th' Sixth Wa-ard. Th' mayor give him th' bound volumes iv th' council proceedings, an' they was a very handsome set. Th' on'y books I seen was th' kind that has th' life iv th' pope on th' outside an' a set iv dominos on th' inside. They're good readin'. Nawthin' cud be better f'r a man whin he's tired out afther a day's wurruk thin to go to his library an' take down wan iv th' gr-reat wurruks iv lithratchoor an' play a game iv dominos f'r th' dhrinks out iv it. Anny other kind iv r-readin', barrin' th' newspapers, which will niver hurt anny onedycated man, is desthructive iv morals.

"I had it out with Father Kelly th' other day in this very matther. He was comin' up fr'm down town with an ar-rmful iv books f'r prizes at th' school. 'Have ye th' Key to Heaven there?' says I. 'No,' says he, 'th' childher that'll get these books don't need no key. They go in under th' turnstile,' he says, laughin'. 'Have ye th' Lives iv th' Saints, or the Christyan Dooty, or th' Story iv Saint Rose iv Lima?' I says. 'I have not,' says he. 'I have some good story books. I'd rather th' kids'd r-read Char-les Dickens than anny iv th' tales iv thim holy men that was burned in ile or et up be lines,' he says. 'It does no good in these degin'rate days to prove that th'

best that can come to a man f'r behavin' himsilf is to be cooked in
a pot or di-gisted be a line,' he says. 'Ye're wrong,' says I. 'Beggin'
ye'er riv'rince's pardon, ye're wrong,' I says. 'What ar-re ye goin'
to do with thim young wans? Ye're goin' to make thim near-
sighted an' round-shouldered,' I says. 'Ye're goin' to have thim believe that, if they behave thimsilves an' lead a virchous life, they'll
marry rich an' go to Congress. They'll wake up some day, an' find
out that gettin' money an' behavin' ye'ersilf don't always go together,' I says. 'Some iv th' wickedest men in th' wur-ruld have
marrid rich,' I says. 'Ye're goin' to teach thim that a man doesn't
have to use an ax to get along in th' wur-ruld. Ye're goin' to teach
thim that a la-ad with a curlin' black mustache an' smokin' a ciga-
reet is always a villyan, whin he's more often a barber with a
lar-rge family. Life, says ye! There's no life in a book. If ye want to
show thim what life is, tell thim to look around thim. There's
more life on a Saturdah night in th' Ar-rchy Road thin in all th'
books fr'm Shakespeare to th' rayport iv th' drainage thrustees.
No man,' I says, 'iver wrote a book if he had annything to write
about, except Shakespeare an' Mike Ahearn. Shakespeare was all
r-right. I niver read anny of his pieces, but they sound good; an' I
know Mike Ahearn is all r-right.'"

"What did he say?" asked Mr. Hennessy.

"He took it all r-right," said Mr. Dooley. "He kind o' grinned,
an' says he: 'What ye say is thrue, an' it's not thrue,' he says.
'Books is f'r thim that can't injye thimsilves in anny other way,' he
says. 'If ye're in good health, an' ar-re atin' three squares a day, an'
not ayether sad or very much in love with ye'er lot, but just lookin'
on an' not carin' a'—he said rush—'not carin' a rush, ye don't
need books,' he says. 'But if ye're a down-spirited thing an' want
to get away an' can't, ye need books. 'Tis betther to be comfortable at home thin to go to th' circus, an' 'tis betther to go to th'
circus thin to r-read anny book. But 'tis betther to r-read a book
thin to want to go to th' circus an' not be able to,' he says. 'Well,'
says I, 'whin I was growin' up, half th' congregation heard mass
with their prayer books tur-rned upside down, an' they were as
pious as anny. Th' Apostles' Creed niver was as convincin' to me

afther I larned to r-read it as it was whin I cudden't read it, but believed it.'" (December 4, 1897)

7. Christmas Gifts

In December 1897 Dunne fell victim to what was for him an annual despondency at the heightened deprivation and forced jollity of the holiday season in Chicago. During that month, which marks the end of the Bridgeport-centered Dooley performances, he faced the familiar demon on three successive Saturdays. This is the first piece of the group.

The approach of Christmas is heralded in Archey Road by many of the signs that are known to the less civilized and more prosperous parts of the city. The people look poorer, colder, and more hopeful than at other times. The bakeries assume an old country appearance of gayety. The saloons are well filled. Also, if you have your eyes about you, you may catch a glimpse, now and then, through a frosted window-pane of a stunted Christmas tree, laden slenderly with glass balls and ropes of red popcorn, the work of painful hands after the childher are abed. Mr. Dooley knew Christmas was coming by the calendar, the expiration of his quarterly license, and Mr. Hennessy coming in with a doll in his pocket and a rocking-chair under his arm.

"Prisints?" said the philosopher.

"Yis," said Mr. Hennessy. "I had to do it. I med up me mind this year that I wudden't buy anny Chris'mas prisints or take anny. I can't afford it. Times has been fearful ha-ard, an' a look iv pain comes over th' ol' woman's face whin I hold out fifty cints fr'm me salary on Saturdah night. I give it out that I didn't want annything, but they'se so much scurryin' ar-round an' hidin' things whin I go in that I know they've got something f'r me. I cudden't stand it no longer, so I wint down town tonight, down be Shekel an' Whooper's place, an' bought these things. This is a fine doll f'r th' money."

"It is," said Mr. Dooley, taking the doll and examining it with the eye of an art critic. "It closes its eyes,—yis, an', bedad, it cries if ye punch it. They're makin' these things more like human bein's ivry year. An' does it say pap-pah an' mam-mah, I dinnaw?"

"No," said Mr. Hennessy, "th' pap-pah an' mam-mah dolls costs too much."

"Well," continued Mr. Dooley, "we can't have ivrything we want in this wurruld. If I had me way, I'd buy goold watches an' chains f'r ivrybody in th' r-road, an' a few iv th' good Germans. I feel that gin'rous. But 'tis no use. Ye can't give what ye want. Ivry little boy ixpects a pony at Chris'mas, an' ivry little girl a chain an' locket' an' ivry man thinks he's sure goin' to get th' goold-headed cane he's longed f'r since he come over. But they all fin'lly land on rockin'-horses an' dolls, an' suspindhers that r-run pink flowers into their shirts an' tattoo thim in summer. An' they conceal their grief Chris'mas mornin' an' thry to look pleasant with murdher in their hearts.

"Some wan has always give me a Chris'mas prisint, though no wan has anny r-right to. But no wan iver give me annything I cud wear or ate or dhrink or smoke or curl me hair with. I've had flasks iv whisky give me,—me that have lashin's iv whisky at me elbow day an' night; an', whin I opined thim, blue an' yellow flames come out an' some iv th' stuff r-run over on th' flure, an' set fire to th' buildin'. I smoke th' best five-cint see-gar that money can buy; yet, whin a good frind iv mine wants to make me a prisint f'r Chris'mas, he goes to a harness shop an' buys a box iv see-gars with excelsior fillin's an' burlap wrappers, an', if I smoked wan an' lived, I'd be arristed f'r arson. I got a pair iv suspinders wanst fr'm a lady,—niver mind her name,—an' I wur-ruked hard that day; an' th' decorations moved back into me, an' I had to take thim out with pumice stone. I didn't lose th' taste iv th' paint f'r weeks an' weeks.

"Wan year I wanted a watch more thin annything in th' wur-ruld. I talked watches to ivry wan that I thought had designs on me. I made it a pint to ask me frinds what time iv night it was, an' thin say, 'Dear me, I ought to get a watch if I cud affoord it.' I used to tout people down to th' jooler's shop, an' stand be th' window with a hungry look in th' eyes iv me, as much as to say, 'If I don't get a watch, I'll perish.' I talked watches an' thought watches an' dhreamed watches. Father Kelly rebuked me f'r bein' late f'r mass. 'How can I get there before th' gospil, whin I don't know what time it is?' says I. 'Why don't ye luk at ye'er watch?' he says. 'I haven't none,' says I. Did he give me a watch? Faith, he did not. He sint me a box iv soap that made me smell like a coon goin' to a ball in a State Sthreet ca-ar. I got a necktie fr'm wan man; an', if I wore it to a meetin' iv th' Young Hebrews' Char'table Society, they'd've thrun me out. That man wanted me to be kilt. Another la-ad sint me a silk handkerchief that broke on me poor nose. Th' nearest I got to a watch was a hair chain that unravelled, an' made me look as if I'd been curryin' a Shetland pony. I niver got what I wanted, an' I niver expect to. No wan does."

"I'll get ye what ye want," said Mr. Hennessy, "if ye'll tell me what it is, an' it don't cost too much."

"Will ye?" said Mr. Dooley, eagerly.

"I will," said Mr. Hennessy, "if 'tis within me means."

"Ye're jokin'," said Mr. Dooley.

"I'm not. I mane it."

"Do ye, honest?"

"I do so."

"Thin," said Mr. Dooley, "get me th' Audjitooroom. I've wanted that to play with f'r manny years."

And Mr. Hennessy went away with the rocking-chair under his arm, the doll in his pocket, and dumb anger in his heart. (December 18, 1897)

8. Christmas Eve: The Constancy of Poverty

On December 22, 1897, the Chicago Salvation Army invited 5,000 homeless people to Christmas dinner. Other charitable organizations soon followed suit. On Christmas Eve, Mr. Dooley studied the roll of sick and unemployed in Bridgeport.

"Merry Chris'mas," said Mr. Hennessy.

"Get away from in undher that mistletoe there," Mr. Dooley answered, "or I'll hit ye with a bung starter. Yes, it's a merry Chris'mas; I think so."

"They's a west win' blowin' that cuts ye like a sickle," Mr. Hennessy went on. "It's gr-reat weather f'r Chris'mas."

"'Tis so," said Mr. Dooley gloomily. "'Tis gr-reat f'r th' Oppenheimers an' me other rilitives on State sthreet. If it hadn't been f'r th' comin' iv th' col' snap they'd not been able to cillybrate their naytional holiday. Chris'mas to thim is like Chicago fire day to us. 'Twas bad whin it happened but it's tur-rned out all r-right since. But is it a merry Chris'mas all round? I see in th' pa-aper where some wan says Chris'mas dinners has been provided f'r twinty thousan' poor people, but thirty thousan' more is needed. It isn't a merry Chris'mas f'r thim. Nor is it f'r poor Flannigan. 'Tis betther f'r his wife. She died to-day; Father Kelly dhropped in on his way home afther givin' extremunction. His hear-rt was sore with sorrow. Half th' people iv Flannigan's neighborhood has been out iv wurruk f'r a year an' th' sight iv th' sivin fatherless little Doyle childher almost made him cry with pain.

"Do? What can he do? He's spint all th' stole money that he ought to be usin' to buy a warm coat f'r his back, spint it on th' poor, an' he dipt into th' Easther colliction that ought to 've gone to pay inthrest on th' church morgedge. It'll be a smooth talk he'll have to give his grace th' archbishop this year. He was goin' to buy himsilf a Chris'mas prisint iv an altar cloth an' he had to spind th' money buyin' shoes f'r th' little Polackies down be Main sthreet. What can he do? What can annywan do, I'd have ye tell me. If ye'd cut up all th' money in th' sixth war-rd in akel parts ye cudden't buy a toy dhrum apiece f'r th' fam'lies iv Bridgeport. It isn't this year or last. 'Tisn't wan day or another. 'Tis th' same ivry year an' ivry day. It's been so iver since I come here an' 'twill be so afther I'm put away an' me frinds have stopped at th' r-road house on th' way back to count up what I owed thim."

"Goo wan," said the light-hearted Mr. Hennessy, whose pockets were stuffed with useful articles for the little Hennessys. "Ye'er an' ol' crab iv a batch. Things ain't near so bad as they look to ye. Come over to th' house Chris'mas an' ate with us. If ye bring whisky an' lemons ye can make th' punch f'r us."

"I'll not," said Mr. Dooley. "I'll not go annywhere but right here. 'Tis all well enough f'r ye to talk about Chris'mas that have eight or tin childher depindent on ye f'r support. But I've none. Nayther chick nor child. I'm a lone man, Hinnissy, a lone ol' man, an' ivry kid that goes hungry pizens me food an' dhrink. I'll set here Chris'mas, as I've done these manny years, an' look out an' think iv Mrs. Flannigan in Calv'ry Cimitry. That'll keep me from thinkin' iv th' Doyles."

Mr. Hennessy walked as far as the door and came back as far as the stove. Then he wheeled and went to the door again. He returned quickly. Mr. Dooley was watching the maneuver, and, as his friend approached, he turned his back on him.

"Martin," said Mr. Hennessy.

"What is it?" (Gruffly.)

"I've got some things here f'r th' childher—"

"Have ye?"

"But th' stores is still open."

"Yes."

"An' I was thinkin'—"

"So was I; so was I," said Mr. Dooley. "If ye'll wait a minyit till I put on me coat. They'se on'y th' polisman on th' beat due here later an' he'll be all th' betther f'r not havin' his twinty-first to-night."

Mr. Dooley pulled on his great coat with an effort and jammed his hat down on his head till his ears projected in flaps. Then he groaned and grunted and fiercely cursed with many a "bad cess to ye," an' "Divvle take this wooly dog," as he dove under the bar and dragged out parcel after parcel—the same assortment of toys and things to wear and eat that he had bought every year for thirty. Meanwhile Mr. Hennessy looked on in open-eyed astonishment.

"Ye'er a sly ol' fox," he said. "Some day ye'll have yirsilf arristed on ye'er own sayin's. We'll give th' things to th' oldest girl. It won't do to have th' little wans get annything befure Chris'mas mornin'."

Mr. Dooley seemed to regard this as the last word of a Solon or a Willum Joyce, for he slapped Mr. Hennessy on the shoulder and crowed: "Bedad, that's r-right; thrue f'r ye; I niver thought of it."

Laden like stevedores the two men tramped out. They coughed a good deal at the door. Then as they marched along the creaking, wooden sidewalks they were silent and held their heads in shame for their unseemly deed. (December 24, 1897)

9. Dooley's New Year Greeting

Mr. Dooley rings in the New Year 1898 with a scornful reference to the upcoming centennial celebration of the Irish Rebellion of 1798 and a parable for the human condition based on the common experience of the Irish-American pick-and-shovel laborer. Glacial drift is a mixture of clay, sand, gravel, and boulders; there is no harder digging.

"'Tis a sthrange thing this here New Year's business," said Mr. Dooley. "Here I am to-day, an' 'tis ninety-sivin. I clane up th' glasses, count th' cash an' get ready to close up th' shop f'r th' night. Suddenly I hear a whistle blow on a tug, a bell r-rings an' somewan comes out iv Schwartzmeister's an' fires a revolver. An' I've passed without knowin' it fr'm wan year to another. Gorry, but I feel a lone place in me stomach ivry time I pick up a paper an' see th' number iv th' year changed—an' I ought to be used to it, f'r I've done it manny a time—more thin I want to say. Whin nineteen hundherd comes in I'm goin' to be scared to death, till it turns out like other years, th' same ol' r-run iv good an' bad luck, no money, ol' frinds dyin', new inimies comin' up an' th' rig'lar daily procission walkin' out to Calv'ry an' racin' back. Glory be, I'm afraid fr'm an' unknown terror to look into ninety-eight, but if I knew th' things that are sure to happen, no betther an' no worse thin ninety-sivin, barrin' me religion, I'd go down to th' bridge an' fall into th' r-river and break me neck. I wud so."

"All th' years is akel an' th' same," said Mr. Hennessy sententiously. "All th' years an' th' days."

"Thrue f'r ye," said Mr. Dooley, "yet 'tis sthrange how we saw our throubles into reg'lar lenths. We're all like me frind O'Brien that had a conthract on th' dhrainage canal. He thought he was biddin' on soft mud, but he sthruck nawthin' but th' dhrift. But he kept pluggin' away. ''Twill soften later,' he says. Th' ingineers tol' him he was a fool. 'Twas dhrift all th' way through. He rayfused to listen. He knew he'd come to th' mud th' nex' day or th' nex' an' so he wint on an' on an' fin'lly he got through an' made a good, clane job iv it. He looked back on his wurruk an' says he: 'I knowed it was dhrift all th' time, but if I'd let mesilf think that what was ahead was as har-rd as what was behind, I'd thrun up th' job an' broke me conthract,' he says. 'I niver borry throuble,' he says, 'but I've had to borry money to pay me men.' So it is with us. We've all taken a conthract to dig through th' glacial dhrift. We know its glacial dhrift to th' ind, but we make oursilves think 'twill come aisy wan iv these days. So we go on, with pick an' shovel, till th' wurruk is done an' we lay it down gladly."

Everybody in the Archy road has the ordinary engineering terms on the end of his tongue and the figure appealed to Mr. Hennessy, who bleated his acknowledgement. Then his face brightened up.

"We have wan thing comin' this year we've not had befure," he said.

"What's that?" Mr. Dooley asked.

"Th' cillybration iv th' ninety-eight," said Mr. Hennessy.

"Ye'er r-right," said Mr. Dooley. "An' 'twill be th' gran' thing to see all th' good la-ads marchin' down Sackville sthreet singin' 'Who fears to speak iv ninety-eight, who blushes at th' name?' No wan, an' that's th' throuble. If they were afeerd to speak iv it, 'twud be dangerous, an' I'm thinkin' th' more public it is th' less it amounts to. I heerd Hogan glorifyin' over somethin' he r-read in th' pa-aper about all th' Scotchies in th' English ar-rmy that's fightin' haythens somewhere in Boolgahria bein' Irishmin. They was Caseys an' Meaneys and Healys in th' lot, an' th' la-ad with bullets in his legs that sat on a rock an' piped whin th' others was chargin' up th' hill was fr'm me own county—which is not in Scotland. 'Well,' says I, 'what iv it,' I says. 'Th' wurruld is full iv fightin' Irishmin,' I says. 'They's O'Donnells in Spain an' Taafes in Austhria an' Lynches in Chile an' Pat MacMahon was wanst Prisidint iv France,' I says. 'Th' English ar-rmy is full iv Irishmin fightin', who? The inimies iv England,' I says. 'D'ye think it's annything to be proud iv f'r a man named Healy to be found dead with th' legs iv him nakid an' a little hootchy-kootchy plaid skirt an' a woman's hat on him?' I says. 'Wud ye like to be laid out like a belly dancer an' have "number eight thousan' an' three, Rile Scotch Highlanders," on th' coffin plate?' I says. 'Goo wan with ye,' I says. An' he was humilyated befure th' crowd. Th' place f'r Irishmin to die is th' place they was bor-rn or in th' sixth wa-ard, or th' like iv that."

"But ye'er goin' over in th' spring?" asked Mr. Hennessy.

"I'll go over," said Mr. Dooley impressively, "if I have to walk ivery fut iv th' way; an' like as not I will." (December 31, 1897)

10. Mr. Dooley Says Good-bye: "An' What's It Come To?"

Strictly speaking, this is the last piece in the original Chicago Dooley series that stretches back to the day in October 1893 when John McKenna first walked into Mr. Dooley's liquor shop on Archer Avenue. The list here of bad men whose successful careers have not been retarded by Mr. Dooley's efforts against them includes streetcar magnate Charles T. Yerkes, Illinois Senator William Lorimer, Chicago Alderman "Bathhouse John" Coughlin, and Governor John R. Tanner. All of these men had been involved in the passage in the Illinois legislature of the notorious Allen bill, which gave the Chicago city council the power to issue franchises for fifty years without considering compensation for the city.

"I'm goin' away," said Mr. Dooley.

"What!" exclaimed Mr. Hennessy, as if he had been shocked by an electric wire.

"I'm goin' away," repeated the philosopher. "Ye needn't take on so. You an' me ain't hitched together with a log-chain be anny means. I know how it is. We all go through th' same ol' game iv havin' fits whin our frinds takes lave. Do ye start f'r a thrip to Milwaukee an' iviry man ye meet asts ye to have a dhrink with him, an' ye'er wife an' eight small childher weeps on ye'er shoulder or ye'er feet—dipindin' on their hite—an' diligations fr'm th' marchin' club an' th' Saint Vincent de Pauls goes to th' thrain to see ye off an' ye'er as full as a goat an' ye quar'l with th' conductor whin he comes around to take up ye'er ticket.

"Why shud it be so? F'r th' land's sake, lave me bid ye good-by without seeing a grimace on ye'er face as if ye was dhrinkin' bitter beer. A man can't stand still in wan place. He makes frinds an' tips a glass with thim, an' whin he tips manny he swears he'll niver lave thim this side iv th' grave. But whin his time comes he goes an' does not look behind him. In th' ol' counthry whin a man got up an' shook th' mud iv his native bog fr'm his feet they used to say that th' Other People was blowin' their horns f'r him in th' mountains an' he had to lave. An' he wint, an' was glad iv it, an' no man was very sorry afther all. I'd have it th' same way whin I'm called f'r good. A crate with me name on it, so I won't be misdirected, a hearse with a lively dhriver that can dodge th' cable ca-ars an' not spill me, an' thin: 'Good-by; if ye'er iver in th' neighborhood dhrop in.'

"I've got a right to quit ye, Hinnissy, though ye'er a good man an' so'm I, be th' same token. F'r years an' years I've been standin' behind this counter tellin' ye thruths ye'd hear nowhere else—no, not in th' good book or in th' Lives iv th' Saints. Why did I do it? Th' Lord on'y knows. But whin I get talkin' I can't stop anny more thin if I'd started to run down th' span iv th' r-red bridge. Some iv th' things I've said was wrong an' some was right, an' most iv thim was foolish, but this much I know, I've thried to give it out sthraight. An' what's it come to? What's all th' histhry an' pothry an' philosophy I've give ye an' th' Archey road f'r all these years come to? Nawthin'. Th' la-ads I abused ar-re makin' money so fast it threatens to smother thim. Th' wans I stud up f'r is some in jail an' some out iv wurruk. I've bore with iverything. I've stud Yerkuss, an' Bill Lorimer and Bath House Jawn an' th' Relief an' Aid Society, an' Schwartzmeister cuttin' th' price iv pints. I've seen all kinds iv onjestice done an' all kinds iv goodness punished. I seen civil service an' I stud that. But I'll not stand Tanner. I've made up me mind on that. Man an' boy, I've lived here f'r thirty-forty year an' paid me taxes an' disthributed liquor that didn't have a fight or a headache in a bar'l iv it, but whin they ask me to live in a state run be a counthry sausage I've got to quit. I've got to go. A man that knowed Stephen A. Douglas an' wanst thried to break up a meetin' where Ab'ram Lincoln was has no place in th' state iv Illinye."

"Where ar-re ye goin'?" asked Mr. Hennessy.

"I dinnaw. To Boolgahria perhaps. Annywhere I won't hear iv Tanner."

"He'll on'y last three years."

"An' how long d'ye think I'd last if I stayed here? I'm goin'. Good-by. I lave ye to Tanner."

"Good-by," said Mr. Hennessy. "Ye'll think betther iv it. I'll see ye again."

"Mebbe," said Mr. Dooley. "'Tis har-rd f'r me to lave off talkin'. Good-by."

As Mr. Hennessy plodded down the street the philosopher locked the door and turned out the lights of his place, perhaps for the last time. (January 22, 1898)

11. Mr. Dooley's Farewell to the Chicago River

The flow of the Chicago River was reversed for sanitation pur-
poses in January 1900, upon the completion of a drainage canal. To
celebrate the event, Dunne wrote his last unsyndicated piece, "exclu-
sively for the Chicago Journal.*" Interpreting the new condition of the*
river as a sign of eternal flux, Mr. Dooley uses the occasion to call up
one more time the old Bridgeport names and places. The piece is an
explicit gesture of farewell.

"Th' Chicago r-river risin' in Benton Harbor an' imtyin' into
th' Mayor iv St. Looey!" exclaimed Mr. Dooley. "What d'ye think
iv that?"

"I don't believe it," said Mr. Hennessy.

"'Tis thrue, though," Mr. Dooley went on. "Whin Tommy
Gahan got through shovelin' mud out iv th' dhrainage canal with
th' help iv ye'er rilitives on th' dhredge, th' river that'd been
coorsin' placidly through its banks an' soap facthries an' carryin'
th' cast-off diseases iv Halsted sthreet to th' proud but timp'rate
people iv th' Lake Shore dhrive was backed up in th' shafts. It's
r-runnin' th' other way now, Hinnissy, an' befure manny months
they won't be a smell iv it left.

"It don't seem right f'r to threat it that way. It's been a good
frind iv Chicago an' what good's th' lake? Th' Illinye Cinthral
owns it an' sare a wave iv it do I iver see but what comes through a
hose. They're turnin' th' river out an' puttin' th' lake in, an' nex'
summer they'll be a mugwump vote in this precinct that niver
knew wan befure. They're deliverin' th' good ol' river over to
Saint Looey an' 'twill be th' makin' iv th' town.

"Man an' boy, I've lived beside th' Chicago river f'r forty year,
Hinnissy, an' if they ain't any wan else to stand up f'r it, thin here
am I. It niver done naught f'r me but good. Manny's the time I've
set on th' bridge smokin' me pipe an' watchin' th' lights iv th' tugs
dancin' in it like stars, an' me knowin' all th' captains, be hivins,
fr'm th' boss iv th' O. B. Green, with th' fine whistle that sounded
like a good keen at a Connockman's fun'ral, to the little Mary Ann

Gray, that had a snow-plow attachment on th' prow f'r to get into th' slip over be th' r-red bridge. I had thim all be name, an' fr'm thim I larned th' news iv th' Boheemyan settlemint down th' crick, where I was not on visitin' terms, fr'm an iliction where we had to use couplin' pins to presarve th' peace. Thim lads will niver sail in anny thin river iv dhrinkin' wather. They wudden't know how to conthrol their tugs. They'd go so fast they cudden't take th' curves at th' lumber yards.

"'Twas th' prettiest river f'r to look at that ye'll iver see. Ye niver was annything iv a pote, Hinnissy, but if ye cud get down on th' Miller dock some night whin ye an' th' likes iv ye was makin' fireworks in th' blast, an' see th' flames blazin' on th' wather an' th' lights dancin', green at th' sausage facthry, blue at th' soap facthry, yellow at th' tannery, ye'd not thrade it f'r annything but th' Liffey, that's thinner but more powerfuller. D'ye mind whin it was on fire? That was a gran' night. It burned like a pitcher-frame facthry. Chief Swenie come down with thruck nine an' chemical fourteen an' a lot more iv th' best, but thry as he wud he cudden't put it out. He was deprissed be th' shtruggle an' me Uncle Mike wint up, that was a gr-reat joker, an' says he, 'Chief,' he says, 'they'se on'y wan way ye can put out that fire.' 'How's that,' says th' chief. 'Tur-rn th' river upside down,' says me Uncle Mike. Well, sir, ye'd have thought th' chief'd die laughin', he was that pleased. He tol' me aftherward me Uncle Mike was a case.

"But ye cudden't burn up th' river. It was as good as ever afther th' fire, on'y a little smoky in its smell. Gran' ol' river! Onhealthy, says ye? Onhealthy! Th' river niver was onhealthy. 'Twas th' lake. Th' river wint sthrollin' out visitin' its frinds, an', though I niver liked th' comp'ny it kept on thim sprees, I'll say that it always come back—lookin' a little pale, 'tis thrue, but it always come back. An' th' lake helped itself to what th' river had on it and handed it to sthrangers an' joods with poor digestions. Onhealthy? Did ye iver see a healthier lot iv childher, or more iv thim, than lives along th' river? If ye think 'twas onhealthy, go up some day an' thry a roll with Willum J. O'Brien. He's been here near as long as I have. Or luk at me! No, sir, ye might jus' as well say I'm onhealthy if I wint down f'r a visit with Schwartzmeister with a package iv rough-on-rats in me pocket, an' he was to steal it from me an' give it his customers. Th' Chicago river niver was intinded as a dhrink. It didn't go ar-round advertisin' itself as a saisonable beverage! It ain't moxie, an' it ain't sasparilly, an' it ain't ice crame soda wather. It had other business more suited to it, an' 'twas consistent in ivery way.

"Now that it's goin' out I'll niver go to th' bridge again. Niver. I feel as though I'd lost an ol' frind an' a sthrong wan. It wasn't so much that I see it ivery day, but I always knew it was there. Night an' day me frind was there!"

"Ah, go on," said Mr. Hennessy. "What diff'rence does it make wan way or th' other?"

"Ye have no pothry," said Mr. Dooley. "Well, here's to it annyhow, an' hopin' that it'll have a good time in Saint Looey. Be hivins, th' ol' la-ad will keep thim awake down there. He will that!" (January 13, 1900)